Foundation Silverlight 2 Animation

friendsof ED™

DESIGNER TO DESIGNER™

an Apress® company

Foundation Silverlight 2 Animation

ISBN-13 (pbk): 978-1-4302-1569-1

ISBN-13 (electronic): 978-1-4302-1570-7

Printed and bound in the United States of America 9 8 7 6 5 4 3 2 1

Trademarked names may appear in this book. Rather than use a trademark symbol with every occurrence of a trademarked name, we use the names only in an editorial fashion and to the benefit of the trademark owner, with no intention of infringement of the trademark.

Original Firefly photograph courtesy of Terry Priest, www.frfly.com.

Distributed to the book trade worldwide by Springer-Verlag New York, Inc., 233 Spring Street, 6th Floor, New York, NY 10013. Phone 1-800-SPRINGER, fax 201-348-4505, e-mail orders-ny@springer-sbm.com, or visit www.springeronline.com.

For information on translations, please contact Apress directly at 2855 Telegraph Avenue, Suite 600, Berkeley, CA 94705. Phone 510-549-5930, fax 510-549-5939, e-mail info@apress.com, or visit www.apress.com.

Apress and friends of ED books may be purchased in bulk for academic, corporate, or promotional use. eBook versions and licenses are also available for most titles. For more information, reference our Special Bulk Sales–eBook Licensing web page at www.apress.com/info/bulksales.

The information in this book is distributed on an "as is" basis, without warranty. Although every precaution has been taken in the preparation of this work, neither the author(s) nor Apress shall have any liability to any person or entity with respect to any loss or damage caused or alleged to be caused directly or indirectly by the information contained in this work.

The source code for this book is freely available to readers at www.friendsofed.com in the Downloads section.

Credits

Lead Editor	**Production Editor**
Ben Renow-Clarke	Laura Esterman
Technical Reviewer	**Compositor**
Rob Houweling	Lynn L'Heureux
Editorial Board	**Proofreader**
Clay Andres, Steve Anglin, Mark Beckner, Ewan Buckingham,	Dan Shaw
Tony Campbell, Gary Cornell, Jonathan Gennick, Michelle Lowman,	
Matthew Moodie, Jeffrey Pepper, Frank Pohlmann,	**Indexer**
Ben Renow-Clarke, Dominic Shakeshaft, Matt Wade, Tom Welsh	Ron Strauss
Project Manager	**Cover Image Designer**
Kylie Johnston	Corné van Dooren
Copy Editor	**Interior and Cover Designer**
Damon Larson	Kurt Krames
Associate Production Director	**Manufacturing Director**
Kari Brooks-Copony	Tom Debolski

CONTENTS AT A GLANCE

CONTENTS

PART TWO **SILVERLIGHT ANIMATION: THE BASICS** 33

ABOUT THE AUTHOR

Jeff Paries has been creating applications in Silverlight since early 2007, and he maintains a blog with example programs and tips at www. designwithsilverlight.com. He is currently employed as a senior digital media developer at Waggener Edstrom Worldwide in Lake Oswego, Oregon.

Prior to joining Waggener Edstrom, Jeff spent six years as a web manager for a company in the Internet domain name space, where he helped the company develop and maintain a strong online identity.

Having worked for a 3D animation software company for six years, Jeff has a strong background in computer graphics and animation. While there, Jeff played a strong role in training and development of new users by developing training materials, teaching a course in 3D animation at a local community college, and authoring three books and numerous magazine articles related to 3D graphics.

Jeff currently makes his home near Portland, Oregon, with his wife, Kate, and son, Nicholas. He enjoys spending his free time hiking, mountain climbing, motorcycling, and writing Silverlight applications and tutorials. You can contact him through his blog or by email at jeffparies@ yahoo.com.

ABOUT THE TECHNICAL REVIEWER

Since the introduction of Silverlight 1.1, **Rob Houweling** has been developing applications and writing articles on his weblog (http://web-snippets. blogspot.com/) and has been an active member of the forums on Silverlight.net, where he likes to help people with their problems.

Currently, Rob is employed by Amercom B.V. in the Netherlands, where he develops many websites and applications in .NET versions 1.1 through 3.5, using Microsoft SQL Server 2000 through 2005 as the database platform. In 2007, he was lead developer on one of the first online corporate portals built on SharePoint 2007.

Prior to his employment at Amercom, Rob spent several years as a Microsoft certified system administrator.

Rob is very grateful to Jeff for giving him this opportunity, to Amercom for giving him the freedom to work on Silverlight, and to his loving family (Piroschka, Mika, and Isabella) for being patient and understanding.

ABOUT THE COVER IMAGE DESIGNER

Corné van Dooren designed the front cover image for this book. Having been given a brief by friends of ED to create a new design for the Foundation series, he was inspired to create this new setup combining technology and organic forms.

With a colorful background as an avid cartoonist, Corné discovered the infinite world of multimedia at the age of 17— a journey of discovery that hasn't stopped since. His mantra has always been "The only limit to multimedia is the imagination," a mantra that is keeping him moving forward constantly.

After enjoying success after success over the past years— working for many international clients, as well as being featured in multimedia magazines, testing software, and working on many other friends of ED books— Corné decided it was time to take another step in his career by launching his own company, Project 79, in March 2005.

You can see more of his work and contact him through www.cornevandooren.com/ or www. project79.com/.

If you like his work, be sure to check out his chapter in *New Masters of Photoshop: Volume 2* (friends of ED, 2004).

ACKNOWLEDGMENTS

It has been my experience in writing four books that the successful completion of a project of this size and scope are rarely the effort of a single person, and this one is no exception. The following people made this book much better than it would have been without them.

Rob Houweling, lead developer at Amercom: Rob served as my technical editor, going through all of the examples in the book in great detail (oftentimes more than once), refactoring code, offering suggestions, and so on. He also tried his best to get me to conform to best practices for coding, and while I didn't always hit the mark, I did better than I would have without him. I got to know Rob personally over the months that it took to get the book done, and for someone who I've never met in person and who lives half a world away, I feel like I can call him a good friend. Rob, my door is always open to you.

Ryan Loghry, illustrator: Ryan's artwork goes a long way to making the example projects in the book move beyond primitive shapes and examples. While I'm responsible for all those wonderful gradient-filled spheres, Ryan created all of the cool-looking stuff—the rockets, scenes, and so forth. I asked him to deliver the sun and moon, and he did—quite literally. Check out his site at www.ryanloghry.com/ to see more of his excellent illustration work.

Keith Peters, author: Any Flash developer should recognize Keith's name. While I've never met him in person, he was kind enough to grant me permission to adapt some of his cool ActionScript examples into Silverlight.

Other people that contributed to the successful completion of the book include Matt Smith of PhotoSpherix, who provided the excellent sample images for the virtual reality object engine in Chapter 11; Trevor McCauley and Andy Beaulieu for permission to include/adapt code they originally developed; all of my coworkers (I'd put all of your names here, but I'd miss someone, and then they'd be mad at me); and everyone at friends of ED—but especially Kylie for keeping me on track and Ben for his guidance.

INTRODUCTION

I have found that one of the hardest goals to achieve when writing a book is to not only describe a technique for doing something, but to do it in a way that gets the creative juices of the reader flowing.

With that in mind, I tried to go a step beyond the concepts with the example projects and show one or more ways to apply the techniques being described. It isn't always about new techniques, but it is often about applying existing techniques in new ways. Along those lines, it is often the case that seeing a couple of different applications of a technique will help a person start thinking about ways to unlock the ideas that they have had floating around in their head for a while and give them a means to bring their ideas to life.

I think this book can do that for you.

There are nearly 200 example projects included in this book, including both "code-along" and "completed" versions that you can take apart, change, and put back together in order to learn how to make the concepts work for you. Don't get locked into what is being demonstrated, though—find ways to move beyond the examples and apply the concepts in new and interesting ways. This is where your applications will really start to shine.

In the end, the goal of the book is to provide a means to realize your ideas using Silverlight as the technology to deliver them.

Have fun. There's a lot to learn.

Who this book is for

This book is ideal for a wide variety of web developers. If you are a Silverlight developer wanting to learn more about animation-specific topics or a Flash developer interested in learning about Silverlight, this book will show you a wide variety of methods that you can use to make objects move and interact with users, and each other.

Through a large assortment of code-along projects that you can work through while reading the book, you will learn the basics of animation in Silverlight, and then step into intermediate and advanced procedural (code-based) animation. If you get stuck, completed versions of the projects are included on the friends of ED website (www.friendsofed.com), so you can compare that code with your own to get back on track in a hurry.

This is the right book for anyone interested in adding rich interactive applications to a website. If you're not sure how to get "there" from "here," you will find a wealth of interesting tips, techniques, and methods to help add some sparkle to your site. You will gain a solid understanding of the techniques used to make objects move, and some ideas for how to apply them in projects of your own.

No need to feel left out if you are a designer—this book will also serve as a valuable reference for those seeking a deeper understanding of how to go about programming Silverlight. This can be a big help when working in a team environment where cross-discipline skills are an asset.

How this book is structured

This book starts out by providing the foundation information necessary for those people new to Silverlight development. The early portion of the book starts out with what you need to know about Silverlight and development software and the basics of animation (transforms, storyboards, and animations).

The middle portion of the book moves toward advanced animation topics—coordinates, vector movement, and frame-based animations. The latter portion of the book describes interesting ways to apply trigonometry, how to simulate simple 3D movements in a 2D environment, different techniques for collision detection, inverse and forward kinematics, and particle systems. The final chapter in the book describes in detail how you can add virtual reality objects to your applications with a Silverlight 2 version of the Silverlight Virtual Reality (SLVR) object engine.

If you have been developing Silverlight applications for a while, do a quick scan of the first chapter or two so you know what information is there in case you need it as a reference, and then dig in.

Each chapter describes concepts through example projects. A description of the technique is provided, and then step-by-step examples walk you through how to code up projects that demonstrate the technique. If you get stuck, most of the projects include a completed version with finalized code that you can take a look at to see how it's done.

Many of the topics are tightly integrated, and you will see some crossover from chapter to chapter. This is unavoidable, although some effort was made to present the information in manageable doses rather than opening the floodgates. There are, of course, additional optimizations and different coding styles that could be applied to the code in the projects—many times, the code in the examples is written in a longer form to make it more readable and easily digested. Feel free to take the examples apart, reorganize, optimize, and put them back together—that's the whole point!

Layout conventions

To keep this book as clear and easy to follow as possible, the following text conventions are used throughout.

Project names, and important words or concepts are normally highlighted on the first appearance in **bold type**.

Code is presented in fixed-width font.

New or changed code is normally presented in **bold fixed-width font**.

Menu commands are written in the form Menu ➤ Submenu ➤ Submenu.

Sometimes code won't fit on a single line in a book. Where this happens, I use an arrow like this: ➡

    This is a very, very long section of code that should be written ➡
    all on the same line without a break.

Downloading the code

The source code for this book is available to readers at www.friendsofed.com/ in the Downloads section of this book's home page. Please feel free to visit the friends of ED website and download all the code there. You can also check for errata and find related titles from friends of ED and Apress.

Part One

GETTING STARTED

Chapter 1

WHAT YOU NEED TO KNOW

Silverlight is a cross-browser, cross-platform browser plug-in developed by Microsoft to deliver multimedia, graphics, and animation on the Web. Content created for Silverlight looks the same on a PC and a Mac, and supports a wide range of browsers. There is even a Microsoft-supported Linux version, called Moonlight.

Silverlight projects can consist of many assets—images, vector graphics, XAML markup, and programming code are all brought together and presented in the browser by the Silverlight plug-in. You may use one program to create the XAML markup, another to create the vector graphics, and another to create the programming code, as shown in Figure 1-1. XAML, the markup language upon which Silverlight applications are built, is to Silverlight what HTML is to a web page. XAML describes the containers, positions, sizes, and other attributes of the objects in a Silverlight application.

You're reading this because you want to learn how to make objects move in Silverlight. Since it's best to start at the beginning, this chapter presents an overview of the software and technologies with which you will be working to create Silverlight content, and the various concepts covered in the book that you will need to know to have success with the examples that are presented. If you are a Flash/Flex developer exploring Silverlight, or if you are new to Silverlight altogether, this chapter is designed to help you get your feet wet without being overwhelmed. If you are a designer, you will likely want to focus on the Expression Blend–based aspects of the text to get up and running quickly. If you are already comfortable developing Silverlight applications and want to get right to business, you can skip ahead to Chapter 2 and start working through the animation-specific topics.

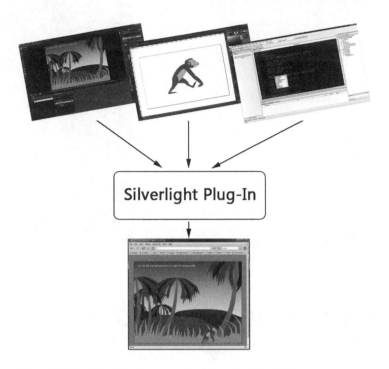

Figure 1-1. The Silverlight browser plug-in renders Silverlight content in the browser.

What you need to know about software

The following tools were created with the goal of making the creation of Silverlight content as easy and fast as possible. While you could use a simple text editor such as Notepad to create the XAML markup that describes the objects you will be using in your applications, a visual design/development environment will save you a lot of time and headaches. With that in mind, you will want to add some of the following software tools to your collection.

Microsoft Expression Blend

Blend, shown in Figure 1-2, is a great tool for developing Silverlight applications. It bridges the gap between designers and developers to speed application development time by providing a visual environment in which to create application interfaces. You can find a free trial version at www.microsoft.com/expression/. For the Silverlight 2 development described in this book, you'll want to use Blend 2.5 or above.

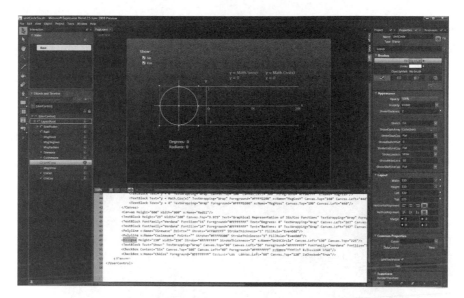

Figure 1-2. The visual interface in Blend makes creating Silverlight interfaces fast and easy.

Microsoft Expression Design

Design, shown in Figure 1-3, is a vector-based drawing tool for designers that can be used to create or edit the various graphical assets you will incorporate into your Silverlight projects. Design directly supports input of common formats such as Illustrator and Photoshop files, and can be utilized to export vector drawings directly to XAML. Like Blend, a free trial of Design is available for download at www. microsoft.com/expression/.

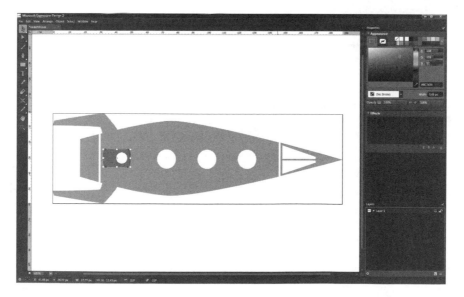

Figure 1-3. Expression Design is a vector-based drawing tool that can export directly to XAML.

Microsoft Visual Studio

Visual Studio, shown in Figure 1-4, is the preferred development environment for creating the C#, Visual Basic, or JavaScript code-behind files that bring Silverlight applications to life. The intuitive interface makes common programming tasks quick and easy. Microsoft offers a 90-day free trial of Visual Studio 2008 Professional, which you can find at http://msdn.microsoft.com/en-us/vs2008/products/.

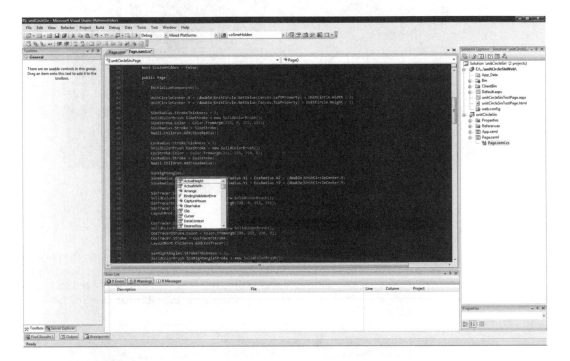

Figure 1-4. Visual Studio is the preferred environment for Silverlight development.

Alternatively, you can download and install Microsoft Visual Web Developer Express Edition, which can be registered free of charge. You can find the download at www.microsoft.com/express/vwd/. By the fall of 2008, Visual Web Developer Express Edition (shown in Figure 1-5) is expected to support Silverlight Tools for Visual Studio (see the following section), which enables Silverlight application development. Visual Web Developer Express will be supporting both Visual Basic and C# development.

Figure 1-5. Microsoft Visual Web Developer is free to register.

Silverlight Tools for Visual Studio 2008

This is a free add-on for Visual Studio specifically for developing Silverlight applications. You can find this download at http://go.microsoft.com/fwlink/?LinkId=120319. Currently, this package includes the Silverlight plug-in, the Silverlight 2 Software Development Kit (SDK), Visual Basic and C# project templates, XAML IntelliSense and code generators, debugging for Silverlight applications, web reference support, and integration with Expression Blend. All this may sound very complicated, but in a nutshell, this add-on makes developing Silverlight applications in Visual Studio much easier. If you develop in Visual Studio, the tools are a must-have.

If you are new to Silverlight development, the relationship between the different software programs will become more apparent as you work through the examples in this book. Expression Blend and Visual Studio are tightly integrated, making movement between the two programs fast and easy.

What you need to know about XAML

So far, I've mentioned XAML a few times, and described it as the markup that describes objects used in a Silverlight application. As a designer or developer new to Silverlight, the biggest question you are probably asking yourself is "Why do I need to learn XAML?" XAML, pronounced *zammel*, is an acronym for Extensible Application Markup Language. XAML is an XML-based language used to describe everything about the elements that are the building blocks of Silverlight applications—their shape, size, color, position, and so forth. Beyond the importance of XAML to a Silverlight application, it also serves as a bridge between designers and developers. Traditionally, the processes of design and development have been separated, as illustrated in Figure 1-6. The designer creates full-fledged mock-ups that, when approved, are sliced up and handed off to a developer for implementation. The designer then waits for the developer to create a working version, and the two collaborate to get any actions or animations just right before the application is released.

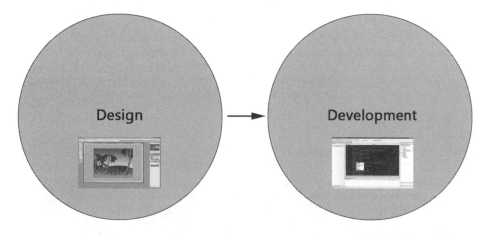

Pre-XAML Development Model

Figure 1-6. The "old way" of doing things: the designer hands off assets to the developer.

In a XAML world, that all changes. XAML is a bridge between design and development. The designer is empowered—no longer are assets sent off into a black hole for processing. With XAML, designers can set up the objects, describe their motions through storyboards, and take part in the development process if they so choose—all without writing any code. The overall development cycle can be accelerated as well. XAML is flexible and easily allows "proxy objects" to stand in for the real thing. In this way, the developer can begin the work of coding an application at the same time the designer is still working on the assets the application will utilize. Figure 1-7 illustrates the XAML-based development model. Of course, there is some cross-discipline training that needs to take place, which is why as a designer, you will want to learn XAML.

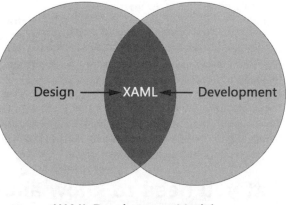

XAML Development Model

Figure 1-7. In a XAML-based development model, the line between designer and developer is blurred.

If you are a developer, it is useful to note that each element described in a XAML file maps to a Microsoft .NET type, and the attributes of an element (such as height, width, opacity, etc.) are equivalent to .NET class properties. Don't worry about what that means now if you're not a developer; we'll cover it in more detail later.

Because XAML is XML-based, all XAML files must be well-formed XML files. This means that XAML declarations are subject to many rules, including case sensitivity, use of whitespace, proper closing tags, and so on. Once you have created a XAML file, the Silverlight plug-in in your web browser is used to parse and render the content contained in the XAML file.

In contrast, Adobe Flex uses a different XML-based language, called MXML. While both XAML and MXML are used to describe application interfaces, the two are not interchangeable.

Silverlight developers write code in files referred to as code-behind files, which manipulate the elements or element attributes described in a XAML file. Depending upon the complexity, you may find yourself using several XAML files within a single project. Using multiple XAML files often makes managing the code base a little easier because tasks unique to each object are separated from the main application logic. Additionally, this creates a situation where multiple designers or developers can work on a single project by dividing tasks. We will be using multiple XAML files in some of our projects.

You will want to have some familiarity with XAML because it is often more convenient to directly edit the XAML file in an environment like Visual Studio or Expression Blend rather than hunt down a specific property pane to change an attribute. Eventually, you will need to roll up your sleeves and get your hands dirty.

There are many more XAML elements available for use in your Silverlight applications than those described here. For simplicity, the examples in this book work mostly with the Canvas, Image, Rectangle, Path, Ellipse, TextBlock, and Line elements. Those of you familiar with XAML are probably already asking "What about TextBox? Or Grid/StackPanel?" The examples presented are intended to focus on the concepts used to make objects move, not various methods for laying out data or the merits of one layout panel over another.

Using Blend to create XAML

Microsoft's Expression Blend tool offers a useful visual environment in which to create Silverlight applications because it automatically generates proper XAML as you work. Let's take a look at some XAML elements we'll be using from the perspective of Blend.

If you already have Blend installed, go ahead and start the program. When Blend opens, you will be given the option of opening a recent project via a list of recent projects displayed on the Projects tab, or choosing from New Project, Open Project, or Open Site. Select the New Project option. Figure 1-8 shows the dialog with which you will be presented.

If it is not already selected, choose the Silverlight 2 Application project type, browse to the location where you would like the project saved, and click the OK button to create a project using the default name. Blend will take a moment to set the project up for you, and then you will be presented with a blank project.

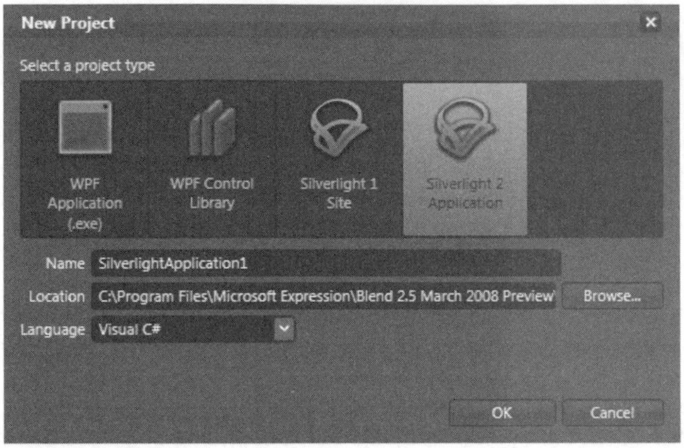

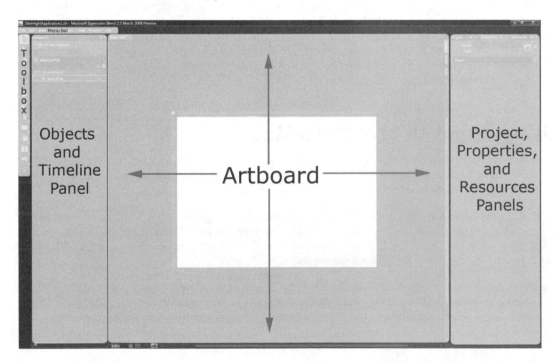

Figure 1-8. Expression Blend New Project dialog

Blend initially presents the interface as the **Design Workspace**, as shown in Figure 1-9, which maximizes the space allotment for the design window. If you find yourself in the **Animation Workspace**, with the Objects and Timeline panel across the bottom, press the F6 key to change back to the Design Workspace. The Design Workspace is laid out such that the left side of the interface contains the toolbox and the Objects and Timeline panel, the center contains the artboard, and the right contains the Project, Properties, and Resources panels, each of which is accessible via a row of tabs across the top. There is also a menu bar across the top.

Figure 1-9. The default interface layout for Blend

One thing you will find out rather quickly is that Blend's interface layout is fairly flexible to suit the way you work. By selecting Window ➤ Active Workspace, you can toggle the main interface layout between the Design Workspace and the Animation Workspace. The Animation Workspace shows a timeline that is helpful when creating animations. Alternatively, the F6 key can be used to toggle between the workspace layouts. Verify that the Design Workspace is the currently selected view.

Along the right side of the artboard, you will see three vertically arranged tabs, labeled Design, XAML, and Split. These tabs allow you to change between the **active document view**. The Design view is the current view and shows only the artboard. Clicking the XAML tab will display only the XAML code for the current file, while selecting Split will show both the artboard and the XAML code. You can click the interface tabs or use the F11 key to switch between active document views. Select Split view so that as you are working through this section you can see how Blend assists in creating XAML code. Figure 1-10 shows what the Blend interface should look like at this point.

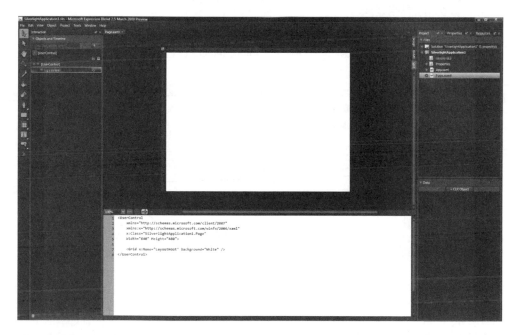

Figure 1-10. Using the Split active document view

Notice in the XAML window that Blend has added some code for you already. This code is the base template for a new project, and is required in all XAML files. The first line is the opening tag for a UserControl element, and the next line defines the namespace used by this XAML file. A namespace defines what elements you can use in a Silverlight application, and always comes after the opening UserControl type.

```
xmlns="http://schemas.microsoft.com/client/2007"
```

This is followed by another namespace declaration. The xmlns:x namespace contains information that controls how XAML interacts with the .NET framework.

```
xmlns:x="http://schemas.microsoft.com/winfx/2006/xaml"
```

The next line identifies this XAML file as an object class within the application that was created when you selected New Project. The name Blend gave this application is SilverlightApplication1, and the default XAML file that is created for every new project is named Page:

```
x:Class="SilverlightApplication1.Page"
```

Finally, there are some properties that are self-explanatory:

```
Width="640" Height="480"
```

You will not typically need to make changes to the first few lines of code within the XAML files you create. If you would like to run your application, select Project ➤ Test Solution, or press the F5 key. Blend will open a browser window that contains your Silverlight application. Currently, the application does not contain any elements, so the browser window will appear blank. Close the browser window and return to Blend.

Select the Properties tab at the top right of the interface. The Properties panel contains the various panes that display the attributes available for the object selected in the Objects and Timeline panel on the left.

Select [UserControl] in the Objects and Timeline panel by clicking it. On the Layout pane of the Properties panel, change Width to 800 and Height to 600. Notice that Blend automatically updates the XAML and the Design view for you, as follows:

```
<UserControl
    xmlns="http://schemas.microsoft.com/client/2007"
    xmlns:x="http://schemas.microsoft.com/winfx/2006/xaml"
    x:Class="SilverlightApplication1.Page"
    Width="800" Height="600">
```

After the opening UserControl tag, the next line in the XAML file defines a container of type Grid:

```
<Grid x:Name="LayoutRoot" Background="White" />
```

Some of the available layout containers, such as Grid and StackPanel, have default behaviors that control the way objects placed in them are laid out. This is not the case with the Canvas container, so for simplicity, we will be using Canvas elements as containers. In the XAML window, change the text that says Grid to Canvas. Double-click the LayoutRoot element in the Objects and Timeline panel. A yellow highlight will appear around the element to indicate that it is selected. Any elements that are added will now automatically be added to the LayoutRoot element.

Let's look at some of the XAML elements in more detail.

The Canvas element

Canvas elements are containers that allow you to define an area into which other elements can be placed. Elements placed in a Canvas are referred to as children of the Canvas in which they reside. Canvases are extremely useful for organizing elements that make up related parts of an interface, and have properties such as Background, Height, IsHitTestVisible, Left, Name, Opacity, Tag, Top, Visibility, and Width.

Locate the Grid element icon in the toolbox. Click and hold the mouse on the Grid icon until the fly-out menu opens, and select the Canvas element, as shown in Figure 1-11.

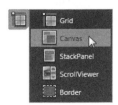

Double-click the Canvas icon to add a Canvas element to your project. Blend will add the new Canvas to the Objects and Timeline panel, and create the XAML for you. Notice that the LayoutRoot Canvas has changed—it now has a matching closing tag, and the new Canvas element has been added within the LayoutRoot element:

Figure 1-11. The Layout panel fly-out menu

```
<Canvas x:Name="LayoutRoot" Background="White">
    <Canvas Height="480" Width="640"/>
</Canvas>
```

Select the newly added [Canvas] item in the Objects and Timeline panel, and use the Layout pane of the Properties panel to change the Width property to 800 and Height to 600. In the XAML view window, edit the new Canvas element to add a Background attribute:

```
<Canvas Height="600" Width="800" Background="#FF0000FF"/>
```

The Brushes pane on the Properties panel will change to show a color picker with the background color you defined for the Canvas element. You may have noticed that the color code Blend added contains more characters than you are used to seeing when defining colors via hexadecimal. Whereas normally you might see a group of three pairs of values for the red, green, and blue values, here you see four pairs of values. This is because the first two numbers indicate the alpha channel (transparency) value for the defined color. To the right of the color picker are the individual values that make up the selected color—Red, Green, Blue, and Alpha. If you have a known value, you may type it in here rather than using the color picker in the interface.

Keep in mind that the alpha transparency defined for any given color is independent from the overall opacity of an object. It is possible to have a color that has an alpha value of 25%, meaning it is 25% visible, while the object to which that color brush is applied has an overall opacity value of 50%, further diminishing the visibility of the color.

We want to name the newly added Canvas element so it will be easily identifiable. At the top of the Properties panel is a field called Name, which currently contains the value <No Name>. When an element is not explicitly named, it appears in the Objects and Timeline panel by its type—in this case, [Canvas]. Click in the Name field, enter myCanvas, and press the Enter key. Both the Objects and Timeline list and XAML code will update. The final XAML for this Canvas element will look something like this:

```
<Canvas Height="600" Width="800" Background="#FF0000FF"
    x:Name="myCanvas"/>
```

Later, when we start getting into adding code to control the objects in our XAML files, you will see that having an x:Name property will make accessing objects extremely easy, since they are referenced by name.

The Image element

XAML Image elements allow you to utilize JPG or PNG images in an application. Image elements have attributes such as Height, IsHitTestVisible, Left, Name, Opacity, Stretch, Tag, Top, Visibility, and Width.

To add an Image element in Blend, click the Asset Library icon on the toolbox, check the Show All check box at the top right of the panel, and then click the Image item, as shown in Figure 1-12. The Image icon will appear on your toolbox and remain there throughout your working session.

Double-click the myCanvas item in the Objects and Timeline panel to select it, and then double-click the Image icon to insert a default Image object. An alternative method for adding elements is to click their icon and then click and drag in the Design Workspace. This allows you to create elements that are sized differently than the default if you prefer.

Figure 1-12. Using the Asset Library to insert an Image element onto the artboard

By default, Image elements do not point to an image, referred to as a **source attribute**. To set the source for an Image object, select the Choose an image button on the Common Properties pane (labeled with ellipses points: . . .) and navigate to a JPG or PNG image on your hard drive. Figure 1-13 shows the Common Properties pane for an Image element.

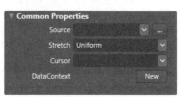

Figure 1-13. The Common Properties pane for a XAML Image element

When you select an image source in Blend, the image is automatically copied as a resource to the directory where the project is saved. Change the newly added Image element's size to 320×240 pixels, and select Fill from the Stretch select box on the Common Properties pane. To move an element around on the artboard, press the V key to change to selection mode, and drag it around using the mouse. Observe the XAML code as you're dragging, and how it changes when you release the mouse button. Blend will add Canvas.Top and Canvas.Left attributes to describe the Image element's relationship to its parent—the myCanvas container.

When you are finished exploring the Image element, your XAML code should look similar to this:

```
<Image Height="240" Width="320" Source="Humpback Whale.jpg"
    Stretch="Fill" Canvas.Top="79" Canvas.Left="247"/>
```

This XAML describes an image that is 320×240, and will display the image Humpback whale.jpg. The image will be squashed or stretched to fill the 320×240 dimensions of the Image object. The

Canvas.top property specifies that the Image object will be placed 79 pixels down from the top of the containing canvas, and the Canvas.Left property will place the image 247 pixels from the left of the containing canvas.

The Rectangle element

Rectangle XAML elements are used, as you might expect, to render rectangular shapes. Rectangle elements have attributes such as Fill, Height, IsHitTestVisible, Left, Name, Opacity, RadiusX, RadiusY, Stroke, Tag, Top, Visibility, and Width.

As with other XAML elements, Rectangles can be added by typing in the appropriate XAML or by using the Rectangle icon on the toolbox. Click the Rectangle icon or press the M key and then click and drag on the artboard to create a rectangle. Holding down the Shift key will lock the Height and Width attributes, which is useful for creating squares.

On the Properties panel, at the top of the Brushes pane, verify that Fill is selected, and then click in the color picker to select a red color.

Move the cursor over the control points on the rectangle's bounding box and notice how the cursor changes to indicate that various properties of the rectangle can be directly modified. By dragging any of the points on the bounding box, the rectangle can be scaled. If the cursor is moved just outside a corner point, the rectangle can be rotated. If the cursor is moved just outside the non-corner points, the rectangle can be skewed vertically or horizontally. By manipulating the handles that appear at the top-left corner of the rectangle, you can modify the radius and round the corners of the rectangle. By default, the radius handles will affect both the x and y radius values equally. By holding down the Shift key, you can modify the radius handles independently of each other. As with other objects and properties, changes can also be typed in directly on the Properties panel. Skew and rotation are referred to as *transforms* and are accessible on the Transform pane. The XAML for a rectangle with rounded corners looks like this:

```
<Rectangle Height="50" Width="147" Canvas.Left="145" Canvas.Top="378"
    Fill="#FFC60000" Stroke="#FF000000" RadiusX="23" RadiusY="23"/>
```

The preceding XAML describes a Rectangle object that is 147×50. The top-left corner of the rectangle will be 145 pixels from the left of the container canvas and 378 pixels from the top. The rectangle will be filled with a dark reddish color, specified by the Argb hex value #FFC60000, and will have a black stroke. The RadiusX and RadiusY values will round the corners of the rectangle.

The Path element

Paths are series of connected lines and curves used to form shapes. Paths have properties such as Fill, Height, IsHitTestVisible, Left, Name, Opacity, Stroke, Tag, Top, Visibility, and Width. If you are familiar with the Pen tool and the way that Bezier paths work in programs such as Photoshop or Illustrator, you will find that creating a path in Blend works in a similar manner.

By selecting the Pen tool from the toolbox, you can create a path by clicking the artboard. Each time you click, a new point is added to the path. By holding down the mouse button after clicking to create a point, dragging the mouse will allow you to change the magnitude and bias of the spline as it passes through the control point. If an endpoint is selected, clicking the opposite endpoint will close the path. You can remove points that are already on a path by clicking them.

Once a path has been drawn, you can press the A key or click the white arrow icon in the toolbox to use the Direct Selection tool and modify the path. Holding down the Alt key while clicking a control point will toggle the point between peaked and smooth, changing the way the spline appears as it passes through that point. Figure 1-14 shows an example of both a smooth and a peaked path.

By default, paths are filled with a solid color, referred to as a solid color brush. To remove the Fill attribute from a path, set the Fill property to No brush. To do this, first select the element by clicking it in the Objects and Timeline list. Select Fill on the Brushes pane to modify the fill, and then click the leftmost tab above the color picker to remove the fill, as shown in Figure 1-15.

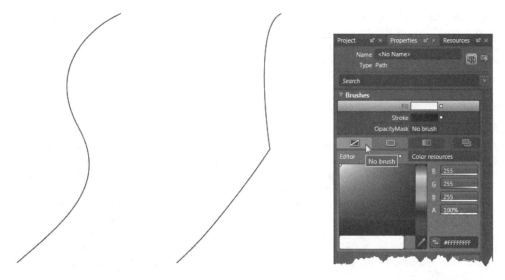

Figure 1-14. The path on the left is made from smooth points. The path on the right has a peaked center point.

Figure 1-15. Setting an object's fill to No brush

In the Name field of the Properties panel, type myPath. The XAML code and Objects and Timeline list will automatically update to reflect the change. The XAML code for the path created in this project will look something like this:

```
<Path Height="163.223" Width="317.816" Canvas.Left="396.684"
    Canvas.Top="306.473" Stretch="Fill" Stroke="#FF000000"
    Data="M714,366 C662,333 660,306 613,307 C566,308 578,354 541,360➡
    C504,366 491,313.00006 452,314.00006 C413,315.00006 ➡
    401,347.00003 399,369 C397,390.99997 391,427.99994➡
    422,442.99991 C453,457.99988 526.00012,477.99988➡
    551.00012,464.99991 C576.00012,451.99994 714,366➡
    714,366 z" x:Name="myPath"/>
```

The Data portion of the Path element is defined with a minilanguage used to describe geometric paths. More information regarding the specifics of the language can be found in the Silverlight MSDN library online, at http://msdn.microsoft.com/en-us/silverlight/default.aspx. Don't feel intimidated by the looks of the path data—it's unlikely you will often find yourself typing in the numbers to manually create Path elements. More likely, you will be using a tool such as the one in Blend to create paths for you.

You may be wondering if it will become necessary for you to re-create your entire collection of path-based Illustrator artwork in Blend for use in your Silverlight applications. You will be happy to know that converting your artwork from Illustrator to Silverlight is fairly easy. To export your Illustrator artwork as XAML, visit www.mikeswanson.com/xamlexport/ and grab Michael Swanson's excellent export plug-in. Once it's installed in Illustrator as per the instructions, open your artwork, select File ➤ Export, and choose Silverlight XAML from the list of available file types. A XAML file will be produced, the contents of which can be copied and pasted into the XAML editor in Blend or Visual Studio. If you are not attached to Illustrator for your graphic design needs, another alternative is the Microsoft Expression Design product. There is a free trial available at www.microsoft.com/expression/. Design will open your Illustrator files and export Silverlight XAML files for use in Blend or Visual Studio as well.

The Ellipse element

The Ellipse element is used to draw ellipse shapes in your Silverlight applications. Like the previous few examples, the Ellipse element also has properties such as Fill, Height, IsHitTestVisible, Left, Name, Opacity, Stroke, Tag, Top, Visibility, and Width. Click and hold the Rectangle icon in the toolbox to access the Ellipse icon. When the Shapes fly-out menu opens, as in Figure 1-16, select the Ellipse icon. The shortcut key to create an Ellipse is L.

Figure 1-16. The Ellipse element icon

With the Ellipse icon selected, click and drag on the artboard to draw an ellipse. As with Rectangle elements, the Width and Height properties are not linked when creating a new ellipse. To link the Height and Width properties in order to create a circle, hold down the Shift key while dragging.

Once you have created an ellipse to your liking, use the color picker on the Brushes pane of the Properties panel to select a shade of green. Select the Stroke item on the Brushes pane, and then click the No brush tab above the color picker to turn off the stroke for this object. The XAML for a green Ellipse element may look like this:

```
<Ellipse Height="68" Width="113" Canvas.Left="82" Canvas.Top="70"
    Fill="#FF5ED221"/>
```

The XAML code shown here will create an ellipse that is 113×68. The ellipse's top-left corner will be 82 pixels from the left of the containing canvas and 70 pixels down. The fill color #FF5ED221 will make the ellipse fill with green. Notice that unlike the Rectangle object, no stroke is defined for the ellipse. This means that the ellipse will not display a stroke line around its edge.

The TextBlock element

XAML currently offers two types of text elements. One is called a TextBox, and the other is called a TextBlock. A TextBox is an editable text box, just like you would find on an HTML form. On the other hand, TextBlocks are used to display a static block of text that cannot be edited by a user. They are typically used for providing instructions or other information, though they can also be useful for debugging by displaying various object property values within an application as it is running. TextBlocks have properties such as Foreground (color), Height, Opacity, Width, and Visibility. There are also properties for Margins, FontFamily, FontSize, Text, and so forth. To add a TextBlock to the artboard, click and hold the TextBox icon in the toolbar until the Text Controls fly-out menu opens. Select the TextBlock item, as shown in Figure 1-17.

Figure 1-17. Adding a TextBlock to the artboard

You can now double-click the TextBlock icon, or click and drag on the artboard to create the new text block. You will notice that the default text, TextBlock, is selected, allowing you to type in the new text immediately. Once you're done typing, click the Selection tool icon in the toolbox, or click outside the TextBlock to deselect it, and then press the V key to change back to selection mode. Alternatively, you can use the Common Properties pane of the Properties panel, shown in Figure 1-18, to change the text in a TextBlock. The Text field displays the text that is in the selected TextBlock element. Typing new text into this field will update the text that is displayed.

Figure 1-18. The Common Properties pane can be used to modify the text in a TextBlock element.

The XAML for a TextBlock typically looks like this:

```
<TextBlock Height="92" Width="332" Canvas.Left="165" Canvas.Top="86"
    Text="This is an example of a TextBlock element."
    TextWrapping="Wrap"/>
```

The code shown here will create a TextBlock object that is 332 pixels wide and 92 pixels high. The TextBlock object will be located 165 pixels from the left of the container canvas and 86 pixels from the top. The text displayed in this TextBlock will be displayed in the default Portable User Interface font, and will read This is an example of a TextBlock element. The TextWrapping is set to wrap the text if it exceeds the width of the TextBlock. Because the height of this TextBlock is hard-coded rather than set to Auto, any wrapped text that exceeds the 92-pixel height will be clipped.

Oftentimes, you may need to use multiple lines of text within the TextBlock, or change styles for different portions of the text. This is done by using the <Run> and <LineBreak> tags within a TextBlock element. When entering text via the Text field on the Common Properties pane, pressing Enter will create a XAML LineBreak tag. Each line of text is separated into its own Run tag. While the Blend interface will create the base tags for you, if you'd like to mix font styles or sizes as shown here, you must modify the XAML directly. In these cases, the TextBlock serves as a container, with an opening and closing tag, and the text runs and line breaks are contained within the TextBlock container, as shown here:

```
<TextBlock TextWrapping="Wrap" Canvas.Top="268" Canvas.Left="245">
<Run FontFamily="Arial" FontSize="12"
    Text="This is Arial 12 point text."/>
<LineBreak/>
<Run FontFamily="Verdana" FontSize="14"
    Text="This is Verdana 14 point text."/>
</TextBlock>
```

Notice how each Run can be used to define a different style for the text if necessary. While changing text styles from line to line is not particularly common, runs and line breaks can be useful for creating bulleted lists.

The Line element

The Line element is used to draw a straight line between two points. Lines are nothing more than simple path segments that contain only two points. As such, they share the same properties as the Path element. You can create Line elements by selecting the Line icon from the Shapes fly-out menu, or by using the Backslash key on the keyboard. Clicking and dragging the mouse on the artboard will draw a line. Holding the Shift key will constrain the angle of the line to 15 degree multiples. XAML for a Line element looks like this:

```
<Path Height="146" Width="146" Canvas.Left="67" Canvas.Top="170"
    Fill="#FFFFFFFF" Stretch="Fill" Stroke="#FF000000"
    Data="M67,317 L212,170"/>
```

The example Line element XAML shown here draws a diagonal line. The top-left corner of the line's bounding box is located at 146,146, but the line itself is drawn diagonally from the bottom left of the box to the top right. This is controlled by the numbers shown in the Data portion of the XAML. The first pair of numbers is the starting point for the line (67,317). The second pair of numbers preceded by the L are the endpoint for the line (212,170). The Stretch property has to do with the way the object is contained within its bounding box and how it is affected by explicitly set Width and Height properties. For a simple two-point path, the fill color won't have any effect—paths are typically filled shapes, rather than simple lines. The stroke color, which is black in this case, will be what gives the line its color.

It should be noted that there is an actual Line element in XAML, which takes four properties in order to create a line: X1, Y1, X2, and Y2. These two coordinate pairs define the line's beginning point and endpoint. We will be using both throughout the various tutorials presented in the book, though the true Line object is typically generated programmatically given that Blend produces paths. A Line object's XAML looks like the following code:

```
<Line X1="0" Y1="0" X2="100" Y2="100"/>
```

The controls elements

In addition to the previously mentioned elements, we will be working with some of the existing user controls in Silverlight 2, such as sliders and buttons. Sliders and buttons are prebuilt controls, and will be used at times to modify properties as applications are running or to reset values. Buttons, sliders, and other prebuilt controls are added from the Controls fly-out menu, shown in Figure 1-19.

In the following example, you can see that the XAML for both sliders and buttons looks very simple. If you add them to your application by selecting them from the Controls fly-out menu and run the application, you will see that they have some built-in behaviors already. The button changes when you mouseover or click, and the slider is draggable. However, to use them for anything, it takes a bit of code to wire them up.

Figure 1-19. The Controls fly-out menu

This built-in behavior you see is inherited from the System.Windows.Controls class, and is referred to as a ControlTemplate. We will not be modifying control styles or ControlTemplates over the course of this book, but it is useful to know that they exist, and that you can find more information on them in the Silverlight MSDN library online.

The following is some sample XAML code for a button and a slider:

```
<Button Height="26" Width="72" Canvas.Left="555"
    Canvas.Top="100" Content="Button"/>
<Slider Height="34" Width="147.5" Canvas.Left="567" Canvas.Top="159"/>
```

More about XAML

As you can see from the preceding simple walkthrough, Blend is a powerful tool that helps cut application design and development time by creating XAML code for you as you work. However, even with the help of Blend, you should take the opportunity to learn more about XAML in general—the available objects and attributes extend well beyond the few discussed here. If you are interested in learning more, explore the elements through Blend and use the Silverlight Development Center at http://msdn.microsoft.com for detailed descriptions of the available attributes of each element. The development center has extensive descriptions of all the available elements.

What you need to know about programming

Teaching programming is beyond the scope of this book, so you will want to have some exposure to it before digging into the more complex examples. While Silverlight supports code-behind files written in C#, Visual Basic, and JavaScript, the examples here are written in C#.

If you are new to programming or the C# language, don't panic. You don't need to have years of programming experience to work through the examples. If you enter the code as it is shown, you should be able to run the projects without too much trouble. If you have experience with a language like JavaScript or Java, the code should be fairly easy to follow because the syntax is fairly similar.

If you consider yourself more of a creative type than a developer, you should still be able to find value in the provided example code and related information. All the examples are available as a download from the friends of ED website (www.friendsofed.com/). You can look at them, dissect them, modify them, and experiment to see how it all goes together.

A good development environment makes the development process faster and easier, so the process described in the book relies on Visual Studio and C#. Visual Studio (or Visual Web Developer Express Edition) is a great way to write code without the editor getting in your way. Visual Studio contains extensive IntelliSense help—small pop-up windows open as you type in the name of objects or properties to show you the options available to you. Coding is often as simple as typing the first couple of letters of your object's name, and then pressing Enter. By then typing a period (.), all the properties and methods for that object will be displayed. The IntelliSense available within the programming environment makes it easy to identify and utilize the properties and methods that are available for various objects. The examples are written in a way that should be easy to absorb and follow. Once you have the techniques and concepts down, you can optimize them as you see fit for use in your own applications.

With regard to specifics of programming, familiarity with the various types of loops, public and private variables, methods, and passing data will be helpful, as will some knowledge of object-oriented programming, though it's not critical.

Silverlight 1.0 applications supported only JavaScript, and in the general context of web development, there are a lot of developers and designers that are familiar with the language. If you are used to programming with JavaScript, you should be able to make the jump to C# fairly easily—the syntaxes of the two languages are very similar, but C# offers a lot more flexibility.

Anatomy of a Silverlight project

We're going to be working with a lot of projects. Some of them are created with Blend, and some with Visual Studio. While the basic structure of a project is common between the programs, there are some important differences, and some important information you need to be aware of. Don't worry too much if you don't get everything in this section just yet. Keep it in the back of your head and refer back to the book if you need to. This is just to get you prepared for what you'll be seeing later.

Both Blend and Visual Studio produce a group of files referred to as a "project." Projects created in Blend contain a smaller number of files than those created in Visual Studio, so we'll start by exploring the anatomy of a project in Blend. When you begin Blend, a startup pane will display a list of recent projects on a Projects tab. You also have the option of selecting New Project, Open Project, or Open Site.

When New Project is selected, a New Project dialog like the one shown in Figure 1-20 opens. You can choose from the following options: WPF Application, WPF Control Library, Silverlight 1 Site, or Silverlight 2 Application. WPF stands for Windows Presentation Foundation, and was the predecessor to Silverlight. Silverlight's capabilities are a subset of WPF intended for online use, whereas WPF is more suited to creating robust Windows applications.

In this book, we will be working exclusively with Silverlight 2 applications. You also have the choice of specifying either the C# or Visual Basic programming language to use in the code-behind files that you will be writing later. Since the code samples in this book are done in C#, you will want to choose Visual C# from the Language drop-down if it is not the default.

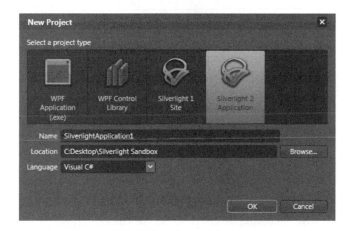

Figure 1-20. The New Project dialog in Blend

Once you have given your application a name, click OK, and Blend will create the project for you. In Blend, the contents of a project are not as obvious as they are in Visual Studio because the list of files appears on the Project tab of the Properties panel. To see or access the list of project-related files while working in Blend, simply click the Project tab on the Properties panel. The file list shown in Figure 1-21 shows an example default file list after creating a new project in Blend.

The topmost file in the list is the solution file. The file is placed in the root directory of the project and has a .sln extension. Solution files can be opened in either Blend or Visual Studio. The solution file contains a reference to the next file in the list, which is in the project directory and has a .csproj extension. This file is an XML file that contains all the various configuration options for the development environment.

Next in the list is the References folder, which contains several mysterious-looking DLL files. These files are referred to as *assemblies*, and contain the libraries that Silverlight needs to run your applications. Three of these files, mscorlib.dll, System.dll, and System.Windows.dll, are required. Three others, System.Core.dll, System.Windows.Browser.dll, and System.Xml.dll, are included to provide application functionality above and beyond the base DLLs that are commonly used.

Inside the Properties folder are two more files— AppManifest.xml and AssemblyInfo.cs. AppManifest.xml is updated when an application is compiled to include the assemblies that are deployed within the client application. The AssemblyInfo.cs file contains metadata that gets embedded into the assembly file that is generated when you compile. The AssemblyInfo.cs file contents look like the following listing:

Figure 1-21. The default list of files associated with a new project in Blend

```
using System.Reflection;
using System.Runtime.CompilerServices;
using System.Runtime.InteropServices;

// General Information about an assembly is controlled through the
// following set of attributes. Change these attribute values to
// modify the information associated with an assembly.
[assembly: AssemblyTitle("BlendSilverlightAnatomy")]
[assembly: AssemblyDescription("")]
[assembly: AssemblyConfiguration("")]
[assembly: AssemblyCompany("")]
[assembly: AssemblyProduct("BlendSilverlightAnatomy")]
[assembly: AssemblyCopyright("Copyright ©  2008")]
[assembly: AssemblyTrademark("")]
[assembly: AssemblyCulture("")]

// Setting ComVisible to false makes the types in this assembly not
// visible  to COM components.  If you need to access a type in
// this assembly from COM, set the ComVisible attribute to
// true on that type.
[assembly: ComVisible(false)]
```

```
// The following GUID is for the ID of the typelib if this
// project is exposed to COM
[assembly: Guid("a1e7ead7-b8f1-4250-bc86-4d6223db9368")]

// Version information for an assembly consists of the
// following four values:
//
//        Major Version
//        Minor Version
//        Build Number
//        Revision
//
// You can specify all the values or you can default the Revision
// and Build Numbers by using the '*' as shown below:
// [assembly: AssemblyVersion("1.0.*")]

[assembly: AssemblyVersion("1.0.0.0")]
[assembly: AssemblyFileVersion("1.0.0.0")]
```

You can see that the listing contains fields for title, description, configuration, copyright, and so on. For Blend-based projects, you can edit this file with any text editor if you have a need.

The next two files in the list are App.xaml and App.xaml.cs. These two files create a class called App, and are required by every Silverlight application. Their purpose is to start the application and show the user interface (UI).

Finally, we come to Page.xaml and Page.xaml.cs. These two files also create a class, called Page. The Page class is where you will typically be creating the UI for your application. Page.xaml is a file containing markup that contains elements of the UI, while Page.xaml.cs is the code-behind file that controls what happens when your application runs. Generally speaking, you won't have to worry about these files too much in the early going. Blend will take care of putting the right XAML code in the right spot for you.

If you take a look at the folder where the application resides, you will see that the root folder contains the solution file, and a folder with the same name. Inside the solution folder is the .csproj file, as well as the App and Page XAML and CS files, like those shown in Figure 1-22. Inside the Properties folder is where the AppManifest.xml and AssemblyInfo.cs files reside.

Notice that there is no References folder as displayed in the file list in Blend. This is because the assemblies are located elsewhere and referenced in the project. When you compile a project, the necessary libraries will be included in the application.

You will also see bin and obj folders. When you compile a Silverlight application in Blend, these folders will contain the final application files Blend uses to display the application to you. The bin\Debug folder in particular may be useful. After compiling, you will find a file with the project name and a .xap (pronounced *zap*) extension. This file is a renamed ZIP archive that contains your application. Also in that folder is a Default.html file, which will load and display the application XAP file. The XAP and HTML files can be used to deploy your application on a web server.

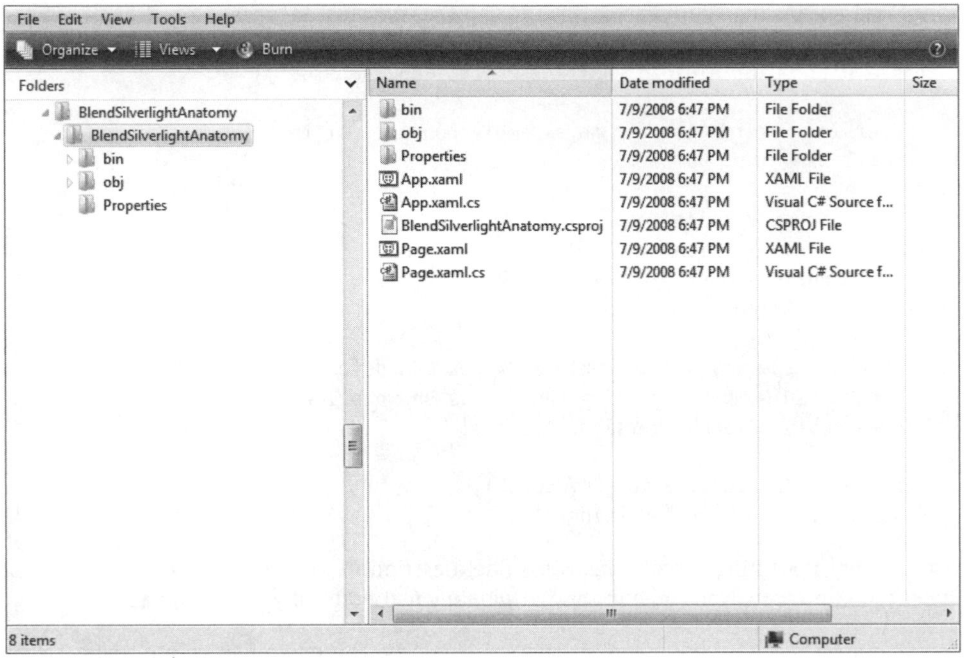

Figure 1-22. The project folder for a Blend-created project

You can edit the HTML file to change the way your application is presented in the page, but use some care—if you edit the file and then recompile in Blend, your HTML file will be overwritten with a new test page that contains the default code. This is not the case with Visual Studio, but Visual Studio creates the page in a slightly different way, as you will see. There are a few pieces of code that are of interest in the HTML file, so we'll take a quick look at those. The first are two of the styles near the top of the page:

```
body {
    padding: 0;
    margin: 0;
}
#silverlightControlHost {
    height: 100%;
}
```

If you're familiar with CSS, you can feel free to edit these as you choose. For the Visual Studio–based projects in this book, the body style has a padding-top: 50px; style applied in order to give the application a little room across the top.

The #silverlightControlHost style is applied to a div that contains the Silverlight object tag:

```
<div id="silverlightControlHost">
    <object data="data:application/x-silverlight,"
            type="application/x-silverlight-2-b2"
            width="100%" height="100%">
```

```
            <param name="source" value="BlendSilverlightAnatomy.xap"/>
            <param name="onerror" value="onSilverlightError" />
            <param name="background" value="white" />

            <a href="http://go.microsoft.com/fwlink/?LinkID=115261"
               style="text-decoration: none;">
                 <img src="http://go.microsoft.com/fwlink/?LinkId=108181"
                      alt="Get Microsoft Silverlight"
                      style="border-style: none"/>
            </a>
        </object>
        <iframe style='visibility:hidden;height:0;width:0;border:0px'>
        </iframe>
    </div>
```

Notice that the object has its height and width set to 100%. This will cause the application to fill the div. The style, in turn, sets the div's width and height to 100%, which will fill the browser. In many cases, you will want to control the size of your application. For the book projects, the applications are 800×600, and the style is adjusted accordingly, as shown:

```
#silverlightControlHost {
    height: 600px;
    width: 800px;
}
```

If you do not adjust the style for the Silverlight application's div container, you may be surprised when you see your content appear to spill outside the bounds of your application.

There are two other small changes made to the HTML for most of the projects in the book. The first is the HTML body tag's background. You can change this via the style tag or the body tag. The background color of the page is typically set to a medium-gray.

```
html, body
{
    background-color: #999999;
    height: 100%;
    overflow: auto;
}
```

Finally, the content of the page is wrapped in another div that is center-aligned on the page. This can also be handled via CSS rather than HTML code.

```
<div align="center">

    <!-- Runtime errors from Silverlight will be displayed here.
         This will contain debugging information and should be
         removed or hidden when debugging is completed -->
    <div id='errorLocation'
         style="font-size: small;color: Gray;"></div>
```

```
            <div id="silverlightControlHost">
                <object data="data:application/x-silverlight,"
                        type="application/x-silverlight-2-b2"
                        width="100%" height="100%">
                    <param name="source" value="BlendSilverlightAnatomy.xap"/>
                    <param name="onerror" value="onSilverlightError" />
                    <param name="background" value="white" />

                        <a href="http://go.microsoft.com/fwlink/?LinkID=115261"
                          style="text-decoration: none;">
                        <img
                            src="http://go.microsoft.com/fwlink/?LinkId=108181"
                            alt="Get Microsoft Silverlight"
                            style="border-style: none"/>
                </a>
                </object>
                <iframe style='visibility:hidden;height:0;width:0;border:0px'>
                </iframe>
            </div>
        </div>
```

Notice that inside the silverlightControlHost div is the object tag that instantiates the Silverlight application. The first line of the object tag declares the type of object and size. The source parameter points directly to the XAP file that contains the application. The onerror parameter points to a JavaScript function that will run if Silverlight encounters an error. This is useful for troubleshooting, but can be removed for release code. The final parameter sets the default background color of the application. These are just the default parameters with which we will be working.

If you're using Visual Studio, you will be presented with a New Project dialog when you select File ➤ New Project in Visual Studio. If you have installed Silverlight Tools for Visual Studio, you will see a Silverlight Application option under the Templates section on the right pane of the dialog box. Figure 1-23 shows the New Project dialog.

Once you have selected the Silverlight Application template, you can give the project a name, select a location, and even change the solution name if you so choose. The biggest difference between Blend and Visual Studio with regard to the project files is what happens when you click OK on the New Project dialog. Visual Studio will open a second dialog called Add Silverlight Application, like the one shown in Figure 1-24.

This dialog allows you to have Visual Studio add a web page to the solution for hosting the Silverlight application. Typically, when this dialog opens, you will want to click OK and accept the defaults. Visual Studio will then go about creating the project for you.

In Visual Studio's Solution Explorer, you will see the same project files as those in the Blend project, as well as the web page and related ClientBin folder, which contains the application XAP file, as shown in Figure 1-25.

Visual Studio will create both an ASPX and an HTML file in the web project. By default, the ASPX file will be used when you compile and run an application. To change this, right-click the HTML file and select Set As Start Page, as shown in Figure 1-26. The next time you compile, the selected file will be used. The example projects throughout the book have been set to use the HTML file as the start page.

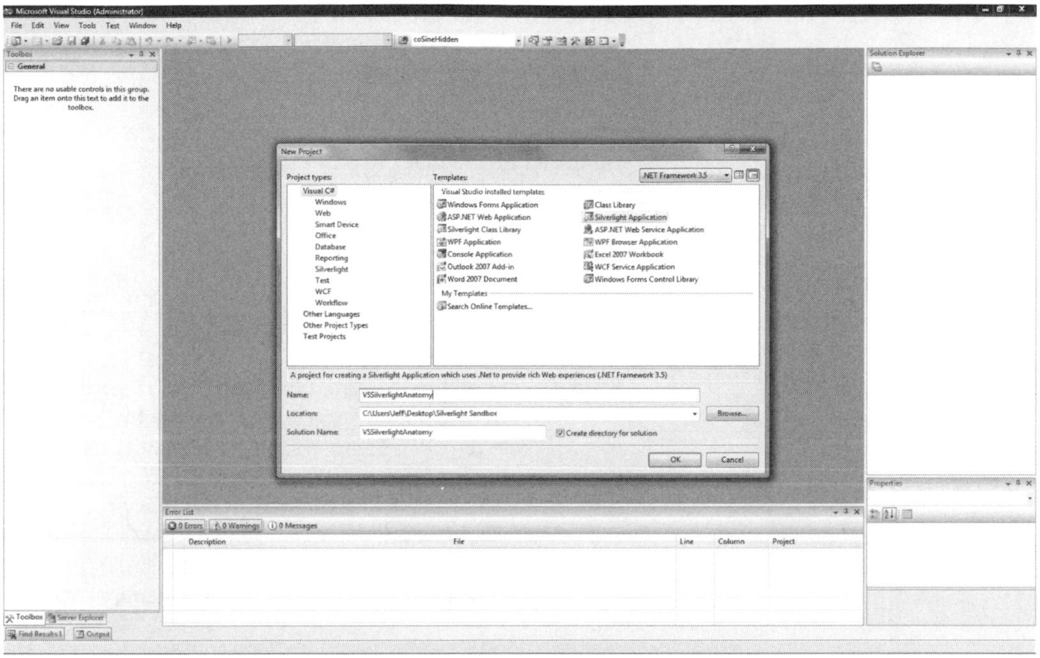

Figure 1-23. The New Project dialog box in Visual Studio 2008

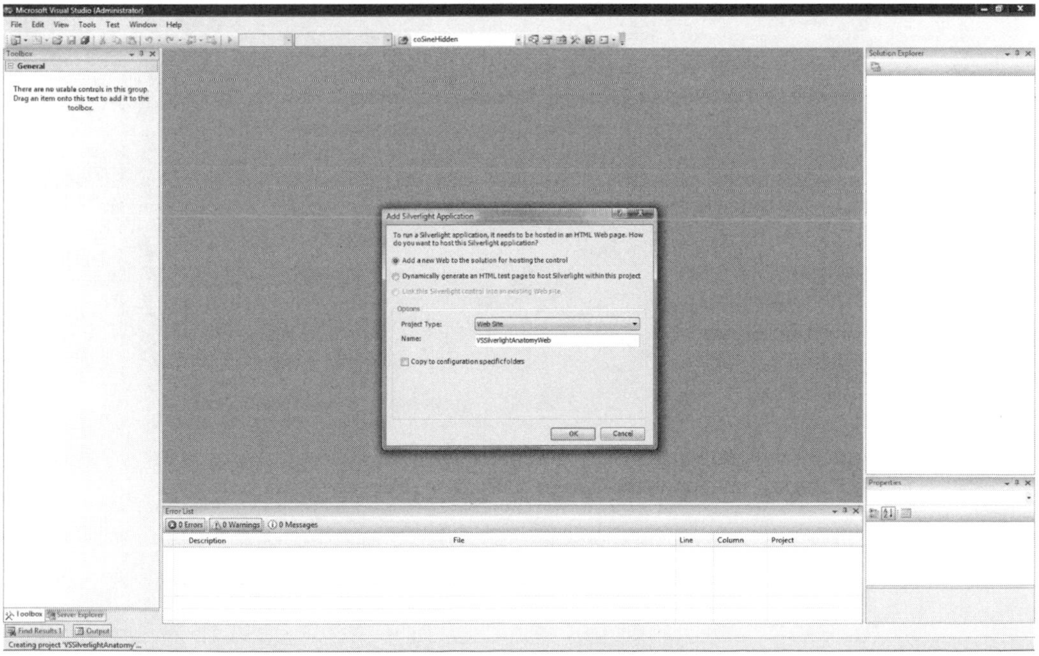

Figure 1-24. The Add Silverlight Application dialog box in Visual Studio 2008

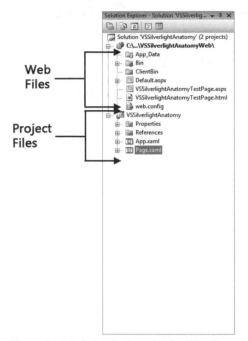

Web
Files

Project
Files

Unlike with Blend, the web files created as part of your project in Visual Studio can be edited, and you will not lose the changes each time you compile your project. This makes it a little easier to see application content as part of a completed web page without risk of having to re-create the web page if you forget to copy files to a backup location.

You will notice in the project's file list that the XAML files are shown, but none of the code-behind files are visible. To view the code-behind files, click the + symbol to the left of the XAML control you want to edit, and the file list will expand. You can then double-click the .cs file to open it for editing.

When you are editing a XAML file, a long list of available user controls shows up in the toolbox. These are the same controls available to you in Blend. At the moment, the interface in Blend is a little more robust when it comes to creating interfaces or objects for your applications. The two programs are well integrated, however. You can open any XAML file for editing in Blend by right-clicking the file in Solution Explorer and selecting Open in Expression Blend from the menu, as shown in Figure 1-27.

Figure 1-25. Solution Explorer in Visual Studio

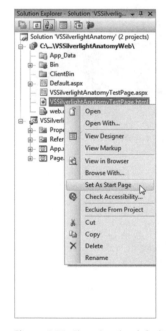

Figure 1-26. Changing the default start page for a Visual Studio project

Figure 1-27. Opening a file from your Visual Studio project in Blend for editing is fast and easy.

Summary

Of the software discussed for creating Silverlight content, Visual Studio and Blend are really must-haves. The benefits they bring to development really smooth out the process for both designers and developers. As the backbone of a Silverlight application, it is critical that both designers and developers familiarize themselves with XAML markup. XAML acts as a bridge between design and development, giving designers more control throughout the application development process.

In our projects, we'll only be using a subset of the XAML objects available. The objects we'll be concentrating on include Canvas, Image, Rectangle, Path, Ellipse, TextBlock and a couple of the prebuilt controls such as Slider and Button. Canvases are generally used as containers for other types of objects. Images allow you to utilize JPG or PNG images in your applications. Rectangles, Paths, and Ellipses are all vector-based drawing objects. TextBlocks are used to display noneditable text within an application.

If you have some experience programming, you should be able to pick up the C# syntax relatively quickly. Working through the projects in the book will help you identify how various objects and properties are accessed through code. If you're used to programming in JavaScript, you should find C# fairly easy to adopt from a coding perspective, but there's a lot to learn with respect to the availability of the .NET libraries. Be patient, and you'll get it!

New Silverlight projects can be created in either Blend or Visual Studio, though there are some differences between the two. Visual Studio will allow you to specify a web project that creates a web page in which your application is automatically hosted. Blend only creates the web page when a project is compiled, and will overwrite the page each time you compile.

In Chapter 2, we'll take a look at the basic transforms available in Silverlight. These include Translate, Scale, Rotate, Skew, Flip, and Center Point. We'll also take a look at object properties, and how to work with the control points of which objects are comprised.

Part Two

SILVERLIGHT ANIMATION: THE BASICS

Chapter 2

BASIC TRANSFORMS

When we talk about animation in Silverlight, we're really talking about the different ways we can manipulate the properties of an object within the applications we build. One of the tools available to change the way an object looks relative to the original is called a **transform**. Basic transforms are used to modify an object's translation (its location relative to the container in which it resides), rotation, scale, or skewing. Basic transforms are a common aspect of application UI development, often used to animate objects over time (such as panels sliding in and out, and objects growing and shrinking).

We will be working with the transform properties located on the Transform pane (shown in Figure 2-1), which can be found near the bottom of the Properties panel. If the full pane is not already visible, you will see a bar that contains an arrowhead pointing to the right and the word Transform. You can expand the pane by clicking anywhere on the Transform header on the bar.

Figure 2-1. The Transform pane of the Properties panel

The Transform pane contains tabs that are used to create transforms that translate, rotate, skew, adjust the center point of, or flip an object. The following sections describe how each of these transforms can be used to make changes to objects on the artboard.

The Translate transform

By translating an object, we're moving that object around the artboard, but moving it in a way that is relative to its original position. This is different than what happens when you drag an object, because dragging an object changes its position relative to the container in which it resides.

This is useful for creating motions that are self-contained. For example, if a panel "opens" by sliding 200 pixels to the right, you can freely reposition the panel anywhere in the layout container without affecting the motion defined by the translation.

Consider an object that is positioned at the x and y coordinates 100,100. If you drag the object 50 pixels to the right and 50 pixels down, the object will now reside at the absolute position of 150,150. However, if the same object has a transform applied that moves it 50 pixels to the right and 50 pixels down from its original position, the object will be *drawn* at 150,150, though its absolute position relative to the container in which it resides will still be 100,100. The Top and Left fields on the Properties panel will show the absolute value of 100,100.

This can be a bit confusing, so let's work through an example that demonstrates the difference between the two:

1. Create a new project in Blend. Change the default Grid container on the artboard to a Canvas by editing the XAML, or by right-clicking the LayoutRoot element in the Objects and Timeline list and selecting Change Layout Type ➤ Canvas, as shown in Figure 2-2.

2. Select the Rectangle tool from the toolbox by pressing M, and then double-click the Rectangle icon to add a Rectangle element to the canvas. By default, a 100×100 rectangle will be placed in the upper-left corner of the canvas on the artboard. Select the rectangle on the Objects and Timelines panel and use the Brushes pane of the Properties panel to give it a background color other than the default white.

Figure 2-2. The Change Layout Type menu in Blend

3. On the Transform pane (shown in Figure 2-1), the square icon on the left with nine points allows you to select the point of origin for the transform. We'll take a closer look at this in another example, but this is useful if you need to make an object scale or rotate about a point other than the default center. In the X field, enter 100 and press Enter. The rectangle should oblige by moving to the right 100 pixels. Notice on the Layout pane that the Left position of the rectangle is still being reported as 0.

Translations define an offset from an object's current position on the artboard. If you press the V key to change to the Selection tool and then drag the rectangle to a different location on the artboard, you will notice the Left property changing in the Layout pane. After dragging, the rectangle is still off-set 100 pixels from the value being displayed in the Layout pane. You can test this by entering 0 into the X field on the Transform pane—without a translation applied, the rectangle returns to the position shown in the Left field of the Layout pane. Y offsets will work the same way as X offsets.

Let's create an animation that will demonstrate a translation that occurs over time:

1. Open the **eclipse** project from Chapter 2 by selecting File ➤ Open ➤ Project/Solution. Locate the eclipse.sln file. This project contains two objects: a sun and a darkened moon.

2. In this project, we will be using a Translate trans-form to move the moon in order to create a lunar eclipse. If the workspace in Blend is not in the Animation Workspace (with the Objects and Timeline panel below the artboard), press F6 to change the layout now. Once you've done that, click the New Storyboard button on the Objects and Timeline panel, as shown in Figure 2-3.

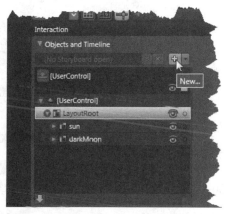

Figure 2-3. Click the New Storyboard button to create a new animation.

3. The Create Storyboard Resource window will open. This window asks for a unique name for the story-board that is about to be created. As you work on the artboard creating motions for your objects, Blend will automatically build out the storyboard for you. We'll take a more in-depth look at storyboards in Chapter 3. For now, just click OK to accept the default name of Storyboard1.

4. The Blend interface will switch to timeline recording mode, as shown in Figure 2-4. A timeline and its associated controls will appear to the right of the Objects and Timeline panel, and the artboard border will turn red, indicating that timeline recording is on. When timeline recording mode is on, any changes you make to the properties of an object will create a keyframe on the timeline. You can toggle timeline recording mode on and off by clicking the red button at the top left of the artboard. Turning off timeline recording will not close the current timeline—it simply stops Blend from recording the changes you make as keyframes on the timeline. This is very useful when you need to make some changes to an object that are not supposed to be part of the animation.

The yellow bar on the timeline is called the timeline play head, and it indicates your current position within the timeline. If you are coming from a Flash background, there is a significant difference in the way timelines works in Silverlight. Here, animations are **time-based** rather than **frame-based**. Time-based animations should offer a more consistent end user experi-ence across a wide array of hardware, as one second is a consistent unit of measure across computers.

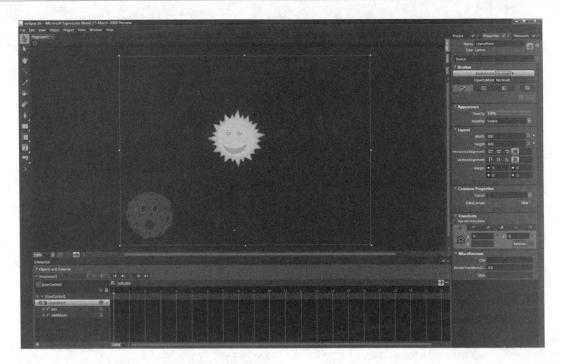

Figure 2-4. The Blend interface showing the eclipse project in timeline recording mode

5. In order to move the timeline play head to a specific point on the timeline, use the mouse to click the triangle at the top of the play head, and then drag it. For this example, we want to move the moon in front of the sun over a 1-second period of time, so drag the timeline play head to the 1-second mark, as shown in Figure 2-5.

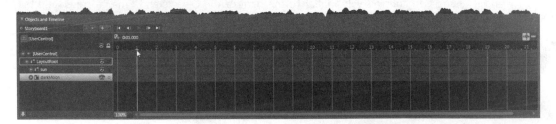

Figure 2-5. Move the timeline play head to the 1-second mark on the timeline.

6. Select the darkMoon element on the Objects and Timeline panel by clicking it. On the Properties panel, make sure that the Transform pane is expanded. On the Translate tab, we want to enter values that cause the moon to be centered over the sun object. In the X field, enter 280 to offset the moon object 280 pixels to the right. In the Y field, enter -245 to offset the moon object up 245 pixels from its current location. Remember that in Silverlight, the x and y offsets are measured from the top-left corner of an object.

7. Press the Play button above the timeline to preview your animation. You defined the start point of the object by its placement on the canvas, and the endpoint by the Translate transform you defined. Blend will handle all the "in-between" frames automatically, and the moon will glide in front of the sun. As you created the time-based translation, Blend automatically generated a storyboard in the background. The storyboard is XAML code that tells Silverlight how the objects in your application should move. I'll talk a lot more about storyboards in Chapter 3, but just so you can see what's going on, the following code listing shows the storyboard that was created for this animation:

```
<Storyboard x:Name="Storyboard1">
    <DoubleAnimationUsingKeyFrames BeginTime="00:00:00"
     Storyboard.TargetName="darkMoon"
     Storyboard.TargetProperty="(UIElement.RenderTransform).➥
     (TransformGroup.Children)[3].(TranslateTransform.X)">
        <SplineDoubleKeyFrame KeyTime="00:00:01" Value="280"/>
    </DoubleAnimationUsingKeyFrames>
    <DoubleAnimationUsingKeyFrames BeginTime="00:00:00"
     Storyboard.TargetName="darkMoon"
     Storyboard.TargetProperty="(UIElement.RenderTransform).➥
     (TransformGroup.Children)[3].(TranslateTransform.Y)">
        <SplineDoubleKeyFrame KeyTime="00:00:01" Value="-245"/>
    </DoubleAnimationUsingKeyFrames>
</Storyboard>
```

8. As mentioned earlier, translations are simply offsets from an object's actual position within its parent object. To illustrate this, drag the timeline play head back to 0 or select the Go to first frame button above the timeline. Click the red button at the top-left corner of the artboard to turn off timeline recording.

9. With the darkMoon element still selected, enter 200 into the Top field on the Layout pane of the Properties panel. Now press the Play button for the timeline again to preview the animation. What happens? The moon moves to the same offset defined in the storyboard, but because the base object's actual position has changed, the final frame of the animation now finds the moon above the sun rather than over it.

This is an important detail to keep in mind when using translations. You may find yourself in need of a relative offset when animating objects, but remember that changes to the location of the object will affect the end position.

The Rotate transform

Rotate transforms are used to rotate objects within an application. Rotational angles are expressed in degrees, and the values input are additive—a value of 720 will fully spin an object around twice (360 × 2). For spinning in the opposite direction (counterclockwise), negative values can be used.

To see a Rotate transform in action, open the **exhaustFan** project from Chapter 2. This project contains a scene comprised of a simple static background element and a fan element that will be made to rotate, as shown in Figure 2-6.

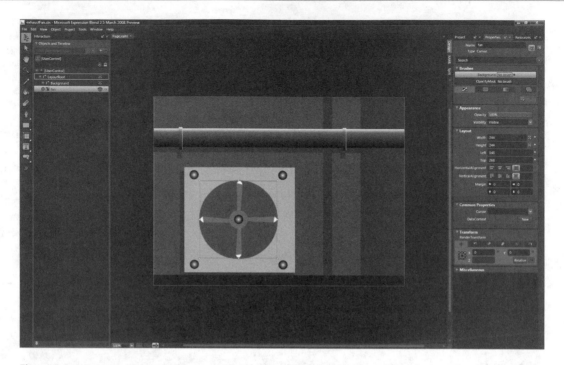

Figure 2-6. A Rotate transform will be used to make the exhaust fan in this project spin.

1. Click the New storyboard button on the Objects and Timeline panel. Click OK when the Create Storyboard Resource dialog opens to accept the default storyboard name. Once again, verify that the Blend layout is set to the Animation Workspace with the timeline open across the bottom of the screen.

2. Drag the timeline play head to 2 seconds. Select the fan element from the Objects and Timeline list. On the Transform pane, select the Rotate tab, and enter 720 into the Angle field. When you click the Play button for the timeline, you will see the fan element perform two rotations over the course of the 2-second animation.

If you are interested in seeing the angle at any given point in time on the storyboard, drag the timeline play head and keep an eye on the Angle field of the Rotate tab. As you move the play head, the value changes to reflect the fan's current angle. Once again, Blend has taken the end value you specified and created all the in-between frames automatically. The storyboard for this project is shown in the following listing:

```
<Storyboard x:Name="Storyboard1">
    <DoubleAnimationUsingKeyFrames BeginTime="00:00:00"
      Storyboard.TargetName="fan"
      Storyboard.TargetProperty="(UIElement.RenderTransform).➥
      (TransformGroup.Children)[2].(RotateTransform.Angle)">
        <SplineDoubleKeyFrame KeyTime="00:00:02" Value="720"/>
    </DoubleAnimationUsingKeyFrames>
</Storyboard>
```

As noted earlier, it is possible to change the point of origin for a transform by relocating the center point. To change the point around which an object is rotating, click the Translate tab of the Transform pane. The small box with nine points located on the left side of the Transform pane allows you to change the location of the pivot to one of nine presets.

3. Click the red button at the top left of the artboard to turn off timeline recording, and drag the timeline play head back to 0.

4. On the Translate tab, click the top-left point, as shown in Figure 2-7.

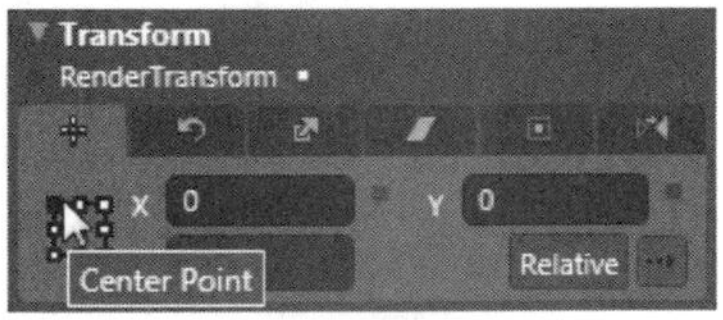

Press the Play button for the timeline. The fan should now be rotating around its top-left corner. This is useful for creating objects that rotate from locations other than their center point. A more accurate term for "center point" is **render transform origin**, as this is how it is specified in XAML code. Changing the location of the center point is really just changing the origin of any transform applied to an object. It just happens that the default position of the point is in the center of an object's bounding box.

Figure 2-7. Changing the center point for a Rotate transform

Try selecting other points for the center point and playing the timeline to see the effect it has on the object. Figures 2-8 through 2-10 show the effect of changing the center point of the fan object if it were rotated 15 degrees.

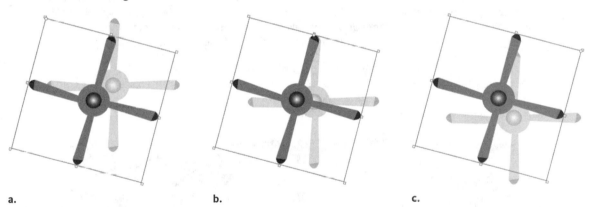

a.   b.   c.

Figure 2-8. Rotation around origin 0,0 (a); rotation around origin .5,0 (b); and rotation around origin 1,0 (c)

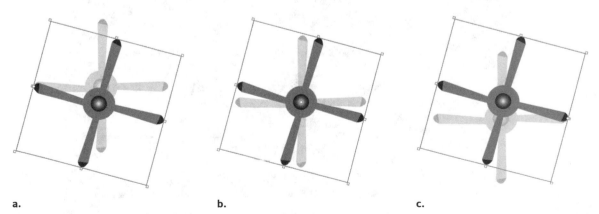

a.   b.   c.

Figure 2-9. Rotation around origin 0,.5 (a); rotation around origin .5,.5 (b); and rotation around origin 1,.5 (c)

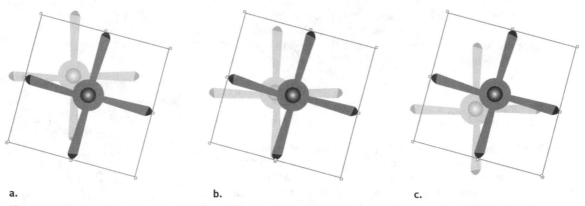

a.   b.   c.

Figure 2-10. Rotation around origin 0,1 (a); rotation around origin .5,1 (b); and rotation around origin 1,1 (c)

The Scale transform

Scale transforms are used to scale objects relative to their original size. The values used in Silverlight for scaling are relative to 1, with 1 being 100%. Therefore, a value of 2 will scale an object to twice its original size. Conversely, a value of .25 will make an object one quarter of its original size. When scaling, values for x and y scale are not linked. This means that to scale an object proportionately, it is necessary to enter the same value in both the X and Y fields of the Scale tab.

Let's take a look at how a Scale transform can be used to modify an object over time in order to simulate perspective. Open the **truck** project from Chapter 2. This project contains a scene that consists of a street backdrop and a truck object, as shown in Figure 2-11. We will be using a Scale transform to make the truck appear as though it is driving away from us.

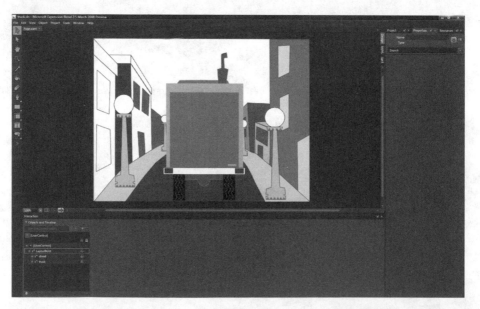

Figure 2-11. Scale transforms can be used to make objects appear as though they are moving away.

1. Click the New storyboard button on the Objects and Timeline panel, and click OK when the Create Storyboard Resource dialog opens. If the Animation Workspace is not set with the timeline displayed below the artboard, press the F6 key.

2. Select the truck element from the Objects and Timeline panel.

3. Move the timeline play head to 3 seconds.

4. On the Transform pane of the Properties panel, select the Scale tab, and enter .15 in both the X and Y fields. This will cause the truck to scale from its current value of 1 (100%) to a value of .15 (15%) over 3 seconds.

5. Click Play to preview the animation. The truck should look as though it is driving down the street, ending near the horizon. Figure 2-12 shows the end position of the truck.

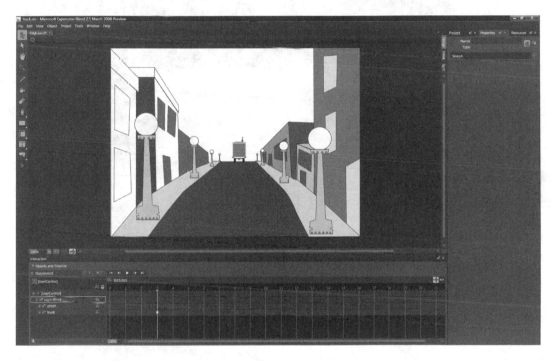

Figure 2-12. A scale translation makes the truck appear to move down the street.

Like Rotate transforms, Scale transforms can also have their center point adjusted. This is useful for making panels that appear to expand and/or collapse to a point other than the center. For this animation, the storyboard is shown in the following listing:

```
<Storyboard x:Name="Storyboard1">
    <DoubleAnimationUsingKeyFrames BeginTime="00:00:00"
     Storyboard.TargetName="truck"
     Storyboard.TargetProperty="(UIElement.RenderTransform).➡
     (TransformGroup.Children)[0].(ScaleTransform.ScaleX)">
        <SplineDoubleKeyFrame KeyTime="00:00:03" Value="0.15"/>
    </DoubleAnimationUsingKeyFrames>
```

```
<DoubleAnimationUsingKeyFrames BeginTime="00:00:00"
 Storyboard.TargetName="truck"
 Storyboard.TargetProperty="(UIElement.RenderTransform).➥
(TransformGroup.Children)[0].(ScaleTransform.ScaleY)">
    <SplineDoubleKeyFrame KeyTime="00:00:03" Value="0.15"/>
 </DoubleAnimationUsingKeyFrames>
</Storyboard>
```

To see an example of this type of scaling, open the **panels** project from Chapter 2. This project contains a canvas with two rectangular "panels," as shown in Figure 2-13.

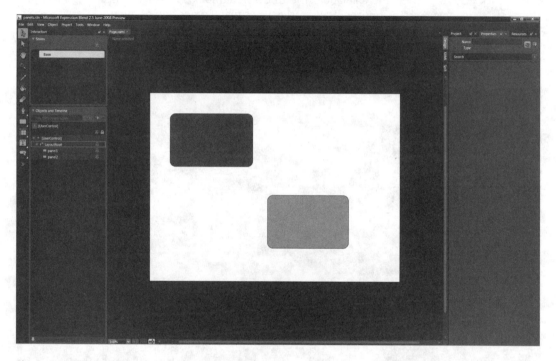

Figure 2-13. The panels project upon opening

1. Click the New storyboard button, and click OK to accept the default name.

2. Select panel1 from the Objects and Timeline panel, and on the Transform pane, change the center point to the middle-left selection (0,.5).

3. On the Scale tab, enter 0 into both the X and Y fields.

4. For the panel2 element, change the center point to the middle-right selection (1,.5).

5. On the Scale tab, scale panel2 down to 0.

Notice that Blend has placed small, oval-shaped keyframe markers on the timeline for both elements, as shown in Figure 2-14.

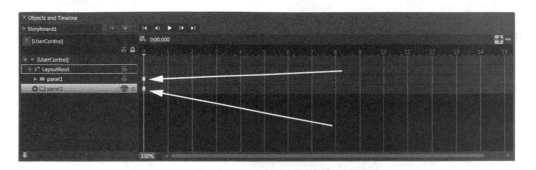

Figure 2-14. Blend adds keyframe markers to the timeline as you manipulate objects on the artboard.

6. Move the timeline play head to 3 seconds, and change the x-y scale for both objects back to 1.

7. Click the Play button on the timeline to see the animation.

Both objects will scale from 0 to 1 over the same time span, but each one scales from a different point of origin. The origin point of the scaling is illustrated with arrows in Figure 2-15. You can create a lot of interesting effects by using different points of origin in a Scale transform that makes use of varied x and y values to expand panels along the different axes at different rates of speed.

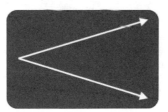

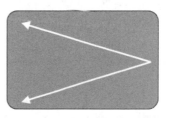

Figure 2-15. The effect of scaling panels from different origin points

The storyboard for this project is a little more complex, since it contains multiple objects with multiple keyframes. It is shown in the following listing:

```
<Storyboard x:Name="Storyboard1">
    <PointAnimationUsingKeyFrames BeginTime="00:00:00"
     Duration="00:00:00.0010000" Storyboard.TargetName="panel1"
```

```
        Storyboard.TargetProperty="(UIElement.RenderTransformOrigin)">
            <SplinePointKeyFrame KeyTime="00:00:00" Value="0,0.5"/>
        </PointAnimationUsingKeyFrames>
        <DoubleAnimationUsingKeyFrames BeginTime="00:00:00"
         Storyboard.TargetName="panel1"
         Storyboard.TargetProperty="(UIElement.RenderTransform).➥
         (TransformGroup.Children)[0].(ScaleTransform.ScaleX)">
            <SplineDoubleKeyFrame KeyTime="00:00:00" Value="0"/>
            <SplineDoubleKeyFrame KeyTime="00:00:03" Value="1"/>
        </DoubleAnimationUsingKeyFrames>
        <DoubleAnimationUsingKeyFrames BeginTime="00:00:00"
         Storyboard.TargetName="panel1"
         Storyboard.TargetProperty="(UIElement.RenderTransform).➥
         (TransformGroup.Children)[0].(ScaleTransform.ScaleY)ᵃ>
            <SplineDoubleKeyFrame KeyTime="00:00:00" Value="0"/>
            <SplineDoubleKeyFrame KeyTime="00:00:03" Value="1"/>
        </DoubleAnimationUsingKeyFrames>
        <PointAnimationUsingKeyFrames BeginTime="00:00:00"
         Duration="00:00:00.0010000" Storyboard.TargetName="panel2"
         Storyboard.TargetProperty="(UIElement.RenderTransformOrigin)">
            <SplinePointKeyFrame KeyTime="00:00:00" Value="1,0.5"/>
        </PointAnimationUsingKeyFrames>
        <DoubleAnimationUsingKeyFrames BeginTime="00:00:00"
         Storyboard.TargetName="panel2"
         Storyboard.TargetProperty="(UIElement.RenderTransform).➥
         (TransformGroup.Children)[0].(ScaleTransform.ScaleX)">
            <SplineDoubleKeyFrame KeyTime="00:00:00" Value="0"/>
            <SplineDoubleKeyFrame KeyTime="00:00:03" Value="1"/>
        </DoubleAnimationUsingKeyFrames>
        <DoubleAnimationUsingKeyFrames BeginTime="00:00:00"
         Storyboard.TargetName="panel2"
         Storyboard.TargetProperty="(UIElement.RenderTransform).➥
         (TransformGroup.Children)[0].(ScaleTransform.ScaleY)">
            <SplineDoubleKeyFrame KeyTime="00:00:00" Value="0"/>
            <SplineDoubleKeyFrame KeyTime="00:00:03" Value="1"/>
        </DoubleAnimationUsingKeyFrames>
    </Storyboard>
```

In addition to using the center point as a static origin for scaling, you can change the location of the center point over time. For example, you could make the truck from the previous example weave down the street by manipulating the center point.

If you would like to try this out, start with the **truckCompleted** project. Above the list of objects on the Objects and Timeline panel, there is a select box that will allow you to open an existing storyboard. Click the Open a Storyboard button, as shown in Figure 2-16.

Blend will present you with a list of available storyboards, as shown in Figure 2-17. This project contains only a single storyboard, Storyboard1, which you should click to open as a starting point. The storyboard will open and Blend will be in timeline recording mode.

Figure 2-16. The Open a Storyboard button on the Objects and Timeline panel

Figure 2-17. The list of available storyboards in the truckCompleted project

1. Select the truck object from the Objects and Timeline list.

2. Drag the timeline play head to .8 seconds.

3. On the Transform pane of the Properties panel, use the Center Point selection presets to pick the point at the middle left (0,.5).

4. Drag the timeline play head to 2 seconds.

5. On the Transform pane of the Properties panel, use the Center Point selection presets to pick the point at the middle right (1,.5).

6. Preview the animation. The point of origin for the Scale transform changes as the truck object scales down from 1 to .15, which causes the truck to appear as though it is swerving as it moves down the road.

The storyboard for this project is shown in the following listing:

```
<Storyboard x:Name="Storyboard1">
    <DoubleAnimationUsingKeyFrames
     Storyboard.TargetName="truck"
     Storyboard.TargetProperty="(UIElement.RenderTransform).➥
     (TransformGroup.Children)[0].(ScaleTransform.ScaleX)"
     BeginTime="00:00:00">
        <SplineDoubleKeyFrame KeyTime="00:00:03" Value="0.15"/>
    </DoubleAnimationUsingKeyFrames>
    <DoubleAnimationUsingKeyFrames
     Storyboard.TargetName="truck"
     Storyboard.TargetProperty="(UIElement.RenderTransform).➥
     (TransformGroup.Children)[0].(ScaleTransform.ScaleY)"
     BeginTime="00:00:00">
        <SplineDoubleKeyFrame KeyTime="00:00:03" Value="0.15"/>
    </DoubleAnimationUsingKeyFrames>
```

```
<PointAnimationUsingKeyFrames BeginTime="00:00:00"
 Storyboard.TargetName="truck"
 Storyboard.TargetProperty="(UIElement.RenderTransformOrigin)">
     <SplinePointKeyFrame KeyTime="00:00:00.8000000" Value="0,0.5"/>
     <SplinePointKeyFrame KeyTime="00:00:02" Value="1,0.5"/>
     <SplinePointKeyFrame KeyTime="00:00:03" Value="0.5,0.5"/>
 </PointAnimationUsingKeyFrames>
 <DoubleAnimationUsingKeyFrames BeginTime="00:00:00"
 Storyboard.TargetName="truck"
 Storyboard.TargetProperty="(UIElement.RenderTransform).➡
 (TransformGroup.Children)[3].(TranslateTransform.X)">
     <SplineDoubleKeyFrame KeyTime="00:00:00.8000000"
     Value="34.342134475708008"/>
     <SplineDoubleKeyFrame KeyTime="00:00:02"
     Value="-109.26261468474225"/>
     <SplineDoubleKeyFrame KeyTime="00:00:03" Value="0"/>
 </DoubleAnimationUsingKeyFrames>
</Storyboard>
```

The Skew transform

Skew transforms can be used to skew an object horizontally, vertically, or both. Open the **skewTransform** project from Chapter 2. This project contains a simple room scene that consists of a background and a door, as shown in Figure 2-18. We will be using a Skew transform to make the door appear as though it has opened.

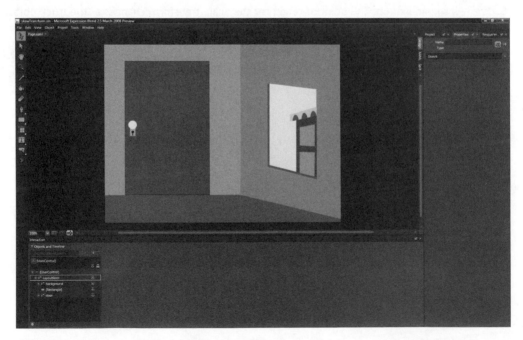

Figure 2-18. Making use of a Skew transform to make a door open

1. Select the door element on the Objects and Timeline panel.

2. On the Transform pane of the Properties panel, select the Translate pane. As with a real door, we want the door in our project to skew along an edge, not the center. On the center point selector, select the control point that is in the middle on the right-hand side (1,.5).

3. On the Objects and Timeline panel, click the New storyboard button, and press Enter to accept the default name.

4. Move the timeline play head to 1 second, and on the Skew pane, enter -10 into the Y field to skew the door canvas −10 units along the y axis. The door should appear to be ajar, as shown in Figure 2-19.

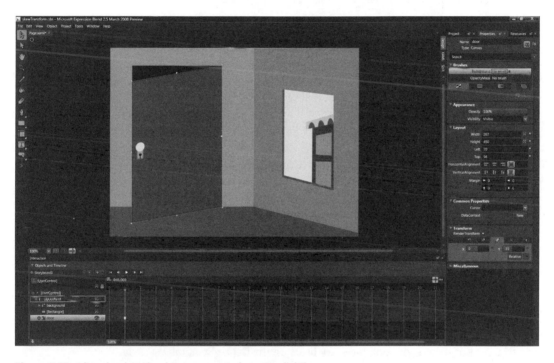

Figure 2-19. After skewing, the door appears to be open slightly.

Press the Play button for the timeline and watch the animation. The door should look like it swings open. Now, you are probably saying to yourself that real-world doors *rotate* about the y axis rather than *skew*, and you are correct. This project is really just a demonstration of how Skew transforms are applied. We're able to get away with it here because we didn't overdo the transform. If you would like to extend the Skew transform to make the door appear as though it has opened wider, you can also apply some scaling to compensate for the warping that will result from the skew. The storyboard for this animation is shown here:

```
<Storyboard x:Name="Storyboard1">
    <DoubleAnimationUsingKeyFrames BeginTime="00:00:00"
     Storyboard.TargetName="door"
```

```
Storyboard.TargetProperty="(UIElement.RenderTransform).➥
    (TransformGroup.Children)[1].(SkewTransform.AngleY)">
        <SplineDoubleKeyFrame KeyTime="00:00:01" Value="-10"/>
    </DoubleAnimationUsingKeyFrames>
</Storyboard>
```

You may have noticed in the projects so far that the objects to which the transforms are being applied are often canvas container objects. In the case of the door, the "door" canvas contains the paths that make up the door, and even a nested canvas that contains the shapes for the doorknob. In this way, canvas layout containers are useful in organizing objects in your projects. They also serve a purpose in that transforms applied to canvases affect all the children inside the canvas being transformed.

The Center Point transform

As you've seen in some of the examples, there is an icon on the Translate tab that allows you to choose one of nine preset locations for the center point of an object. In addition to the presets used to move the center point, there is a Center Point tab. The presets available on the Translate tab are really just shortcuts—as you choose different points, Blend fills the fields on the Center Point tab with appropriate values.

The location of the center point for a selected item's bounding box is changed by manipulating x and y values between 0 and 1. As with the rotating fan example, the top-left position is 0,0; the top center is .5,0; and the top right is 1,0. In the middle row, the values are 0,.5; .5,.5; and 1,.5. The bottom row is 0,1; .5,1; and 1,1. These values are the same and have the same effect whether your object is big or small.

The Center Point tab is useful when you want to place the center point of a transform at a position other than one of the presets—if you have an oddly shaped object that is supposed to appear as though it is swinging, for example.

There are two ways to manipulate the center point of an object. The first way is to type values into the available fields on the Center Point tab. The second way is to select the element on the Objects and Timeline panel on the artboard with the Selection tool (V), and then manipulate the center point with the mouse. Because it is more visual, it is often easier to "rough in" the position with the mouse, and then fine-tune as necessary using the entry fields on the Center Point tab.

When the mouse is over the center point, the cursor will change to a small square with four arrows on it, as shown in Figure 2-20. The center point can then be dragged to a new location. Center points can even be located outside of an object's bounding box. This is useful in situations where you have objects rotating around other objects.

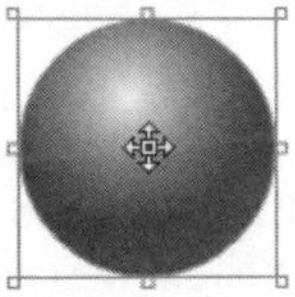

Changes to the location of an element's center point don't cause any visual changes to the element itself. They will, however, change the way that transforms affect the element.

Figure 2-20. An object's center point can be dragged with the mouse.

The **centerpointTransform** project contains two elements for you to experiment with—an ellipse with a gradient fill and a simple black line. On the ellipse, simply use the Selection tool (V) to select the center point with the mouse and then drag it to a different location.

The line element is a little trickier—by default, an object's center point location is in the middle of the object's bounding box, and lines don't have large enough bounding boxes to make their center points easily accessible for clicking and dragging. Since a line element's bounding box doesn't have any height, the center point is not visible.

If you need to move the center point of a line, resize the line's bounding box by dragging the center point of the bounding box border, as shown in Figure 2-21. This will make the center point of the line's bounding box visible/accessible, and you can then drag it where you would like. If you resize the line object by manipulating the bounding box, the center point will move in relation to the size of the bounding box.

Figure 2-21. Expand the bounding box of a Line object to access its center point.

The Flip transform

The Flip tab on the Transform pane, shown in Figure 2-22, has shortcut buttons that allow you to flip an object along the x or y axis. When you use the buttons on the Flip tab, Blend simply creates a Scale transform for you. Using the Flip X axis button, for example, will cause Blend to simply invert the scale of the selected element along the x axis. If an object is scaled to 1x, it will be 100% of its size along the x axis. When you click the Flip X axis button, Blend will make the scale −1x, inverting the object's scale. You can see this by clicking the button and then selecting

Figure 2-22. The Flip tab is used to scale an object along the x or y axis.

the Scale tab. Because an object's scale can be adjusted over time, you can use Flip to create keyframes on a storyboard.

Animating object properties

In addition to transforming objects over time, it is also possible to modify an object's properties over time. Different types of objects have different properties. For example, when working with rectangles, you might change the Color, Opacity, RadiusX, RadiusY, StrokeThickness, Width, Height, Left, or Top values.

Changes to an object's properties are different than transforms because they change the object itself. For example, changing an object's Left property or margins will move the object relative to the container in which it resides. As shown, this is in contrast to a Translate *transform*, where an object moves relative to its original position.

You can animate object properties by creating a new timeline, moving the play head to the appropriate time, and making changes to the properties on the Properties panel. Blend will record the change by placing a keyframe on the timeline.

Property animations can be used to make animations for use as button rollovers, sliding panels, menus dropping down, and so on. Take a look at the **propertyAnimations** project for Chapter 2. This project contains a couple of panels and a couple of ellipses, as shown in Figure 2-23.

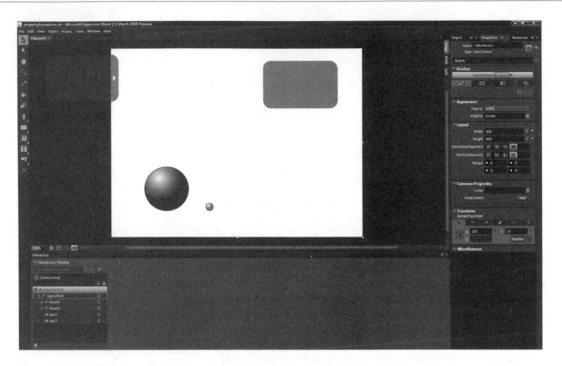

Figure 2-23. An object's properties can be animated in a manner similar to creating transforms.

Notice that Panel1 at the top left of the artboard is positioned partially off the main canvas. If the Silverlight object in the base ASP or HTML file is styled appropriately, only the part of an object that is on canvas will show up when the application runs. Positioning an object partially off-canvas is a useful way to hide parts of that object when an application runs. In this project, we will be creating an animation that will slide Panel1 onto the main canvas, bringing it into view. We'll also change some properties on the other objects in the project to see how they are affected.

1. Begin by creating a new storyboard.

2. Move the timeline play head to 2 seconds.

3. Click Panel1 in the Objects and Timeline panel.

4. Change to selection mode by pressing V on the keyboard, and then use the right arrow key on the keyboard to move the panel to the right. The Shift key modifier will move an object by 10 pixels each time an arrow key is pressed. Move the panel to the right until it is mostly on the main canvas, leaving just the left side positioned off-canvas.

5. Preview the animation—you should see a nice little slide action for that panel. The storyboard that Blend automatically creates is shown here:

```
<Storyboard x:Name="Storyboard1">
    <DoubleAnimationUsingKeyFrames
     BeginTime="00:00:00"
     Storyboard.TargetName="Panel1"
     Storyboard.TargetProperty="(UIElement.RenderTransform).➥
     (TransformGroup.Children)[3].(TranslateTransform.X)">
```

```
    <SplineDoubleKeyFrame KeyTime="00:00:02" Value="190"/>
  </DoubleAnimationUsingKeyFrames>
</Storyboard>
```

6. Move the play head to 3 seconds.

7. Select Panel2 in the Objects and Timeline panel, and enter 0 into the Opacity field on the Appearance pane of the Properties panel.

8. Play the animation again, and you will now see Panel2 slowly fade out as Panel1 slides in from the left. Blend once again creates the XAML code for the animation that was just added:

```
<Storyboard x:Name="Storyboard1">
    <DoubleAnimationUsingKeyFrames
     BeginTime="00:00:00"
     Storyboard.TargetName="Panel1"
     Storyboard.TargetProperty="(UIElement.RenderTransform).➥
     (TransformGroup.Children)[3].(TranslateTransform.X)">
        <SplineDoubleKeyFrame KeyTime="00:00:02" Value="190"/>
    </DoubleAnimationUsingKeyFrames>
    <DoubleAnimationUsingKeyFrames
     BeginTime="00:00:00"
     Storyboard.TargetName="Panel2"
     Storyboard.TargetProperty="(UIElement.Opacity)">
        <SplineDoubleKeyFrame KeyTime="00:00:03" Value="0"/>
    </DoubleAnimationUsingKeyFrames>
</Storyboard>
```

9. In order to make Panel2 delay the fadeout a bit, and then fade a little more quickly, move the play head to 2 seconds, and enter 100 into the Opacity field. When you preview storyboard, Panel1 will now slide in, and then Panel2 will begin to fade.

10. Move the timeline play head to 1 and select ball1.

11. Select Fill on the Brushes pane, and change the color of the gradient that is being used to fill the ellipse shape. It doesn't make any difference which color you choose. For reference, I changed the right gradient stop color to #FF3E6A01.

12. Move the timeline play head to 4 seconds, and select ball2.

13. Change the Width and Height properties to 100.

Now when you click Play, you should have quite a bit of action occurring on your artboard! Blend continues to augment the storyboard as you make changes to the object properties over time. The storyboard currently looks like the one shown in the following listing:

```
<Storyboard x:Name="Storyboard1">
    <DoubleAnimationUsingKeyFrames
     BeginTime="00:00:00"
     Storyboard.TargetName="Panel1"
     Storyboard.TargetProperty="(UIElement.RenderTransform).➥
     (TransformGroup.Children)[3].(TranslateTransform.X)">
        <SplineDoubleKeyFrame KeyTime="00:00:02" Value="190"/>
    </DoubleAnimationUsingKeyFrames>
```

```
<DoubleAnimationUsingKeyFrames
 BeginTime="00:00:00"
 Storyboard.TargetName="Panel2"
 Storyboard.TargetProperty="(UIElement.Opacity)">
    <SplineDoubleKeyFrame KeyTime="00:00:02" Value="1"/>
    <SplineDoubleKeyFrame KeyTime="00:00:03" Value="0"/>
</DoubleAnimationUsingKeyFrames>
<ColorAnimationUsingKeyFrames
 BeginTime="00:00:00"
 Storyboard.TargetName="ball1"
 Storyboard.TargetProperty="(Shape.Fill).➥
(GradientBrush.GradientStops)[1].(GradientStop.Color)">
    <SplineColorKeyFrame KeyTime="00:00:01" Value="#FF3E6A01"/>
</ColorAnimationUsingKeyFrames>
<DoubleAnimationUsingKeyFrames
 BeginTime="00:00:00"
 Storyboard.TargetName="ball2"
 Storyboard.TargetProperty="(FrameworkElement.Width)">
    <SplineDoubleKeyFrame KeyTime="00:00:04" Value="100"/>
</DoubleAnimationUsingKeyFrames>
<DoubleAnimationUsingKeyFrames
 BeginTime="00:00:00"
 Storyboard.TargetName="ball2"
 Storyboard.TargetProperty="(FrameworkElement.Height)">
    <SplineDoubleKeyFrame KeyTime="00:00:04" Value="100"/>
</DoubleAnimationUsingKeyFrames>
</Storyboard>
```

Let's take a quick look at the timeline. At the moment, it should look similar to the one shown in Figure 2-24.

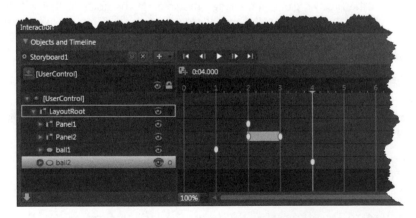

Figure 2-24. The timeline window shows objects and their keyframes.

You can see that each time you make a change to one of the object's properties, Blend adds a keyframe to the timeline. From the storyboard code, you can also see that each keyframe on the timeline represents an entry, or animation, in the storyboard. Not only are keyframes useful visual cues for when actions are taking place and which objects they will affect; but they can also be directly manipulated in the timeline. You can do this by grabbing the small oval-shaped markers and dragging them. If, for example, you decide that ball2 isn't changing size quickly enough, you can drag the marker on the timeline to the left to speed up the action. Try dragging the keyframe for ball2 to 2 seconds and playing the timeline. The ball will now resize a little more quickly, and you don't have to do very much work at all!

If you decide that you want ball2 to grow taller faster than it gains width, you can modify individual property keyframes as well. Expand the ball2 object in the Objects and Timeline panel. You should see entries for Height and Width and their associated markers on the timeline. Drag the oval keyframe marker for the Height property to 1 second. Your timeline should look similar to the one shown in Figure 2-25. Now when you press Play, ball2 will expand vertically more quickly than it expands horizontally.

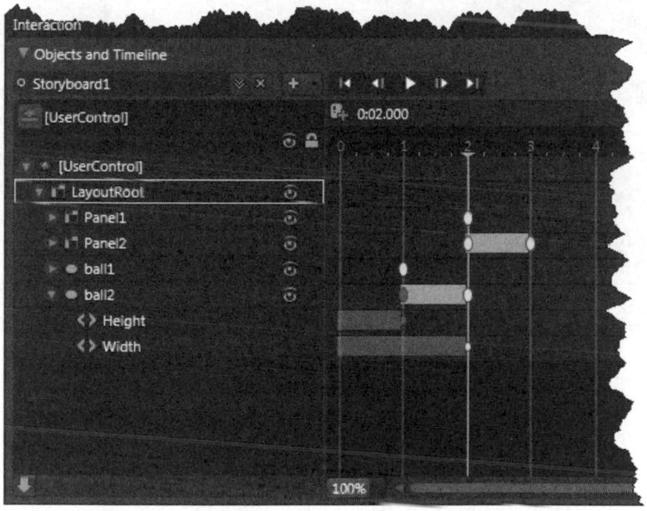

Figure 2-25. Keyframe markers are easy to modify in the timeline.

As you spend time fine-tuning animations in the timeline, you may find yourself needing to manipulate several keyframe markers at once. To do this, simply hold down the Ctrl key as you click keyframe markers to select/deselect multiple keyframes. You can then reposition the selected markers as a group.

Animating control points

In addition to the transform and property animations available to you in Blend/Silverlight, you can also manipulate the individual points that make up an object. Technically speaking, you are simply manipulating the properties of the control points that make up a path, but it is broken out here to a separate section for the sake of clarity.

Open the **controlpointAnimation** project from Chapter 2. This project contains a sunset ocean scene, as shown in Figure 2-26. We'll use the Direct Selection tool to add a control point animation that makes the waves roll a bit.

Figure 2-26. You can use the Direct Selection tool to animate the control points that make up an object.

1. Once the project is open, press the A key to change to the Direct Selection tool.
2. Click the water element on the Objects and Timeline panel. The element will change to display the control points that make up the path for this object.
3. Create a new storyboard and move the timeline play head to 3 seconds.
4. Along the top of the water object path, Shift-click to select the two uppermost points at the top of the swells. The control points will turn blue as they are selected.
5. Use the down arrow key to move those two points down about 20 pixels.
6. Click one of the two corner points along the top of the object, and then Shift-click the opposite corner and center point so that you have selected the inverse three points along the top of the wave.
7. Move the selected points upward about 20 pixels.
8. Press Play, and the swells should gently invert over the 3 seconds of the timeline.

The storyboard for this project looks pretty complex. This is because manipulating the points of a path-based object not only affects the points you are manipulating directly, but also the lines that pass through the control points. I'll talk more about that in Chapter 3, but for now, here's a look at the storyboard for this project:

```
<Storyboard x:Name="Storyboard1">
    <PointAnimationUsingKeyFrames
     BeginTime="00:00:00"
     Storyboard.TargetName="water"
     Storyboard.TargetProperty="(Path.Data).➥
     (PathGeometry.Figures)[0].(PathFigure.StartPoint)">
        <SplinePointKeyFrame KeyTime="00:00:03" Value="0.5,0.5"/>
    </PointAnimationUsingKeyFrames>
    <PointAnimationUsingKeyFrames
     BeginTime="00:00:00"
     Storyboard.TargetName="water"
     Storyboard.TargetProperty="(Path.Data).➥
     (PathGeometry.Figures)[0].(PathFigure.Segments)[0].➥
     (BezierSegment.Point1)">
        <SplinePointKeyFrame KeyTime="00:00:03" Value="0.5,0.5"/>
    </PointAnimationUsingKeyFrames>
    <PointAnimationUsingKeyFrames
     BeginTime="00:00:00"
     Storyboard.TargetName="water"
     Storyboard.TargetProperty="(Path.Data).➥
     (PathGeometry.Figures)[0].(PathFigure.Segments)[0].➥
     (BezierSegment.Point2)">
        <SplinePointKeyFrame KeyTime="00:00:03"
         Value="111.5,25.5000228881836"/>
    </PointAnimationUsingKeyFrames>
    <PointAnimationUsingKeyFrames
     BeginTime="00:00:00"
     Storyboard.TargetName="water"
     Storyboard.TargetProperty="(Path.Data).➥
     (PathGeometry.Figures)[0].(PathFigure.Segments)[0].➥
     (BezierSegment.Point3)">
        <SplinePointKeyFrame KeyTime="00:00:03"
         Value="184.5,25.5000228881836"/>
    </PointAnimationUsingKeyFrames>
    <PointAnimationUsingKeyFrames
     BeginTime="00:00:00"
     Storyboard.TargetName="water"
     Storyboard.TargetProperty="(Path.Data).➥
     (PathGeometry.Figures)[0].(PathFigure.Segments)[1].➥
     (BezierSegment.Point1)">
        <SplinePointKeyFrame KeyTime="00:00:03"
         Value="257.5,25.5000228881836"/>
    </PointAnimationUsingKeyFrames>
    <PointAnimationUsingKeyFrames
     BeginTime="00:00:00"
     Storyboard.TargetName="water"
     Storyboard.TargetProperty="(Path.Data).➥
     (PathGeometry.Figures)[0].(PathFigure.Segments)[1].➥
     (BezierSegment.Point2)">
```

```
        <SplinePointKeyFrame KeyTime="00:00:03"
         Value="371.5,11.4999856948853"/>
</PointAnimationUsingKeyFrames>
<PointAnimationUsingKeyFrames
 BeginTime="00:00:00"
 Storyboard.TargetName="water"
 Storyboard.TargetProperty="(Path.Data).➡
 (PathGeometry.Figures)[0].(PathFigure.Segments)[1].➡
 (BezierSegment.Point3)">
        <SplinePointKeyFrame KeyTime="00:00:03"
         Value="445.5,7.49999141693115"/>
</PointAnimationUsingKeyFrames>
<PointAnimationUsingKeyFrames
 BeginTime="00:00:00"
 Storyboard.TargetName="water"
 Storyboard.TargetProperty="(Path.Data).➡
 (PathGeometry.Figures)[0].(PathFigure.Segments)[2].➡
 (BezierSegment.Point1)">
        <SplinePointKeyFrame KeyTime="00:00:03"
         Value="519.5,3.49999713897705"/>
</PointAnimationUsingKeyFrames>
<PointAnimationUsingKeyFrames
 BeginTime="00:00:00"
 Storyboard.TargetName="water"
 Storyboard.TargetProperty="(Path.Data).➡
 (PathGeometry.Figures)[0].(PathFigure.Segments)[2].➡
 (BezierSegment.Point2)">
        <SplinePointKeyFrame KeyTime="00:00:03"
         Value="603.5,27.5000171661377"/>
</PointAnimationUsingKeyFrames>
<PointAnimationUsingKeyFrames
 BeginTime="00:00:00"
 Storyboard.TargetName="water"
 Storyboard.TargetProperty="(Path.Data).➡
 (PathGeometry.Figures)[0].(PathFigure.Segments)[2].➡
 (BezierSegment.Point3)">➡
        <SplinePointKeyFrame KeyTime="00:00:03"
         Value="668.5,27.5000171661377"/>
</PointAnimationUsingKeyFrames>
<PointAnimationUsingKeyFrames
 BeginTime="00:00:00"
 Storyboard.TargetName="water"
 Storyboard.TargetProperty="(Path.Data).➡
 (PathGeometry.Figures)[0].(PathFigure.Segments)[3].➡
 (BezierSegment.Point1)">
        <SplinePointKeyFrame KeyTime="00:00:03"
         Value="733.5,27.5000171661377"/>
</PointAnimationUsingKeyFrames>
```

```
<PointAnimationUsingKeyFrames
 BeginTime="00:00:00"
 Storyboard.TargetName="water"
 Storyboard.TargetProperty="(Path.Data).➡
 (PathGeometry.Figures)[0].(PathFigure.Segments)[3].➡
 (BezierSegment.Point2)">
     <SplinePointKeyFrame KeyTime="00:00:03"
      Value="802.499694824219,3.5007905960083"/>
</PointAnimationUsingKeyFrames>
<PointAnimationUsingKeyFrames
 BeginTime="00:00:00"
 Storyboard.TargetName="water"
 Storyboard.TargetProperty="(Path.Data).➡
 (PathGeometry.Figures)[0].(PathFigure.Segments)[3].➡
 (BezierSegment.Point3)">
     <SplinePointKeyFrame KeyTime="00:00:03"
      Value="802.499694824219,3.5007905960083"/>
</PointAnimationUsingKeyFrames>
<PointAnimationUsingKeyFrames
 BeginTime="00:00:00"
 Storyboard.TargetName="water"
 Storyboard.TargetProperty="(Path.Data).➡
 (PathGeometry.Figures)[0].(PathFigure.Segments)[4].➡
 (BezierSegment.Point1)">
     <SplinePointKeyFrame KeyTime="00:00:03"
      Value="802.499694824219,3.5007905960083"/>
</PointAnimationUsingKeyFrames>
<PointAnimationUsingKeyFrames
 BeginTime="00:00:00"
 Storyboard.TargetName="water"
 Storyboard.TargetProperty="(Path.Data).➡
 (PathGeometry.Figures)[0].(PathFigure.Segments)[4].➡
 (BezierSegment.Point2)">
     <SplinePointKeyFrame KeyTime="00:00:03"
      Value="803.166687011719,103.834053039551"/>
</PointAnimationUsingKeyFrames>
<PointAnimationUsingKeyFrames
 BeginTime="00:00:00"
 Storyboard.TargetName="water"
 Storyboard.TargetProperty="(Path.Data).➡
 (PathGeometry.Figures)[0].(PathFigure.Segments)[4].➡
 (BezierSegment.Point3)">
     <SplinePointKeyFrame KeyTime="00:00:03"
      Value="803.5,158.501022338867"/>
</PointAnimationUsingKeyFrames>
<PointAnimationUsingKeyFrames
 BeginTime="00:00:00"
 Storyboard.TargetName="water"
```

59

```
Storyboard.TargetProperty="(Path.Data).➡
(PathGeometry.Figures)[0].(PathFigure.Segments)[5].➡
(LineSegment.Point)">
   <SplinePointKeyFrame KeyTime="00:00:03"
    Value="0.5,157.501022338867"/>
</PointAnimationUsingKeyFrames>
</Storyboard>
```

Summary

The basic transforms available in Blend allow you to change the properties of an object over time, creating simple animations. The transforms include Translate, Rotate, Scale, Skew, as well as two special shortcut transforms—Center Point and Flip. Transforms can be applied individually or in combinations to achieve different effects. As you work in Blend's visual interface, the software works "behind the scenes" for you, adding the necessary XAML to your file in the form of storyboards and animations.

Now that you have had a chance to become more familiar with the types of transforms available to you in Blend/Silverlight, it's time to take a closer look at what is happening under the hood. As you have seen, Blend is creating sometimes complex-looking storyboard and animation XAML code in the background. Like other objects in Silverlight, storyboards also have properties associated with them. In Chapter 3, we will take an in-depth look at how all of the storyboard code works, the types of keyframes and keyframe interpolation available, and how events are used to make storyboards play. We'll also start exploring the development aspect of Silverlight a little more by writing some code.

Chapter 3

STORYBOARDS AND ANIMATIONS

As you have seen, Blend does the heavy lifting when it comes to creating animations and storyboards while you concentrate on manipulating objects on the artboard. In this regard, Blend is a great time-saving tool. However, the default animations produced in Blend may not be ideal in all situations. There are multiple types of animation available to you in Blend/Silverlight, and being aware of the different types will make it easier for you to select the appropriate match for your projects. In this chapter, we will be taking an in-depth look at storyboards and each of the different types of animation provided by Silverlight. To complete the discussion, you will also learn how each type of animation can be written entirely in the code-behind file, with no XAML. Your main take-away should be a deep understanding of the various animation types and how each affects the motion of your objects.

Before you get started

A brief heads up before you begin: Despite the deep integration between Blend and Visual Studio, they are still separate environments, and as such, invite nuances between user experiences when working with project files. Blend 2.5 doesn't persist the files that were open in Visual Studio or the start page. Because of this, you are likely to open a project and find a blank screen staring at you. Don't panic! The project is open. To work through the examples, click the Projects tab in Blend, and then right-click the HTML file and select Startup—this will ensure that Blend uses the correct page when you run a project. After that, double-click the Page.xaml file, and you should be ready to go.

Storyboards and storyboard properties

When you think of a storyboard, think of it as a container that will hold a set of animations. As you move objects around on the artboard in timeline recording mode, Blend automatically adds animations to the storyboard container for you. In some of the previous examples, you used the New storyboard button in Blend and the default name Storyboard1 to create new storyboard containers. When you do this, an empty storyboard is created in the XAML file that looks like this:

```
<Storyboard x:Name="Storyboard1"/>
```

Each storyboard you create must have a unique name, which is assigned through the x:Name property. As you create storyboards, it is a good idea to use descriptive names. In the event that you have a project containing many storyboards, you will find it much easier to locate the correct one when it comes time to play them.

Storyboards can contain any number of animations, from a few to dozens. They can also be left blank and used as timers.

Like other objects in a Silverlight application, storyboards have properties that affect the way the storyboard behaves. Let's work through some examples to explore these properties further.

1. Open the **StoryboardProperties** project from Chapter 3. If you open the project in Blend, you may need to double-click the Page.xaml file on the Project tab to open the XAML. This project contains a gradient-filled ellipse named GreenBall and a simple storyboard with one animation that causes the ball to move from left to right in 2 seconds. The storyboard is named MoveBall, and looks like this:

```
<Storyboard x:Name=" MoveBall">
  <DoubleAnimationUsingKeyFrames Storyboard.TargetName="GreenBall"
    Storyboard.TargetProperty="(UIElement.RenderTransform).➥
    (TransformGroup.Children)[3].(TranslateTransform.X)"
    BeginTime="00:00:00">
  <SplineDoubleKeyFrame KeyTime="00:00:02" Value="540"/>
  </DoubleAnimationUsingKeyFrames>
</Storyboard>
```

2. Click the Open a storyboard button to open the list of available storyboards, and select MoveBall.

3. Play the storyboard to see how it moves the Ball object across the canvas.

We'll talk more about the types of animation that go into storyboards later in this chapter. Right now, we want to concentrate just on the Storyboard tag and its available properties. Like most objects in Silverlight, some storyboard properties have default values. You know that when you add an ellipse to the artboard, you do not need to specify the Opacity or Visibility, for example. Even though those properties are not explicitly written in the XAML code, the ellipse will still show up and have an opaque fill by default.

Similarly, storyboards have properties that are not explicitly coded in XAML, but still affect the way a storyboard behaves. This is the case for the first property we'll look at: FillBehavior. FillBehavior describes how a storyboard acts when it reaches its end. The default value for this property is HoldEnd, which will cause a storyboard to hold its end position when it has completed playing.

Because it is default behavior, it is not necessary to code, but `<Storyboard x:Name="MoveBall">` is the functional equivalent to `<Storyboard x:Name="MoveBall" FillBehavior="HoldEnd">`.

The other possible value for the `FillBehavior` property is Stop. Using Stop causes a storyboard to return objects to the position at which they were located prior to the storyboard playing. Using Stop will cause all the objects affected by a storyboard to return to their initial positions. Let's take a look.

4. Change to Split view and scroll to the top of the XAML window.

5. Modify the `FillBehavior` property for the MoveBall storyboard. After the storyboard name, type in FillBehavior="Stop". Hand-editing the XAML may cause Blend to close the storyboard. If this happens, just reopen the storyboard by selecting Open a storyboard on the Objects and Timeline panel once again. If you are using an early release version of Blend, the storyboard list may improperly display multiple listings for the storyboard. In this case, select the last one in the list.

```
<Storyboard x:Name="MoveBall" FillBehavior="Stop">
    [...]
</Storyboard>
```

Test the animation. The ball should move across the canvas to the right, and then move to its starting position on the left.

You should see a significant difference in the end position for the Ball object when using Stop rather than the default "HoldEnd" `FillBehavior`.

The next storyboard property we will take a look at is `AutoReverse`. As you might expect, `AutoReverse` will cause a storyboard to play backward when it reaches the end. By default, the value for `AutoReverse` is False, and like the `FillBehavior` property, is not written into the XAML tag for the storyboard.

6. In Split view, scroll to the top of the XAML window and remove the `FillBehavior` tag that was previously added.

7. After the storyboard name, type in AutoReverse="True" so that the storyboard looks like the one in the following code. Click Play to see how the behavior has changed.

```
<Storyboard x:Name="MoveBall" AutoReverse="True">
    [...]
</Storyboard>
```

The ball moves to the right, and when the storyboard reaches the end, it reverses and proceeds to play backward until the ball is brought to a stop at the original starting position. The movement of the timeline play head will mimic this motion.

Oftentimes, `AutoReverse` is used in conjunction with the next property we'll be looking at, called `RepeatBehavior`. The default value for `RepeatBehavior` is 1, meaning that a storyboard will play one time. There are three ways to specify the `RepeatBehavior` for a storyboard. You can enter duration, a number of iterations, or the string value Forever.

8. Remove the `AutoReverse` property added in step 7.

9. Change the storyboard so that the `RepeatBehavior` is set to Forever, as shown here:

```
<Storyboard x:Name="MoveBall" RepeatBehavior="Forever">
    [...]
</Storyboard>
```

Press the F5 key to compile and view the project in a browser. The storyboard that moves the ball from left to right will play repeatedly. Close the browser when you're done looking at the application.

While you can certainly edit the XAML directly in XAML or Split view as we have done, you can also access storyboard properties inside Blend's interface, as shown in Figure 3-1. To change a storyboard's properties, click the storyboard name at the top of the Objects and Timeline list, and then make any necessary changes on the Common Properties pane of the Properties panel.

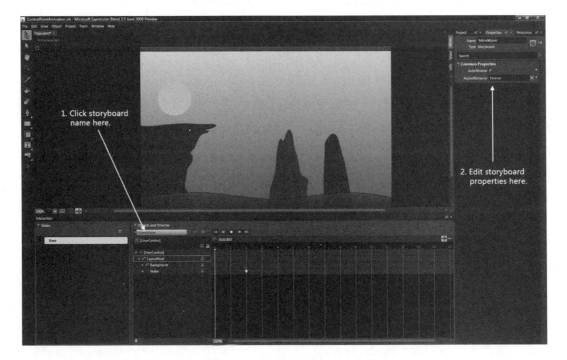

Figure 3-1. Storyboard properties can be edited in the Blend interface.

If you have a case where an animation needs to play a specific number of times, you can change the value of RepeatBehavior to get the necessary behavior.

10. In the example project, change the RepeatBehavior value to 4x, like so:

```
<Storyboard x:Name="MoveBall" RepeatBehavior="4x">
    [...]
</Storyboard>
```

11. Press the F5 key to compile the project and view it in a browser. The MoveBall storyboard will play four times. Close the browser when you're done looking at the application.

Use caution when using iteration values. If you forget the x that lets Silverlight know you are using iterations, the value is instead interpreted as a duration value, and you may be left wondering why your animation continues to play for a number of hours.

Duration values for RepeatBehavior are expressed as a string, specified as *hours:minutes:seconds*. When a duration value is used for RepeatBehavior, a storyboard will play for the amount of time specified.

12. To play the example storyboard animation for 4 seconds, change the value of RepeatBehavior to 00:00:04, as shown:

```
<Storyboard x:Name="MoveBall" RepeatBehavior="00:00:04">
    [...]
</Storyboard>
```

13. Press the F5 key to run the project. In this case, the animation of the ball moving only lasts for 2 seconds, so the storyboard is played through twice. Close the browser when you're done looking at the application. What will happen if you specify a duration of 3 seconds (00:00:03)? The animation will play through 1.5 times, stopping halfway through the second iteration.

The next property we'll look at is called BeginTime, and is used to delay a storyboard from starting for some period of time. Like the duration values for RepeatBehavior, values for BeginTime are also expressed as *hours:minutes:seconds*.

14. Remove the RepeatBehavior property from the storyboard.

15. Delay the start of the MoveBall storyboard for 5 seconds by adding the following property to the storyboard tag:

```
<Storyboard x:Name="MoveBall" BeginTime="00:00:05">
    [...]
</Storyboard>
```

16. Press the F5 key to run the project. The ball will stay to the left of the canvas for 5 seconds, and then the storyboard will move the ball across the screen. When you're done viewing the application, close the browser window.

SpeedRatio is a property that can be used to speed up the playback of a storyboard. Values for SpeedRatio are expressed as a multiplier, with 1 being normal speed.

17. Remove the BeginTime property set in step 15.

18. To play an animation 8 times faster, set the value as shown here:

```
<Storyboard x:Name="MoveBall" SpeedRatio="8">
    [...]
</Storyboard>
```

19. Press F5 once again to view the effect this change has on the storyboard. The ball should move across the screen pretty quickly. Close the browser window when you're done.

Using SpeedRatio on a storyboard can help if the overall storyboard playback needs to be adjusted. SpeedRatio offers an easy way to adjust the playback for all the animations in the storyboard at once.

Combining storyboard properties

Although we examined the storyboard properties individually in the previous exercises, you will often find yourself combining them to achieve different effects. Let's look at how to use multiple storyboard properties at once:

1. Open the **ControlPointAnimation** project. In Blend, double-click the Page.xaml file on the Project tab to open the XAML. This is the same project used in Chapter 2 to animate some wave swells. This project already contains an animation called MoveWaves that moves the control points that make up the wave object. Press F5 to run the application if you'd like to see the animation.

2. Change to Split mode and scroll through the XAML window. You will see that the MoveWaves storyboard is fairly complex, containing over a dozen separate point animations.

3. Since the main wave motion is already created, we are going to focus on adding some properties to the storyboard that will cause the animation to play to the end, reverse and play backward to the beginning, and then play forward again, looping this behavior forever. We can do that by adding two properties to the storyboard—AutoReverse and RepeatBehavior—as shown here:

```
<Storyboard x:Name="MoveWaves" AutoReverse="True"
        RepeatBehavior="Forever">
    [...]
</Storyboard>
```

4. Press the F5 key to compile and run the application. The storyboard will play forward until it reaches the end, at which time the AutoReverse property will cause the storyboard to play backward. When it reaches the beginning, the RepeatBehavior property will cause the storyboard to play forward again, and this cycle will repeat endlessly.

Take a look at the following storyboard and try to determine what kind of behavior will result from using the values shown.

```
<Storyboard x:Name="MoveWaves" BeginTime="00:00:10"
        RepeatBehavior="4x"
        AutoReverse="True" SpeedRatio="2">
    [...]
</Storyboard>
```

BeginTime is unaffected by the SpeedRatio value set for a storyboard. As such, this example will delay 10 seconds when the storyboard begins, after which the storyboard will play a total of four times at twice the speed. In this example, AutoReverse and SpeedRatio will essentially cancel each other out— AutoReverse doubles the duration of any animations contained in the storyboard, while a SpeedRatio of 2 will play them twice as fast.

5. Paste the properties shown in the listing into the MoveWaves storyboard and run the project to see the result.

As containers, storyboards are not the real workhorses when it comes to making things move in Silverlight. For that, animations are used. In the next section, we'll take an in-depth look at the types of animation available to you within Silverlight.

Types of animation

One of the important concepts to understand with Silverlight is that all the values you can modify for objects are of a particular type of data. The C# code we'll be using later is considered **strongly typed**, which means that every object and variable must have a declared data type.

Some common data types are **Boolean**, which contains **true** or **false** values; **integer**, which contains values between −2147483648 and 2147483647; **double**, which contains values between −1.79769313486232E+308 and 1.79769313486232E+308; and **byte**, which contains values between 0 and 255. We'll be dealing with different types of data later when we start doing more programming, but for the time being, just be aware that different data types exist. In Silverlight, most numeric values used for properties such as Opacity, Height, and Width are of the double type.

When it comes to animations, Silverlight offers three main types, double, Color, and Point, each of which has two variations: **from/to** and **using keyframes**. If you are using keyframes, there are three further variations: **linear**, **spline**, and **discreet**. While that seems like a lot to keep track of, Blend goes a long way in making animations easier to sort through and use. Unfortunately, no software can do it all, and Blend does not offer the ability to work with the very useful from/to type of animation. Luckily, from/to animations are relatively straightforward to code in XAML. Let's look at all these animation types in more detail now.

Double

As you might expect, the DoubleAnimation type changes properties of type double over time.

There are two types of double animations: DoubleAnimation and DoubleAnimationUsingKeyFrames. The former is a from/to animation, and simply works by providing target values. The latter becomes a container for a set of keyframes that define values at specific points along the timeline.

The code for a storyboard with a DoubleAnimation might look something like the following listing:

```
<Storyboard x:Name="Storyboard1">
    <DoubleAnimation Storyboard.TargetName="MyEllipse"
    Storyboard.TargetProperty="(UIElement.Opacity)"
    Duration="00:00:01"
    From="1"
    To="0.5"/>
</Storyboard>
```

From/to animations animate the property of an object from one value to another—hence the name. The example code specifies a property required for all animations called TargetName. This property is the x:Name property of an object in your project. In this case, the object that will be affected by this animation is called MyEllipse.

Following the target name is a TargetProperty. This tells Silverlight which property of the object will be affected by this animation. This code tells Silverlight we will be changing the opacity.

As with a storyboard, the Duration specifies how long this animation will take, while the From and To properties are the beginning and ending values used in the animation. This animation can be read as "Change the opacity of MyEllipse from 1 to .5 in 1 second."

The From property is not required, and is often left off. When omitted, From becomes whatever the current value is. When used this way, paired from/to animations are effective for creating animations that need to smoothly reverse on some user action, such as panels that slide in and out as the mouse enters or leaves an object.

To take a closer look at how from/to animations work, open the **DoubleFromTo** project for Chapter 3. The project contains a Canvas object called Slider that contains a panel shape. Press F5 to run the project. As the mouse enters the panel, the panel will slide out, and when the mouse leaves the panel, it will slide back in. The animations work if the mouse enters or leaves the object at any point. These movements are created with two DoubleAnimations, both of which omit the From value. The following code listing shows the storyboards and their animations:

```
<Storyboard x:Name="SlideOut">
    <DoubleAnimation Storyboard.TargetName="Slider"
    Storyboard.TargetProperty="(UIElement.RenderTransform).➥
    (TransformGroup.Children)[3].(TranslateTransform.X)"
    Duration="00:00:00.50"
    To="150"/>
</Storyboard>

<Storyboard x:Name="SlideIn">
    <DoubleAnimation Storyboard.TargetName="Slider"
    Storyboard.TargetProperty="(UIElement.RenderTransform).➥
    (TransformGroup.Children)[3].(TranslateTransform.X)"
    Duration="00:00:00.50"
    To="0"/>
</Storyboard>
```

When the mouse enters the Slider object, the SlideOut animation plays, moving the panel from its current position to 150 over a duration of .5 seconds. If the mouse leaves the panel at any point, the SlideIn animation begins, moving the panel from whatever the current value is to 0 over a duration of .5 seconds. In this particular animation, the double value being manipulated is the X Translate transform.

As noted earlier, Blend does not produce from/to animations by default. Instead, Blend generates a type of animation called a DoubleAnimationUsingKeyFrames. To see what one of these looks like, open the **DoubleUsingKeyframes** project from Chapter 3. This project contains a single Rectangle object and a storyboard that moves the rectangle 150 pixels to the right over a .5-second duration. You can test it out by pressing F5.

```
<Storyboard x:Name="Storyboard1">
    <DoubleAnimationUsingKeyFrames Storyboard.TargetName="Rectangle"
    Storyboard.TargetProperty="(UIElement.RenderTransform).➥
    (TransformGroup.Children)[3].(TranslateTransform.X)"
    BeginTime="00:00:00">
        <SplineDoubleKeyFrame KeyTime="00:00:00.50" Value="150"/>
    </DoubleAnimationUsingKeyFrames>
</Storyboard>
```

Keyframe animations are containers that hold keyframe definitions. If you are using Blend, each time a keyframe is created on the timeline, a corresponding entry is made into an animation container.

Like the DoubleAnimation type, DoubleAnimationUsingKeyFrames animations also define TargetName and TargetProperty values. However, the length of the animation is determined by the keyframes within the animation, not by a duration value.

BeginTime is specified to tell Silverlight when the animation should start. In this example, BeginTime is 00:00:00, so it will start with no delay when called.

Within the DoubleAnimationUsingKeyframes container is a SplineDoubleKeyFrame KeyTime definition that defines a keyframe at .5 seconds and specifies that the value of the X Translate transform should be 150.

Color

Color animations are animations that change colors over time. Instead of manipulating values of type double, color animations change the hex values that define a color. Like animations that use double, color animations also come in two varieties: ColorAnimation and ColorAnimationUsingKeyFrames.

With color values in Silverlight, hex values are preceded by a value representing the alpha transparency of the color being defined. For example, #FFFF0000 is 100% opaque red, while #7FFF0000 is 50% red. If the alpha transparency value is left off of a hex color, Silverlight will assume the color to be 100% opaque.

The **ColorFromTo** project for Chapter 3 contains an example ColorAnimation. Open the project and press F5 to run it. When you move the mouse over the red ellipse, it will begin to turn dark blue. If the mouse leaves the ellipse, it will turn back to red. Each of the two color animations happens over .5 seconds, and as with the DoubleAnimation example, the From attribute is omitted from the ColorAnimation to give a smooth animation effect.

```
<Storyboard x:Name="TurnBlue">
    <ColorAnimation Storyboard.TargetName="RedEllipse"
    Storyboard.TargetProperty="(Shape.Fill).(SolidColorBrush.Color)"
    Duration="00:00:00.50"
    To="#FF0D0874"/>
</Storyboard>

<Storyboard x:Name="TurnRed">
    <ColorAnimation Storyboard.TargetName="RedEllipse"
    Storyboard.TargetProperty="(Shape.Fill).(SolidColorBrush.Color)"
    Duration="00:00:00.50"
    To="#FFFF0000"/>
</Storyboard>
```

When working with color animations in Blend, the default type of animation that will be created is ColorAnimationUsingKeyFrames. Like DoubleAnimationusingKeyFrames, this type of animation will create a container within your storyboard that contains entries for each keyframe you create.

In the following code listing, a keyframe has been created at .5 seconds and contains a pure blue value of #FF0000FF. When the animation runs, the SplineColorKeyFrame specifies that the ellipse's color is to change from the current color to the blue defined by the keyframe in .5 seconds.

```
<Storyboard x:Name="TurnBlue">
    <ColorAnimationUsingKeyFrames Storyboard.TargetName="RedEllipse"
    Storyboard.TargetProperty="(Shape.Fill).(SolidColorBrush.Color)"
```

```
    BeginTime="00:00:00">
        <SplineColorKeyFrame KeyTime="00:00:00.50" Value="#FF0000FF"/>
    </ColorAnimationUsingKeyFrames>
</Storyboard>
```

Point

Like double and color animations, point animations also come in two flavors: PointAnimation and
PointAnimationUsingKeyFrames. From a code perspective, they also become significantly more complex to work with since you are now dealing with the individual points that sit along a path and form
an object. Even simple objects can become complex when viewed in the context of point animations.
Open the **PointFromTo** project for Chapter 3. This project contains a simple path that is in the shape
of an ellipse, the XAML for which is shown following:

```
<Path Height="277" Width="200" Canvas.Left="306" Canvas.Top="65"
    Fill="#FFFF0000" Stretch="None" x:Name="RedPath" Cursor="Hand">
    <Path.Data>
        <PathGeometry>
            <PathFigure IsClosed="True" StartPoint="200,100">
            <BezierSegment Point1="200,155.228469848633"
            Point2="155.228469848633,200" Point3="100,200"/>
            <BezierSegment Point1="44.7715263366699,200"
            Point2="0,155.228469848633" Point3="0,100"/>
            <BezierSegment Point1="0,44.7715263366699"
            Point2="44.7715263366699,0" Point3="100,0"/>
            <BezierSegment Point1="155.228469848633,0"
            Point2="200,44.7715263366699" Point3="200,100"/>
            </PathFigure>
        </PathGeometry>
    </Path.Data>
</Path>
```

The BezierSegment containers describe the points along the path that make up a simple circle shape.
Run the project by pressing F5. When the pointer is placed in the red ellipse, the bottom point will
drop down, as shown in Figure 3-2. When the pointer leaves the red circle, the bottom point returns
to its original position, as shown in Figure 3-3.

Figure 3-2. The bottom point
of the circle drops when the
mouse pointer enters the circle.

Figure 3-3. The bottom point of the
circle returns to its starting position
when the mouse pointer leaves the circle.

PointAnimation definitions are a little more complex than the DoubleAnimation and ColorAnimation examples shown. The following code shows the storyboards and animations:

```xml
<Storyboard x:Name="MovePointDown">
    <PointAnimation Storyboard.TargetName="RedPath"
        Storyboard.TargetProperty="(Path.Data).➡
        (PathGeometry.Figures)[0].(PathFigure.Segments)[1].➡
        (BezierSegment.Point1)"
        Duration="00:00:00.50"
        To="44.7715263366699,277"/>

    <PointAnimation Storyboard.TargetName="RedPath"
        Storyboard.TargetProperty="(Path.Data).➡
        (PathGeometry.Figures)[0].(PathFigure.Segments)[0].➡
        (BezierSegment.Point2)"
        Duration="00:00:00.50"
        To="155.228469848633,277"/>

    <PointAnimation Storyboard.TargetName="RedPath"
        Storyboard.TargetProperty="(Path.Data).➡
        (PathGeometry.Figures)[0].(PathFigure.Segments)[0].➡
        (BezierSegment.Point3)"
        Duration="00:00:00.50"
        To="100, 277"/>
</Storyboard>

<Storyboard x:Name="MovePointUp">
    <PointAnimation Storyboard.TargetName="RedPath"
        Storyboard.TargetProperty="(Path.Data).➡
        (PathGeometry.Figures)[0].(PathFigure.Segments)[1].➡
        (BezierSegment.Point1)"
        Duration="00:00:00.50"
        To="44.7715263366699,200"/>

    <PointAnimation Storyboard.TargetName="RedPath"
        Storyboard.TargetProperty="(Path.Data).➡
        (PathGeometry.Figures)[0].(PathFigure.Segments)[0].➡
        (BezierSegment.Point2)"
        Duration="00:00:00.50"
        To="155.228469848633,200"/>

    <PointAnimation Storyboard.TargetName="RedPath"➡
        Storyboard.TargetProperty="(Path.Data).➡
        (PathGeometry.Figures)[0].(PathFigure.Segments)[0].➡
        (BezierSegment.Point3)"
        Duration="00:00:00.50"
        To="100,200"/>
</Storyboard>
```

To this point, the storyboards used to create from/to animations have been relatively simple. The PointAnimation type has become full of confusing numbers and a very complex looking TargetProperty. The values shown in these two storyboards directly relate to values in the XAML markup for the object. Let's take a closer look at the pieces that make up the TargetProperty for the first animation in the MovePointDown storyboard.

```
Storyboard.TargetProperty="(Path.Data).➥
    (PathGeometry.Figures)[0].(PathFigure.Segments)[1].➥
    (BezierSegment.Point1)"
```

The XAML for our object contains a PathGeometry section, which in turn contains a PathFigure. A more complex object might contain several PathFigure elements. Inside of the PathFigure are four BezierSegment entries, each one of which refers to a point on the path and its associated spline, as shown in Figure 3-4.

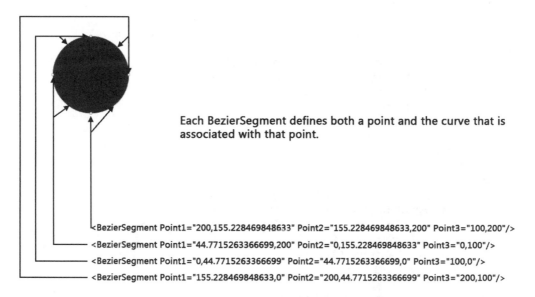

Each BezierSegment defines both a point and the curve that is associated with that point.

```
<BezierSegment Point1="200,155.228469848633" Point2="155.228469848633,200" Point3="100,200"/>
<BezierSegment Point1="44.7715263366699,200" Point2="0,155.228469848633" Point3="0,100"/>
<BezierSegment Point1="0,44.7715263366699" Point2="44.7715263366699,0" Point3="100,0"/>
<BezierSegment Point1="155.228469848633,0" Point2="200,44.7715263366699" Point3="200,100"/>
```

Figure 3-4. The BezierSegments that make up the Sphere object

When referencing PathFigures in the PathGeometry container, they are numbered starting from 0. In our case, we only have a single PathFigure, so the first portion of the TargetProperty for the storyboard is saying, "In the path data section, I want the first figure from the PathGeometry list."

```
(Path.Data).(PathGeometry.Figures)[0]
```

Inside of the PathFigure container, we can see four segments, numbered from 0 to 3. The next portion of the TargetProperty tells Silverlight to which segment the animation will apply:

```
(PathFigure.Segments)[1]
```

This information directs Silverlight to the second segment in the list (the first segment is [0]), which is shown here:

```
<BezierSegment Point1="44.7715263366699,200"
    Point2="0,155.228469848633" Point3="0,100"/>
```

Finally, the TargetProperty tells Silverlight which point values are being modified:

```
(BezierSegment.Point1)
```

The duration value is the same as it has been for the other animation types, but notice that the To value is a pair of numbers separated by a comma:

```
To="44.7715263366699,277"
```

This is the x,y coordinate where the point will end up. With both DoubleAnimation and ColorAnimation, it is relatively simple to make changes to an object using just a single animation. This is not the case with PointAnimation, because each point affects its adjoining spline segment. As a result, more animations are necessary.

When creating PointAnimations that return points to their original position, it is important to pay attention to the values being used. Unlike a DoubleAnimation that "undoes" a translation by returning it to 0, the values used for PointAnimations need to come from the XAML markup because they represent the x,y location of the point being manipulated.

This becomes especially difficult when the XAML for an object is written in the traditional path mini-language notation. For example, the preceding elliptical path typically appears in XAML as follows:

```
<Path Height="278" Width="200" Canvas.Left="306" Canvas.Top="64"
    Fill="#FFFF0000" Stretch="None" x:Name="RedPath" Cursor="Hand"
    Data="M200,101 C200,156.22847 155.22847,201 100,201 ➡
    C44.771526,201 0,156.22847 0,101 C0,45.771526 44.771526,1 ➡
    100,1 C155.22847,1 200,45.771526 200,101 z">
```

For this reason, it is often easier to utilize Blend when creating PointAnimationUsingKeyFrames animations, and then convert them to PointAnimations as opposed to trying to hand-code PointAnimation XAML.

Blend generates the PointAnimationUsingKeyFrames animation type when the points of an object are manipulated over time. As points are moved, keyframes are added to the timeline.

The **PointUsingKeyframes** project from Chapter 3 contains a red path similar to the one in the last project, as well as a storyboard that will move the bottom point of the ellipse down. As demonstrated in the previous PointAnimation example, three animations are necessary to move a single point down.

In Blend, use the Open a storyboard icon on the Objects and Timeline panel to open the MovePointDown storyboard. Click Play to see the bottom of the path deform downward. The MovePointDown storyboard is shown in the following listing for reference:

```
<Storyboard x:Name="MovePointDown">
<PointAnimationUsingKeyFrames Storyboard.TargetName="RedPath"
    Storyboard.TargetProperty="(Path.Data).➡
        (PathGeometry.Figures)[0].(PathFigure.Segments)[0].➡
        (BezierSegment.Point2)"
```

```
            BeginTime="00:00:00">
        <SplinePointKeyFrame KeyTime="00:00:00.50"
            Value="155.228469848633,263"/>
    </PointAnimationUsingKeyFrames>

    <PointAnimationUsingKeyFrames Storyboard.TargetName="RedPath"
        Storyboard.TargetProperty="(Path.Data).➥
            (PathGeometry.Figures)[0].(PathFigure.Segments)[0].➥
            (BezierSegment.Point3)"
            BeginTime="00:00:00">
        <SplinePointKeyFrame KeyTime="00:00:00.50"
            Value="100,263"/>
    </PointAnimationUsingKeyFrames>

    <PointAnimationUsingKeyFrames Storyboard.TargetName="RedPath"
        Storyboard.TargetProperty="(Path.Data).➥
            (PathGeometry.Figures)[0].(PathFigure.Segments)[1].➥
            (BezierSegment.Point1)"
            BeginTime="00:00:00">
        <SplinePointKeyFrame KeyTime="00:00:00.50"
            Value="44.7715263366699,263"/>
    </PointAnimationUsingKeyFrames>
</Storyboard>
```

Once you have spent a little time working with paths and PointAnimations, the code will become a little easier to read. It is best to spend some time with a few simple objects in order to get a feel for how the code changes in relation to changes you make to an object. As you can imagine, point animations can get complex very quickly.

A note about from/to

The from/to animation types with which you have been working have an additional attribute called By that you can use in lieu of a To value. The **DoubleByAnimation** project contains a storyboard that moves an ellipse using a DoubleAnimation that is declared as a from/by.

When using the By property, leave the To property off. The animation will alter the TargetProperty of an object by the specified amount. In this example, the ellipse's X transform property is moved from a value of 0 by 150 pixels over 1 second. One use for this type of animation may be specifying a range of motion for an object.

Open the project and press F5 to see the animation in a browser. The storyboard that moves the ellipse is shown following:

```
<Storyboard x:Name="Storyboard1">
    <DoubleAnimation Storyboard.TargetName="Ellipse"
    Storyboard.TargetProperty="(UIElement.RenderTransform).➥
        (TransformGroup.Children)[3].(TranslateTransform.X)"
        From="0" By="150" Duration="00:00:01"/>
</Storyboard>
```

If you wanted to generalize the starting position for the ellipse in this animation, you could remove the From property. The object would then move from wherever it is located by 150 pixels.

Types of keyframes

When working with UsingKeyFrames animations, each animation contains a number of keyframes. Silverlight has three types of keyframes, each of which creates a unique type of motion for an object. Depending upon user action, Blend may change the keyframe type behind the scenes. This section will take a look at each of the keyframe types and the type of motion they create.

Linear

Linear keyframes do what you might expect from their name—provide a way to move in a linear fashion from one keyframe to the next.

Open the **LinearKeyframe** project for Chapter 3. This project contains an example of a rectangle that uses linear keyframes to move in a diamond pattern. Press the F5 key to compile and run the application.

The storyboard is shown in the following listing. Even though the rectangle moves to four positions, if you look through the code listing, you can count eight. This is because there are two sets of animations: one handles the X transform, and the other the Y. Each one is four keyframes, for a total of eight.

```
<Storyboard x:Name="Storyboard1">
    <DoubleAnimationUsingKeyFrames Storyboard.TargetName="Rectangle"
    Storyboard.TargetProperty="(UIElement.RenderTransform).➥
        (TransformGroup.Children)[3].(TranslateTransform.X)"
        BeginTime="00:00:00">
        <LinearDoubleKeyFrame KeyTime="00:00:00.5000000" Value="200"/>
        <LinearDoubleKeyFrame KeyTime="00:00:01" Value="526"/>
        <LinearDoubleKeyFrame KeyTime="00:00:01.5000000" Value="253"/>
        <LinearDoubleKeyFrame KeyTime="00:00:02" Value="13"/>
    </DoubleAnimationUsingKeyFrames>
    <DoubleAnimationUsingKeyFrames Storyboard.TargetName="Rectangle"
    Storyboard.TargetProperty="(UIElement.RenderTransform).➥
        (TransformGroup.Children)[3].(TranslateTransform.Y)"
        BeginTime="00:00:00">
        <LinearDoubleKeyFrame KeyTime="00:00:00.5000000" Value="-121"/>
        <LinearDoubleKeyFrame KeyTime="00:00:01" Value="55"/>
        <LinearDoubleKeyFrame KeyTime="00:00:01.5000000" Value="305"/>
        <LinearDoubleKeyFrame KeyTime="00:00:02" Value="84"/>
    </DoubleAnimationUsingKeyFrames>
</Storyboard>
```

When using linear keyframes, Silverlight simply calculates the value of the TargetProperty between keyframes using linear interpolation. The preceding code illustrates LinearDoubleKeyFrame, but LinearColorKeyFrame and LinearPointKeyFrame are also available.

Spline

If you work in Blend, you will typically see spline keyframes added to your animations, even if the animations define linear movements for your objects. This is because without an additional property called KeySpline, spline and linear keyframes produce the same results. If you open and run the **SplineKeyframe** project for Chapter 3, you will see that it contains the same rectangle and animation as the linear keyframe example. However, in this project, the animations are defined as a series of spline keyframes. From the code listing, you can see that all the values are the same; only the type of keyframe has changed:

```
<Storyboard x:Name="Storyboard1">
    <DoubleAnimationUsingKeyFrames Storyboard.TargetName="Rectangle"
    Storyboard.TargetProperty="(UIElement.RenderTransform).➥
        (TransformGroup.Children)[3].(TranslateTransform.X)"
        BeginTime="00:00:00">
        <SplineDoubleKeyFrame KeyTime="00:00:00.5000000" Value="200"/>
        <SplineDoubleKeyFrame KeyTime="00:00:01" Value="526"/>
        <SplineDoubleKeyFrame KeyTime="00:00:01.5000000" Value="253"/>
        <SplineDoubleKeyFrame KeyTime="00:00:02" Value="13"/>
    </DoubleAnimationUsingKeyFrames>
    <DoubleAnimationUsingKeyFrames Storyboard.TargetName="Rectangle"
    Storyboard.TargetProperty="(UIElement.RenderTransform).➥
        (TransformGroup.Children)[3].(TranslateTransform.Y)"
        BeginTime="00:00:00">
        <SplineDoubleKeyFrame KeyTime="00:00:00.5000000" Value="-121"/>
        <SplineDoubleKeyFrame KeyTime="00:00:01" Value="55"/>
        <SplineDoubleKeyFrame KeyTime="00:00:01.5000000" Value="305"/>
        <SplineDoubleKeyFrame KeyTime="00:00:02" Value="84"/>
    </DoubleAnimationUsingKeyFrames>
</Storyboard>
```

So if the motion is the same between linear and spline keyframes, what's the difference? Why use one over the other? Where LinearDoubleKeyframes create linear motion, it's possible to add a property to a SplineDoubleKeyFrame called KeySpline. The KeySpline property affects the way an object moves as it approaches or leaves a keyframe, and can be added to a spline keyframe by directly editing the XAML or by modifying the keyframe via Blend's interface.

Test it out—in the example project, edit the XAML and modify the first SplineDoubleKeyFrame to include a KeySpline property:

```
<SplineDoubleKeyFrame KeySpline="1,0 0,1" KeyTime="00:00:00.5000000"
    Value="200"/>
```

Play the animation and notice the change in motion. Spline animations are used to add what is known as **ease** to an object's motion. I'll talk more about ease in the next section of this chapter.

Discrete

Discrete keyframes create a type of motion that holds an object in place until a keyframe is reached, at which time the object is moved to the value of the new keyframe. This type of motion is useful when creating frame-by-frame animations.

The **DiscreteKeyframe** project contains the same storyboard as the linear and spline projects, only this time the storyboard is written with discrete keyframes, as shown in the code listing.

Once again, you will see that none of the values changed, only the type of keyframe being used. Press F5 to compile and run the project, and notice how the rectangle holds its position until a keyframe is reached, at which time it jumps to the value specified in the next keyframe.

```xml
<Storyboard x:Name="Storyboard1">
    <DoubleAnimationUsingKeyFrames Storyboard.TargetName="Rectangle"
    Storyboard.TargetProperty="(UIElement.RenderTransform).➥
      (TransformGroup.Children)[3].(TranslateTransform.X)"
      BeginTime="00:00:00">
      <DiscreteDoubleKeyFrame KeyTime="00:00:00.5000000" Value="200"/>
      <DiscreteDoubleKeyFrame KeyTime="00:00:01" Value="526"/>
      <DiscreteDoubleKeyFrame KeyTime="00:00:01.5000000" Value="253"/>
      <DiscreteDoubleKeyFrame KeyTime="00:00:02" Value="13"/>
    </DoubleAnimationUsingKeyFrames>
    <DoubleAnimationUsingKeyFrames Storyboard.TargetName="Rectangle"
    Storyboard.TargetProperty="(UIElement.RenderTransform).➥
      (TransformGroup.Children)[3].(TranslateTransform.Y)"
      BeginTime="00:00:00">
      <DiscreteDoubleKeyFrame KeyTime="00:00:00.5000000" Value="-121"/>
      <DiscreteDoubleKeyFrame KeyTime="00:00:01" Value="55"/>
      <DiscreteDoubleKeyFrame KeyTime="00:00:01.5000000" Value="305"/>
      <DiscreteDoubleKeyFrame KeyTime="00:00:02" Value="84"/>
    </DoubleAnimationUsingKeyFrames>
</Storyboard>
```

Even though each of the example projects shown here uses a specific type of keyframe, you can freely mix and match them in your storyboards to achieve different effects. When working with KeySpline curves for spline keyframes, motion control can be a little tricky to accomplish by hand-coding XAML; this is where a tool such as Blend comes in very handy. In the next section, we will take a look at how to use Blend to modify keyframe types, and take a closer look at how the different types of keyframes affect the objects you are animating.

Keyframe interpolation in blend

Up to this point, all the animations created in our projects have had a bit of a mechanical feel due to the fact that they are linear in nature. Silverlight is simply calculating the in-between frames (called "tweening" in traditional animation) from a start value to an end value specified by various keyframes. For example, if a rectangle scales to two times its original size over the span of 1 second, every 1/10th of a second, the rectangle will increase in size by the same amount (1.1, 1.2, 1.3, 1.4, etc.).

We know that motion in the real world is not always linear, however. Cars don't just immediately go from standing still to moving at 60 MPH. Nonlinear motion is important in giving objects an organic, natural feel. Silverlight offers several types of interpolation between keyframes: **linear** (the default), **ease-in**, **ease-out**, and **hold-in**.

1. Open the **Ease** project from Chapter 3. This project contains an image of a desktop along with two folders positioned off the desktop to the left, as shown in Figure 3-5. There is also a basic storyboard in place that will make both folders move onto the desktop over a 2-second span, hold them there for 1 second, and then move them both off the desktop to the right over the next 2 seconds.

2. Open the storyboard by selecting MoveFolders from the Open a storyboard list on the Objects and Timeline panel.

3. Play the storyboard to see the default motion that occurs, which is linear in nature and similar to the type of motion in the projects to this point.

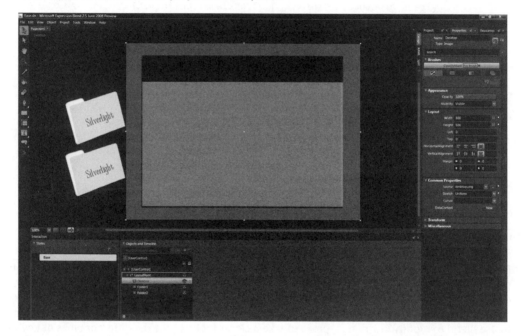

Figure 3-5. The Ease project demonstrates different types of keyframe interpolation.

4. When using Blend, changes are made to keyframe interpolation via a menu accessed by right-clicking a keyframe marker on the timeline. Right-click the keyframe at 2 seconds for Folder1, and from the pop-up menu, select Ease In ➤ 50%, as shown in Figure 3-6.

Figure 3-6. Change the ease-in value by right-clicking a keyframe marker to get the menu shown here.

5. Play the timeline, and notice how Folder1 now moves just a bit faster than Folder2, and "eases" as it approaches the keyframe at 2 seconds.

6. Set the ease-in value for Folder2 at 2 seconds to 100%. Folder2 now moves ahead of Folder1, and both ease into the keyframe. As you can see, ease-in is used to affect the way a property changes as a keyframe is approached.

7. To alter the way a property changes as you move away from a keyframe, edit the ease-out value for that keyframe. Right-click the keyframe for Folder1 at 3 seconds and change Ease Out to 100%.

Upon playing the storyboard, Folder1 will now leave the keyframe more slowly, but both folders reach the next keyframe at the same time, since no ease has been set for that keyframe. Behind the scenes, Blend is adding KeySpline elements to the animations in this storyboard that control the motion of the object. For the keyframe at 2 seconds on Folder1, the added XAML can be seen inside the SplineDoubleKeyFrame container shown here:

```
<SplineDoubleKeyFrame KeyTime="00:00:02" Value="500">
    <SplineDoubleKeyFrame.KeySpline>
        <KeySpline ControlPoint1="0,0" ControlPoint2="0.75,1"/>
    </SplineDoubleKeyFrame.KeySpline>
</SplineDoubleKeyFrame>
```

The values represented in the XAML just shown can be seen in Blend as keyframe markers are selected on the timeline. Select the keyframe marker at 2 seconds for Folder1. On the Properties panel, you will see the Easing pane, which looks like Figure 3-7.

As you select ease values from the pop-up menu, Blend will adjust the ease spline for you. If you find that you would like different ease values than what the pop-ups afford, you can make changes manually by dragging the yellow handles at each end of the spline in the Easing pane.

The x axis of the graph is representative of the time between the previous keyframe and the one you have selected, while the y axis is representative of the property you are animating. Alternatively, you can type values into the boxes at the bottom of the pane. As you can imagine, modifying the values for a KeySpline without a visual tool like Blend would be quite difficult.

Unlike easing, Hold In does not cause a property to change over time, but instead causes an abrupt change to the value of a property when the play head reaches the modified keyframe. This should sound familiar to you because it describes the exact behavior of a discrete keyframe type.

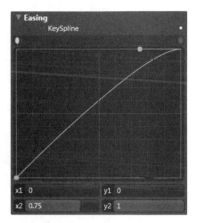

Figure 3-7. Manually editing the spline on the Easing pane allows fine control over ease values.

8. Change the view to Split. Scroll in the XAML window until you can see the code for the MoveFolders storyboard.

9. For Folder1, right-click the keyframe at 2 seconds and select the Hold In item from the pop-up menu. Did you see what happened to the code? Blend added a DiscreteDoubleKeyFrame for you!

   ```
   <DiscreteDoubleKeyFrame KeyTime="00:00:02" Value="500"/>
   ```

10. Change the remaining two keyframes for Folder1 to use Hold In and play the animation. Folder2 will slide along as expected, while Folder1 leaps from keyframe to keyframe.

From this look at storyboards, animations, keyframes, and keyframe interpolation, you should have a pretty good idea of the types of tools available to you when making objects move using XAML in Silverlight. You should also be able to see that a tool like Blend does a lot of behind-the-scenes work for you to make the job of animating objects easier. With a solid grip on how storyboards work, it's time to take a look at how to go about making storyboards play when you want them to. The next section takes a look at events and how they are captured in order to give you control over when the storyboards you have created will play.

Events

To this point, we have worked with animations fairly extensively, but always within the confines of Blend. We haven't yet done anything to get our animations running in the browser, where Silverlight applications are usually presented. Events are used to add interactivity to applications, whether from user input or based on some condition within the application itself. In this section, we're going to take a look at what events are, and how they can be wired up.

1. Open the **Truck** project from Chapter 3. This project contains the truck scene from Chapter 2, as well as a storyboard that will scale the truck down in order to make it appear to be moving away.

2. Use the Open a storyboard icon and select the ScaleTruck item from the storyboard list.

3. Play the timeline to preview the animation.

4. Now press F5 to test the project. A browser window will open . . . and nothing happens. This is because there is nothing telling Silverlight to play the timeline in the application.

The way to go about telling Silverlight what to do with various storyboards is through events. Events consist of three parts: an event listener, an event, and an event handler. The event listener, as you may have guessed, tells Silverlight to "listen" for a particular event, such as MouseEnter, MouseLeave, MouseLeftButtonUp, or Loaded.

When the specified event occurs, the event listener tells Silverlight which event handler to use. The event handler is a set of instructions that tells Silverlight what to do. Events can be caused by users, as is the case with a mouse click, or they can occur from within the application, such as when a storyboard has ended. When an event occurs, it is said to be "raised."

There are two ways to create events for objects in Silverlight. One is by adding them directly in the XAML, and the other is by creating them entirely in the code-behind file. When created using XAML, a typical event hookup looks like this:

```
<Rectangle Height="100" Width="100" Fill="#FFFF0000"
    x:Name="MyRect" MouseEnter="MyRect_MouseEnter"/>
```

This code creates a small red square named MyRect. An event listener is added to listen for the MouseEnter event. If the pointer is placed over this object, the MouseEnter event will be raised, and the event handler—in this case, a set of instructions (or function) called MyRect_MouseEnter—will be executed.

Remember earlier when you were told that as a designer, a time would come when you'd have to roll up your sleeves and get your hands dirty? Start rolling.

The following sections describe adding events first from a designer's perspective, and then from a developer's perspective. If you are a designer, there isn't really a way around having to add some code to create interactivity, so after reading through your section, take the time to go through the developer section and see that it's not difficult or scary to do. You will probably find that it is faster, easier, and far more flexible.

Getting back to the **Truck** project, we want to find an event that will cause the storyboard we created to play when the application is opened in a browser. The appropriate event in this case is called Loaded, and will be attached to our main Canvas object, called LayoutRoot. When the Canvas loads, a trigger will be used to play our storyboard.

For designers

1. With the **Truck** project open, press F11 until you are in XAML view. Scroll to the top of the XAML window, and beginning around line 6 you will see a section that contains the storyboard resources that have been created for this project. It looks like this:

```
<UserControl.Resources>
    <Storyboard x:Name="scaleTruck">
        <DoubleAnimationUsingKeyFrames Storyboard.TargetName="truck"
    Storyboard.TargetProperty="(UIElement.RenderTransform).➡
        (TransformGroup.Children)[0].(ScaleTransform.ScaleX)"
        BeginTime="00:00:00">
            <SplineDoubleKeyFrame KeyTime="00:00:03" Value="0.15"/>
        </DoubleAnimationUsingKeyFrames>
        <DoubleAnimationUsingKeyFrames
        Storyboard.TargetName="truck"
            Storyboard.TargetProperty=➡
            "(UIElement.RenderTransform).➡
            (TransformGroup.Children)[0].➡
            (ScaleTransform.ScaleY)"
            BeginTime="00:00:00">
            <SplineDoubleKeyFrame KeyTime="00:00:03" Value="0.15"/>
        </DoubleAnimationUsingKeyFrames>
    </Storyboard>
</UserControl.Resources>
```

We are trying to avoid diving into the code-behind file, so the goal is to create an event trigger that is automated as part of the XAML file. To do this, it is necessary to relocate the storyboard and included animations to a new section of XAML code that we will create. The new section of XAML will define what are known as triggers for this application. To save you some typing, a blank triggers section has been provided in the TriggersDocument.txt file for Chapter 3.

2. Open TriggersDocument.txt, and then cut the storyboard from your Blend project and paste it into the TriggersDocument.txt code, where it says <!--Insert Storyboard here -->. You will have something that looks like the following code listing:

```
<Canvas.Triggers>
<EventTrigger RoutedEvent="Canvas.Loaded">
<EventTrigger.Actions>
<BeginStoryboard>

 <!-- Insert Storyboard here. -->
<Storyboard x:Name="ScaleTruck">
        <DoubleAnimationUsingKeyFrames Storyboard.TargetName="Truck"
            Storyboard.TargetProperty=➡
            "(UIElement.RenderTransform).➡
            (TransformGroup.Children)[0].➡
            (ScaleTransform.ScaleX)"
            BeginTime="00:00:00">
            <SplineDoubleKeyFrame KeyTime="00:00:03" Value="0.15"/>
        </DoubleAnimationUsingKeyFrames>
```

```
<DoubleAnimationUsingKeyFrames Storyboard.TargetName="Truck"
    Storyboard.TargetProperty=➡
    "(UIElement.RenderTransform).➡
    (TransformGroup.Children)[0].➡
    (ScaleTransform.ScaleY)"
    BeginTime="00:00:00">
    <SplineDoubleKeyFrame KeyTime="00:00:03" Value="0.15"/>
</DoubleAnimationUsingKeyFrames>
</Storyboard>

</BeginStoryboard>
</EventTrigger.Actions>
</EventTrigger>
</Canvas.Triggers>
```

3. Once the storyboard has been copied into the text file, hop back over to Blend and remove the entire UserControl.Resources section, starting from and including the opening <UserControl. Resources> tag, to the closing </UserControl.Resources> tag.

4. Paste the entire contents from the text file just after the opening tag for the LayoutRoot Canvas in Blend. Don't panic if Blend reports that the XAML is invalid—as of the June 2008 release, the trigger section will compile and run correctly.

5. Press F5 to run the project again, and when the browser opens, you should see the truck high-tailing it away.

That was a lot of cutting, copying, and pasting of code. What just happened?

By default, storyboards are available to an application as a global resource. Rather than have the storyboard available this way, we placed it inside of a trigger, which is a XAML method for attaching an event. The RoutedEvent="Canvas.Loaded" tag in the XAML sets up an event handler that waits for the Canvas to be loaded, which occurs when an application runs. When the Loaded event is raised for the Canvas, the <EventTrigger.Actions> actions are performed—in this case, the actions list our storyboard animations.

There's a significant limitation to using triggers—at this time, Loaded is the only trigger available directly within XAML. This means that at the moment, if you are hoping for anything more than basic animations that run when an application loads, it will be necessary to wire them up in the code-behind file.

If you are now questioning your ability to use Silverlight because it requires some programming, don't fret—hooking up events in the code-behind is more automated (and therefore less tedious) than the process you just worked through. The tight integration between Blend and Visual Studio makes wiring events easier than you may have thought, so work through the next section to get a feel for how events are added in C#.

For developers

1. Start in Blend with the freshly opened **Truck** project.

2. Select the Project tab to the left of the Properties tab, and expand the Page.xaml item so you can see the Page.xaml.cs code-behind file.

3. Right-click the code-behind and select Edit in Visual Studio from the menu, as shown in Figure 3-8.

Figure 3-8. Using Visual Studio to open a code-behind file from within Blend

Once Visual Studio opens, you will be looking at the code-behind file for the XAML file from the **Truck** project.

4. Position the cursor at the end of the InitializeComponent() code and press Enter to move the cursor to a new line. You will be adding an event listener to the LayoutRoot Canvas.

5. Type lay. As you type, an IntelliSense window will open that shows all the available objects, properties, methods, and so on to which you have access. Inside the IntelliSense window, LayoutRoot will become highlighted, as shown in Figure 3-9.

Figure 3-9. IntelliSense in Visual Studio helps cut down on the time it takes to wire up events.

6. Since the LayoutRoot Canvas is the object to which we want to attach an event, press the period (.) key.

7. Visual Studio will finish typing the name of the element for you, and the IntelliSense window will display a list of properties and methods for this object. We already know we will be using the Loaded event, so type lo. Loaded will become highlighted in IntelliSense, so press Enter and Visual Studio will fill in the rest of the text.

8. To finish adding the event, type += and press the Tab key twice. The first time, Visual Studio will add the event listener to the code, and the second time, Visual Studio will add a basic event handler function that is called when the event is raised. The following code listing shows what you should have at this point:

```
public partial class Page : UserControl
{
    public Page()
    {
        // Required to initialize variables
        InitializeComponent();
        LayoutRoot.Loaded += new RoutedEventHandler(LayoutRoot_Loaded);
    }

    void LayoutRoot_Loaded(object sender, RoutedEventArgs e)
    {
        throw new NotImplementedException();
    }
}
```

9. We'll talk more about private vs. public variables and/or functions later, but for now, add a private protection modifier to the LayoutRoot_Loaded event handler, as follows. This protects the function from being available anywhere other than the Page.xaml.cs file.

```
private void LayoutRoot_Loaded(object sender, RoutedEventArgs e)
```

The LayoutRoot_Loaded function that Visual Studio just added is what will be called when the LayoutRoot Canvas loads when the application runs. The function needs to contain a set of instructions to tell Silverlight what to do—right now it contains some simple, default place-holder code.

10. Remove the throw new NotImplementedException(); code. In its place, start typing the story-board name—ScaleTruck. As soon as you see the storyboard name highlighted in IntelliSense, press the period key to see the list of properties and methods available. To make a storyboard play, the Begin() method is used, so type in Beg, then a set of empty parentheses, and end the line with a semicolon:

```
ScaleTruck.Begin();
```

You can now test the project in Visual Studio by pressing F5, or save the project and test it from Blend. Either way, the storyboard will now play when the application loads. The **TruckCompleted** project includes the code described in this example.

The previous process used only the code-behind to hook up an event to an object, but it is possible to create the event listener in XAML, and only use the code-behind for the event handler. This makes it a little easier when working in a team to identify which objects have event listeners. It also offers some flexibility in that a designer may create the event listeners, and then hand off the project for the developer to create the event handlers. I bet that every developer reading this right now is cringing at that thought (and so are the designers who prefer to avoid any more code than necessary). The important take-away is that there is a lot of flexibility in the workflow, and there is more than one way to get the job done. Find out which one is the most comfortable for you, and run with it.

Let's take a look at how we can wire up one event listener to a mouse click, and another to the end of a storyboard.

1. Open the **Events** project from Chapter 3. This project contains three rectangles, each of which has an associated storyboard that defines a simple Translate transform to slide the rectangle to the right. We will be hooking up an event listener that causes a storyboard to play when one of the rectangles is clicked.

2. Begin by selecting the RedRectangle element on the Objects and Timeline panel. At the top of the Properties panel, select the Events icon, as shown in Figure 3-10.

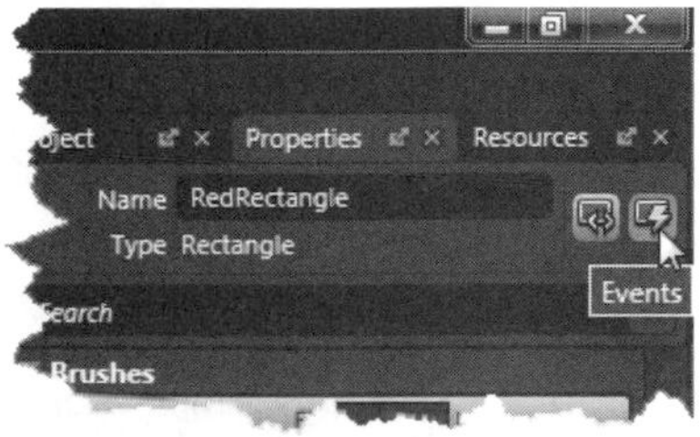

The Events pane displays a list of the available events for this object, such as GotFocus, KeyDown, KeyUp, LayoutUpdated, and Loaded. If you look down the list, you will see both MouseLeftButtonDown and MouseLeftButtonUp. When utilizing clicks for input, it is typically preferred to use the "up" event for the click to avoid performing an action before the user has released the mouse button.

Figure 3-10. The Events icon on the Properties panel can be used to add events.

3. In the MouseLeftButtonUp field, type Red_MouseUp and press Enter. Two things will happen. First, Blend will add some XAML to the definition of the RedRectangle object that attaches an event handler to this object:

```
MouseLeftButtonUp="Red_MouseUp"
```

Next, if you have Visual Studio installed, it will load the project and automatically create the basic event handler code for you:

```
private void Red_MouseUp(object sender, MouseButtonEventArgs e)
{

}
```

4. The storyboards in this project are named MoveRed, MoveBlue, and MoveGreen. In order to tell Silverlight to play the storyboard for the red rectangle, place the cursor between the curly braces and type mo. IntelliSense will open a dialog like the one shown in Figure 3-11. You can see all three storyboards listed alphabetically in the window.

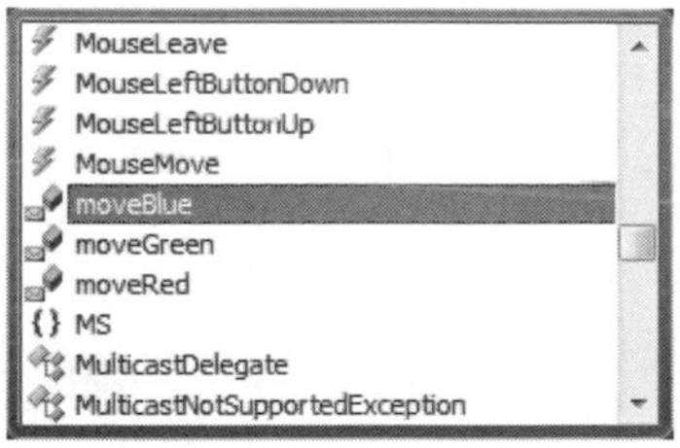

5. Select the MoveRed item with the arrow keys, and then press the period key to see what methods are available for storyboard elements. You know from the previous example that the method to call in order to play a storyboard is Begin(), so start typing beg. When Begin becomes highlighted in the IntelliSense window, type an empty set of parentheses, and end the line with a semicolon so that the completed line looks like this:

```
MoveRed.Begin();
```

Figure 3-11. The IntelliSense window shows all the objects in a project, including storyboards.

6. Press F5 to test the project. When the browser window opens, click the red rectangle—it should glide smoothly across the screen to the right.

7. Use Blend to add an event handler to the blue rectangle in a similar manner. Select BlueRectangle in the Objects and Timeline panel or by clicking the object on the artboard, and then click the Events icon on the Properties panel.

8. In the MouseLeftButtonUp field, type Blue_MouseUp and press Enter. Once again, Blend will add the event listener to the XAML for you, and Visual Studio will create the event handler. All you need to add is a call to the Begin() method for the MoveBlue storyboard:

```
private void Blue_MouseUp(object sender, MouseButtonEventArgs e)
{
    MoveBlue.Begin();
}
```

Repeat this process for the green rectangle as well. Once all three events have been hooked up, run the project. As you click each rectangle, the specified storyboard will play. Since each rectangle has its own event listener awaiting a mouse click, the Rectangle objects can be clicked in any order or at any speed, and the storyboards will play. A completed version of this project with all the event code in place is available in the Chapter 3 projects as **EventsCompleted**.

Storyboard events

Applications that offer a lot of user interaction often use many storyboards and animations, making them quite complex. In these cases, it can be useful to segment the storyboards, chaining them together by using the end of one storyboard to start another. Like most objects in Silverlight, storyboards also have events associated with them. The event listeners can be added to storyboards in XAML, but like the previous example, you will still need to add some code to execute the desired action.

The **StoryboardEvents** project for Chapter 3 contains the same rectangles and storyboards as the previous example. The MouseLeftButtonUp event listener for the red rectangle has already been added, and the event handler will play the storyboard to move the rectangle. Running the project will allow you to click the red rectangle and see it move across the screen.

For this project, we want to add an event listener to the MoveRed storyboard so that when ends, it calls an event handler that contains code to play the MoveBlue storyboard. When a storyboard ends, it raises a Completed event.

1. Adding the code to attach an event listener to a storyboard is relatively straightforward, but must be done in the XAML code. With the **StoryboardEvents** project open, press F11 until you are in XAML view.

2. Scroll to the top of the window until you see the MoveRed storyboard.

```
<Storyboard x:Name="MoveRed">
[...]
</Storyboard>
```

3. The Completed event listener is written into the opening tag of a storyboard. Edit the XAML code for the storyboard to look like the following:

```
<Storyboard x:Name="MoveRed" Completed="MoveRed_Completed">
```

4. Save the project. On the Projects panel, expand the file list under Page.xaml, and then right-click Page.xaml.cs and select Edit in Visual Studio.

5. Unlike using the Events pane in Blend to add events to objects, directly editing the XAML code does not automatically add any event handler code in the code-behind files. Below the Red_MouseUp event handler code, add the following event handler for the Completed event of the MoveRed storyboard:

```
private void MoveRed_Completed(object sender, EventArgs e)
{
    MoveBlue.Begin();
}
```

6. Run the application and click the red rectangle. The rectangle will slide across the screen, and when it reaches the end of its storyboard, the Completed event will be raised. At that point, Silverlight will execute the code in the event handler that was just added, and the blue rectangle will move.

7. To hook up a Completed event listener on the MoveBlue storyboard that starts the MoveGreen storyboard, begin by adding the appropriate event listener to the MoveBlue storyboard in Blend:

```
<Storyboard x:Name="MoveBlue" Completed="MoveBlue_Completed">
```

8. Save the project and once again edit the Page.xaml.cs code-behind file in Visual Studio. Add the event handler function that the Completed event listener will call when the Completed event is raised:

```
private void MoveBlue_Completed(object sender, EventArgs e)
{
    MoveGreen.Begin();
}
```

9. Run the application and click the red rectangle. Now what you will see is that when the MoveRed storyboard completes, the code will start the MoveBlue storyboard, which in turn has code that will start the MoveGreen storyboard. For reference, **StoryboardEventsCompleted** contains the completed version of this example.

As you can see from working through the event examples, the XAML and code-behind files are integrated and work together to capture user interactions and let Silverlight know what to do. Developers may prefer to keep the event listeners entirely in the code-behind where they can be easily edited or changed if the need arises.

As demonstrated with the Loaded event listener, event listeners and event handlers can be hooked up completely from the code-behind file. Let's take a closer look at how the same event listeners look in XAML and in the code-behind. The XAML for the RedRectangle object used in the previous example is shown following, and includes an event listener for a mouse button release:

```
<Rectangle Height="54" Width="149" Canvas.Left="65" Canvas.Top="58"
    Fill="#FFFF0000" Stroke="#FF000000" RadiusY="12" RadiusX="12"
    x:Name="RedRectangle" RenderTransformOrigin="0.5,0.5"
    MouseLeftButtonUp="Red_MouseUp">
```

The event listener can be removed from the XAML and added to the Page() constructor in the code-behind file. The Page() constructor is a method that is called when the Page.xaml object is created in the Silverlight application. Any user control you add to a project has a constructor, and each control's constructor is called when that control is instantiated in your applications. Any code you want to have executed when a control is loaded is placed inside the constructor.

When creating event listeners in code, let the IntelliSense and code snippets do the work. In this example, you would type RedRectangle., and then start typing the mouse event name until it was highlighted. Type += and press the Tab key twice, and a lot of the code will be created for you:

```
public Page()
{
    // Required to initialize variables
    InitializeComponent();

    RedRectangle.MouseLeftButtonUp +=
        new MouseButtonEventHandler(Red_MouseUp);
}
```

Whether coded in XAML markup or completely in the code-behind, the same function is called: Red_MouseUp. Similarly, the MoveBlue Completed event listener could be moved to the code-behind. The XAML event listener would be removed so that <Storyboard x:Name="MoveBlue" Completed="MoveBlue_Completed"> becomes <Storyboard x:Name="MoveBlue">.

Then an appropriate event listener is added to the code-behind:

```
public Page()
{
    // Required to initialize variables
    InitializeComponent();

    RedRectangle.MouseLeftButtonUp +=
        new MouseButtonEventHandler(Red_MouseUp);
    MoveBlue.Completed += new EventHandler(MoveBlue_Completed);
}
```

As with the Red_MouseUp event handler, the MoveBlue.Completed event listener calls the MoveBlue_Completed event handler the same way the XAML did. This project would function exactly as it did with the XAML event handlers.

Being able to add event listeners via XAML or the code-behind offers a lot of flexibility when working on a team comprised of both designers and developers, but it also means that it's a good idea to agree upon a preferred method for dealing with events to avoid unnecessary work.

The examples in this chapter have demonstrated just how much work Blend does behind the scenes making application development easier by building out storyboards and animations. As a developer, you may have a desire or need to create storyboards and animations entirely in code. In the next section, we'll take a look at how you can do this.

Programming storyboards and animations

This section of the chapter will be useful to anyone interested in learning how to program storyboards. As you have seen, there is quite an array of information that goes into storyboards and the animations they contain. All the storyboards and animations you have worked through can be created entirely from code. While it is perfectly acceptable to create storyboards in XAML as you have done to this point, there may be times when you want a little more flexibility in creating animations that are essentially reusable—"reusable" meaning more of a "code once, use many times" approach than, say, using one storyboard on 20 objects. Let's dig right in with storyboards.

Storyboards

As you are already aware, storyboards are containers for animations, and they may contain one animation, many animations, or no animations at all in order to function as a timer. When coding storyboards, you are creating an empty container to which you will be adding animations. Declaring a storyboard is as simple as creating a new object of type Storyboard, and giving it a name, which is done with the following code. Remember that even though your storyboards are being created from code, they still must each have a unique name.

```
Storyboard MyStoryboard = new Storyboard();
```

Once a storyboard has been declared, you can set any of the properties you did with XAML. For example, adding a Duration property to MyStoryboard would look like the following listing. When coding, durations are typically expressed as TimeSpan objects. TimeSpan objects represent an interval or period of time expressed as days, hours, minutes, seconds, and fractions of a second. Here, the duration is being set to .5 seconds by defining a duration from just the seconds component of a TimeSpan:

```
MyStoryboard.Duration = new Duration(TimeSpan.FromSeconds(0.5));
```

Once a storyboard has been defined, it needs to be made available to the application as a resource. This is done by adding the storyboard to the resources for the root object by calling the Resources.Add() method for the root object and passing a string key and value to the method. The string key can be any string identifier you wish to use, and the value is the storyboard name:

```
LayoutRoot.Resources.Add("MyStoryboard", MyStoryboard);
```

You can also add event listeners to the storyboard using the same type of code as you did in the exercises from the last section:

```
MyStoryboard.Completed += new EventHandler(MyStoryboard_Completed);
```

Now that you know how to define a storyboard with code, the next section will take a close look at how to add animations to the storyboard.

DoubleAnimation

Use Visual Studio to open the **DoubleFromToWithCode** project. As you might guess from the name, this project demonstrates how to create a DoubleAnimation with code. As you can see from the code listing shown following, this project contains the same sliding panel from an earlier project with event listeners for MouseEnter and MouseLeave. The event handler code is in place, but currently contains no code.

```
public partial class Page : UserControl
{
    public Page()
    {
        // Required to initialize variables
        InitializeComponent();

        Slider.MouseEnter += new MouseEventHandler(Slider_MouseEnter);
        Slider.MouseLeave += new MouseEventHandler(Slider_MouseLeave);
    }

    private void Slider_MouseLeave(object sender, MouseEventArgs e)
    {

    }

    private void Slider_MouseEnter(object sender, MouseEventArgs e)
    {

    }
}
```

1. To begin, we will create the SlideOut storyboard from earlier in the chapter. The code for that looks like this:

```
<Storyboard x:Name="SlideOut">
    <DoubleAnimation Storyboard.TargetName="Slider"
    Storyboard.TargetProperty="(UIElement.RenderTransform).➥
        (TransformGroup.Children)[3].(TranslateTransform.X)"
        Duration="00:00:00.50" To="150"/>
</Storyboard>
```

2. Open the Page.xaml.cs code-behind file and create the Storyboard object just above the Page() constructor:

```
private Storyboard SlideOut = new Storyboard();
```

This creates a Storyboard object named SlideOut that is accessible to the Page.xaml.cs file in the application. Checking our original XAML for reference, you can see that there are no other properties assigned for this storyboard.

3. You can see in the original code that the storyboard contains a single DoubleAnimation. Add code just after the storyboard declaration to create a new DoubleAnimation object:

```
private DoubleAnimation SlideOutAnim = new DoubleAnimation();
```

This creates an animation object named SlideOutAnim that we need to set a few properties on. The first property we will be setting is TargetName, which is referred to as a **dependency property**. Dependency properties provide a way to compute values based on values of other inputs such as user preferences.

4. Set the TargetName property inside the Page() constructor, just after the IntializeComponent() method, by using the SetValue() method on the DoubleAnimation object. The following code tells Silverlight we are using Slider as the TargetName:

```
SlideOutAnim.SetValue(Storyboard.TargetNameProperty, "Slider");
```

5. Next, set another dependency property, TargetProperty. TargetProperty is declared through a PropertyPath. This code tells Silverlight that the property this animation will be affecting is the third item in the transform group, which is the Translate transform. The transform group in the XAML looks like this, and is numbered from 0 (numbers were added for reference).

```
<Canvas.RenderTransform>
    <TransformGroup>
Child Number 0     <ScaleTransform/>
Child Number 1     <SkewTransform/>
Child Number 2     <RotateTransform/>
Child Number 3     <TranslateTransform/>
    </TransformGroup>
</Canvas.RenderTransform>
```

The code for this property looks like this:

```
SlideOutAnim.SetValue(Storyboard.TargetPropertyProperty,
    new PropertyPath("(UIElement.RenderTransform).➡
(TransformGroup.Children)[3].(TranslateTransform.X)"));
```

6. Finally, the Duration and To properties of the animation are set:

```
SlideOutAnim.Duration = new Duration(TimeSpan.FromSeconds(0.5));
SlideOutAnim.To = 150;
```

Aside from the formatting of the code, the values assigned to the DoubleAnimation object are the same ones from the XAML.

7. Now that the animation has been defined, it can be added to the Storyboard object. The following code uses the Add() method to place the SlideOutAnim DoubleAnimation object in the collection of children for the SlideOut storyboard:

```
SlideOut.Children.Add(SlideOutAnim);
```

8. The storyboard is now made available to the root element of our application. In this case, the root element is a Canvas object named LayoutRoot:

```
LayoutRoot.Resources.Add("SlideOut", SlideOut);
```

At this point, the main code looks like the following listing. The application will compile and run, but you will find that nothing happens when you move the pointer over the panel. This is because the event handlers do not contain any code.

```
public partial class Page : UserControl
{
    private Storyboard SlideOut = new Storyboard();
    private DoubleAnimation SlideOutAnim = new DoubleAnimation();
```

```
public Page()
{
    InitializeComponent();

    SlideOutAnim.SetValue(Storyboard.TargetNameProperty, "Slider");
    SlideOutAnim.SetValue(Storyboard.TargetPropertyProperty,
        new PropertyPath("(UIElement.RenderTransform).➡
        (TransformGroup.Children)[3].(TranslateTransform.X)"));
    SlideOutAnim.Duration = new Duration(TimeSpan.FromSeconds(0.5));
    SlideOutAnim.To = 150;
    SlideOut.Children.Add(SlideOutAnim);
    LayoutRoot.Resources.Add("SlideOut", SlideOut);

    Slider.MouseEnter += new MouseEventHandler(Slider_MouseEnter);
    Slider.MouseLeave += new MouseEventHandler(Slider_MouseLeave);
}

private void Slider_MouseLeave(object sender, MouseEventArgs e)
{

}

private void Slider_MouseEnter(object sender, MouseEventArgs e)
{

}
}
```

9. The event handler functions are already in place, and need only to have code added that calls the newly created storyboard. In the Slider_MouseEnter event handler, add the following code to call the newly created storyboard:

```
SlideOut.Begin();
```

10. Press F5 to test the project. When the pointer moves over the panel, the storyboard plays. When you're done testing, close the browser window and return to Visual Studio.

11. Let's add a second storyboard that will slide the panel back in when the MouseLeave event is raised. Begin by creating the Storyboard object. This code goes near the top of the listing, where the SlideOut storyboard was declared:

```
private Storyboard SlideIn = new Storyboard();
```

12. Declare a new DoubleAnimation called SlideInAnim:

```
private DoubleAnimation SlideInAnim = new DoubleAnimation();
```

13. Inside the Page() constructor, assign TargetName, TargetProperty, Duration, and To properties to the new animation:

```
SlideInAnim.SetValue(Storyboard.TargetNameProperty, "Slider");
SlideInAnim.SetValue(Storyboard.TargetPropertyProperty,
```

```
new PropertyPath("(UIElement.RenderTransform).➥
    (TransformGroup.Children)[3].(TranslateTransform.X)"));
SlideInAnim.Duration = new Duration(TimeSpan.FromSeconds(0.5));
SlideInAnim.To = 0;
```

14. Add the animation to the storyboard, and the storyboard to the root object in the application:

```
SlideIn.Children.Add(SlideInAnim);
LayoutRoot.Resources.Add("SlideIn", SlideIn);
```

15. Finish up by adding a call to the Begin() method of the SlideIn storyboard to the event handler for the MouseLeave event:

```
SlideIn.Begin();
```

You should now have something that looks like the code listing shown following:

```
public partial class Page : UserControl
{
    private Storyboard SlideOut = new Storyboard();
    private DoubleAnimation SlideOutAnim = new DoubleAnimation();
    private Storyboard SlideIn = new Storyboard();
    private DoubleAnimation SlideInAnim = new DoubleAnimation();

    public Page()
    {
        InitializeComponent();

        SlideOutAnim.SetValue(Storyboard.TargetNameProperty, "Slider");
        SlideOutAnim.SetValue(Storyboard.TargetPropertyProperty,
            new PropertyPath("(UIElement.RenderTransform).➥
            (TransformGroup.Children)[3].(TranslateTransform.X)"));
        SlideOutAnim.Duration = new Duration(TimeSpan.FromSeconds(0.5));
        SlideOutAnim.To = 150;
        SlideOut.Children.Add(SlideOutAnim);
        LayoutRoot.Resources.Add("SlideOut", SlideOut);

        SlideInAnim.SetValue(Storyboard.TargetNameProperty, "Slider");
        SlideInAnim.SetValue(Storyboard.TargetPropertyProperty,
            new PropertyPath("(UIElement.RenderTransform).➥
            (TransformGroup.Children)[3].(TranslateTransform.X)"));
        SlideInAnim.Duration = new Duration(TimeSpan.FromSeconds(0.5));
        SlideInAnim.To = 0;
        SlideIn.Children.Add(SlideInAnim);
        LayoutRoot.Resources.Add("SlideIn", SlideIn);

        Slider.MouseEnter += new MouseEventHandler(Slider_MouseEnter);
        Slider.MouseLeave += new MouseEventHandler(Slider_MouseLeave);
    }
```

```
        private void Slider_MouseLeave(object sender, MouseEventArgs e)
        {
            SlideIn.Begin();
        }

        private void Slider_MouseEnter(object sender, MouseEventArgs e)
        {
            SlideOut.Begin();
        }
    }
```

Press F5 to test the project out. When the pointer is placed over the panel, the SlideOut storyboard plays, and when the pointer leaves the panel, the SlideIn storyboard plays. Since both animations are defined with only a To property and omit the From property, the transition between storyboards is seamless and results in a smooth animation. Take a look at the **DoubleFromToWithCodeCompleted** project if you'd like to see the final code from this example.

Using functions to create animation

As you can probably imagine, a complex application may have many storyboards, each with many animations inside them. One of the benefits of using code to produce storyboards and animations is that you can create generic functions that can be passed variables in order to create the animations for you.

1. Use Visual Studio to open the **GeneratingAnimationsWithCode** project. This project is identical to the skeleton project used in the previous example. This time, you are going to code up a function that will create an animation for you.

2. In the Page.xaml.cs code-behind, start by declaring a storyboard before the Page() constructor:

    ```
    private Storyboard SlideOut = new Storyboard();
    ```

3. Below the closing curly brace for the Page() constructor, declare a function that accepts a string and a double value, and returns a type DoubleAnimation. This function will be passed a name and a value, from which it will create a DoubleAnimation and return it to the calling code:

    ```
    private DoubleAnimation CreateSlidingAnim(string elementName,
        double toValue)
    {

    }
    ```

4. Inside this function, declare a new DoubleAnimation type:

    ```
    DoubleAnimation animation = new DoubleAnimation();
    ```

5. The next step is to use the value passed into the function as elementName to set the TargetProperty for the animation. This is done by adding the following code:

    ```
    animation.SetValue(Storyboard.TargetNameProperty, elementName);
    ```

6. In this case, we already know what our target property is since the panel simply slides to the right. The function could be altered to accept an argument for the target property in order to make it a little more flexible, but for clarity we will simply hard-code the property here. Add the following code to specify that the target property is once again the third child in the transform group for our object, which specifies the Translate transform:

```
animation.SetValue(Storyboard.TargetPropertyProperty,
        new PropertyPath("(UIElement.RenderTransform).➥
        (TransformGroup.Children)[3].(TranslateTransform.X)"));
```

7. Next, code up the Duration property:

```
animation.Duration = new Duration(TimeSpan.FromSeconds(0.5));
```

8. Use the value that was passed to the function to create the To property:

```
animation.To = toValue;
```

9. Finish up the function by returning the newly created animation to the calling code:

```
return animation;
```

You now have a compact, generic function that will create animations on demand. Now all you need is some code to call it with.

10. In the Page() constructor, add a child animation to the desired storyboard by calling the function that was just created inside the Add() method. It looks like this:

```
SlideOut.Children.Add(CreateSlidingAnim("Slider", 150));
```

11. In the last step, the CreateSlidingAnim() function we created is passed the element name Slider and value 150, which it uses to create a DoubleAnimation that is returned to the Add() method. Now that the animation has been added to the storyboard, we need to add the storyboard to the root element resources. This code goes in the Page() constructor, right after the code from step 10:

```
LayoutRoot.Resources.Add("SlideOut", SlideOut);
```

12. Finish up by calling the Begin() method for this storyboard in the MouseEnter event handler code:

```
SlideOut.Begin();
```

Press F5 to run the project. When the browser window opens with the application, place the mouse pointer over the panel, and it will slide out.

The really attractive thing about creating animations in this manner is that the hard work is already done. Another animation can be added with just a few lines of code. Let's create the SlideIn storyboard using the same function.

13. Above the Page() constructor, declare another storyboard:

```
private Storyboard SlideIn = new Storyboard();
```

14. Inside the Page() constructor, create the animation with a call to the automated function and add it to the storyboard, and then add the storyboard to the resources for the root element:

```
SlideIn.Children.Add(CreateSlidingAnim("Slider", 0));
LayoutRoot.Resources.Add("SlideIn", SlideIn);
```

15. Add a call to the Begin() method in the event handler, and you're done:

```
SlideIn.Begin();
```

Your completed code should look like the following listing:

```
public partial class Page : UserControl
{
    private Storyboard SlideOut = new Storyboard();
    private Storyboard SlideIn = new Storyboard();

    public Page()
    {
        InitializeComponent();

        SlideOut.Children.Add(CreateSlidingAnim("Slider", 150));
        LayoutRoot.Resources.Add("SlideOut", SlideOut);

        SlideIn.Children.Add(CreateSlidingAnim("Slider", 0));
        LayoutRoot.Resources.Add("SlideIn", SlideIn);

        Slider.MouseEnter += new MouseEventHandler(Slider_MouseEnter);
        Slider.MouseLeave += new MouseEventHandler(Slider_MouseLeave);
    }

    private DoubleAnimation CreateSlidingAnim(string elementName,
        double toValue)
    {
        DoubleAnimation animation = new DoubleAnimation();
        animation.SetValue(Storyboard.TargetNameProperty, elementName);
        animation.SetValue(Storyboard.TargetPropertyProperty,
            new PropertyPath("(UIElement.RenderTransform).➥
            (TransformGroup.Children)[3].(TranslateTransform.X)"));
        animation.Duration = new Duration(TimeSpan.FromSeconds(0.5));
        animation.To = toValue;
        return animation;
    }


    private void Slider_MouseLeave(object sender, MouseEventArgs e)
    {
        SlideIn.Begin();
    }
```

```
private void Slider_MouseEnter(object sender, MouseEventArgs e)
{
    SlideOut.Begin();
}
}
```

If you run the project at this point, you will find that both the MouseEnter and MouseLeave events start the storyboards as expected when the pointer enters or leaves the Slider object. The beauty in this approach is that you could use the CreateSlidingAnim function to create animations that will affect any object, so you could quickly and easily populate multiple storyboards that target many objects. The code is generalized, so it is reusable and can easily be augmented. The final code for this project is in the **GeneratingAnimationsCompleted** project.

DoubleAnimationUsingKeyframes

As noted earlier, each type of animation you've worked with in this chapter can be replicated in code. Let's take a look at a few examples, starting with the **DoubleUsingKeyframesWithCode** project, which will be used to code up the C# equivalent of the following storyboard, which transforms an object 150 pixels along the x axis over .5 seconds:

```
<Storyboard x:Name="Storyboard1">
    <DoubleAnimationUsingKeyFrames Storyboard.TargetName="Rectangle"
        Storyboard.TargetProperty="(UIElement.RenderTransform).➥
        (TransformGroup.Children)[3].(TranslateTransform.X)"
        BeginTime="00:00:00">
        <SplineDoubleKeyFrame KeyTime="00:00:00.5000000" Value="150"/>
    </DoubleAnimationUsingKeyFrames>
</Storyboard>
```

Adding keyframes to an animation makes the coding of storyboards a little more complex, but they still follow the same general pattern. Create a storyboard, create an animation, create some keyframes, and add the keyframes to the animation, the animation to the storyboard, and the storyboard to the resources.

1. Begin work in this project by declaring the Storyboard object as we did in the previous example. This code goes above the Page() constructor in the Page.xaml.cs file.

   ```
   private Storyboard MoveRight = new Storyboard();
   ```

2. Inside the Page() constructor, beneath the Initialize() method, create a new DoubleAnimationUsingKeyframes object called Anim, and set the TargetName and TargetProperty values. This code will once again be targeting the X transform property of the object being animated.

   ```
   DoubleAnimationUsingKeyFrames Anim =
       new DoubleAnimationUsingKeyFrames();
   Storyboard.SetTargetName(Anim, "Rectangle");
   Anim.SetValue(Storyboard.TargetPropertyProperty,
       new PropertyPath("(UIElement.RenderTransform).➥
       (TransformGroup.Children)[3].(TranslateTransform.X)"));
   ```

3. Declaration of the preceding DoubleAnimationUsingKeyFrames object is similar to previous examples. The next step differs a bit, though. Here, you declare the BeginTime for the animation, which is expressed as a TimeSpan object. As per the example storyboard, this keyframe begins at an offset time of 0. This code goes into the Page() constructor after the code added in step 2.

```
Anim.BeginTime = new TimeSpan(0, 0, 0);
```

4. Now you need to declare any keyframes that will live inside the animation. Begin by declaring a new SplineDoubleKeyFrame object called SKeyFrame. The KeyTime is set to .5 seconds, and the value of the keyframe is 150. This tells Silverlight to move the rectangle 150 pixels along the x axis in .5 seconds.

```
SplineDoubleKeyFrame SKeyFrame = new SplineDoubleKeyFrame();
SKeyFrame.KeyTime = KeyTime.FromTimeSpan(TimeSpan.FromSeconds(0.5));
SKeyFrame.Value = 150;
```

5. After that is done, the keyframe object can be added to the animation. Keep in mind that if you have many keyframes in an animation, each one needs to have a unique name.

```
Anim.KeyFrames.Add(SKeyFrame);
```

6. Add the animation to the storyboard and the storyboard to the LayoutRoot object:

```
MoveRight.Children.Add(Anim);
LayoutRoot.Resources.Add("MoveRight", MoveRight);
```

7. All that's left is to add an event listener and an associated event handler. Add the event listener at the bottom of the Page() constructor.

8. If you are using the method described earlier, Visual Studio will create the event handler function for you. All you need to do is add the code that calls the storyboard:

```
private void Rectangle_MouseEnter(object sender, MouseEventArgs e)
{
    MoveRight.Begin();
}
```

9. Compile and run the project and place the pointer over the rectangle. The MoveRight storyboard will play, moving the rectangle 150 pixels to the right. If you wanted to make the rectangle move at an angle, it would be as simple as adding a second animation that changes the Y transform of the object.

10. Add the following code to the project, just after MoveRight.Children.Add(Anim);. Notice that the new animation's name is yAnim and the TargetProperty has been adjusted to affect the Y transform of the Rectangle object.

```
DoubleAnimationUsingKeyFrames YAnim =
    new DoubleAnimationUsingKeyFrames();
Storyboard.SetTargetName(YAnim, "Rectangle");
YAnim.SetValue(Storyboard.TargetPropertyProperty,
    new PropertyPath("(UIElement.RenderTransform).➥
    (TransformGroup.Children)[3].(TranslateTransform.Y)"));
```

```
YAnim.BeginTime = new TimeSpan(0, 0, 0);
SplineDoubleKeyFrame SKeyFrame1 = new SplineDoubleKeyFrame();
SKeyFrame1.KeyTime = KeyTime.FromTimeSpan(TimeSpan.FromSeconds(0.5));
SKeyFrame1.Value = 150;
YAnim.KeyFrames.Add(SKeyFrame1);
MoveRight.Children.Add(YAnim);
```

Use F5 to compile and run the program again. With the second animation in place, the rectangle now moves down and to the right, holding the position at the end of the storyboard.

Remember that the FillBehavior on storyboards is set to HoldEnd, meaning that the storyboard will stay at its last frame when it has finished playing through. If you would like to change the FillBehavior for a storyboard, you can do this through code as well. The following line of code will change the FillBehavior for the storyboard you just created so that when it reaches the end, the rectangle will return to the starting position of the animation:

```
MoveRight.FillBehavior = FillBehavior.Stop;
```

If you'd like to take a look at the final version of the code described here, it's in the **DoubleUsingKeyframesCompleted** project.

ColorAnimation

Now let's take a look at how color animations can be implemented via code. The **ColorFromToWithCode** project illustrates how to work with ColorAnimation objects. In this example, we will create a ColorAnimation that turns a red ellipse blue when the MouseEnter event is raised. The storyboard equivalent for this animation looks like this:

```
<Storyboard x:Name="TurnBlue">
    <ColorAnimation Storyboard.TargetName="RedEllipse"
        Storyboard.TargetProperty="(Shape.Fill).➥
        (SolidColorBrush.Color)" Duration="00:00:00.50"
        To="#FF0D0874"/>
</Storyboard>
```

1. In Visual Studio, open the Page.xaml.cs file for editing. Just above the Page() constructor, add the following code, which declares a storyboard:

```
private Storyboard TurnBlue = new Storyboard();
```

2. On the next line, declare a new ColorAnimation object called BlueColor:

```
private ColorAnimation BlueColor = new ColorAnimation();
```

3. Next, code the animation object's properties inside the Page() constructor. In this case, the TargetName for the BlueColor animation is the RedEllipse object, and the TargetProperty is the object's fill.

```
BlueColor.SetValue(Storyboard.TargetNameProperty,"RedEllipse");
BlueColor.SetValue(Storyboard.TargetPropertyProperty,
    new PropertyPath("(Shape.Fill).(SolidColorBrush.Color)"));
```

4. In the previous example, double data types were being used. In this example, data of type Color will be manipulated. To change a color fill for an object, define the target color as a color from alpha, red, green, and blue color values. Note that the code shown here is using an Argb value (alpha, red, green, blue) to specify a color, whereas the storyboard produced in Blend utilizes a hex value. Argb color values get their value from four byte values (0 through 255), separated by commas. This is probably a familiar format for you if you've worked in almost any paint program. Once a color has been defined, it can be assigned to the To property in the animation.

```
Color ToColor = Color.FromArgb(255, 13, 8, 116);
BlueColor.To = ToColor;
```

5. The animation can now be added to the storyboard, and the storyboard added to the LayoutRoot element:

```
TurnBlue.Children.Add(BlueColor);
LayoutRoot.Resources.Add("TurnBlue", TurnBlue);
```

6. All that's left is an event listener and a little bit of event handler code. The event listener goes inside the Page() constructor:

```
RedEllipse.MouseEnter += new MouseEventHandler(RedEllipse_MouseEnter);
```

7. The event handler is placed after the closing curly brace of the Page() constructor method:

```
private void RedEllipse_MouseEnter(object sender, MouseEventArgs e)
{
    TurnBlue.Begin();
}
```

Compile and run this project and place the pointer on the red ellipse. The object's color will shift to blue. Take a few minutes to add another storyboard and ColorAnimation that will turn the ellipse's color to red when the MouseLeave event is raised. If you need a little help, look in the **ColorFromToWithCodeCompleted** project.

As with the DoubleAnimationUsingKeyFrames type, you can also create keyframe-based color animations using the ColorAnimationUsingKeyFrames type in the same manner.

PointAnimation

The final type of animation we will be producing with code is a PointAnimation. In the following exercise, we will be coding up the equivalent of the following storyboard. This is the storyboard we worked with earlier that causes the lower point of a circular red path shape to droop down when the mouse pointer enters the shape.

```
<Storyboard x:Name="MovePointDown">
    <PointAnimation Storyboard.TargetName="RedPath"
    Storyboard.TargetProperty="(Path.Data).➥
    (PathGeometry.Figures)[0].(PathFigure.Segments)[1].➥
    (BezierSegment.Point1)" Duration="00:00:00.50"
    To="44.7715263366699,277"/>
    <PointAnimation Storyboard.TargetName="RedPath"
```

```
Storyboard.TargetProperty="(Path.Data).➡
(PathGeometry.Figures)[0].(PathFigure.Segments)[0].➡
(BezierSegment.Point2)" Duration="00:00:00.50"
To="155.228469848633,277"/>
<PointAnimation Storyboard.TargetName="RedPath"
Storyboard.TargetProperty="(Path.Data).➡
(PathGeometry.Figures)[0].(PathFigure.Segments)[0].➡
(BezierSegment.Point3)" Duration="00:00:00.50" To="100, 277"/>
</Storyboard>
```

PointAnimation is handled a bit differently than DoubleAnimation or ColorAnimation. One of the things to notice in the XAML listing is that each PointAnimation within the storyboard has a TargetName and TargetProperty. You will need to take this into account when creating PointAnimation in code.

1. Open the **PointFromToWithCode** project in Visual Studio. Open the Page.xaml.cs file for editing.

2. As with DoubleAnimation and ColorAnimation, everything begins with the declaration of a storyboard. Before the Page() constructor, add the following code to declare a storyboard called MovePointDown:

   ```
   private Storyboard MovePointDown = new Storyboard();
   ```

3. Inside the Page() constructor, the TargetName property for the storyboard is set to the RedPath object. This is a deviation from the previous examples where the target was set on the individual animations. While it is also acceptable to set the target for each PointAnimation object, all three animations affect the same object, so it saves a couple of lines of code doing it this way.

   ```
   Storyboard.SetTargetName(MovePointDown, "RedPath");
   ```

4. Next, each of the three PointAnimation objects is created. Let's go through each of them in order. Begin by declaring a new PointAnimation object for the first point. Place this code just below the storyboard declaration before the Page() constructor:

   ```
   private PointAnimation P1Anim = new PointAnimation();
   ```

5. Now the animation must tell Silverlight which property will be affected. The following code specifies that we are setting the value for Point1 of segment 1.

   ```
   P1Anim.SetValue(Storyboard.TargetPropertyProperty,
       new PropertyPath("(Path.Data).(PathGeometry.Figures)[0].➡
       (PathFigure.Segments)[1].(BezierSegment.Point1)"));
   ```

6. As with the DoubleAnimation and ColorAnimation types, Duration is assigned:

   ```
   P1Anim.Duration = new Duration(TimeSpan.FromSeconds(0.5));
   ```

7. Then the To property value is assigned. Because this is a PointAnimation, the data type is expressed as an x,y point. This means that the To property must be created as type Point.

   ```
   P1Anim.To = new Point(45, 277);
   ```

8. Finish up by adding the animation to the storyboard:

   ```
   MovePointDown.Children.Add(P1Anim);
   ```

9. Points 2 and 3 from the XAML example are coded in the same way. Start by declaring two more PointAnimation objects before the Page() constructor:

```
private PointAnimation P2Anim = new PointAnimation();
private PointAnimation P3Anim = new PointAnimation();
```

10. Inside the Page() constructor, use the values from the XAML as a guide to assign values to the properties of the animation. The code for that looks like the following:

```
P2Anim.SetValue(Storyboard.TargetPropertyProperty,
    new PropertyPath("(Path.Data).(PathGeometry.Figures)[0].➥
    (PathFigure.Segments)[0].(BezierSegment.Point2)"));
P2Anim.Duration = new Duration(TimeSpan.FromSeconds(0.5));
P2Anim.To = new Point(155, 277);
MovePointDown.Children.Add(P2Anim);

P3Anim.SetValue(Storyboard.TargetPropertyProperty,
    new PropertyPath("(Path.Data).(PathGeometry.Figures)[0].➥
    (PathFigure.Segments)[0].(BezierSegment.Point3)"));
P3Anim.Duration = new Duration(TimeSpan.FromSeconds(0.5));
P3Anim.To = new Point(100, 277);
MovePointDown.Children.Add(P3Anim);
```

11. Once all three PointAnimations have been defined and added to the storyboard, the storyboard can be added to the LayoutRoot resources:

```
LayoutRoot.Resources.Add("MovePointDown", MovePointDown);
```

12. As with the previous examples, an event listener and event handler are used to play the storyboard when the MouseEnter event is raised. Inside the Page() constructor, place the following event listener code:

```
RedPath.MouseEnter += new MouseEventHandler(RedPath_MouseEnter);
```

13. Just after the closing brace of the Page() constructor, add the following code to the event handler:

```
private void RedPath_MouseEnter(object sender, MouseEventArgs e)
{
    MovePointDown.Begin();
}
```

Compile and run the program by pressing F5. When you place the mouse pointer over the red ellipse, the bottom point will move downward.

One of the nuances in working with PointAnimation types is that an animation to return the point to its starting location does not return the values to 0, as was done in the examples that used translations. Instead, the points need to be returned to the locations that are specified in the XAML definition of the object. Here's the code for the object:

```
<Path Height="277" Width="200" Canvas.Left="306" Canvas.Top="65"
    Fill="#FFFF0000" Stretch="None" x:Name="RedPath" Cursor="Hand">
  <Path.Data>
    <PathGeometry>
      <PathFigure IsClosed="True" StartPoint="200,100">
```

```
    <BezierSegment Point1="200,155.228469848633"
        Point2="155.228469848633,200" Point3="100,200"/>
    <BezierSegment Point1="44.7715263366699,200"
        Point2="0,155.228469848633" Point3="0,100"/>
    <BezierSegment Point1="0,44.7715263366699"
        Point2="44.7715263366699,0" Point3="100,0"/>
    <BezierSegment Point1="155.228469848633,0"
        Point2="200,44.7715263366699" Point3="200,100"/>
      </PathFigure>
    </PathGeometry>
  </Path.Data>
</Path>
```

Let's do a quick walkthrough to see what happens when the points are returned to 0,0.

14. Add a second Storyboard object to the project above the Page() constructor:

```
private Storyboard MovePointUp = new Storyboard();
```

15. Inside the Page() constructor, set the target on the storyboard rather than the individual PointAnimation objects:

```
Storyboard.SetTargetName(MovePointUp, "RedPath");
```

16. Above the Page() constructor, declare three new PointAnimation objects:

```
private PointAnimation P1AnimBack = new PointAnimation();
private PointAnimation P2AnimBack = new PointAnimation();
private PointAnimation P3AnimBack = new PointAnimation();
```

17. Assign the same properties used in the PointAnimations from the MovePointDown storyboard. Notice that the To property for each of the three PointAnimations has been set to an x,y point value of 0, 0.

```
P1AnimBack.SetValue(Storyboard.TargetPropertyProperty,
    new PropertyPath("(Path.Data).(PathGeometry.Figures)[0].➥
    (PathFigure.Segments)[1].(BezierSegment.Point1)"));
P1AnimBack.Duration = new Duration(TimeSpan.FromSeconds(0.5));
P1AnimBack.To = new Point(0, 0);
MovePointUp.Children.Add(P1AnimBack);

P2AnimBack.SetValue(Storyboard.TargetPropertyProperty,
    new PropertyPath("(Path.Data).(PathGeometry.Figures)[0].➥
    (PathFigure.Segments)[0].(BezierSegment.Point2)"));
P2AnimBack.Duration = new Duration(TimeSpan.FromSeconds(0.5));
P2AnimBack.To = new Point(0, 0);
MovePointUp.Children.Add(P2AnimBack);

P3AnimBack.SetValue(Storyboard.TargetPropertyProperty,
    new PropertyPath("(Path.Data).(PathGeometry.Figures)[0].➥
    (PathFigure.Segments)[0].(BezierSegment.Point3)"));
P3AnimBack.Duration = new Duration(TimeSpan.FromSeconds(0.5));
P3AnimBack.To = new Point(0, 0);
MovePointUp.Children.Add(P3AnimBack);
```

18. The newly created storyboard needs to be added to the page resources:

```
LayoutRoot.Resources.Add("MovePointUp", MovePointUp);
```

19. Finally, an event listener and associated event handler code are created for the MouseLeave event. The event listener goes inside the Page() constructor:

```
RedPath.MouseLeave += new MouseEventHandler(RedPath_MouseLeave);
```

20. And the event handler code to call the new animation goes outside of the Page() constructor:

```
private void RedPath_MouseLeave(object sender, MouseEventArgs e)
{
    MovePointUp.Begin();
}
```

Press F5 to run the project. Place the pointer inside the RedEllipse object. The bottom point will glide down as the MousePointDown storyboard plays. Now move the pointer off the RedEllipse object. The point returns to the specified coordinate of 0,0, which is located at the top-left corner of the Path object's bounding box, rather than its starting point on the ellipse (see Figure 3-12).

So how do you know which point from the XAML is the right one to use? Each BezierSegment has three sets of point data that describe the curve. With the reference storyboard for this project and a bit of detective work, we can identify the corresponding points between the object and those being modified by the storyboard.

The first PointAnimation in the MovePointUp storyboard has the following TargetProperty:

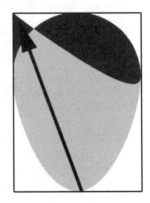

Figure 3-12. Returning points to 0,0 via a PointAnimation

```
(Path.Data).(PathGeometry.Figures)[0].(PathFigure.Segments)[1].➥
    (BezierSegment.Point1)
```

The BezierSegments in the object are numbered as follows:

0. `<BezierSegment Point1="200,155.228469848633" Point2="155.228469848633,200" Point3="100,200"/>`

1. `<BezierSegment Point1="44.7715263366699,200" Point2="0,155.228469848633" Point3="0,100"/>`

2. `<BezierSegment Point1="0,44.7715263366699" Point2="44.7715263366699,0" Point3="100,0"/>`

3. `<BezierSegment Point1="155.228469848633,0" Point2="200,44.7715263366699" Point3="200,100"/>`

21. From the TargetProperty, we know that the P1Back animation is working with segment 1, and needs the coordinates for point 1, which are 44.7715263366699,200 (which we will clean up to 45,200). Update the To property for the P1AnimBack animation as shown:

    P1AnimBack.To = new Point(45, 200);

22. The P2Back animation targets segment 0, point 2, which is located at 155.228469848633,200 (155,200). The P2Back animation is updated to the following:

    P2AnimBack.To = new Point(155, 200);

23. The P3Back animation targets segment 0, point 3, which is the point 100,200. Updating the P3Back animation makes the code look like this:

    P3AnimBack.To = new Point(100, 200);

After plugging in those three sets of coordinates and recompiling, the object now behaves as expected when the MouseLeave event is raised, returning our point to its starting position.

Summary

If you are new to Silverlight, the amount of information that was presented here may be overwhelming. You can probably see where the visual interface in Blend can be a big help when getting started—take the time to create some of your own examples to see how Blend works behind the scenes for you.

Remember that storyboards are just containers for animations, and animations are containers for keyframes. I talked about the three main types of animations provided by Silverlight—double for manipulating many of an object's properties; color for changing an object's fill color using a series of four 1-byte values to represent the alpha, red, green, and blue channels; and point for moving the points that make up paths.

Each animation type has two variations: from/to animations move an object from one position to another, while animations using keyframes define a series of keyframes that contain positions to which an object will move. With keyframe animations, there are different methods of interpolating the movement from keyframe to keyframe. Linear interpolation will move an object smoothly from keyframe to keyframe in a linear fashion. Spline keyframes define ease, which describes how an object might accelerate or decelerate as it approaches or leaves a keyframe. Discrete keyframes cause an object to hold the position of the last keyframe until the next keyframe is reached.

We also took a good look at how storyboards and animations can be created entirely with code. This is useful if you need to create animations on the fly, or create a reusable generic function that produces animations for you.

As you gain some experience with storyboards and animations, you will find that they become easier to manipulate. In Chapter 4, we will take a look at a variety of animation techniques that make use of the methods described in Chapters 2 and 3.

Chapter 4

ANIMATION TECHNIQUES

In this chapter, we're going to take a little time and look at some ways to animate objects using the techniques covered already. The projects presented here should help open the door for you a bit when it comes to thinking through the different ways to work with objects that you want to include in your own animations.

Converting objects to paths

Any shape object you work with in Blend can be converted to a path. This can be used if you want to manually deform an object or text outside of the standard deformations available via the built-in transforms. Let's take a look at how to go about converting a couple of text objects to paths and create some storyboards to deform them.

Open the **ObjectToPath** project for Chapter 4. It contains two text elements—one says TEXT, and the other WARP. Both text elements in this project are currently TextBlock objects, meaning that the text is currently live and can be edited. Once a text object has been converted to a path, the text will no longer be editable.

1. Click the TxtText element in the Objects and Timeline panel, and then Ctrl-click the TxtWarp object so that both items are selected.

2. Right-click the grouped elements in the Objects and Timeline panel and select Path ➤ Convert to Path from the pop-up menu, as shown in Figure 4-1. Blend

will convert both text elements to paths and update the Objects and Timeline list and the artboard. Note that when an object is converted to a path, its type changes, and Blend will change the name of the text objects to [Path] in the Objects and Timeline list.

3. It's a good idea to rename the two text elements to something meaningful in order to keep track of them, so rename the two paths to TxtText and TxtWarp.

4. Create a new storyboard and move the timeline play head to 1 second.

5. Select the TxtText element on the Objects and Timeline panel and press A to change to the Direct Selection tool. The control points that make up the path will become visible, allowing you to manipulate them. You can now modify the objects in whatever way you'd like. Figure 4-2 shows a quick-and-dirty bulge deformation.

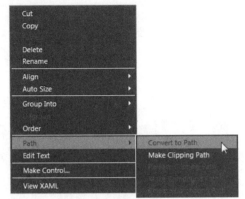

Figure 4-1. Select Path ➤ Convert to Path to convert objects to editable paths.

Figure 4-2. Simulating a bulge deformation on a Path object

Converting objects to paths with the intention of deforming them works well either as a design technique, or for animation, as we've done here. If you'd like to take a closer look at the final animation shown here, look at the **ObjectToPathCompleted** project in Chapter 4. Storyboard1 is the animated deformation.

One thing you may find helpful when deforming text is to use a tool like Photoshop or Illustrator to create an image of text deformed in a way you like. You can then add the image to Blend as a background layer and lock it from selection in the Objects and Timeline panel in order to avoid accidentally moving it. Once the image is in place, you can move the timeline play head and start moving the control points for the object.

If you find yourself needing to animate individual letters, it will be necessary to create a text object for each letter, and then convert each one to a path. After that, the process is the same.

Ghosting effects

Ghosting is an effect that is used in a lot of interactive applications—you click a button or element, and a copy of the element scales up and fades out over a second or two. This lets a user know that the action they took was recognized. The effect can also be used when an application first loads in order to draw attention to a particular part of the interface.

In order to create this type of effect, a copy of an object is created and hidden. Event listeners on the original object are used to capture user input. When the desired action takes place on the original, the copy is unhidden and animated.

The **GhostingEffects** project contains a TextBlock that mimics an "About Us" text menu item, and a gradient-filled ellipse. When performing this action on a text object, remember that TextBlock objects have their Width and Height properties set to Auto, so any transforms you apply may look as though they do not originate from the correct center point. To correct this, add an actual value to the Width and Height property of your TextBlock. In the example project, the text object already has height and width values.

1. Once the project is open, use Ctrl+C and Ctrl+V to copy and paste the TxtAboutUs object in the Objects and Timeline list. The new object will paste as TxtAboutUs_Copy.

2. Create a new storyboard named AboutUs_Clicked, and move the timeline play head to 1.

3. Use the Scale tab on the Transform pane to change both the x and y scale for the TxtAboutUs_ Copy object to 3.

4. Enter 0 in the Opacity field.

5. Click Play to preview the storyboard. The copy of the text object should scale up to three times its original size as it fades out.

6. Close the storyboard, and change the object's visibility to Collapsed on the Appearance pane. This will effectively hide the object from view until it is needed.

7. To add event listeners, select TxtAboutUs in the Objects and Timeline list and click the Events icon. In the MouseLeftButtonUp field, type AboutUs_MouseUp and press Enter. Visual Studio should open with the appropriate function already added:

```
private void AboutUs_MouseUp(object sender, MouseButtonEventArgs e)
{

}
```

8. The code in this event handler will run when the user releases the mouse button on this object. The event handler code should start by changing the Visibility property of the copied object to Visible. To change the Visibility property of an object, call the object followed by the property, and then specify which visibility setting to use, as shown:

```
TxtAboutUs_Copy.Visibility = Visibility.Visible;
```

9. Next, the event handler needs a bit of code to play the animation. The storyboard was called AboutUs_Clicked, and you should already know how to make storyboards play from previous examples.

```
AboutUs_Clicked.Begin();
```

10. Press F5 to run the project. Click the About Us text, and you should see the animation play. The action will only work one time, though—why is that?

Behind the scenes, the animation actually does play each time you click. However, you can't see it because the first time the animation plays, the opacity value of the object is animated to a value of 0, and is left there when the animation completes. So every other time you click the object, the animation plays, but the object is totally transparent. This can be fixed by listening for the storyboard to finish and then resetting the object's state.

11. In Blend, press F11 to enter XAML view, and locate the AboutUs_Clicked storyboard.

12. Attach an event listener to the Completed event for the storyboard that calls a function called AboutUs_Clicked_Completed:

```
<Storyboard x:Name="AboutUs_Clicked"
    Completed="AboutUs_Clicked_Completed">
```

13. In Visual Studio, add the new function to the code:

```
private void AboutUs_Clicked_Completed(object sender, EventArgs e)
{

}
```

14. Inside that function, add some code to hide the copied text object. This is done by setting the Visibility property to Collapsed:

```
TxtAboutUs_Copy.Visibility = Visibility.Collapsed;
```

15. Stop the storyboard in order to reset it to the beginning for the next time it plays:

```
AboutUs_Clicked.Stop();
```

16. Next, reset the Opacity for the text object. Remember that in code, Opacity values range from 0 to 1.

```
TxtAboutUs_Copy.Opacity = 1;
```

Now when the project runs, you can click the text element as often as you'd like and the storyboard will play repeatedly.

17. Repeat the process for the RedBall object to add the effect there as well. In Blend, copy and paste the object to create RedBall_Copy.

18. Create a new storyboard called RedBall_Clicked and move the timeline play head to 1.

19. On the RedBall_Copy object, set the x and y scale values to 3, and the opacity to 0.

20. Test the animation to be sure it works as expected, and then close the storyboard.

21. Set the Visibility of RedBall_Copy to Collapsed to hide it until needed.

22. Next, add the event listeners to the original object. Select the RedBall element in the Objects and Timeline list, and click the Events icon.

23. Add an event handler called RedBall_MouseUp to the MouseLeftButtonUp event listener.

24. In Visual Studio, wire up the event just as you did for the text object:

```
private void RedBall_MouseUp(object sender, MouseButtonEventArgs e)
{
    RedBall_Copy.Visibility = Visibility.Visible;
    RedBall_Clicked.Begin();
}
```

25. In Blend, add a Completed event listener to the RedBall_Clicked storyboard:

```
<Storyboard x:Name="RedBall_Clicked"
    Completed="RedBall_Clicked_Completed">
```

26. Finally, add the event handler code to reset the object in the code-behind file:

```
private void RedBall_Clicked_Completed(object sender, EventArgs e)
{
    RedBall_Copy.Visibility = Visibility.Collapsed;
    RedBall_Clicked.Stop();
    RedBall_Copy.Opacity = 1;
}
```

Press F5 to run the application. Now you can click either object and see the effect, as shown in Figure 4-3. Notice that it doesn't really matter what type of object you are working with—the process is the same for each. A finalized version of the code shown here is available in the **GhostingEffectsCompleted** project.

Figure 4-3. Scaling/fading effects applied to a TextBlock and an Ellipse

Image effects

Given that Silverlight is still essentially a new product, it's not entirely surprising that built-in bitmap image filters such as blur aren't yet available. However, with a little help from your favorite photo-editing program, you can still accomplish some interesting image effects.

Creating effects by cross-fading

Using the following technique, you can easily create animations that make images appear to pull focus, or make blurry images come into focus when a user selects them.

Figure 4-4 shows an image of a yellow flower. Figure 4-5 shows a blurred version of the same image, which had a 3.0 pixel radius Gaussian blur applied in Photoshop. For this project, we need event listeners for MouseEnter and MouseLeave that will be used to cross-fade the two images when a user places the pointer over the image, and fade back when the pointer leaves the image.

Figure 4-4. An image of a yellow flower that will be used to simulate a blur effect

Figure 4-5. The same image with a 3.0-pixel Gaussian blur filter applied in Photoshop

Open the **ImageBlur** project from Chapter 4 to follow along with this example. This project already has the basic structure in place, which consists of a Canvas element named CanvasFlower that contains the two images: FlowerBlur and Flower. The intended action for this project is that when the user moves the pointer over the image, it will scale up slightly as it comes into focus. When the pointer leaves the image, the image will scale back down and become blurred.

There are a couple of things to keep in mind when setting up this type of effect. The first is to make sure the object hierarchy is correct—the Flower element is "on top" of FlowerBlur. Objects in the Objects and Timeline list are organized such that items on the bottom will appear on top of objects beneath them. This is referred to as **Z-order**, and can be coded explicitly in XAML, or implied by the order the objects appear in the list. For this project, the implied order is adequate. The second thing to remember is to set the opacity of the topmost object (the object at the bottom of the Objects and Timeline list) to 0. In this case, it is the Flower element that is at 0% opacity.

Transparent objects will remain visible to the mouse and will accept mouse events, unlike objects that have their visibility set to Collapsed. While this won't affect us here since we'll be working with the canvas container, this is an important distinction when you are trying to capture events on a particular object. Objects that are not transparent can be made invisible to the mouse by using the IsHitTestVisible flag. As with most object properties, there are three ways to set this flag. The first is to expand the Common Properties pane on the Properties panel, and check or uncheck the IsHitTestVisible check box. The second is to type the property directly into the XAML for the object you wish to make invisible to the mouse, and the third is to set the property in the code-behind file. As you have probably already guessed, toggling the check box in Blend simply adds or modifies the XAML for the selected element.

1. Create a new timeline called CanvasFlower_MouseEnter.

2. Move the timeline play head to .5 seconds.

3. With the CanvasFlower element selected, change both the X and Y scale fields on the Transform pane to .65.

4. Select the Flower element and change the Opacity value to 100%.

5. Play the timeline. This is the effect that will be seen when the mouse is placed over the canvas.

   The only problem is that this storyboard, shown following, is keyframe-based, and the effect works more smoothly if it is done as a from/to animation.

```xml
<Storyboard x:Name="CanvasFlower_MouseEnter">
    <DoubleAnimationUsingKeyFrames BeginTime="00:00:00"
        Storyboard.TargetName="CanvasFlower"
        Storyboard.TargetProperty="(UIElement.RenderTransform).➥
        (TransformGroup.Children)[0].(ScaleTransform.ScaleX)">
        <SplineDoubleKeyFrame KeyTime="00:00:00.5000000" Value="0.65"/>
    </DoubleAnimationUsingKeyFrames>
    <DoubleAnimationUsingKeyFrames BeginTime="00:00:00"
        Storyboard.TargetName="CanvasFlower"
        Storyboard.TargetProperty="(UIElement.RenderTransform).➥
        (TransformGroup.Children)[0].(ScaleTransform.ScaleY)">
        <SplineDoubleKeyFrame KeyTime="00:00:00.5000000" Value="0.65"/>
    </DoubleAnimationUsingKeyFrames>
    <DoubleAnimationUsingKeyFrames BeginTime="00:00:00"
```

```
            Storyboard.TargetName="Flower"
            Storyboard.TargetProperty="(UIElement.Opacity)">
        <SplineDoubleKeyFrame KeyTime="00:00:00.5000000" Value="1"/>
    </DoubleAnimationUsingKeyFrames>
</Storyboard>
```

Let's change this storyboard so that it is no longer keyframe-based.

6. Use F11 to change to XAML mode and scroll to the top of the window. I talked about the differences between DoubleAnimation (from/to) and DoubleAnimationUsingKeyFrames in Chapter 3.

7. To convert between DoubleAnimationUsingKeyFrames and DoubleAnimation, change the animation type from DoubleAnimationUsingKeyFrames to DoubleAnimation, delete the BeginTime property, and add Duration and To properties. The Duration value to use for this conversion is the value shown in the SplineDoubleKeyFrame's KeyTime. The value for To is the SplineDoubleKeyFrame's Value field.

8. Once the new DoubleAnimation item is converted, make it self-closing by adding a slash before the closing bracket: />. You will also need to delete the SplineDoubleKeyFrame and closing DoubleAnimationUsingKeyFrames tag.

While all this may sound like a lot of complex work, it's not too difficult and only takes a moment before the previous storyboard listing becomes the following:

```
<Storyboard x:Name="CanvasFlower_MouseEnter">
    <DoubleAnimation Duration="00:00:00.50" To="0.65"
        Storyboard.TargetName="CanvasFlower"
        Storyboard.TargetProperty="(UIElement.RenderTransform).➥
        (TransformGroup.Children)[0].(ScaleTransform.ScaleX)"/>
    <DoubleAnimation Duration="00:00:00.50" To="0.65"
        Storyboard.TargetName="CanvasFlower"
        Storyboard.TargetProperty="(UIElement.RenderTransform).➥
        (TransformGroup.Children)[0].(ScaleTransform.ScaleY)"/>
    <DoubleAnimation Duration="00:00:00.50" To="1"
        Storyboard.TargetName="Flower"
        Storyboard.TargetProperty="(UIElement.Opacity)"/>
</Storyboard>
```

This also makes it super-easy for us to create the MouseLeave storyboard, because it does the exact opposite action of the MouseEnter storyboard.

9. While still in XAML view, copy and paste the CanvasFlower_MouseEnter storyboard. Change the storyboard name to CanvasFlower_MouseLeave.

10. Change the values in each of the three animations. The To property for both the ScaleX and ScaleY transforms become .5, and the To property for the Flower element's opacity is 0. That's it, the second storyboard is done!

```
<Storyboard x:Name="CanvasFlower_MouseLeave">
    <DoubleAnimation Duration="00:00:00.50" To="0.5"
        Storyboard.TargetName="CanvasFlower"
        Storyboard.TargetProperty="(UIElement.RenderTransform).➥
        (TransformGroup.Children)[0].(ScaleTransform.ScaleX)"/>
    <DoubleAnimation Duration="00:00:00.50" To="0.5"
```

```
            Storyboard.TargetName="CanvasFlower"
            Storyboard.TargetProperty="(UIElement.RenderTransform).➥
            (TransformGroup.Children)[0].(ScaleTransform.ScaleY)"/>
        <DoubleAnimation Duration="00:00:00.50" To="0"
            Storyboard.TargetName="Flower"
            Storyboard.TargetProperty="(UIElement.Opacity)"/>
    </Storyboard>
```

All that's left for this project is to create some event listeners and event handler code. Since both of our images are organized in a containing canvas, we will place event listeners on the Canvas element.

11. Switch to Design view in Blend, and select the CanvasFlower object in the Objects and Timeline list.

12. On the Properties panel, click the Events icon, and in the MouseEnter field, type Flower_ MouseEnter. Visual Studio should open up and contain the empty event handler code. Inside the event handler, add the code to play the CanvasFlower_MouseEnter storyboard, as shown:

```
private void Flower_MouseEnter(object sender, MouseEventArgs e)
{
    CanvasFlower_MouseEnter.Begin();
}
```

13. Repeat this process to add the MouseLeave event listener to the CanvasFlower object. For the MouseLeave event, the event handler is called Flower_MouseLeave.

14. Add code to play the CanvasFlower_MouseLeave storyboard, shown here:

```
private void Flower_MouseLeave(object sender, MouseEventArgs e)
{
    CanvasFlower_MouseLeave.Begin();
}
```

You can now run the project to see the result. As you move the pointer over the image, it will scale up slightly and come into focus. Moving the pointer off the image will cause the image to scale down and go out of focus. The **ImageBlurCompleted** project contains all the code shown here.

Don't feel boxed into only doing blurs with this technique—there are a wide variety of image filters that can be used in conjunction with cross-fades to create interesting image effects, and while less flexible, a cross-fade will take less processing overhead than a live bitmap effect.

Simulating drop shadow effects

Drop shadows require two parts: an object and the shadow. As noted when working with blurs, there are currently no bitmap effects available to do drop shadows directly. There are several options for creating them, however. You can create a shadow PNG image file, a rectangle with a gray fill and lighter gray stroke, multiple border objects of varying opacity, shades, or a series of line or border objects that vary in color/opacity. We'll take a look at all these techniques in the next example project.

I have found the path of least resistance to be creating an image file in Photoshop and placing the image layer behind the object that needs the shadow. Shadow image layers scale reasonably well, they are easy to implement, and they look nice. Whatever method you choose to create the shadows is up to you—what we're going to talk about is how we can work with an object that has a shadow when the object is clicked.

Drop shadows have been around forever, and everybody has seen this type of effect—a button or image has a drop shadow, and when the object is clicked, it looks like it is pressed because of the change between the object and shadow. When the mouse button is released, the image pops back up. The description I just gave should clue you in as to which events you will need to use: MouseLeftButtonDown and MouseLeftButtonUp. To follow along with this example, open the **DropShadows** project.

We'll start by creating event listeners for each of the flower image objects in the project.

1. In Blend, select the Flower object in the Objects and Timeline list. Add an event listener called Flower1_MouseDown for the mouse down event, and another called Flower1_MouseUp for the mouse up event. Since we have several events to add and we're not coding up the event handlers just yet, type the code directly into the XAML, as shown:

```
<Image Height="240" x:Name="Flower" Width="320" Canvas.Left="50"
    Canvas.Top="27" Source="yellowFlower.jpg" Stretch="Fill"
    MouseLeftButtonDown="Flower1_MouseDown"
    MouseLeftButtonUp="Flower1_MouseUp" Cursor="Hand"/>
```

2. Select the Flower2 object in the Objects and Timeline list. Add an event listener called Flower2_MouseDown for the mouse down event, and another called Flower2_MouseUp for the mouse up event:

```
<Image Height="240" x:Name="Flower2" Width="320"
    Source="yellowFlower.jpg" Stretch="Fill"
    Canvas.Left="420" Canvas.Top="27" Cursor="Hand"
    MouseLeftButtonDown="Flower2_MouseDown"
    MouseLeftButtonUp="Flower2_MouseUp"/>
```

3. Select the Flower3 object in the Objects and Timeline list. Add an event listener called Flower3_MouseDown for the mouse down event, and another called Flower3_MouseUp for the mouse up event:

```
<Image Height="240" x:Name="Flower3" Width="320"
    Source="yellowFlower.jpg" Stretch="Fill"
    Canvas.Left="-1" Canvas.Top="-1" Cursor="Hand"
    MouseLeftButtonDown="Flower3_MouseDown"
    MouseLeftButtonUp="Flower3_MouseUp"/>
```

4. Next, we'll write the code for the event handlers. Open the Page.xaml.cs file for editing in Visual Studio, and add the following code just before the Page() constructor. This code is used to store the original coordinates of the objects. For storing coordinate data, Point data types seem like a good choice.

```
Point Origin1 = new Point();
Point Origin2 = new Point();
Point Origin3 = new Point();
```

5. In the event handler for the mouse down event, begin by capturing the mouse on the Flower object. This will ensure that we don't lose mouse control if the pointer moves off of the image before the mouse button is released. Continue by storing the original position of the object that was clicked. Once we have done that, we can move the object to the same x,y coordinates as the shadow. That covers our functionality for when the mouse button is pressed.

```
private void Flower1_MouseDown(object sender, MouseButtonEventArgs e)
{
Flower1.CaptureMouse();
Origin1.X = Convert.ToDouble(Flower1.GetValue(Canvas.LeftProperty));
Origin1.Y = Convert.ToDouble(Flower1.GetValue(Canvas.TopProperty));
Flower1.SetValue(Canvas.LeftProperty,
    Shadow1.GetValue(Canvas.LeftProperty));
Flower1.SetValue(Canvas.TopProperty,
    Shadow1.GetValue(Canvas.TopProperty));
}
```

6. When the mouse button is released, the mouse capture on the Flower1 object is released, and the image is returned to its original location. Since these coordinates have been stored in a point object, this is easy to do.

```
private void Flower1_MouseUp(object sender, MouseButtonEventArgs e)
{
    Flower1.ReleaseMouseCapture();
    Flower.SetValue(Canvas.LeftProperty, Origin1.X);
    Flower.SetValue(Canvas.TopProperty, Origin1.Y);
}
```

This method works with all three of the examples in the **DropShadows** project. Each one uses a different way of displaying a drop shadow, but the third example is a little more complex as it uses a canvas full of border objects to create the drop shadow for the object. The technique still works because the origin values of the Shadow3 Canvas are relative to the object's location within its parent Canvas—in this case, the x,y coordinate of −1,−1. When the image is moved to x,y 3,3 on MouseLeftButtonDown, those coordinates are also relative to the container canvas.

7. Add the code for the Flower2 event handlers, shown here:

```
private void Flower2_MouseDown(object sender, MouseButtonEventArgs e)
{
    Flower2.CaptureMouse();
    Origin2.X = Convert.ToDouble(Flower2.GetValue➥
        (Canvas.LeftProperty));
    Origin2.Y = Convert.ToDouble(Flower2.GetValue(Canvas.TopProperty));
    Flower2.SetValue(Canvas.LeftProperty,
        Shadow2.GetValue(Canvas.LeftProperty));
    Flower2.SetValue(Canvas.TopProperty,
        Shadow2.GetValue(Canvas.TopProperty));
}

private void Flower2_MouseUp(object sender, MouseButtonEventArgs e)
{
    Flower2.ReleaseMouseCapture();
    Flower2.SetValue(Canvas.LeftProperty, Origin2.X);
    Flower2.SetValue(Canvas.TopProperty, Origin2.Y);
}
```

119

8. Finish up by adding the event handler code for the Flower3 events:

```
private void Flower3_MouseDown(object sender, MouseButtonEventArgs e)
{
    Flower3.CaptureMouse();
    Origin3.X = Convert.ToDouble(Flower3.GetValue➡
        (Canvas.LeftProperty));
    Origin3.Y = Convert.ToDouble(Flower3.GetValue(Canvas.TopProperty));
    Flower3.SetValue(Canvas.LeftProperty,
        Shadow3.GetValue(Canvas.LeftProperty));
    Flower3.SetValue(Canvas.TopProperty,
        Shadow3.GetValue(Canvas.TopProperty));
}

private void Flower3_MouseUp(object sender, MouseButtonEventArgs e)
{
    Flower3.ReleaseMouseCapture();
    Flower3.SetValue(Canvas.LeftProperty, Origin3.X);
    Flower3.SetValue(Canvas.TopProperty, Origin3.Y);
}
```

9. Run the project. As you click each of the three images, the image will depress. When the mouse button is released, the image will pop back up, just like common button behavior.

The event handlers could be generalized into a generic set of functions since the functionality for the event handlers is common between objects. I left them separated here for illustrative purposes. The finalized version of the code for this example is in the **DropShadowsCompleted** project.

Creating custom, animated cursors

We haven't talked much about cursors, so let's do a quick overview before looking at how to create custom animated cursors. All the objects used in your Silverlight applications currently have eight cursors to choose from, plus the ability to turn the cursor off altogether—Arrow, Eraser, Hand, IBeam, None, SizeNS, SizeWE, Stylus, and Wait. In order to change the cursor that is displayed for an object, you simply add a Cursor property to the object, and specify the type of cursor you would like displayed when the pointer is over that object, like this:

```
<Ellipse Height="100" Width="100" Fill="#FFFF0000" Cursor="Hand"/>
```

The default cursor for all objects is Arrow, so when a cursor is not specified, it will be an Arrow. This means that both of the following XAML snippets will produce an identical red ellipse that has an Arrow cursor when the pointer is over the object.

```
<Ellipse Height="100" Width="100" Fill="#FFFF0000"/>
<Ellipse Height="100" Width="100" Fill="#FFFF0000" Cursor="Arrow"/>
```

The display of cursors is hierarchical and inherited—if an ellipse with no cursor specified in the XAML is placed within a canvas that has the cursor set to None, no cursor will be displayed. However, if the ellipse is given a cursor property of Arrow, the pointer will display an Arrow when over the Ellipse object. Alternatively, if the Canvas object has IsHitTestVisible set to False, the cursor will display normally.

When working with cursors, just associate them mentally with the MouseEnter and MouseLeave events for an object, and you should have no problems with their hierarchical nature. Anywhere a MouseEnter or MouseLeave event can be raised, cursors can be controlled.

With that said, animated cursors aren't really cursors as far as Silverlight is concerned. In order to make custom cursors, the actual cursor for an object is hidden by setting its property to None. A custom object is then built that will become the cursor, and it can even have animations associated with it. Then a bit of code is used to "attach" the object to the mouse location via the MouseMove event.

Take a look at the **AnimatedCursors** project to follow along with this example. It contains a duck, an ellipse, and two objects that will be turned into custom animated cursors each in its own canvas—one is an arrow, and the other is a simple crosshair.

1. We'll start with the arrow. Create a new storyboard called ArrowCursor.

2. Move the timeline play head to .5 seconds. Select the Arrow object inside the CurArrow Canvas.

3. Use the Direct Selection tool to select the two points at the bottom of the arrow shape, and move them to the right 10 pixels.

4. Move the timeline play head to 1.5 seconds, and move the same two points left 20 pixels.

5. When you click Play, the tail of the arrow should swing right, and then back to the left.

6. We want this animation to play constantly. Select the storyboard by clicking the ArrowCursor name in the storyboard list. The Properties panel will change to show the available properties for the selected object.

7. Place a check in the AutoReverse check box, and from the RepeatBehavior select box, choose Forever, as shown in Figure 4-6.

Figure 4-6. The Common Properties pane for a Storyboard object

8. Change back to Design view.

   With the Arrow object inside the CurArrow Canvas still selected, the artboard will show the object and its bounding box. At the moment, both the object and its container canvas are the same size. Thinking ahead to our implementation, our custom cursor will be attached to the mouse pointer at the top-left corner. To ensure that out pointer is accurate, we want to rotate the arrow within the canvas so that the point of the arrow is right at the top-left corner of the canvas container.

9. With the arrow selected, enter a rotation value of -35. You'll get a result something like the one shown in Figure 4-7. It's rotated correctly, but not yet positioned where it needs to be.

10. A slight adjustment to the Top and Left properties will place it in the right spot. −2 left and −3 top should place the tip of the arrow right at the corner of the canvas, as shown in Figure 4-8.

   Earlier in this chapter, I talked about the IsHitTestVisible flag and how it can be used to hide an object from the mouse when the pointer is positioned over it. In this case, when the pointer enters the Ball object's bounds, we are going to display another object at the mouse's location. Because the custom cursor is an object, and will always be located under the pointer location, it will always be hit-tested as True.

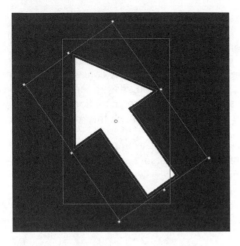

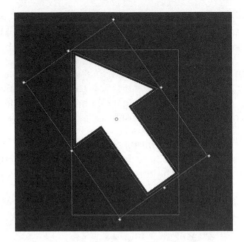

Figure 4-7. The arrow path is rotated within a container canvas.

Figure 4-8. The arrow path after being repositioned within the container canvas

11. To avoid conflicting hit tests between the object using the custom cursor and the cursor itself, we want to set the IsHitTestVisible flag to False for both the CurArrow Canvas and the Arrow object. The check box to change this flag is located near the bottom of the Common Properties pane on the Properties panel. You may need to expand the pane to see it. If you forget to set this flag, you may get some undesirable behavior when the custom cursor is displayed.

12. Once you have set each object's IsHitTestVisible flag to False, select the CurArrow object and change the Visibility property to Collapsed to hide it from view until needed.

13. Select the Ball object from the Objects and Timeline list and use the Common Properties pane of the Properties panel to select None from the Cursor drop-down. The object is now set so that when the pointer is placed over it, no cursor will appear. If you run the project at this point, you can confirm that as the pointer enters the ellipse, the cursor will disappear.

14. With the ball still selected, add an event listener for MouseEnter, and call the event handler Ball_MouseEnter. Visual Studio will open and create the shell of the event handler for you.

15. Inside the handler, add some code that will place the custom cursor object at the current mouse position, begin the animation for the cursor, and then display the cursor:

```
private void Ball_MouseEnter(object sender, MouseEventArgs e)
{
    ArrowCursor.Begin();
    Point MousePoint = e.GetPosition(this);
    Canvas.SetLeft(CurArrow, MousePoint.X);
    Canvas.SetTop(CurArrow, MousePoint.Y);
    CurArrow.Visibility = Visibility.Visible;
}
```

16. Create a MouseLeave event listener that will call an event handler called Ball_MouseLeave when raised. Inside this event handler, we want to hide the cursor, and then stop the animation that is associated with it.

```
private void Ball_MouseLeave(object sender, MouseEventArgs e)
{
    CurArrow.Visibility = Visibility.Collapsed;
    ArrowCursor.Stop();
}
```

At this point, placing the pointer inside the ellipse will display the custom cursor and its animation, while moving the pointer out of the ellipse will hide the cursor and stop the animation. All that's left is to position the cursor at the current mouse position as the mouse is moved inside the Ball object.

17. Add an event listener to the MouseMove event for the Ball object. The event handler should be called Ball_MouseMove. This is an event that will fire continuously while the mouse is moving inside the Ball object. In order to place the custom cursor in the right spot, get the mouse position from the arguments passed to the event handler, and then place the cursor at that location.

```
private void Ball_MouseMove(object sender, MouseEventArgs e)
{
    Point MousePoint = e.GetPosition(this);
    Canvas.SetLeft(CurArrow, MousePoint.X);
    Canvas.SetTop(CurArrow, MousePoint.Y);
}
```

18. That's all there is to it. Run the project. When you place the mouse over the Ball object, the cursor will change to the custom, animated arrow.

For the other object in the project—the Duck—we want to do the same thing using the crosshair cursor. Rather than work through this one step by step, we'll just touch on a couple of things you need to keep an eye on. To follow along with the code, look in the **AnimatedCursorsCompleted** project. While the concept for the duck is identical to the ball, the technique is a little bit different, because unlike the Ball object, the duck is a collection of paths inside a container canvas.

If we try to use the Canvas to capture the MouseEnter, MouseLeave, and MouseMove events, we'll run into two problems. First, events won't register on the Canvas, because it has no fill brush, and is therefore invisible to the mouse. If the Canvas is given a fill color with an alpha value of 0 to make it visible to the mouse, the Canvas will register events, but bring us to the second problem. The mouse events will be raised any time the pointer enters the canvas. Since the Duck object does not fill the entire canvas, the cursor will show at inappropriate places, as shown in Figure 4-9.

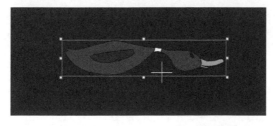

Figure 4-9. Make certain to attach the event listeners to the appropriate objects when using custom cursors; otherwise, the cursors may show up in unintended places.

The best way to handle this is to attach the event listeners to the path or paths that make up the object itself. In this case, the paths that form the duck's body and bill are adequate. Remember to turn off IsHitTestVisible for the wing, collar, and eye. This will allow the event listeners for the body to bubble up to the top.

Using clipping paths

In Silverlight, clipping paths allow you to take one shape and use it to clip another. The overlapping area remains visible, while the rest of the clipped object is hidden from view. I have found that a great way to make use of clipping paths is to apply them to a container object such as a Canvas. Then, as objects are added to the canvas, they can be positioned outside the boundaries of the canvas to keep them hidden, or inside to bring them into view. You can also position objects within a clipped canvas to display only parts of an object, such as a formed media element in a video player.

There are three ways to create clipping paths. The first is from the code-behind file. Since we'll be working with clipping paths specifically in Blend, we won't be going into code-based clipping paths here.

The second method is to select an object you want to clip on the artboard in Blend, and then Ctrl-click a second object.

By then right-clicking the grouped objects in the Objects and Timeline list and selecting Path ➤ Make Clipping Path from the pop-up menu, the second object will clip the first. This operation adds a Clip property to the XAML object, as shown here:

```
<Canvas Height="240" Width="320" Canvas.Top="96"
    Canvas.Left="157" Background="#FF9A9A9A"
    Clip="M0.5,0.5 L319.5,0.5 L319.5,239.5 L0.5,239.5 z"/>
```

The third way to go about creating a clipping path is to add a clipping region to the XAML directly. Functionally, the following code is exactly the same as the preceding code, only it is a little easier to read and figure out what the code is doing. Both of these code snippets will create a 320×240 canvas that is clipped. Any objects placed on the canvas will show, while those objects that lie outside of the canvas bounds will be clipped, as illustrated in Figure 4-10.

```
<Canvas Height="240" Width="320" Canvas.Top="96"
    Canvas.Left="157" Background="#FF9A9A9A">
    <Canvas.Clip>
        <RectangleGeometry Rect="0, 0, 320, 240"/>
    </Canvas.Clip>
</Canvas>
```

Clipping paths are not limited to Canvases and Rectangles—you can clip any object with a Rectangle, Ellipse, Line, or Path geometry. Of course, they can also be animated; otherwise there's little need to include them in a book about animation, right?

Let's take a look at how we can break apart a larger image into 16 equal parts. From a clipping path perspective, one problem is that only a single clipping path can be applied per object. This means that to make a mosaic of an image, we will need 16 Image objects, each with a clipping path defined that will allow a different part of the image to display. The **ClippingPaths** project contains just such a setup for you. While it looks like a single image on the artboard, there are actually 16.

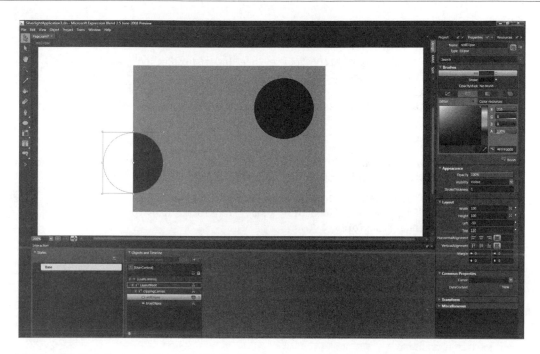

Figure 4-10. Only the parts of an object inside the bounds of a clipping canvas will show.

The quickest way to do this is to copy and paste the XAML, adjusting the clipping paths as you go along.

1. Switch to XAML editing mode and locate the first Image object, named Row0Col0. It starts on line 14.

2. To add a clipping path to the first Image object, add the following code:

```
<Image Width="320" Height="240" Source="beeFlower640x480.jpg"
    Stretch="Fill" x:Name="Row0Col0" RenderTransformOrigin="0.5,0.5">
    <Image.RenderTransform>
        <TransformGroup>
            <ScaleTransform/>
            <SkewTransform/>
            <RotateTransform/>
            <TranslateTransform/>
        </TransformGroup>
    </Image.RenderTransform>
    <Image.Clip>
        <RectangleGeometry Rect="0, 0, 80, 60"/>
    </Image.Clip>
</Image>
```

This creates a visible "window" over the image that starts at 0,0 and is 80×60. For each clipping path across the row, you want to locate the clipping region 80 pixels over from the previous one.

3. To create the second object, copy and paste the first item, change the name to Row0Col1, and adjust the clipping path to start at 80,0:

```
<Image Width="320" Height="240" Source="beeFlower640x480.jpg"
    Stretch="Fill" x:Name="Row0Col1">
    <Image.Clip>
        <RectangleGeometry Rect="80, 0, 80, 60"/>
    </Image.Clip>
</Image>
```

4. The third item, row 0 column 2, has a clip of 160,0; 80,60. See the pattern here? The code is creating an 80×60 window for each object, and you're just moving the window around.

```
<Image Width="320" Height="240" Source="beeFlower640x480.jpg"
    Stretch="Fill" x:Name="Row0Col2" RenderTransformOrigin="0.5,0.5">
    <Image.RenderTransform>
        <TransformGroup>
            <ScaleTransform/>
            <SkewTransform/>
            <RotateTransform/>
            <TranslateTransform/>
        </TransformGroup>
    </Image.RenderTransform>
    <Image.Clip>
        <RectangleGeometry Rect="160, 0, 80, 60"/>
    </Image.Clip>
</Image>
```

5. Add the fourth item (row 0 column 2) with a clipping path of 240,0; 80,60, as shown:

```
<Image Width="320" Height="240" Source="beeFlower640x480.jpg"
    Stretch="Fill" x:Name="Row0Col3" RenderTransformOrigin="0.5,0.5">
    <Image.RenderTransform>
        <TransformGroup>
            <ScaleTransform/>
            <SkewTransform/>
            <RotateTransform/>
            <TranslateTransform/>
        </TransformGroup>
    </Image.RenderTransform>
    <Image.Clip>
        <RectangleGeometry Rect="240, 0, 80, 60"/>
    </Image.Clip>
</Image>
```

Once the first row is done, you can copy and paste the whole row, rename the elements, and change the second value of the clipping region to 60, since you want to clip the next row of the image starting at 60 y. Here's what row 1 column 0 looks like:

```
<Image.Clip>
    <RectangleGeometry Rect="0, 60, 80, 60"/>
</Image.Clip>
```

The third row is at 120 y, and the fourth row is at 180. Once you've finished all four rows, you will have what looks like a single image, but is really 16 parts. You can now create a timeline that animates each of the 16 parts in order to blow apart the image. The **ClippingPathsCompleted** project has an example storyboard in it that you can take a look at. Just run the project and click the main canvas to see the animation. Because the HTML page for the project does not have the styles adjusted, the pieces will move off the main canvas, but you'll get a feel for the type of motion we're creating. In addition to animating objects that have clipping paths applied to them, you can animate the points that make up the clipping paths themselves. This allows you to create some interesting effects such as wipes or reveals. To animate a clipping path, create a new storyboard, select the clipped object, and then click the Direct Selection tool. Clipping paths will be drawn in red on the artboard, and they have white control points, as shown in Figure 4-11.

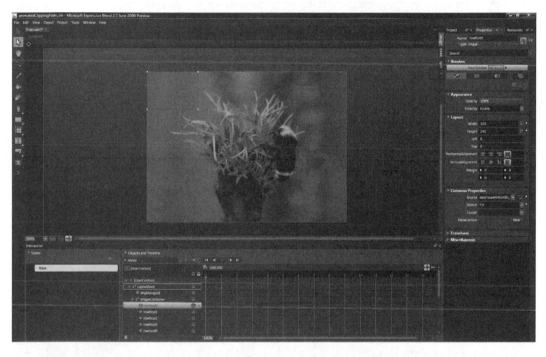

Figure 4-11. Clipping paths can be animated with the Direct Selection tool.

If an image is placed behind the image mosaic constructed from clipped regions, the clipped regions can be animated to look as though they are peeling back, creating a sort of checkerboard effect. I've provided an example of this type of effect in the **AnimatedClippingPaths** project for you to take a look at. Clicking anywhere on the application will start the animation for you.

You're probably asking yourself, "Why go about doing it this way? Why not just go into Photoshop and slice up an image there?" You certainly have the option of doing that. It takes more work to re-assemble the image that way, but the key reason to do it this way is because it's reusable. In both of the example projects, only a single image file was used. If you want to change the effect out, all you need to do is change the image name that is being used.

If you wanted to make it even easier to change images, you could set all the image source attributes to empty strings (""), add the image to your project in Visual Studio or Blend, and use code to assign the image name across all the elements being used. In this way, you could create slideshow or video effects, transitions, and so on. If you took an image and physically cut it into 16 or more parts, you would create a lot more work for yourself because you would need to cut up each image you wanted to work with.

Creating user controls

Before digging into the next two topics, I need to take a moment and talk about user controls. When I say "user control," I'm not referring to elements such as buttons or check boxes specifically, though those are examples of user controls. I'm referring to them more as a general method we will be using to add objects to a project.

To this point, the majority of projects we've looked at have had the object just added to the main XAML file in the project, called Page.xaml. Moving forward, what we will be doing is adding objects as their own unique XAML file, each of which will have its own code-behind file. This makes working with the objects programmatically much easier—creating copies, or instances, of an object takes only a few lines of code. More importantly, adding functionality to an object becomes relatively easy—you add code to the base object, and any copies of it anywhere in your project will immediately gain the same functionality. The best part is that user controls are really easy to add.

1. Open the **MakeUserControl** project to follow along with this section. It contains an ellipse named EllipseElement.

2. There are two ways to add user controls within Blend. The first is to select an object on the artboard or in the Objects and Timeline list, right-click, and select Make Control, as shown in Figure 4-12. Try this out with the EllipseElement item.

3. The Make Control dialog will open and prompt you to name the new control. For this example, use the name EllipseControl and then click OK. Blend will open the new control for editing in a new tab on the artboard.

4. By default, the new control is placed into a Grid layout container that has a white background. Change the background color to No Brush and save the project.

Figure 4-12. Any object in Blend can be turned into a user control.

5. Select the Page.xaml tab at the top of the interface to return to that file for editing. You will see that the control is currently not visible because of the change you made. Press Ctrl+Shift+B to rebuild the project and the ellipse will be redrawn. That's all there is to it. The new user control you created from an existing item is built and ready to be used.

The second method for creating a new user control is to build one from scratch. If you change to the Project tab in Blend, you will see a list of all the files associated with this project.

6. Right-click the project name (**MakeUserControl**), and add a user control by selecting Add New Item, as shown in Figure 4-13.

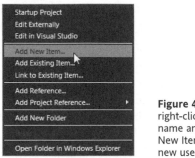

Figure 4-13. In Blend, right-click the project name and select Add New Item to create a new user control.

7. Blend will open the New Item dialog box, which allows you to create a new user control. Type in RectangleControl and click OK. Once again, Blend will open the control on a new tab. This time, the control is blank since it was not created from an existing object.

8. Change the background color of the LayoutRoot element to No Brush, and make the size 200×200.

9. Add a 200×200 blue rectangle named RectangleElement to the LayoutRoot element and save the project.

10. When you return to the Page.xaml tab, you will see that the Rectangle control has not yet been added to the artboard. Press Ctrl+Shift+B to build the project.

11. The new control will become available to you on the Custom Controls tab of the Asset Library, which is accessed through the toolbox, as shown in Figure 4-14.

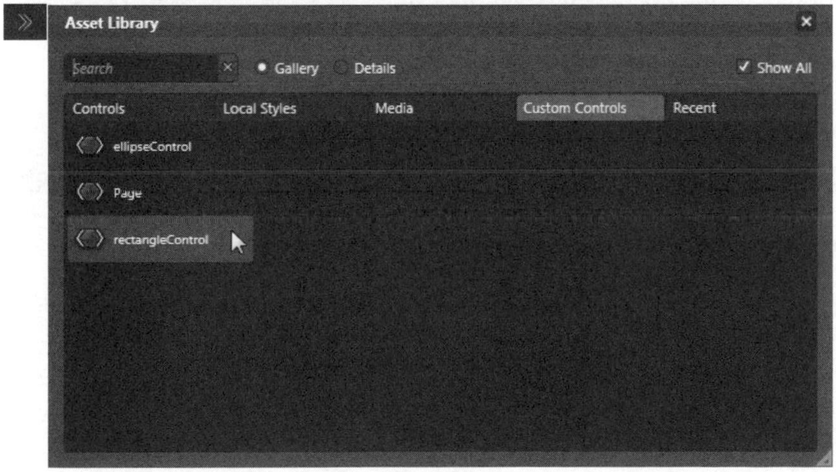

Figure 4-14. The Asset Library contains all the controls available to your project.

12. Selecting a control from the Asset Library will add an icon to the toolbox that you can use to add the control to your project. Select the RectangleControl object from the asset list. Once the icon shows up in the toolbox, double-click it. A new 200×200 blue rectangle will be added to the artboard.

This turns into a lot of fun when the controls are added programmatically, because each instance of a control exists in its own space and can have its own color, size, and so on.

13. On the Project tab, right-click Page.xaml.cs, and select Edit in Visual Studio from the pop-up menu.

    In Visual Studio, we'll add an instance of this custom control in the same place as variables—just above the Page() constructor. Each instance that we create is a copy of the original object, but each copy has its own set of unique properties. Once an object instance has been declared, it is available for use in the application. To make it visible within the application, it must be added to the LayoutRoot Canvas. This is done by calling the Add() method for LayoutRoot.Children.

14. Just above the Page() constructor, add the following code to declare an instance of the Rectangle object:

    ```
    RectangleControl MyRect = new RectangleControl();
    ```

15. To add the user control to the LayoutRoot Canvas, add the following code inside the Page() constructor, just after the InitializeComponent() line:

    ```
    LayoutRoot.Children.Add(MyRect);
    ```

    Now the rectangle will be displayed on the canvas when the project runs.

16. A second instance is equally simple to add—create an object called GreenRect and add it to the canvas.

17. This time, we'll add a little code to modify the object a bit. Because we named the elements that make up the user control, they are easy to access from code by referencing the object name and then the member name. In the case of GreenRect, we want to place the rectangle at 400,200. To do this, add some code before the rectangle is added to the canvas:

    ```
    GreenRect.SetValue(Canvas.LeftProperty, 400.00);
    GreenRect.SetValue(Canvas.TopProperty, 200.00);
    ```

    This code tells Silverlight to position the GreenRect object so that it is 400 pixels from the left of the canvas in which it is being placed, and 200 pixels down. Be careful to use double values when setting properties or the project may throw an error.

    Our object is called GreenRect, so it should probably be green. If you recall when you created the object, you named the rectangle inside the user control RectangleElement. This is the object you want to target when changing properties, and it is accessed through the GreenRect object as GreenRect.RectangleElement. Since we want to change the fill type/color, the code becomes GreenRect.RectangleElement.Fill. From there, it becomes a matter of assigning a SolidColorBrush to the Fill property.

18. Add the following code to the project to change the fill color of the GreenRect object:

    ```
    GreenRect.RectangleElement.Fill = new SolidColorBrush➡
        (Color.FromArgb(255, 0, 255, 0));
    ```

19. Add the GreenRect object to the Children collection of the LayoutRoot element with the following code:

    ```
    LayoutRoot.Children.Add(GreenRect);
    ```

You can compile and run the project to see the results, which should be pretty close to those shown in Figure 4-15.

Figure 4-15. The UserControlsCompleted project creates two instances from a single Rectangle user control.

You have now created two instances of the same base object. Even though both objects are derived from the same base object, they look different. You can create as many instances of an object as you would like, and each one can have its own unique properties! The **MakeUserControlCompleted** project has a function in it called CreateRectangles() that will generate a group of rectangle objects all with different colors. The comments in the project explain what you need to do to use the function.

Implementing drag-and-drop

Drag-and-drop is ubiquitous—people expect to be able to open an application and move things around. If you're coming over from Flash, you will find that drag-and-drop operations in Silverlight aren't quite as simple to implement as those in Flash, but they're not difficult by any measure. Open the **DragAndDrop** project and we'll take a look at how to go about making an object draggable.

If you open the project in Blend, you won't see much—it contains the layout canvas and the Rectangle user control created in the previous section of this chapter. The rectangle is instanced three times when the project runs, with each instance being positioned and filled randomly. What we are about to do is to add the drag-and-drop functionality described in Microsoft's Silverlight documentation to the base control, which will then enable drag-and-drop for all three instances of the object.

1. If you're in Blend, use the Project tab to locate the code-behind for the rectangleControl. xaml file. It's called rectangleControl.xaml.cs.

2. Right-click and select Edit in Visual Studio. The code-behind for this object looks just like the code-behind for the Page.xaml file, only here you are coding behaviors that will be specific to this object.

3. The first two things we will need are a Boolean value to determine if the selected object is being dragged, and a Point object that will be used to help determine the offset between the selected object's current location and the mouse pointer location. These variables are considered **private** because they belong to the Rectangle user control, so they will not be accessible from the main code-behind file. These are placed above the public RectangleControl() constructor:

```
private bool IsMouseCaptured;
private Point MousePosition;
```

4. Next, we need to register three event listeners inside the RectangleControl() function. We will need to know when the mouse button is pressed, when the mouse is moving, and when the mouse button is released. Notice that we're using the keyword this to wire up event listeners rather than an object name. When this is used, it tells Silverlight that the code refers to this object. Since all this code is placed within the RectangleControl, this always refers to RectangleControl.

```
this.MouseLeftButtonDown += new
    MouseButtonEventHandler(RectangleControl_MouseLeftButtonDown);
this.MouseLeftButtonUp +=
    new MouseButtonEventHandler(RectangleControl_MouseLeftButtonUp);
this.MouseMove += new MouseEventHandler(RectangleControl_MouseMove);
```

In the mouse down event handler, the selected object is the sender passed to the function. This function sets up a reference to the sender as Item. The position of the mouse is then stored, and the Boolean flag indicating whether or not dragging is occurring is set to true. The CaptureMouse() method ensures that while the mouse button is down, any events being raised are exclusively owned by the selected object, even if the pointer goes outside the bounds of the object. Finally, the object's cursor is changed to a hand.

5. Add the following code to the MouseLeftButtonDown event handler:

```
private void RectangleControl_MouseLeftButtonDown➧
    (object sender, MouseButtonEventArgs e)
{
    FrameworkElement Item = sender as FrameworkElement;
    MousePosition = e.GetPosition(null);
    IsMouseCaptured = true;
    Item.CaptureMouse();
    Item.Cursor = Cursors.Hand;
}
```

While dragging is occurring (the mouse button is down and the mouse is moving), the code in the event handler once again creates a reference called Item to the sender object before checking to see if a drag is in process. If so, the difference between the stored mouse position and the current mouse position is applied to the selected object. Once the object has been moved, the stored mouse position is updated for the next time the function is called. As the mouse is moving, this function is executing repeatedly—calculating the mouse position, moving the object, and getting the current mouse position again for the next time through.

6. Add the following code that contains the functionality described previously to the MouseMove event handler:

```
private void RectangleControl_MouseMove➡
    (object sender, MouseEventArgs e)
{
    FrameworkElement Item = sender as FrameworkElement;
    if (IsMouseCaptured)
    {
        // Calculate the current position of the object.
        double DeltaV = e.GetPosition(null).Y - MousePosition.Y;
        double DeltaH = e.GetPosition(null).X - MousePosition.X;
        double NewTop = DeltaV + (double)Item.GetValue➡
            (Canvas.TopProperty);
        double NewLeft = DeltaH + (double)Item.GetValue➡
            (Canvas.LeftProperty);

        // Set new position of object.
        Item.SetValue(Canvas.TopProperty, NewTop);
        Item.SetValue(Canvas.LeftProperty, NewLeft);

        // Update position global variables.
        MousePosition = e.GetPosition(null);
    }
}
```

When the mouse is released, the sender object is once again captured as Item, and the Boolean flag used to determine that a drag operation is in progress is set to false. Mouse capture for the selected object is released, and the Point variable MousePosition is cleared. Finally, the selected item's cursor is returned back to whatever the default value is. In this case, the cursor is not defined in the XAML, so the default arrow will be displayed.

7. Add the following code to the MouseLeftButtonUp event handler to add the functionality described:

```
private void RectangleControl_MouseLeftButtonUp➡
    (object sender, MouseButtonEventArgs e)
{
    FrameworkElement Item = sender as FrameworkElement;
    IsMouseCaptured = false;
    Item.ReleaseMouseCapture();
    MousePosition.X = MousePosition.Y = 0;
    Item.Cursor = null;
}
```

If you now run the project, you will see that even though you only wrote drag-and-drop code once, you can drag and drop any of the three Rectangle user controls. Notice that when the selected rectangle passes behind another, you do not lose control of the drag operation. This is the result of using the `CaptureMouse()` method.

If you wanted to augment the code so that the selected object is always on top, you could add a function that would manipulate the z-index for each of the objects, setting them all to 0, for example, except for the selected object, which would be set to 1.

One of the nice things about this bit of code is that it's generic. You can place the `MouseLeftButtonDown`, `MouseLeftButtonUp`, and `MouseMove` handlers' code in any user control hosted in a canvas, or place it in the main code and call it from any object, and it will enable dragging. This means that once you have it coded up, it's as simple as copying and pasting a bit of code, and hooking up the event listeners for the object you want to be able to drag and drop. The completed example project is saved as **DragAndDropCompleted**.

Frame-based animation sequences

I've talked a lot about how to make things move, but haven't spent a lot of time dealing with actual frame-based animation. This is the kind of animation that comes to mind when you think of how classic animation is created. A series of frames is drawn, each one slightly different. As you flip through the frames, the slight changes from frame to frame create the illusion of motion. Depending upon your approach to using Silverlight, you have a few choices in how you decide to implement your own frame-based animations. Because of the flexibility, we will explore three different ways to create frame-based animations.

Let's begin by taking a look at the character we'll be animating. Figure 4-16 shows a series of poses for a duck. In the first pose, the wings are up. The second pose shows the wings in mid-flap, and the final pose shows the wings down. To make the flap animation, we'll create an animation that moves forward through the frames, then backward, and then repeats.

Figure 4-16. The duck poses that will animate into a wing flap cycle

This is one of those situations where having an illustrator or animator handy is useful, because getting the motion to look right if an animation is longer than a few frames can be a little tricky.

The first method for creating frame-based animations is done entirely with a storyboard. This technique is great if you're a designer or just prefer to stick entirely to Blend to create your applications. In your project, you create a new user control that will be the animated item. In the user control, a canvas container is created, into which the poses for the action you're creating are placed. Since most objects are made up of many paths, it makes organization easier to place each pose inside of its own descriptively named canvas.

Open the **DiscreteFrameBasedAnimation** project to build this example. The project contains the Page.xaml file, as well as a Duck user control that is in the Duck.xaml file. Open the Duck.xaml file and take a look at how the object is organized. There is a main container canvas named DuckFlyingPoses, inside of which are three more canvases, each of which contains a pose for the duck. The WingsUp canvas has the duck with its wings up—the leftmost pose shown in Figure 4-16. The WingsMid pose is shown in the center, and WingsDown is on the right. The poses are spaced equally horizontally.

1. Click the DuckFlyingPoses canvas. Notice how the canvas is just large enough to contain a single duck pose—in this case, the WingsUp pose.

2. Create a new storyboard named FlapWings, and move the play head to .3 seconds.

3. In the Objects and Timeline list, click WingsUp, and then Ctrl-click WingsMid and WingsDown. All three poses should be selected.

4. On the Transform pane of the Properties panel, type -300 into the X field. All three poses will slide to the left 300 pixels.

5. Move the play head to .6 seconds.

6. With all three poses still selected, enter -600 into the X field on the Transform pane.

7. Play the animation.

   Not quite what you expected, right? All three duck poses simply slide to the left, and you're wondering if you missed something in the instructions. It's doing what it's supposed to—we're not quite done yet!

   Currently, the animation is at a point where the duck's wings started in the up position, pushed through the mid position, and are now at the down position. To complete the flap cycle, we need to work back through the poses in the opposite direction.

8. Move the timeline play head to .9.

9. Enter -300 into the X field on the Transform pane.

10. Move the timeline play head to 1.2 seconds.

11. Enter 0 into the X transform field. The canvases will be back in their original positions at this point.

    At this point, playing the timeline will continue to give you some unexpected results, as the duck poses simply slide back and forth along the x axis. In fact, it doesn't look much like the duck is flying at all.

    What we need to finish off our animation is a tool that can help us change between poses only when a keyframe is reached, rather than smoothly interpolating the motion between the frames like we're currently seeing.

    Are you with me here? The tool we need is the reliable discrete keyframe that we discussed earlier. Remember that discrete keyframes hold their position until the next keyframe is reached, at which time the object being animated jumps to the position in the next keyframe.

12. To change the type of keyframe being used to a discrete keyframe, hold down the Ctrl key and click all 12 of the keyframe markers on the timeline.

13. With all the markers selected, right-click and select Hold In from the pop-up menu, as shown in Figure 4-17. Alternatively, you could switch to XAML mode and edit the storyboard by hand to use DiscreteDoubleKeyFrames rather than SplineDoubleKeyFrames. Either way, once the change has been made, playing the storyboard again has it looking a little more like what we were expecting—the poses jump from keyframe to keyframe rather than sliding. We're almost done!

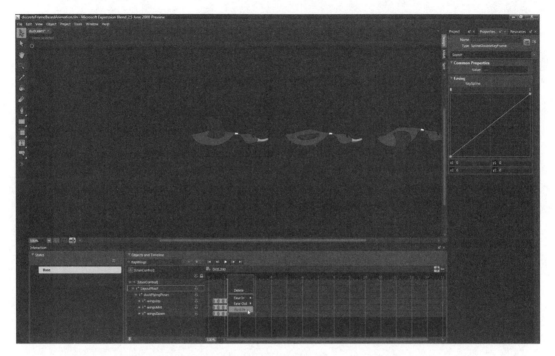

Figure 4-17. Change the keyframes in the animation so that they become DiscreteDoubleKeyFrames.

The last thing needed to finish off this particular animation is a clipping path applied to the DuckFlyingPoses Canvas in order to hide the poses that are positioned outside of the main canvas. Assuming the canvas was sized appropriately prior to having the poses added, this is easy to do.

14. Close the FlapWings storyboard.

15. Double-click the DuckFlyingPoses Canvas to select it. It will display a yellow border. This means that any new objects created will automatically be placed in the selected canvas.

16. The DuckFlyingPoses Canvas is 257×130. Double-click the Rectangle icon in the toolbox to add a rectangle to the project.

17. In the Width field on the Layout pane, enter 257. For Height, enter 130. The new rectangle now covers the canvas, as shown in Figure 4-18.

18. With the rectangle selected in the Objects and Timeline list, Ctrl-click the DuckFlyingPoses Canvas so that both are selected.

19. Right-click the selected group and choose Path ➤ Make Clipping Path from the pop-up menu.

Figure 4-18. Create a clipping region over the container canvas to hide the poses that are not in view.

Now when the FlapWings storyboard is opened and played, there is a nice flapping animation.

20. The animation seems a little slow and needs to be sped up a bit. Switch to XAML view and scroll up to find the storyboard. Add a SpeedRatio property to the storyboard and set it to play the storyboard twice as fast as it does by default. You can go up or down with the SpeedRatio value depending upon what you need to do with your animation. For now, SpeedRatio="2" will do.

21. We also know that this will be a repeating animation, so add a RepeatBehavior property to the storyboard as well. At this point, the opening tag for the storyboard looks like the following:

```
<Storyboard x:Name="FlapWings" SpeedRatio="2" RepeatBehavior="Forever">
```

The duck is flying and looks pretty good in Blend, but how do we put it to work in our application? All that's necessary is to create an instance of the user control, add it to the root canvas, and start the animation. We'll start the storyboard in the Duck user control. Every time the duck is added to an application, it will begin flapping automatically.

22. Press Ctrl+S to save the project. On the Project panel in Blend, expand Duck.xaml so you can see the Duck.xaml.cs file. Right-click Duck.xaml.cs and select Edit in Visual Studio.

23. Just after the InitializeComponent(); line, add this.FlapWings.Begin();. This line tells Silverlight to start the FlapWings storyboard each time a Duck object is instanced. The this keyword always means "this object"—since we're calling FlapWings.Begin() from inside the Duck object, saying this.FlapWings.Begin() tells Silverlight to play the animation for this object.

24. Next, open the `Page.xaml.cs` file for editing in Visual Studio.

25. Just before the `Page()` constructor, create an instance of the Duck object called `MyDuck`.

```
Duck MyDuck = new Duck();
```

26. Because this duck isn't moving relative to the underlying canvas, it needs to be positioned where we can get a good look at it—200,200 seems like as good a spot as any. Place the following three lines of code after the `InitializeComponent();` code. This will position the duck at 200,200, and add it to the LayoutRoot Canvas so that it is visible within the application.

```
MyDuck.SetValue(Canvas.LeftProperty, 200.00);
MyDuck.SetValue(Canvas.TopProperty, 200.00);
LayoutRoot.Children.Add(MyDuck);
```

Press F5 to compile and run the program. You should get a white canvas with the duck flapping away. Want another duck that's not working quite as hard? No problem! Keep working in the `Page.xaml.cs` file.

27. Create a new instance of the Duck user control:

```
Duck SlowDuck = new Duck();
```

28. To separate the ducks a bit, position this one at 300,300. Before adding it to the canvas, however, tell Silverlight you want the `FlapWings` animation of SlowDuck to have a `SpeedRatio` of 1, meaning that this duck will flap one-half as fast as the first duck.

```
SlowDuck.SetValue(Canvas.LeftProperty, 300.00);
SlowDuck.SetValue(Canvas.TopProperty, 300.00);
SlowDuck.FlapWings.SpeedRatio = 1;
LayoutRoot.Children.Add(SlowDuck);
```

Now when the project runs, there are two ducks: one is flapping frantically, while the other takes her sweet time.

What's that? Now you want a whole flock of ducks? No problem!

29. Start by declaring a random number generator above the `Page()` constructor.

```
Random Rng = new Random();
```

30. Create a function that accepts an integer argument and uses it to generate the specified number of ducks. Here, the ducks are placed at random positions and given a random flap speed between 1 and 3.

```
void MakeDucks(int NumDucks)
{
    for (int i = 0; i < NumDucks; i++)
    {
        Duck NewDuck = new Duck();
        Point Position = new Point(Rng.NextDouble() *
            (LayoutRoot.Width - NewDuck.Width),
            Rng.NextDouble() * (LayoutRoot.Height -
            NewDuck.Height));
        Canvas.SetLeft(NewDuck, Position.X);
        Canvas.SetTop(NewDuck, Position.Y);
        int Speed = Rng.Next(1,3);
        NewDuck.FlapWings.SpeedRatio = Speed;
        LayoutRoot.Children.Add(NewDuck);
    }
}
```

31. To call this function and use it to create 20 ducks in addition to the 2 we already have, add the code MakeDucks(20); to the Page() constructor. Changing the number inside the parentheses will change the number of ducks that are added to the application.

The full code for this project is in the **DiscreteFrameBasedCompleted** project. There are some comments in the code that explain how to enable the MakeDucks() function shown previously so you can see it in action.

Animation with the Visual State Manager

The next technique we'll look at for working with frame-based animations uses the Visual State Manager that found its way into Silverlight 2. This tool can be used very effectively for frame-based animations—it provides a quick-and-easy visual tool with which you can quickly set up an animation cycle. The interface for the Visual State Manager available in Blend allows you to take a series of objects and create snapshots of their properties. Once the snapshots have been created, code can be used to flip through them, giving the illusion of animation.

The setup for this method is a little bit different than the last. We will once again be working with the duck poses from the previous example, but in the last example objects were spread horizontally, and then flipped through via keyframes. This time, we want all the duck's poses piled on top of one another. The main hierarchy of objects is still the same—there is a Canvas called DuckFlyingPoses, and three Canvases inside that. Once again, the container Canvases are called WingsUp, WingsMid, and WingsDown. Figure 4-19 shows the base setup for the project.

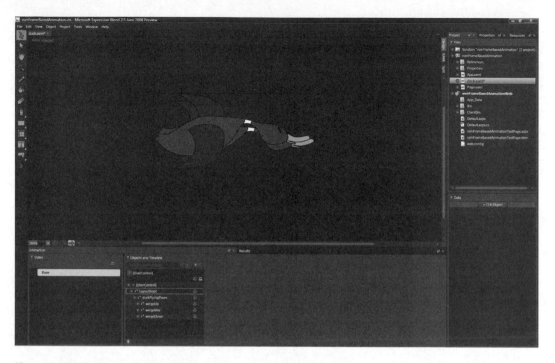

Figure 4-19. When using the Visual State Manager for frame-based animations, all the poses are aligned directly on top of one another.

Open the **VSMFrameBasedAnimation** project to follow along with this example. The Visual State Manager is accessed on the States panel, which is located to the left of the Objects and Timeline panel when your workspace is set up for animation. In the default design workspace, the States panel is located on the left side of the interface, above the Objects and Timeline panel.

1. With the **VSMFrameBasedAnimation** project open, open the Duck.xaml file for editing. Create a state group by clicking the Add State Group button located at the top right of the States panel, as shown in Figure 4-20. The new state group will automatically be added to the pane.

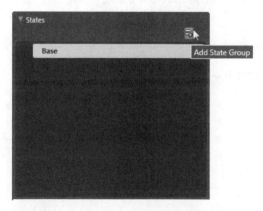

Figure 4-20. Use the States panel to add named snapshots of objects.

2. As soon as the group is added, the name is selected by default, so you can begin typing to give the newly added state group a unique name right away. Type in WingFlap. The state group is a container. The group is now created but does not yet contain any state definitions.

3. To add a state to the state group, click the Add State icon, shown in Figure 4-21.

4. When you click the Add State icon, the interface in Blend will change to State recording mode, and a new state will be added to the selected state group. Name the first state in the duck project Up.

5. Expand the DuckFlyingPoses Canvas in the Objects and Timeline list, and select both the WingsMid and WingsDown poses.

6. On the Properties panel, set the Visibility to Collapsed. Only the WingsUp pose will now be visible on the artboard. A snapshot of the user control was just created that uses XAML to describe how this view of the user control now differs from the original state of the object. In this case, the default base state had all three poses visible.

Figure 4-21. Use the Add State button to save snapshots of your object's properties.

7. Create a second state named Mid.

8. For this state, set the Visibility for both WingsUp and WingsDown to Collapsed. Only the middle pose will remain visible on the artboard.

9. Create a third state named Down.

10. For this state, set the Visibility of both the WingsUp and WingsMid poses to Collapsed. Once you're done adding states for a user control, you can turn off State recording mode by clicking the red button at the top left of the artboard.

In the previous example, we moved forward through the frames and then back to the middle pose before repeating the animation. Here, we will control the states the same way, in the order 1, 2, 3, 2, 1, 2, 3, 2, 1 . . . , which gives essentially the same effect as the previous example.

What exactly does Blend do to the code when you use the state manager? Each time you create a state group, Blend creates a container for the group in the XAML. Each time you add a state, Blend adds a container for that state. Inside our state containers go . . . you guessed it: discrete keyframes!

The following listing shows the XAML code for the Up state. You can identify the familiar properties with which you have been working in storyboards and animations.

```
<vsm:VisualState x:Name="Up">
    <Storyboard>
        <ObjectAnimationUsingKeyFrames BeginTime="00:00:00"
          Duration="00:00:00.0010000" Storyboard.TargetName="WingsMid"
          Storyboard.TargetProperty="(UIElement.Visibility)">
        <DiscreteObjectKeyFrame KeyTime="00:00:00">
            <DiscreteObjectKeyFrame.Value>
                <Visibility>Collapsed</Visibility>
            </DiscreteObjectKeyFrame.Value>
        </DiscreteObjectKeyFrame>
        </ObjectAnimationUsingKeyFrames>
```

141

```
        <ObjectAnimationUsingKeyFrames BeginTime="00:00:00"
            Duration="00:00:00.0010000" Storyboard.TargetName="WingsDown"
            Storyboard.TargetProperty="(UIElement.Visibility)">
            <DiscreteObjectKeyFrame KeyTime="00:00:00">
                    <DiscreteObjectKeyFrame.Value>
                        <Visibility>Collapsed</Visibility>
                    </DiscreteObjectKeyFrame.Value>
            </DiscreteObjectKeyFrame>
        </ObjectAnimationUsingKeyFrames>
    </Storyboard>
</vsm:VisualState>
```

Let's take a look at how to actually use these states to create an animation. We need a timer, which is just a storyboard that doesn't contain any animations. Each time the timer raises a completed event, a set of actions will be performed.

11. To create a new timer storyboard in Blend, change to Split view and scroll to the top of the XAML window.

12. Still working with the Duck.xaml file, click the New storyboard button, type in FlapWings, and then click OK. The storyboard XAML will appear in the code you see in the XAML portion of the Split view. The timer storyboard needs to have an interval defined via the Duration property. For the duck project, a Duration of 00:00:00.50 was added to the storyboard:

```
<Storyboard x:Name="FlapWings" Duration="00:00:00.50"/>
```

With this particular example, there's a bit more code involved than with the prior method that used a storyboard only. The majority of the code here is unique to the Duck user control, and is located in the Duck.xaml.cs code-behind file, so press Ctrl+S to save the project, and then open Duck.xaml.cs for editing in Visual Studio.

13. There are two variables initialized. One is an integer used to change the visible state, and the second is a string used to keep track of the current state by name, because the method to change the state on screen needs a string passed to it. Add the following two lines of code just above the Duck() constructor:

```
private int DuckState = 1;
private string CurrentState;
```

14. In the public Duck() class that is called when the Duck object is instantiated, the empty storyboard we're using as a timer is started, and a Completed event listener is wired up. Every half-second (500ms), this storyboard will raise a Completed event that is used to change the visible state of the duck in the project.

```
this.FlapWings.Begin();
this.FlapWings.Completed += new EventHandler(FlapWings_Completed);
```

15. The event handler code for the Completed event does all the work. The DuckState integer is used as a counter to keep track of which pose should be in view, and is tested by a switch statement. When the correct switch statement is triggered, the CurrentState variable is updated with the name of the state that should be displayed. VisualStateManager is then invoked to change the state. The false flag at the end of the VisualStateManager.GoToState() method tells Silverlight that these state changes do not use transitions.

```
void FlapWings_Completed(object sender, EventArgs e)
{
    switch(DuckState)
    {
        case 1:
            CurrentState = "Up";
            break;
        case 2:
            CurrentState = "Mid";
            break;
        case 3:
            CurrentState = "Down";
            break;
        case 4:
            CurrentState = "Mid";
            break;
    }

    VisualStateManager.GoToState(this, CurrentState, false);

    DuckState += 1;
    if (DuckState > 4) DuckState = 1;

    this.FlapWings.Begin();
}
```

When called, the Visual State Manager does the work of changing the view rendered on the screen. After that, the counter is incremented to get ready for the next pose, and checked to keep it within the bounds of our animation, which is four poses. To finish, the timer storyboard is restarted once again.

The timer storyboard is the real workhorse here. Every half-second, it causes the code in the Completed event handler to execute in order to control the state of the object shown on the screen.

With the code in place for the Duck object, move to the Page.xaml.cs code-behind for the main application. The code here is very simple.

16. First, declare a new Duck object:

```
Duck MyDuck = new Duck();
```

17. When the application initializes, a bit of prep is done on the duck. First, it is positioned on the canvas. In this example, it's being placed at 200,200. Inside the Page() constructor, add the following two lines of code to position the duck:

```
MyDuck.SetValue(Canvas.LeftProperty, 200.00);
MyDuck.SetValue(Canvas.TopProperty, 200.00);
```

18. Next, do a little preset on the object by calling upon the Visual State Manager to set the duck to the WingsUp pose. Remember that the Duck object has all three poses visible, and they are piled on top of one another. We do not want the duck to appear on screen with all three poses showing, so the call to the state manager sets the initial view for us. Add the following line of code immediately after the two lines added in step 17:

```
VisualStateManager.GoToState(MyDuck, "Up", false);
```

19. After that, add the Duck object to the LayoutRoot Canvas. This line of code goes immediately after the one added in step 18:

```
LayoutRoot.Children.Add(MyDuck);
```

Compile and run the application. The white background canvas will be drawn, and the animated duck will be added. The Duck user control object is completely self-contained—it starts itself and hooks up the Completed event for the storyboard automatically. As with the last project, you can customize the speed of the flapping wings animation by tweaking the SpeedRatio property of the FlapWings storyboard in the Duck user control. To speed up the flap, increase the SpeedRatio property. Alternatively, you may decrease the Duration value—this will have essentially the same effect. All the code covered in this example is available in the **VSMFrameBasedCompleted** project. One of the nice things about coding up an animation in this manner is that the code is relatively easy to follow. It's fairly easy to track what the animation is going to do when looking through the switch statement in the Duck user control code. The Visual State Manager in Blend makes it really easy to see what a user will see on the screen in each state as it's added to a state group. This makes the whole development process flow very smoothly.

A code-based Visual State Manager

Some of you may prefer a solution that is purely code-based. The last frame-based animation method that we're going to look at describes a way of creating your own state manager using only code.

The setup for this project is almost identical to the previous example. The hierarchy and organization for the Duck user control is the same, only it does not contain the state group and associated states that were created in the last project. This time, we'll be controlling the visible state entirely with code. There are two differences. For this project, we don't have the Visual State Manager to set our initial pose for us, so the WingsMid and WingsDown Canvases are set to Collapsed. In addition, the FlapWings storyboard is already in place.

1. The differences between this project and the last one are confined to the Duck user control code-behind. Open the **CodeFrameBasedAnimation** project.

2. The integer used for tracking the state is still declared at the beginning of the file. Add the following code just before the Duck() constructor:

```
private int DuckState = 1;
```

3. When initialized, the object will start the storyboard that controls the animation and wire up a Completed event to that storyboard. Add the following code to the Duck() constructor:

```
this.FlapWings.Begin();
this.FlapWings.Completed += new EventHandler(FlapWings_Completed);
```

4. The difference between the code-based control and the Visual State Manager's control is in the Completed event handler. The event handler begins by changing the visibility for each of the three poses to Collapsed to hide them. The switch statement then manually sets the visibility for the appropriate pose, based on the DuckState variable. The rest of the code remains the same as it was with the Visual State Manager example. The following listing shows the code for the event handler on the FlapWings storyboard's Completed event.

```
void FlapWings_Completed(object sender, EventArgs e)
{
    this.WingsUp.Visibility = Visibility.Collapsed;
    this.WingsMid.Visibility = Visibility.Collapsed;
    this.WingsDown.Visibility = Visibility.Collapsed;

    switch (DuckState)
    {
        case 1:
            this.WingsUp.Visibility = Visibility.Visible;
            break;
        case 2:
            this.WingsMid.Visibility = Visibility.Visible;
            break;
        case 3:
            this.WingsDown.Visibility = Visibility.Visible;
            break;
        case 4:
            this.WingsMid.Visibility = Visibility.Visible;
            break;
    }

    DuckState += 1;
    if (DuckState > 4) DuckState = 1;

    this.FlapWings.Begin();
}
```

5. In the Page.xaml.cs file, the code to create an instance of the Duck object is shown following. This code goes before the Page() constructor.

```
Duck MyDuck = new Duck();
```

6. Position the Duck object and add it to the root canvas in the same way as the previous example. Add the following code inside the Page() constructor, right after the InitializeComponent() line:

```
MyDuck.SetValue(Canvas.LeftProperty, 200.00);
MyDuck.SetValue(Canvas.TopProperty, 200.00);

LayoutRoot.Children.Add(MyDuck);
```

If you want to change the speed at which the duck is moving, you can still adjust the SpeedRatio property of the FlapWings storyboard, just as with the prior example. The **CodeFrameBasedCompleted** project contains the completed code for this example of frame-based animation.

So there you have it: three different methods for creating frame-based animations.

The first example is probably well suited to designers, but has a tendency to hide the content a bit because it's using a clipping path to avoid showing the individual frames that make up the animation. If a project containing this style of animation were handed off or stored away and referenced later, it might take a bit of time to recall the technique being used.

The second method, which uses the Visual State Manager, is easy to set up with a tool like Blend, and makes it easy to see exactly what Silverlight will be presenting on the screen when any given state is called. It still requires a small amount of code in the code-behind to make it go, but easily adapts to an object with a large number of poses.

The entirely code-based solution shown in the final example is extremely fast to set up, and works in a manner very similar to the Visual State Manager. If you're a code junkie or don't have access to Blend to create state groups and states, this one may be your answer.

Summary

In this chapter, I talked about ways to apply some of the techniques discussed in earlier chapters. You saw how objects can be converted into paths and how the points of the paths can be animated to create text effects. We also explored how we can use copies of objects to create interesting ghosting effects for objects when clicked.

Though Silverlight doesn't yet offer easily accessible built-in bitmap effects, it's still possible to create drop shadows and blurs by using a couple of images and storyboards to transition between them. The code that enables these effects is relatively simple and transportable.

Individual animated objects can be turned into custom cursors by hiding the default cursor for the object that will display the custom cursor and attaching the animated object to the mouse position in the code-behind. The various mouse event listeners can then be used to show and hide the animated/ custom cursor.

Clipping paths allow you to take one shape and use it to clip the visible area of another. They will serve a wide variety of purposes in your application development, from clipping a canvas in order to show or hide content, to creating custom transition or image mosaic effects.

User control objects allow you to "divide and conquer" development tasks—separating objects and their associated code from the main code base of an application. Object-oriented design in Silverlight makes it very easy to utilize a single code source to create numerous instances of an object, each with its own set of properties. With user controls, it's possible for several developers to work on a single project, each focusing on separate objects and their associated behavior, all of which can be brought together in the final application.

Drag-and-drop is something you are likely to use quite often. While at the moment it is not as directly accessible as it is in Flash, it's still easy to create a set of generalized functions that can be quickly pasted into the code-behind for an object in order to implement drag-and-drop functionality.

I closed out this chapter by talking about three different techniques for implementing frame-based animation. The first technique showed how you can utilize discrete keyframes to create the illusion of motion by jumping between the different frames of an object. The second technique used the Visual State Manager to define state views for an object. We then used code to call upon the Visual State Manager to flip between the poses in order to animate our object. Finally, we employed a code-only technique for performing the same function as the Visual State Manager.

Now that we've looked at different ways to apply the concepts described in the first few chapters, it's time to break free of the storyboard animation techniques a bit and have some fun exploring vectors and angles in Silverlight, and how they're used to work with objects programmatically.

Part Three

ADVANCED ANIMATION

Chapter 5

COORDINATES IN SILVERLIGHT

Our journey into animating from the code-behind begins with a better look at Silverlight's angle and coordinate system. You've seen a little bit of this in some of the earlier examples, but now that you will be directly manipulating objects, it is important to have a firm understanding of the ideas presented here in order to make objects move the way you want them to.

The Silverlight coordinate system

It's a little bit easier to understand coordinates in Silverlight if you first get a little bit of a refresher of the Cartesian coordinate system. You should remember Figure 5-1 from your school days—it represents a traditional, two-dimensional (2D) coordinate system. The x axis runs horizontally, and the y axis runs vertically. The point at which the two axes intersect is referred to as the **origin**, and has an x,y coordinate of 0,0. The arrows at the end of each axis indicate that they extend forever in their respective directions. The intersection of the two axes divides the Cartesian plane into four quadrants, numbered from the upper right (the northeast quadrant), counterclockwise.

The points that lie within quadrant I are positive along both the x and y axes. In quadrant II, points are –x,+y. Quadrant III contains points that are negative for both x and y, and quadrant IV is positive along the x axis and negative along the y.

Silverlight's coordinate system, shown in Figure 5-2, is like working in quadrant IV of the Cartesian coordinate system, except that the y axis is flipped. This means that in order to move an object toward the bottom of a canvas, you increase the y coordinate (top property) for that object. Placing an object at 0,0 will position the object such that the top-left corner of the object is aligned with the top-left corner of the canvas. You can use negative x,y values or x,y values that exceed the width or height of the canvas to place objects outside of the visible area. This assumes that the styled width and height for the Silverlight application matches the height and width of the container canvas.

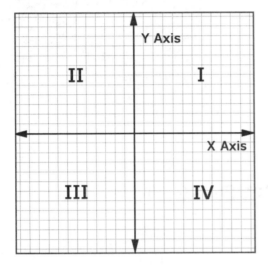

Figure 5-1. The four-quadrant Cartesian coordinate system

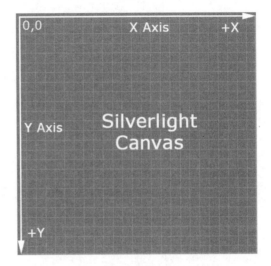

Figure 5-2. The Silverlight coordinate system uses a flipped y axis.

Vectors and velocity

When we talk about vectors in Silverlight, we're really talking about velocity and direction. Using vectors gives us a simple way to describe a direction and distance an object will be traveling over a given period of time, though time is not specifically a component of vector movement. For our purposes, the time component of code-based animations will be provided by a timer storyboard, as described in Chapter 4.

It's logical at this point to wonder what a vector is. Vectors describe motion by defining the size and direction of distance. Let's take a look at a one-dimensional (1D) vector. A 1D vector can be represented along the number line we all remember from school. We start at 0, and draw a line to the number 3, as Figure 5-3 shows. This is vector 3. It has direction and distance.

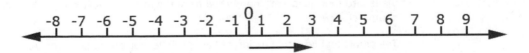

Figure 5-3. The vector 3

Let's draw another vector. This vector extends from 3 to 6, as shown in Figure 5-4. It is also vector 3. Vectors do not have a position—they simply describe direction and distance. Objects, however, do have a position, and when a vector is applied to an object, the object's position will be altered.

Vectors can be added—when the two vectors that were just drawn are added, we get vector 6. The speed of an object traveling along this new vector would be twice what it is for vector 3.

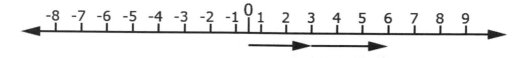

Figure 5-4. Vector 3, followed by vector 3 again

As you might expect, vectors that point to the left are defined with negative numbers. Negative and positive vectors can be added together just as two positive vectors are. For example, vector 5 + vector –3 = vector 2.

The terms that define a vector are referred to as **components**. This is because they are different from points, which define a position in 2D space. Vectors can begin anywhere, but their distance and direction do not change based on the location of the object to which they are applied.

As you can probably imagine, 2D vectors work in much the same way as 1D vectors, only they specify both an x and y component. The vector 5,5 is shown in Figure 5-5.

Figure 5-5. A 2D vector

The concept of making an object move in Silverlight by using vectors is relatively simple. Place the object on the canvas and start a timer. Each time the specified period of time passes, move the object by the distance defined in the vector. Let's take a look at an example of a 1D vector.

One-dimensional vector movement

In this project, we'll create some code that moves a simple ellipse particle across the screen using a vector for movement.

1. Open the **oneDimensionalVector** project to code along with this example. The project contains the main page XAML, as well as a user control called "particle" that is a simple yellow ellipse. The particle object also contains a storyboard called Move, which will be used as a timer to make the particle move.

2. Open the Page.xaml.cs file for editing. Before the Page() constructor, declare an instance of the particle object:

```
particle myParticle = new particle();
```

3. Inside the Page() constructor, after the InitializeComponent(); code, add the following code to position the particle instance on the main canvas:

```
Canvas.SetLeft(myParticle, 25);
Canvas.SetTop(myParticle, 300);
```

4. Follow that up with the code that adds the particle to the main canvas:

```
LayoutRoot.Children.Add(myParticle);
```

5. Finally, start the particle's timer. For this example, the particle has its own timer—if you're moving multiple objects on the screen, you would want to place the timer in the Page.xaml file and call it from there.

```
myParticle.Move.Begin();
```

6. Now that our particle is on the canvas, we need to add a bit of code in the code-behind for the particle. Open the particle.xaml.cs file for editing. Before the particle() constructor, declare a variable that will be used to store the vector:

```
private double VectorX = 2;
```

7. Next, add an event handler for the Completed event on the particle's storyboard timer inside the particle() constructor:

```
this.Move.Completed += new EventHandler(Move_Completed);
```

8. Following the closing curly brace of the particle() constructor, add the event handler function:

```
private void Move_Completed(object sender, EventArgs e)
{

}
```

9. The code inside the event handler function will run each time the timer completes. Add the following code inside the function, which will reposition the particle to its current location plus the value of the vector variable, and then restart the timer storyboard:

```
Canvas.SetLeft(this, Canvas.GetLeft(this) + VectorX);
this.Move.Begin();
```

Press F5 to compile and run the project. The particle will be drawn on the screen, and as the Move storyboard timer completes, the particle will move across the screen. The completed version of the code for this project is available in the **oneDimensionalVectorCompleted** project.

Two-dimensional vector movement

Working with a 2D vector uses the exact same technique, except that 2D vectors utilize variables for both the x and y components of the movement vector. Let's throw down some code that allows a user to fly a particle around the screen.

1. Open the **twoDimensionalVector** project to code along with the example. This project has a similar setup as the last one, except that the Move storyboard is now on the main page. There is also an instruction screen, which you won't need to worry about. If you run the project, you'll see I've already added code to take care of hiding the instruction pane when the OK button is clicked. We will just concentrate on placing the particle and making it move.

2. Open the particle.xaml.cs file for editing. In this file, we're going to take care of storing the particle's velocity, and also add some boundary-checking code. We'll start with the variable declarations, which go before the particle() constructor. The first two will store the x and y velocity, and the last two will store the height and width of the application.

```
public double VelocityX = 0;
public double VelocityY = 0;
public double rootWidth;
public double rootHeight;
```

3. Create a new public function called MoveParticle() after the closing curly brace of the particle() constructor. This function will be used to update the position of the particle on the screen, and check to see if the particle has gone beyond the boundaries of the application.

```
public void MoveParticle()
{

}
```

4. Inside the function, start with the following two lines of code. This will update the position of the particle on the main canvas.

```
Canvas.SetLeft(this, Canvas.GetLeft(this) + VelocityX);
Canvas.SetTop(this, Canvas.GetTop(this) + VelocityY);
```

5. Follow that up with the following two if...else statements that check to see if the particle has gone beyond the edge of the application. If it has, the particle is repositioned to the opposite side of the canvas.

```
if (Canvas.GetLeft(this) > this.rootWidth)
{
    Canvas.SetLeft(this, 0);
}
else if (Canvas.GetLeft(this) < 0)
{
    Canvas.SetLeft(this, this.rootWidth);
}

if (Canvas.GetTop(this) > this.rootHeight)
{
    Canvas.SetTop(this, 0);
}
else if (Canvas.GetTop(this) < 0)
{
    Canvas.SetTop(this, this.rootHeight);
}
```

6. Save the file, and open the Page.xaml.cs file for editing. Before the Page() constructor, declare an instance of the particle object:

```
particle myParticle = new particle();
```

7. Inside the Page() constructor, add the following code to position the particle at the center of the main canvas, and initialize the particle's rootWidth and rootHeight variables with the size of the main canvas before adding it to the main canvas:

```
Canvas.SetLeft(myParticle, LayoutRoot.Width / 2);
Canvas.SetTop(myParticle, LayoutRoot.Height / 2);
myParticle.rootWidth = LayoutRoot.Width;
myParticle.rootHeight = LayoutRoot.Height;
LayoutRoot.Children.Add(myParticle);
```

8. If you press F5 to compile and run the project at this point, you should see the instruction pane. Clicking OK closes the pane, and the particle should be positioned at the center of the main canvas. All that's left is to make it move. Begin by adding the following code inside the Page() constructor. This code will set up an event handler for the Completed event on the Move storyboard, and start the storyboard.

```
Move.Completed += new EventHandler(Move_Completed);
Move.Begin();
```

9. After the closing curly brace of the Page() constructor, create the Move_Completed() event handler function:

```
private void Move_Completed(object sender, EventArgs e)
{

}
```

10. Inside the event handler function, call the particle's MoveParticle() function, and restart the storyboard:

```
myParticle.MoveParticle();
Move.Begin();
```

11. If you run the project again, you'll see that the particle is on the canvas. Even though the storyboard timer is running, the particle isn't moving. This is because the velocity of the particle is still 0,0. We're going to control the particle's vector with the arrow keys. Start coding this up by adding an event handler inside the Page() constructor that listens for the KeyDown event on the main canvas:

```
this.KeyDown += new KeyEventHandler(Page_KeyDown);
```

12. After the closing curly brace of the Page() constructor, create the event handler function:

```
private void Page_KeyDown(object sender, KeyEventArgs e)
{

}
```

13. Inside the function, add the following switch() statement. This statement handles the up, down, left, or right arrow keys, and then updates the particle's velocity and the on-screen text appropriately.

```
switch (e.Key)
{
    case Key.Up:
        myParticle.VelocityY -= 1;
        msgYVector.Text = Convert.ToString(myParticle.VelocityY);
        break;
    case Key.Down:
        myParticle.VelocityY += 1;
        msgYVector.Text = Convert.ToString(myParticle.VelocityY);
        break;
    case Key.Left:
        myParticle.VelocityX -= 1;
        msgXVector.Text = Convert.ToString(myParticle.VelocityX);
        break;
    case Key.Right:
        myParticle.VelocityX += 1;
        msgXVector.Text = Convert.ToString(myParticle.VelocityX);
        break;
}
```

Press F5 to compile and run the program. As you press the arrow keys, the velocity of the particle will change, as will the motion of the particle on the canvas. The final code for this example can be found in the **twoDimensionalVectorCompleted** project. As you can see from this application, vectors are relatively easily manipulated as an application is running, and will affect the movement of the object to which they are applied in real time.

Changing the direction of a vector

When manipulating objects moving along vectors programmatically, you can change their direction by multiplying one or both components by –1. For example, given a positive vector of 3, the vector is effectively reversed when multiplied by –1. This will reverse the vector, as 3 × –1 = –3.

The multiplication of two negative numbers results in a positive, so a negative vector multiplied by –1 will become positive. For example, –3 × –1 = 3. This is a very useful way to reverse an object's direction completely, or just along a single axis if necessary.

Take a look at Figure 5-6, which shows the vector 5,5. In the image, you can also see what the effect would be on the vector if one or both of the vector components were reversed by multiplying the component by –1. The vectors shown are all the same length, but describe four different directions, all with a simple math operation.

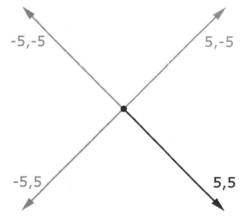

Figure 5-6. The effect of reversing the components of vector 5,5

So when might you find yourself needing to reverse vectors? The two most likely answers to that question are (1) based on user input, which you have already seen in the particle flight demonstration project, and (2) application boundaries, where an object should "bounce" if a wall is encountered in order to stay within the bounds of an application.

In the next example, we will implement directional changes using this technique. The directional changes are going to be fairly easy to implement, because we're going to invoke the law of reflection. The law of reflection deals with rays of light, and states that a ray of light will leave a surface at the same angle at which it approached, as illustrated in Figure 5-7. You may be more familiar with this when it is stated as "The angle of incidence is equal to the angle of reflection."

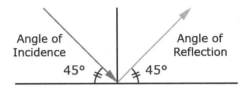

Angle of Incidence   45°   Angle of Reflection   45°

Figure 5-7. The law of reflection

Granted, we are not dealing with rays of light, but this is a common technique for boundary handling. If you view the law of reflection image in terms of vectors, the angle of incidence could be an approach vector of 5,5, while the angle of reflection is a vector of 5,–5. Let's modify the particle project to make the particle bounce back when it hits a boundary, rather than wrapping to the opposite side.

1. Open the **VectorBounce** project to code along with this example. We will be making all of our changes in the particle user object, so open the particle.xaml.cs file for editing.

2. Currently, the code to move the particle looks like the following listing. The particle is moved, and then tests are done to see if the particle has moved outside the boundaries of the application. If it has, it is placed on the opposite side of the canvas.

```
public void MoveParticle()
{
    Canvas.SetLeft(this, Canvas.GetLeft(this) + VelocityX);
    Canvas.SetTop(this, Canvas.GetTop(this) + VelocityY);

    if (Canvas.GetLeft(this) > this.rootWidth)
    {
        Canvas.SetLeft(this, 0);
    }
    else if (Canvas.GetLeft(this) < 0)
    {
        Canvas.SetLeft(this, this.rootWidth);
    }

    if (Canvas.GetTop(this) > this.rootHeight)
    {
        Canvas.SetTop(this, 0);
    }
    else if (Canvas.GetTop(this) < 0)
    {
        Canvas.SetTop(this, this.rootHeight);
    }
}
```

3. Remove the two if...else statements that currently do the boundary checking and wrap the particle to the other side of the Canvas. We'll add some new code to replace them. In order to make the particle bounce, there are really only two ways the vector needs to be manipulated.

The first is to reverse the x component. This happens if the particle hits either the left or right boundary of the application. The second is to reverse the y component. This happens if the particle hits either the top or bottom boundary of the application.

4. Start by doing a check for the right side boundary by taking the particle's left position plus its width, and test to see if it is greater than or equal to the application width, which is stored in the rootWidth variable. If so, we multiply the x vector by –1.

```
if (Canvas.GetLeft(this) + this.Width >= this.rootWidth)
{
    VelocityX *= -1;
}
```

5. To test for the left boundary, add an else clause to the if statement that tests to see if the particle's left property is less than or equal to 0. If so, the x vector is multiplied by –1.

```
else if (Canvas.GetLeft(this) <= 0)
{
    VelocityX *= -1;
}
```

It's important to remember that the position of the object may not always be exactly equal to the boundary width or height values, which is why we use >= or <=. If an object is at left position 10 with a vector of –3, its left position will be 10, 7, 4, 1, –2, and so on. Note that 0 is never hit, and we don't want to leave a hole there in the logic.

6. For the top and bottom boundaries, the idea is the same. We'll test the particle's top location plus its height to see if it is greater than or equal to the application height. If so, the y vector is multiplied by –1. Another check is done to see if the particle's top location is less than or equal to 0. If so, we multiply the y vector by –1.

```
if (Canvas.GetTop(this) + this.Height >= this.rootHeight)
{
    VelocityY *= -1;
}
else if (Canvas.GetTop(this) <= 0)
{
    VelocityY *= -1;
}
```

That's all it takes. Press F5 to compile and run the application, and watch the particle bounce around the application. You'll be seeing variations on this boundary checking code throughout the book. I put the code changes covered here into the **vectorBounceCompleted** project so you can examine them.

When you run the application, one of the things you may notice is that it can become difficult to control the particle when large velocity vectors are reached—the particle will cross the application rather quickly, reversing the vector. Once the vector is reversed, the key you need to use to change the direction also changes, so user control can become difficult. In these cases, it's a good idea to place an upper limit on the vector in order to define a maximum speed an object can take.

Now that you've seen how vectors can be used to make objects move in Silverlight, let's take a look at a classic implementation: a single-player paddle game.

Single-player paddle game

The classic paddle-and-ball game is a great example of how vectors can be used to move objects around the screen. It also demonstrates how you can begin putting different pieces together to create a more complete animation experience. In this section, I'll talk about how to create a simple single-player paddle game that uses drag-and-drop for the paddle, vectors for the movement of the ball, and boundary checking to keep the ball on the screen in front of the paddle.

1. Open the **PaddleGame** project to code along with this example. The project is partially stubbed out, and contains ball, paddle, and wall user objects. The ball object contains a 25✕25 white ellipse. The paddle object contains a filled rectangle with slightly rounded corners. The wall object contains a series of rectangles arranged to look like a red brick wall. There is a storyboard timer on the main page called Move, which will be used to create the action. If you run the project right now, you'll see the instruction page, which I've already coded up. You can click the Play button, and the pane will hide, but nothing further will happen.

2. We'll start by coding up the objects we will be controlling from the Page.xaml.cs file. The wall has no function other than providing a visual barrier, so there's nothing to do there. The paddle object already contains drag-and-drop code, and has no other behaviors, so there's nothing to do there either. That leaves the ball object. Open ball.xaml.cs for editing. Inside the ball control, we'll add some variables to store the application height, the velocity of the ball, and a random number generator, as well as a function to place the ball randomly on the game board. Start by declaring the following variables before the ball() constructor.

```
public double AppHeight;
public double VelocityX;
public double VelocityY;
private Random rng = new Random();
```

3. After the closing curly brace of the ball() constructor, create a publicly accessible function called init(). This code will be called each time the ball needs to be placed on the screen—at the beginning of the game and each time it gets by the paddle.

```
public void init()
{

}
```

4. Inside the function, add the following code to initialize the velocity for the ball. The x velocity will always be 5, and the y velocity will be a random number between 1 and 8.

```
VelocityX = 5;
VelocityY = rng.Next(1, 8);
```

5. Finish up the init() function with the following two lines. This will position the ball 65 pixels from the left of the screen, and at a random vertical location.

```
Canvas.SetLeft(this, 65);
Canvas.SetTop(this, rng.Next(Convert.ToInt16(this.Height),
                             Convert.ToInt16(AppHeight -
                             this.Height)));
```

6. Save the file and open Page.xaml.cs for editing. At the moment, nothing is here except for the instruction pane messaging. Let's add some elements to the game board. Start by declaring an instance of the ball, the paddle, and the wall object before the Page() constructor. We're also going to be tracking "lives," so declare an integer to store that value.

    ```
    private paddle gamePaddle = new paddle();
    private wall bricks = new wall();
    private ball gameBall = new ball();
    private int lives = 3;
    ```

7. Inside the Page() constructor, initialize the paddle object by setting its position on the main canvas and assigning a value to the rootHeight variable we created in the object. We'll hide it until it's needed, so set the Visibility to Collapsed before adding the object to the gameElements canvas:

    ```
    gamePaddle.SetValue(Canvas.LeftProperty, 44.00);
    gamePaddle.SetValue(Canvas.TopProperty, 92.00);
    gamePaddle.rootHeight = LayoutRoot.Height;
    gamePaddle.Visibility = Visibility.Collapsed;
    gameElements.Children.Add(gamePaddle);
    ```

8. Follow that up with code that positions the bricks object and adds it to the gameElements canvas:

    ```
    bricks.SetValue(Canvas.LeftProperty, 735.00);
    bricks.SetValue(Canvas.TopProperty, -60.00);
    gameElements.Children.Add(bricks);
    ```

9. Next, we'll hide the ball, set the ball's AppHeight variable, and add it to the gameElements canvas. We won't need to worry about positioning the ball since the init() function we wrote will do that for us when called.

    ```
    gameBall.Visibility = Visibility.Collapsed;
    gameBall.AppHeight = LayoutRoot.Height;
    gameElements.Children.Add(gameBall);
    ```

10. If you look at the event handlers set up inside the Page() constructor, you'll see one for the Click event on the Play button, and one for the Completed event of the hideMessages storyboard. The flow of the program is that it loads and displays the instruction pane with the Play button. The Play button is clicked, which plays the hideMessages storyboard in order to hide the instruction pane. Once that storyboard is completed, control goes to the hideMessages_Completed() function, which is coded but currently empty.

    So what needs to happen there? First, the instruction pane is gone, so we'll show the ball and paddle. Next, we'll initialize the ball by calling the init() function. Finally, we'll start the timer storyboard to get everything moving.

    ```
    gameBall.Visibility = Visibility.Visible;
    gamePaddle.Visibility = Visibility.Visible;
    gameBall.init();
    Move.Begin();
    ```

11. If you run the application, you'll see the instruction pane disappear when the button is clicked, and the ball and paddle show up, but nothing happens. You started the storyboard in step 10—what's happening? The storyboard runs, but only for one tick. We need to set up an event handler that keeps it going. Inside the Page() constructor, add an event handler for the Completed event on the Move storyboard:

```
Move.Completed += new EventHandler(Move_Completed);
```

12. Add the Move_Completed() event handler function after the closing curly brace of the Page() constructor. This is where all of the action will take place.

```
private void Move_Completed(object sender, EventArgs e)
{

}
```

13. Inside the function, update the position of the ball, and restart the timer:

```
Canvas.SetLeft(gameBall, Canvas.GetLeft(gameBall)
            + gameBall.VelocityX);
Canvas.SetTop(gameBall, Canvas.GetTop(gameBall) + gameBall.VelocityY);

Move.Begin();
```

14. Run the application again, and this time, when you click the Play button, the ball will move. In fact, it keeps moving until it goes right off the screen. Let's add some boundary checks for the top and bottom of the application. In the Move_Completed() function, remove the code that starts the timer, and add the following if...else statement. This will test for the top and bottom of the application, just as with the particle project. If the ball encounters either, the y velocity is reversed.

```
if (Canvas.GetTop(gameBall) <= 0)
{
    Canvas.SetTop(gameBall, 0);
    gameBall.VelocityY *= -1;
}
else if (Canvas.GetTop(gameBall) + gameBall.Height
        >= LayoutRoot.Height)
{
    Canvas.SetTop(gameBall, LayoutRoot.Height - gameBall.Height);
    gameBall.VelocityY *= -1;
}
```

15. Next, we'll test for the right side of the application, which in this case is really the left side of the bricks object. If the bricks are encountered, the x velocity of the ball is reversed.

```
if (Canvas.GetLeft(gameBall) + gameBall.Width
    >= Canvas.GetLeft(bricks))
{
    Canvas.SetLeft(gameBall, Canvas.GetLeft(bricks) - gameBall.Width);
    gameBall.VelocityX *= -1;
}
```

16. Now we have the ball bouncing off the top and bottom of the application, and the bricks along the right. We want to test to see if the ball hit the paddle. That starts out with an if statement that checks to see if the ball is inside the upper and lower bounds of the paddle:

```
if (Canvas.GetTop(gameBall) >= Canvas.GetTop(gamePaddle)
    && Canvas.GetTop(gameBall) <= Canvas.GetTop(gamePaddle) +
    gamePaddle.Height)
{

}
```

17. Inside of the if statement goes another if statement. This one tests to see if the paddle and ball are contacting. If they are, the x velocity of the ball is reversed.

```
if (Canvas.GetLeft(gameBall) <= Canvas.GetLeft(gamePaddle)
    + gamePaddle.Width && Canvas.GetLeft(gameBall)
    >= Canvas.GetLeft(gamePaddle))
{
    gameBall.VelocityX *= -1;
}
```

18. We are recognizing the game boundaries and the paddle. Now we need to figure out if the ball gets by the paddle, and if so, what we'll do about it. The following if statement checks to see if the ball makes it all the way off the screen. If so, the timer will be stopped, and we'll call a function called nextBall() (which we'll create in a moment). If the ball doesn't make it off the screen, then the timer will be restarted.

```
if (Canvas.GetLeft(gameBall) <= -gameBall.Width)
{
    Move.Stop();
    nextBall();
}
else
{
    Move.Begin();
}
```

19. Create the nextBall() function after the closing curly brace of the Move_Completed() function. The ball has made it off the game board, so this is where we'll put our reaction code:

```
private void nextBall()
{

}
```

20. Inside the function, start out by hiding the ball and paddle:

```
gameBall.Visibility = Visibility.Collapsed;
gamePaddle.Visibility = Visibility.Collapsed;
```

21. Next, decrement the number of lives left and update the messaging on the screen:

```
lives -= 1;
msgRemaining.Text = "Balls Remaining: " + lives;
```

22. Next, add some code to taunt the player with a different message each time they lose a life. The messages will show up on the instruction pane. If a player loses all three lives (zero remaining), the Play button on the instruction pane will be hidden so they cannot enter back into the game loop.

```
switch (lives)
{
    case 2:
        msgGameText.Text = "Swing and a miss...";
        break;
    case 1:
        msgGameText.Text = "One ball left!";
        break;
    case 0:
        msgGameText.Text = "Game Over.";
        btnPlay.Visibility = Visibility.Collapsed;
        break;
}
```

23. The function finishes up by starting the showMessages storyboard, which is the opposite of hideMessages. At this point, the messaging has updated, the pane is visible, and the game is awaiting user input to go back into the game loop.

```
showMessages.Begin();
```

This completes the code for the single-player paddle game. Run the application and test it out. Figure 5-8 shows the game in action.

Figure 5-8. A single-player paddle game in action

One of the things this version of the game does *not* do is allow the paddle to influence the direction of the ball. The ball simply bounces off the paddle in the opposite direction based on our application of the law of reflection. It would be nice to add a bit of code so that the direction the paddle is moving when the ball hits it will influence the ball's direction. To do this, we need a way to determine a movement vector for the paddle. Luckily, this just takes a few lines of code.

24. Open the paddle.xaml.cs code-behind for editing. We'll need a couple of variables: one for the old position of the paddle and one for the current position of the paddle. Add these variables above the paddle() constructor:

```
private double oldY;
private double posY;
```

25. We'll also need a publicly accessible double to hold the paddle's y velocity:

```
public double paddleYVelocity;
```

26. Inside the paddle_MouseMove() event handler code for the paddle, we'll keep track of where the paddle was and where it is now. The difference between the two will give us the magnitude of the movement, and we'll dampen that a bit by dividing it in half. The following code goes at the top of the if statement in the event handler:

```
oldY = posY;
posY = e.GetPosition(null).Y;
paddleYVelocity = (posY - oldY) / 2;
```

27. Now we just add a bit of code to the paddle hit check in the page.xaml.cs code-behind file. The code shown in bold takes the calculated velocity of the paddle and adds it to the y component of the ball when it hits the paddle.

```
if (Canvas.GetLeft(gameBall) <=
    Canvas.GetLeft(gamePaddle) + gamePaddle.Width &&
    Canvas.GetLeft(gameBall) >= Canvas.GetLeft(gamePaddle))
{
    gameBall.VelocityX *= -1;
    gameBall.VelocityY += gamePaddle.paddleYVelocity;
}
```

Now when the game runs, the direction and speed of the paddle will affect the reflected angle the ball travels after hitting the paddle.

All of the code for this project is available in the **PaddleGameCompleted** project. It compiles into a tidy little 8K package.

Think about some of the ways you could modify the program. Can you make the ball speed up the longer it is on the screen? What about making each successive level more difficult by making the paddle smaller?

Dressing up the game

This game helps highlight one of the strengths in using XAML for the objects. Each object—the paddle, ball, and wall—is contained within its own canvas, in its own user control. That offers a lot of flexibility because you could very easily go into the XAML file for each object and change the look of the object, or change the type of object being used altogether, and simply recompile the game to get a version that looks completely different.

For example, if you had a rendered image of a wall that you wanted to use, you could replace the entire set of rectangles that comprise the wall object and the game would still act the same. This is because the boundary location values being used are based upon the positions of the canvases that contain the objects, not the objects themselves. The same would be the case if you elected to use an animated ball in the game. Take a bit of time to experiment with changes to the look and feel of the game so you can see how easy the XAML structure makes it to edit the game pieces.

Code-controlled vectors

Let's take a look at an application of vector movement that you will probably find more interesting. We'll use some vectors to move a ball object around the screen, but add some interactivity by allowing the user to drag the ball, and add some interest by applying the force of gravity to the ball.

1. To code along with this example, open the **gravityBall** project—the project contains the main Page.xaml file, which provides a background gradient color, and a ball.xaml object, which is a simple red ellipse. The ball object contains drag-and-drop code as well as a storyboard timer called Move.

2. Begin in the Page.xaml.cs file. Before the Page() constructor, declare an instance of the ball object:

```
private ball redBall = new ball();
```

3. Inside the Page() constructor, position the ball and add it to the main canvas:

```
Canvas.SetLeft(redBall, 100);
Canvas.SetTop(redBall, 100);
LayoutRoot.Children.Add(redBall);
```

4. Run the application and see that you can use the mouse to drag the ball around the screen and release it. What we are going to do now is add some code to the ball.xaml.cs file so that when the mouse button is released following a drag operation, the ball is affected by the force of gravity. Start with publicly accessible variables to store the gravity, width, and height properties of the main application.

```
public double Gravity;
public double appHeight;
public double appWidth;
```

5. Follow those up with private variables to store the ball's position and velocity:

```
private Point ballPosition;
private double VelocityX = 0;
private double VelocityY = 0;
```

6. Next, we'll add some code to the ball_MouseLeftButtonDown() event handler so that when the mouse button is pressed to begin a drag operation, the velocity variables used to move the ball are set to 0. The lines to add to the function are shown in bold in the following listing.

```
private void ball_MouseLeftButtonDown(object sender,
                                      MouseButtonEventArgs e)
{
    FrameworkElement item = sender as FrameworkElement;
    mousePosition = e.GetPosition(null);
    isMouseCaptured = true;
    item.CaptureMouse();
    item.Cursor = Cursors.Hand;

    VelocityX = 0;
    VelocityY = 0;
}
```

7. In the ball_MouseLeftButtonUp() event handler, add code to store the current position of the ball object, and begin the Move storyboard:

```
private void ball_MouseLeftButtonUp(object sender,
                                    MouseButtonEventArgs e)
{
    FrameworkElement item = sender as FrameworkElement;
    isMouseCaptured = false;
    item.ReleaseMouseCapture();
    mousePosition.X = mousePosition.Y = 0;
    item.Cursor = null;

    ballPosition.X = Canvas.GetLeft(this);
    ballPosition.Y = Canvas.GetTop(this);

    Move.Begin();
}
```

8. To keep the ball moving, add an event handler for the Completed event on the Move storyboard in the ball() constructor:

```
Move.Completed += new EventHandler(Move_Completed);
```

9. Create the event handler function after the closing curly brace of the ball() constructor. Inside the function, add code to add the gravity constant to the current y velocity vector of the ball object, and then update the values stored in the ballPosition variable. After that, the position of the ball can be updated on the screen and the storyboard restarted. This will cause the ball to accelerate as it falls.

```
private void Move_Completed(object sender, EventArgs e)
{
    VelocityY += Gravity;

    ballPosition.X += VelocityX;
    ballPosition.Y += VelocityY;
```

```
        Canvas.SetLeft(this, ballPosition.X);
        Canvas.SetTop(this, ballPosition.Y);

        Move.Begin();
    }
```

10. While the code you've added will move the ball, we haven't yet assigned a value to the Gravity variable in this object. Open the Page.xaml.cs file and declare a variable for gravity before the Page() constructor.

```
private double globalGravity = .6;
```

11. Inside the Page() constructor, initialize the Gravity value of the ball object with the value of the globalGravity variable you just declared:

```
redBall.Gravity = globalGravity;
```

Run the program and take a look at it. When the program runs, the ball is drawn on the screen and can be dragged around. When the mouse is released, gravity takes over and the ball falls . . . and keeps falling, right out of the application!

12. We already talked about how to reverse the vector along which an object is traveling. For the ball, we're trying to emulate what a real ball does when it bounces—each successive bounce a ball makes is going to be a bit lower than the previous bounce. In our case, we're going to declare a variable to diminish the bounces, called restitution, which we will set to .6. This code goes inside the ball.xaml.cs file, before the ball() constructor:

```
private double restitution = .6;
```

13. Back in step 4, we added variables in the ball.xaml.cs file called appHeight and appWidth, which will be used to store the height and width of the application. Before we can add in our boundary checks, we need to initialize these variables. In the Page() constructor inside the Page.xaml.cs file, add the following two bold lines of code to the section where the ball is initialized:

```
Canvas.SetLeft(redBall, 100);
Canvas.SetTop(redBall, 100);
redBall.Gravity = globalGravity;
redBall.appWidth = LayoutRoot.Width;
redBall.appHeight = LayoutRoot.Height;
LayoutRoot.Children.Add(redBall);
```

14. Now that the ball object is aware of the size of the application, we can start doing boundary checking. Inside the Move_Completed() event handler in the ball.xaml.cs file, add the following bold code to check for the top and bottom boundaries. Notice that the velocity is being reversed by multiplying it not by −1, but by the value of our restitution variable, .6. This won't have an obvious effect when the ball bounces off the top of the application because it is being drawn down by gravity, but it will make a difference when the ball hits the bottom and bounces up, as it will bounce only a portion of the distance it fell.

```
private void Move_Completed(object sender, EventArgs e)
{
    VelocityY += Gravity;

    ballPosition.X += VelocityX;
    ballPosition.Y += VelocityY;

    if (ballPosition.Y <= 0)
    {
        ballPosition.Y = 0;
        VelocityY *= -restitution;
    }

    else if ((ballPosition.Y + this.Height) >= appHeight)
    {
        ballPosition.Y = appHeight - this.Height;
        VelocityY *= -restitution;
    }

    Canvas.SetLeft(this, ballPosition.X);
    Canvas.SetTop(this, ballPosition.Y);

    Move.Begin();
}
```

15. Follow that code up with the boundary-checking code for the right and left sides of the application:

```
else if ((ballPosition.X + this.Width) >= appWidth)
{
    ballPosition.X = appWidth - this.Width;
    VelocityX *= -restitution;
}

else if (ballPosition.X <= 0)
{
    ballPosition.X = 0;
    VelocityX *= -restitution;
}
```

16. Now when the application runs, the ball can be dragged, and when released, will drop straight down and bounce in a fairly realistic fashion until it comes to rest. Trying to drag the ball again at this point will cause the ball to snap back to its resting location, because the storyboard that makes the ball drop is still running. To correct this, add code to the ball_MouseLeftButtonDown() event handler that will stop the storyboard when the mouse button is pressed. The application will then permit repeated dragging and dropping of the ball, though you will still need to drag the ball straight up to avoid the lower boundary-checking code:

```
Move.Stop();
```

17. So far, our application is looking pretty good. One of the things that you may notice is that the ball always releases straight down, though. We're going to add some code that allows us to throw the ball around the application. In order to do this, we're going to need to capture the x and y velocity components of the mouse as the ball is dragged around the screen. To store the mouse velocity, add a Point variable at the top of the ball.xaml.cs file to store the last position of the mouse:

```
private Point oldMouse;
```

18. In the ball_MouseMove() event handler code, add the following bold code to store the last known mouse position:

```
if (isMouseCaptured)
{
    oldMouse.X = mousePosition.X;
    oldMouse.Y = mousePosition.Y;

    // Calculate the current position of the object.
    double deltaV = e.GetPosition(null).Y - mousePosition.Y;
    double deltaH = e.GetPosition(null).X - mousePosition.X;
    double newTop = deltaV + Canvas.GetTop(item);
    double newLeft = deltaH + Canvas.GetLeft(item);

    // Set new position of object.
    Canvas.SetTop(this, newTop);
    Canvas.SetLeft(this, newLeft);

    // Update position global variables.
    mousePosition = e.GetPosition(null);
}
```

19. Now that we have the variable and we're storing the position of the mouse as it drags, we can calculate and x and y velocity from the movement and speed of the mouse. This is done at the very bottom of the if statement inside the ball_MouseMove() event handler.

```
if (isMouseCaptured)
{
    oldMouse.X = mousePosition.X;
    oldMouse.Y = mousePosition.Y;

    // Calculate the current position of the object.
    double deltaV = e.GetPosition(null).Y - mousePosition.Y;
    double deltaH = e.GetPosition(null).X - mousePosition.X;
    double newTop = deltaV + Canvas.GetTop(item);
    double newLeft = deltaH + Canvas.GetLeft(item);

    // Set new position of object.
    Canvas.SetTop(this, newTop);
    Canvas.SetLeft(this, newLeft);

    // Update position global variables.
    mousePosition = e.GetPosition(null);
```

```
VelocityX = (mousePosition.X - oldMouse.X) / 2;
VelocityY = (mousePosition.Y - oldMouse.Y) / 2;
}
```

Does this code look familiar? It should—we used the same technique for the y component in the paddle game to get the direction and speed of the paddle to influence the direction the ball traveled when hit.

20. Run the application again and check it out. We've made only a few small changes, and now we can use the mouse to drag the ball and throw it around the screen. It will bounce off of the application boundaries until it no longer bounces. It will then continue to roll along the base of the application until it goes beyond either the left or right side of the application. This is because the ball no longer has any y velocity, but does still have an x velocity. No friction has been applied to slow the ball after it has stopped bouncing. Two small lines of code will correct this. The first is a variable declared in the ball.xaml.cs file that will contain a friction value:

```
private double friction = .9;
```

21. The second is a bit of code to slow the ball down when it comes in contact with the ground in our application. This code goes into the logic that tests for the bottom of the application, and simply multiplies the x velocity vector of the ball by the friction value. This will have little to no effect on the normal bounce action for the ball when the ball is only in momentary contact with the boundary, but will bring the ball to a stop when it is no longer bouncing.

```
else if ((ballPosition.Y + this.Height) >= appHeight)
{
    ballPosition.Y = appHeight - this.Height;
    VelocityY *= -restitution;
    VelocityX *= friction;
}
```

At this point, there are a couple of holes in the logic for the application that we need to plug. If you played with the application long enough, you would probably find them yourself, but I will save you a little bit of time. The holes in the logic are quite literally "corner cases." In each of the application's four corners, the ball can be made to contact two boundaries at once. For example, if the ball is rolling along the bottom boundary and also touches one of the sides, it will be permitted to continue to roll off the screen. You may have seen this before adding the friction code. This is because the logic tests for one boundary or the other, but not both.

While the situation exists for all four corners, we really only need to worry about correcting the bottom two for this application, as it is highly unlikely that the ball will touch the top boundary and one of the sides at the same time. Figure 5-9 illustrates the corner cases.

Figure 5-9. If the ball touches the lower boundary of the application at the same time it touches one of the sides, the boundary-checking logic will allow the ball to roll off the screen.

171

22. To fix these holes, we can add two more checks in the Completed event handler code for the storyboard. These two checks test for the following conditions: (1) if the ball is touching the bottom and right boundaries at the same time, and (2) if the ball is touching the bottom and left boundaries at the same time.

```
// test corners
if (ballPosition.Y + this.Height >= appHeight &&
    (ballPosition.X + this.Width) >= appWidth)
{
    ballPosition.X = appWidth - (this.Width + 1);
}

if (ballPosition.Y + this.Height >= appHeight && ballPosition.X <= 0)
{
    ballPosition.X = 0;
    VelocityX *= -restitution;
}
```

That's all it takes to correct the problem with the corners. The ball will no longer be permitted to leave the application even if it is contacting the lower boundary and one of the side boundaries at the same time.

Now we can turn our attention to polishing the application. One more bit of functionality we would like to add is to disallow the ball object from going off the screen while being dragged. This means that in the ball_MouseMove() event handler, we need to add a bit of code that checks to see if the ball is outside of the boundaries, and if it is, start the Move storyboard.

23. Because each boundary check runs the same code, we'll create a function to do the dirty work for us. The following function is a pared-down version of the code in the ball_ MouseLeftButtonUp() function. Go ahead and add this function to the application. The code inside the function basically releases the mouse capture, updates the ballPosition variables, and starts the timer so that the ball's movement is then under the control of the application.

```
private void outOfBounds(FrameworkElement item)
{
    isMouseCaptured = false;
    item.ReleaseMouseCapture();
    item.Cursor = null;
    ballPosition.X = Canvas.GetLeft(this);
    ballPosition.Y = Canvas.GetTop(this);
    Move.Begin();
}
```

24. With that function in place, we can update the ball_MouseMove() event handler to check for the boundaries while dragging, and call the outOfBounds() function if one is encountered. Once this code is in place, test it out—run the program, grab the ball, and drag the mouse off the canvas. The ball should bounce off of the boundary and fall.

```
if (isMouseCaptured)
{
    oldMouse.X = mousePosition.X;
    oldMouse.Y = mousePosition.Y;

    // Calculate the current position of the object.
    double deltaV = e.GetPosition(null).Y - mousePosition.Y;
    double deltaH = e.GetPosition(null).X - mousePosition.X;
    double newTop = deltaV + Canvas.GetTop(item);
    double newLeft = deltaH + Canvas.GetLeft(item);

    // Set new position of object.
    Canvas.SetTop(this, newTop);
    Canvas.SetLeft(this, newLeft);

    // check for left and top boundary
    if (Canvas.GetLeft(this) < 0 || Canvas.GetTop(this) < 0)
    {
        outOfBounds(item);
    }

    // check for right and bottom boundaries
    if (Canvas.GetLeft(this) + this.Width >= appWidth)
    {
        outOfBounds(item);
    }
    if (Canvas.GetTop(this) + this.Height >= appHeight)
    {
        outOfBounds(item);
    }

    // Update position global variables.
    mousePosition - e.GetPosition(null);

    VelocityX = (mousePosition.X - oldMouse.X) / 2;
    VelocityY = (mousePosition.Y - oldMouse.Y) / 2;
}
```

25. We're going to make one final tweak to this program before calling it done. To have a little bit of fun with it, we will add a slider to the Page.xaml file that will allow a user to manipulate the gravity value in real time. At the bottom of the Page.xaml file, just above the closing Canvas tag, add the following code to create a slider and associated label:

```
<Slider Width="150" Canvas.Top="38" Canvas.Left="12"
        x:Name="gravitySlider"/>
<TextBlock Text="Gravity: " TextWrapping="Wrap" Canvas.Left="14"
        Canvas.Top="10" x:Name="msgGravity"/>
```

26. Inside the Page() constructor in the Page.xaml.cs file, set the minimum, maximum, and initial values for the slider object. We'll also update the label for the slider to indicate the current gravity value being used.

```
gravitySlider.Minimum = 0;
gravitySlider.Maximum = 2;
gravitySlider.Value = globalGravity;
msgGravity.Text = "Gravity: " + globalGravity;
```

27. Following that code, add an event listener for the ValueChanged event of the slider:

```
gravitySlider.ValueChanged +=
    new RoutedPropertyChangedEventHandler<double>➡
    (gravitySlider_ValueChanged);
```

28. Add an event handler function. Inside the function, the code will change the globalGravity value, update the value of the variable in the ball object, and update the text on the screen as the slider is manipulated.

```
private void gravitySlider_ValueChanged➡
    (object sender, RoutedPropertyChangedEventArgs<double> e)
{
    globalGravity = gravitySlider.Value;
    redBall.Gravity = globalGravity;
    msgGravity.Text = "Gravity: " + globalGravity.ToString("0.00");
}
```

That's it! Now when the application runs, you can manipulate the gravity value in real time via the slider control. Set the gravity low and throw the ball, and crank up the gravity while the ball is arcing near the top of the application to see it in action.

All of the code shown here is available in the **gravityBallCompleted** project. Once again, the application is really small—it compiles into a package that is only about 7K. It's also pretty flexible. All the behavior for the ball is stored inside the ball user control, meaning you could easily add a second ball to the application if you wanted. You need only declare a second instance of the ball object, and add it to the LayoutRoot of Page.xaml.

Vectors and frame-based animations

In Chapter 4, we talked about different ways to do frame-based animation in Silverlight. Regardless of which method you choose, objects that are animated with a series of frames can use vector motion, too. For instance, one of the examples we discussed was a duck flapping its wings. Once you have the duck flap animation going, you still need a way to move the object on the screen. This would be done via vectors.

In this example, we'll take a look at a frame-based animation that is a little more complex than the duck example. We will be working with a monkey walk cycle that spans 12 frames, each of which is shown in the following series of illustrations.

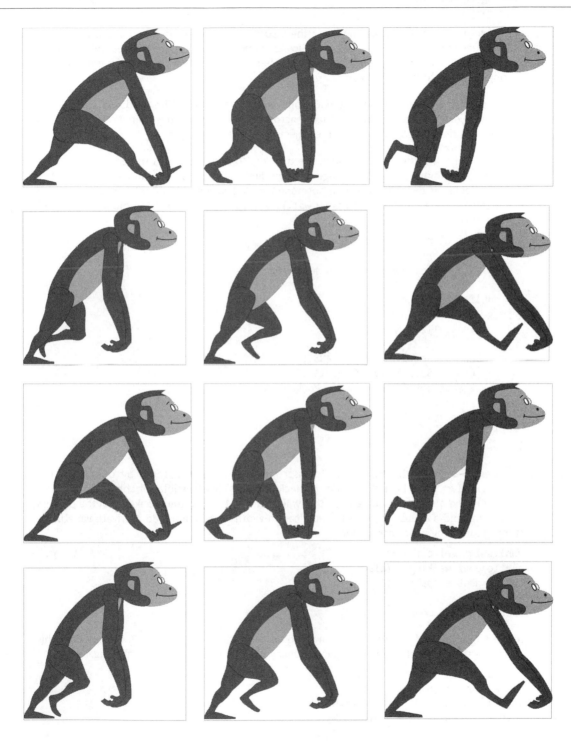

For this example, the monkey was animated via the Visual State Manager in Blend and a storyboard timer that switches frames every 5 milliseconds. Slower frame switching still preserves the illusion of animation, but you will find that you need to balance between the speed of the animation and the speed the object travels across the screen.

For an object such as a duck that is flying, you won't notice it as much. With an object such as our monkey, the figure may have a tendency to "skate" across the screen while the animation plays. This is why the storyboard timing and x velocity of the object need to be managed.

1. To code along with this example, open the **monkeyWalk** project. This project contains a bit of code to get things going. In the Page.xaml.cs file, an instance of the monkey user control called myMonkey is declared. It is then positioned, added to the LayoutRoot Canvas, and made to start walking via the storyboard timer walkTimer, which is located in the monkey user control file.

```
public partial class Page : UserControl
{
    private monkey myMonkey = new monkey();

    public Page()
    {
        InitializeComponent();

        Canvas.SetTop(myMonkey, 488);
        Canvas.SetLeft(myMonkey, 150);
        LayoutRoot.Children.Add(myMonkey);

        myMonkey.walkTimer.Begin();
    }
}
```

2. In order to augment this application for user input, we'll need to add a bit of code to the monkey.xaml.cs code-behind file. Start by declaring publicly accessible variables to store the x velocity of the monkey, a Boolean flag that will be tested to see if the monkey is in the process of walking, and a double to store the application width. In addition, add a private variable to store the monkey's current position.

```
public int velocityX = 1;
public bool walking = false;
public double appWidth;

private double monkeyPosition;
```

3. In the Page.xaml.cs file, add the following bold code shown to the Page() constructor. This code sets the appWidth property of the myMonkey user control for bounds checking.

```
Canvas.SetTop(myMonkey, 488);
Canvas.SetLeft(myMonkey, 150);
myMonkey.appWidth = LayoutRoot.Width;
LayoutRoot.Children.Add(myMonkey);
```

4. At the top of the `walkTimer_Completed()` event handler, add code to change the walking flag to true, and update the value of the `monkeyPosition` variable:

```
this.walking = true;
monkeyPosition = Canvas.GetLeft(this);
```

5. After the closing curly brace of the `switch()` statement, add a line of code to update the location of the monkey object on the screen:

```
Canvas.SetLeft(this, monkeyPosition += velocityX);
```

6. If you run the project at this point, the monkey will be drawn on the screen and animated, and will move very slowly to the right. We want the monkey to walk based on user input, so let's modify the `Page.xaml.cs` file to add this capability. Start by removing the line of code in the `Page()` method that causes the monkey animation to begin:

```
myMonkey.walkTimer.Begin();
```

7. Instead of beginning on its own, we will make the animation begin when a key is pressed. To do this, add a KeyDown event to the `Page()` constructor:

```
this.KeyDown += new KeyEventHandler(Page_KeyDown);
```

8. Create the `Page_KeyDown()` event handler function:

```
private void Page_KeyDown(object sender, KeyEventArgs e)
{

}
```

9. When the left or right arrow keys are pressed, the monkey will be made to move in the direction of the arrow key that was pressed. The walking flag you just added to the monkey code-behind will be used to determine if the monkey is already moving. If it is not, the timer that moves the monkey through its frame poses is started. Of note is the way the monkey is turned if the left arrow key is pressed—it is scaled to −1 along the x axis, effectively flipping the object. Because the scaling is applied to the canvas that contains all of the poses for the monkey, all of the poses inside that canvas are reversed as well. All of this functionality is handled by placing the following `switch()` statement inside the `Page_KeyDown()` event handler function:

```
switch (e.Key)
{
    case Key.Left:
        if (!myMonkey.walking) myMonkey.walkTimer.Begin();
        myMonkey.monkeyScale.ScaleX = -1;
        break;

    case Key.Right:
        if (!myMonkey.walking) myMonkey.walkTimer.Begin();
        myMonkey.monkeyScale.ScaleX = 1;
        break;
}
```

10. Run the application. After clicking the canvas area, you will be able to use the arrow keys to control the direction in which the monkey points, but not the direction in which it moves. To add this functionality, we're going to add a variable called strideLength to the Page.xaml.cs file:

```
private int strideLength = 8;
```

11. The reason why a variable is being used is because movements to the left and right both need access to the value, and based on the object being animated, it may take a little bit of tweaking to get the value set just right. It's much easier to change a single value than to hunt through code for multiple instances of a number. The strideLength value will be assigned to the x velocity value of the monkey so that the monkey will move 8 pixels with each completion cycle of the storyboard timer. To change direction and move the monkey to the left, a negative strideLength value is assigned to the x velocity vector of the object. To move to the right, the strideLength value is assigned to the x velocity of the monkey as-is. Update the switch() statement with the two bold lines in the following code:

```
switch (e.Key)
{
    case Key.Left:
        if (!myMonkey.walking) myMonkey.walkTimer.Begin();
        myMonkey.monkeyScale.ScaleX = -1;
        myMonkey.velocityX = -strideLength;
        break;

    case Key.Right:
        if (!myMonkey.walking) myMonkey.walkTimer.Begin();
        myMonkey.monkeyScale.ScaleX = 1;
        myMonkey.velocityX = strideLength;
        break;
}
```

In the code, each time the storyboard completes, the monkey is moved the distance defined by the strideLength variable. Remember that depending upon your object's motion, you may end up needing to use a larger or smaller value. The idea is to get a number that works well in order to keep the object from looking as though it is skating across the screen.

After clicking the application to get focus, you will be able to control the monkey with the left and right arrows, as shown in Figure 5-10.

The problem is that given the chance, the monkey will walk right off the edge of the screen. Once again, we will need to add a bit of code to control where our object is allowed to travel. In this case, if the left or right edge is encountered, we want to stop the walk cycle timer in order to stop the monkey from advancing. This code is added in the monkey.xaml.cs code-behind file, near the bottom of the walkTimer_Completed() event handler code.

12. Remove the code that updates the monkey's position:

```
Canvas.SetLeft(this, monkeyPosition += velocityX);
```

Figure 5-10. Scaling an object to −1 along the x axis makes it possible to reverse a frame-based object's direction.

13. Add an `if...else` statement to test for the left and right sides of the application. In this example, we're modifying the edge values by 1 to account for the border around the main canvas.

```
if (Canvas.GetLeft(this) <= 1)
{
    Canvas.SetLeft(this, 1);
    walkTimer.Stop();
}
else if (Canvas.GetLeft(this) + this.Width > appWidth - 1)
{
    Canvas.SetLeft(this, appWidth - this.Width);
    walkTimer.Stop();
}
```

14. Next, wrap the existing Visual State Manager code in an `else` statement:

```
else
{
    VisualStateManager.GoToState(this, whichState, false);
    frame += 1;
    if (frame > 12) frame = 1;
}
```

15. Finish up by adding the following line of code shown in bold back in to update the monkey's position on the screen. This code will be executed if no boundary is encountered.

```
else
{
    Canvas.SetLeft(this, monkeyPosition += velocityX);
    VisualStateManager.GoToState(this, whichState, false);
    frame += 1;
    if (frame > 12) frame = 1;
}
```

Finally, the last line of the function is the existing code that restarted the walkTimer. Notice that the code to restart the timer is going to run even if the code to stop the timer due to a boundary is encountered. This is deliberate, because the application is still "live" and awaiting input. If the walkTimer were started inside the else clause in the preceding code, when a boundary was reached, pressing the opposite key would turn the object, but it would stick to the wall since the boundary checks are still valid conditions. The final code for the function is shown in the following listing:

```
private void walkTimer_Completed(object sender, EventArgs e)
{
    this.walking = true;
    monkeyPosition = Canvas.GetLeft(this);

    switch (frame)
    {
        case 1:
            whichState = "pose_1";
            break;
        case 2:
            whichState = "pose_2";
            break;
        case 3:
            whichState = "pose_3";
            break;
        case 4:
            whichState = "pose_4";
            break;
        case 5:
            whichState = "pose_5";
            break;
        case 6:
            whichState = "pose_6";
            break;
        case 7:
            whichState = "pose_7";
            break;
        case 8:
            whichState = "pose_8";
            break;
```

```
        case 9:
            whichState = "pose_9";
            break;
        case 10:
            whichState = "pose_10";
            break;
        case 11:
            whichState = "pose_11";
            break;
        case 12:
            whichState = "pose_12";
            break;
    }

    if (Canvas.GetLeft(this) <= 1)
    {
        Canvas.SetLeft(this, 1);
        walkTimer.Stop();
    }
    else if (Canvas.GetLeft(this) + this.Width > appWidth - 1)
    {
        Canvas.SetLeft(this, appWidth - this.Width);
        walkTimer.Stop();
    }
    else
    {
        Canvas.SetLeft(this, monkeyPosition += velocityX);
        VisualStateManager.GoToState(this, whichState, false);
        frame += 1;
        if (frame > 12) frame = 1;
    }
    this.walkTimer.Begin();
}
```

Now you can run the final version of the **monkeyWalk** project. Click the application so it receives focus for input, and then use the arrow keys. When the right arrow key is pressed, the monkey will walk until the right side of the screen is reached, at which time it will stop.

If the left arrow key is pressed, the monkey will continue to the left until the edge of the application is encountered. All of the code covered here is available in the **monkeyWalkCompleted** project.

Vectors and storyboard animations

The majority of what we've done with storyboard animations is use them to move objects around the screen or modify their existing properties. However, don't be afraid to experiment with mixing up storyboard animations with vector-based animations that you are controlling from code.

Combining both methods can help bring a level of interactivity to an application that neither one would manage to do really well on its own. The next example we'll look at combines storyboards with vector animation to create a mechanical claw that the user can control.

1. Open the **clawGame** project to code along with this example. The project contains two user controls. The first is a rail across which a tram will move. The second object is a tram to which the claw is attached. The rail is really just there as a visual guide—all the action for this project will take place in the tram user control.

2. Start out in the Page.xaml.cs file by declaring instances of each object before the Page() constructor:

```
rail rail = new rail();
tram tram = new tram();
```

3. Inside the Page() constructor, position each object's top property, and add it to the main canvas. The rail does not move, and we'll be controlling the tram with code, so there's no need to set the left properties. You can run the project and take a look at the objects at this point if you'd like.

```
Canvas.SetTop(rail, 20);
Canvas.SetTop(tram, 20);

LayoutRoot.Children.Add(tram);
LayoutRoot.Children.Add(rail);
```

4. Next, we'll code up the tram.xaml.cs file. Start with a publicly accessible double to hold the application width. Following that, add a private velocity integer variable, and a Boolean that will be used to determine if the claw is in motion:

```
public double appWidth;

private int velocityX;
private bool clawMoving = false;
```

5. Inside the tram() constructor, add code to begin the tramTimer storyboard, and create event handlers for the Completed event of the tramTimer storyboard and the Completed event of the clawDown storyboard. The clawDown storyboard contains an animation that opens the claw as it drops toward the bottom of the screen, and then closes the claw and rises back up.

```
this.tramTimer.Begin();
this.tramTimer.Completed += new EventHandler(tramTimer_Completed);
this.clawDown.Completed += new EventHandler(clawDown_Completed);
```

6. Create the clawDown_Completed() event handler function. The code that goes inside the function is simple. It does nothing more than switch our Boolean flag clawMoving to false.

```
private void clawDown_Completed(object sender, EventArgs e)
{
    this.clawMoving = false;
}
```

7. Create the tramTimer_Completed() event handler function. This function handles the motion and boundary checking for the tram object. At each completion cycle of the timer storyboard, the tram is moved by the current value contained in the velocityX variable. Tests are done to see if either the left or right walls were hit, and if so, the direction of the velocity vector is reversed. The function finishes off by restarting the timer that is used to move the tram.

```
private void tramTimer_Completed(object sender, EventArgs e)
{

    Canvas.SetLeft(this, Canvas.GetLeft(this) + velocityX);

    // check if hit right wall
    if (Canvas.GetLeft(this) + this.Width >= (this.appWidth - 20))
    {
        velocityX *= -1;
    }

    // check if hit left wall
    if (Canvas.GetLeft(this) <= -5)
    {
        velocityX *= -1;
    }

    this.tramTimer.Begin();
}
```

8. Two more functions need to be added to this code-behind. The first, SetTramVel(), will accept an integer argument. When called, this function checks to see if the clawMoving flag is true, which will only happen if the storyboard animation for the claw is playing. If the storyboard for the claw is not playing, the current value of velocityX is increased by the velocity amount passed to the function. Then some simple tests are done to keep the speed of the tram within the range of +2 and −2.

```
public void setTramVel(int velocity)
{
    if (!clawMoving)
    {
        velocityX += velocity;
        // keep the velocity within +2/-2 range
        if (velocityX > 0 && velocityX > 2)
        {
            velocityX = 2;
        }
        else if (velocityX < 0 && velocityX < -2)
        {
            velocityX = -2;
        }
    }
}
```

9. The final function to add to this code-behind will be called when the down arrow key is pressed on the keyboard. The function is called downKey(). When called, the code will check to see if the claw storyboard is playing. If not, it will set the x velocity vector of the tram object to 0, set the clawMoving Boolean to true, and start the clawDown animation.

```
public void downKey()
{
    if (!clawMoving)
    {
        velocityX = 0;
        this.clawMoving = true;
        this.clawDown.Begin();
    }
}
```

10. That does it for the tram object. Since we added the appWidth property, we'll need to add that into the Page.xaml.cs file, in the Page() constructor:

```
public Page()
{
    InitializeComponent();

    Canvas.SetTop(rail, 20);
    Canvas.SetTop(tram, 20);
    tram.appWidth = this.Width;

    LayoutRoot.Children.Add(tram);
    LayoutRoot.Children.Add(rail);
}
```

11. The input for the application will be handled via the keyboard, so inside the Page() constructor, add a KeyUp event listener to gather user input from the keyboard:

```
this.KeyUp += new KeyEventHandler(keyHandler);
```

12. Create the event handler function after the closing curly brace of the Page() constructor:

```
private void keyHandler(object sender, KeyEventArgs e)
{

}
```

13. The event handler code for the keyboard input handles three cases. When the left arrow key is pressed, the tram's x velocity is adjusted by a value of –1. If the right arrow key is pressed, the tram's x velocity is incremented by 1. Remember that the setTramVel() function is passed a value that is added to the current x velocity. This means that if the tram's velocity is 2, when the left arrow key is pressed, the velocity gets decremented by –1, which results in a slowing motion (and an eventual change of direction if the arrow key is pressed repeatedly). When the down arrow key is pressed, the downKey() method for the tram object is called.

```
switch (e.Key)
{
    case Key.Left:
        tram.setTramVel(-1);
        break;
    case Key.Right:
        tram.setTramVel(1);
        break;
    case Key.Down:
        tram.downKey();
        break;
}
```

Compile and run the project. Click the main application to gain focus, and then use the arrow keys to manipulate the tram's direction. The claw will drop when you press the down arrow key.

The finalized code for this project is available in the **clawGameCompleted** project. Take some time to examine the XAML for the objects. The tram object is composed of three parts: the roller tram, which is the main part of the object, the claw that hangs below the tram, and the cable that lowers and raises the claw.

The cable canvas has a clipping region applied that hides the cable. Figure 5-11 shows the tram object with the cable selected. Notice that only the area where the cable should be allowed to show is inside the clipping region. The clipping region is what helps to give the illusion that the cable is dropping when the storyboard is played, as shown in Figure 5-12.

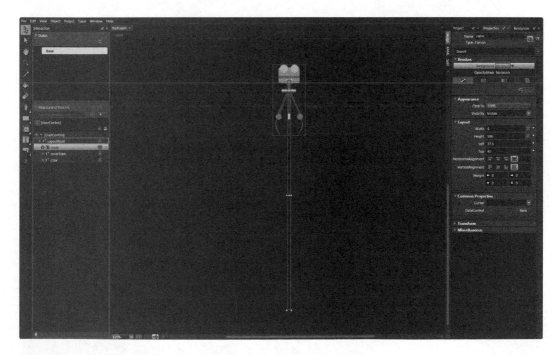

Figure 5-11. The cable portion of the tram is hidden with a clipping region.

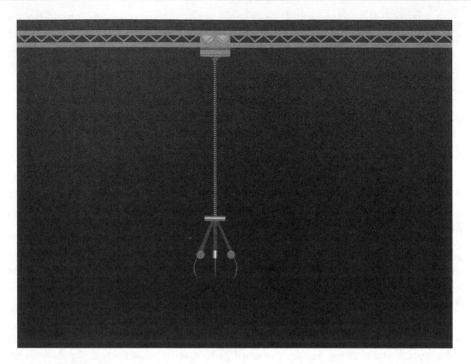

Figure 5-12. The claw project in action. The user controls the movement of the claw and when it drops.

Vector math

How you choose to store vectors for your objects is entirely up to you—you can store vectors as individual x,y components in different variables, as in the previous examples, or you can use a Point object to store both vector components in a single variable. One caveat to be aware of is that if you attempt to store a vector as a Point property using a getter and setter, you will not be able to access the individual components of the point. However, using Point data types as shown here—as public variables—will work OK. Whichever method you choose to store your vectors, there is a bit of math that can be done with them. Next, we're going to take a look at how that is done.

We'll start with vector addition. Vectors are pretty simple to add—you simply add the x components of the vectors and the y components of the vectors. Figure 5-13 illustrates an example. Given the pair of vectors drawn in white, which are 8,10 and 0,10, the resultant vector, 8,20, is drawn in black. The magnitude of the vectors used in this example are exaggerated a bit to demonstrate the addition, but the idea is what we're after. Vector addition can be used to "look ahead" and see where your object will be the next time it moves.

Vectors can also be scaled by multiplying. To scale a vector by 2, for example, you multiply both of the vector's components by 2. This will result in a vector that points in the same direction but is twice as long.

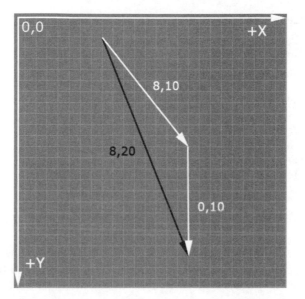

Figure 5-13. To add vectors, add the individual components.

The **vectorMath** project contains a couple of examples for you to experiment with. There's nothing that you really need to code up here, so you can take a breather. I'll just go through the code so you can modify it if you'd like.

In the Page.xaml.cs file, two Point objects are declared, each of which will be used to store a vector:

```
Point vector1 = new Point();
Point vector2 = new Point();
```

To get started, I assigned some arbitrary values to the vector objects. The first is 8,10, and the second is 0,10.

```
vector1.X = 8;
vector1.Y = 10;
vector2.X = 0;
vector2.Y = 10;
```

Once that's done, both vectors are passed to a function called writeVectors(), which simply outputs the values to the screen:

```
private void writeVectors(Point vectorA, Point vectorB)
{
    msgBlock.Text = "Vector 1: " + vectorA;
    msgBlock.Text += "\nVector 2: " + vectorB;
}
```

Following that, the values are passed to the addVectors() function:

```
addVectors(vector1, vector2);
```

This function takes both vectors, adds their components, and places the result on the screen:

```
private void addVectors(Point vectorA, Point vectorB)
{
    Point newVector = new Point();
    newVector.X = vectorA.X + vectorB.X;
    newVector.Y = vectorA.Y + vectorB.Y;
    msgBlock.Text += "\nVector Addition: " + newVector;
}
```

Once that's done, a vector and a scaling factor are passed to the scaleVector() function:

```
scaleVector(vector1, 2);
```

The scaleVector() function multiplies each component of the vector passed by the scale value that was passed, and then writes the output to the screen:

```
private void scaleVector(Point vectorA, int scale)
{
    Point newVector = new Point();
    newVector.X = vectorA.X * scale;
    newVector.Y = vectorA.Y * scale;
    msgBlock.Text += "\nVector 1 Scaled by " + scale + ": "
                    + newVector + "";
}
```

Take a little time and play around with the values that are set for the vectors to see what type of results the math operations you're performing will have.

Angles in Silverlight

As you saw earlier when working through the transform types, rotational angles in Silverlight are expressed in degrees and can be additive or subtractive—for example, both 720 and –720 degrees will rotate an object around twice. The former will rotate an object clockwise, while the latter will rotate an object counterclockwise.

As you have seen along the way, Rotate transforms are accessible through code. By adding an x:Name property to an object's Rotate transform, you can easily access the angle of rotation. Take, for example, the following rectangle XAML:

```
<Rectangle x:Name="myRect" Height="100"
           HorizontalAlignment="Left"
           VerticalAlignment="Top"
           Width="100" Fill="#FFFFFFFF"
           Stroke="#FF000000"
           RenderTransformOrigin="0.5,0.5">
```

```
    <Rectangle.RenderTransform>
            <TransformGroup>
                <RotateTransform x:Name="myRectRotate" Angle="90"/>
            </TransformGroup>
    </Rectangle.RenderTransform>
    </Rectangle>
```

You should be able to tell from this code that the rectangle has been rotated 90 degrees via a Rotate transform. Notice that an x:Name attribute, myRectRotate, was added to the RotateTransform definition. To modify this value via code, you can directly access the Angle member of myRectRotate as follows:

```
    myRectRotate.Angle = -20;
```

You may have noticed when working with vectors that the line a vector makes kind of looks like an angle. With just a bit of code, you can convert a vector into an angle. To do this, however, you'll need to know three things.

First off, mathematics uses a unit of measure called a **radian** to measure angles—1 radian is equal to about 57.2958 degrees. Second, we use a math function called Atan2() (arctangent) to determine the radians. Finally, we need a way to convert the radians to a useful number that represents an angle for us.

If you're starting to get nervous because we're using some mathematics, don't worry. It's presented here as kind of a "plug-and-play" solution. For now, we want to focus on how vectors and angles are related.

All of this radian and Atan2 talk is a fancy way of saying we need the following two lines of code, into which we plug a vector. The result will be the angle of the vector.

```
    double radians = Math.Atan2(vectorLength.Y, vectorLength.X);
    angle = Convert.ToInt16(180 / Math.PI * radians);
```

The first line uses the Atan2() math method to calculate the radians from the vector that was passed. You can see the usage of the Atan2() function, and how we pass the vector to the function. Notice that the vector is passed y,x; not x,y. The second line of code contains the formula for converting radians to degrees.

Converting vectors to angles

To see this code in action, visit the **vectorAngleConversion** project. This is a simple project that sets up a Point object that contains a vector, and a variable called angle:

```
    Point vectorLength = new Point();
    double angle;
```

A value that represents a vector is assigned to the vectorLength variable, and the angle of the vector is calculated and output to a TextBlock:

```
    vectorLength.X = 5;
    vectorLength.Y = 5;
```

189

```
double radians = Math.Atan2(vectorLength.Y, vectorLength.X);
angle = Convert.ToInt16(180 / Math.PI * radians);
msgBlock.Text = angle + "";
```

The result produced by this bit of code is 45, which is the correct angle (in degrees) for a vector of 5,5. Go ahead and play with the values of the vectorLength variable and run the program to see what kind of results you get. Don't worry if you see a few results that surprise you—we'll be visiting these two math functions again later.

Let's take a look at a project that graphically illustrates the math. This project allows a user to adjust the endpoints of a line. As the endpoints are adjusted, the application calculates the length of the vector that the line creates, calculates the angle of that vector, and applies the angle to a separate line object as a sanity check for the calculations. All the code we're about to discuss is available in the **vectorAngles** project.

The Page.xaml file for this project contains four sliders and several TextBlock objects that are used to provide user feedback. In addition, there is a Path object that is used to draw a simple line. The default orientation for the line is horizontal.

In the Page.xaml.cs file, the objects needed in the project are declared. The first one is the user-adjustable line, called myLine. The next two objects are Point objects, p1 and p2, and are used to store the endpoints of the myLine object. The last two declarations are similar to those illustrated in the previous project—vectorLength is used to determine the length of the line as a user manipulates it, and angle is used to store the angle of the line.

```
Line myLine = new Line();
Point p1 = new Point();
Point p2 = new Point();
Point vectorLength = new Point();
double angle;
```

The code starts by assigning some default values to the p1 and p2 Point objects:

```
p1.X = 0;
p1.Y = 0;
p2.X = 250;
p2.Y = 250;
```

Next, the values in the p1 and p2 Point objects are used to create starting and ending points for the myLine object. In Silverlight, a line is defined by two pairs of coordinates: the start point and the endpoint. They are referenced as X1, Y1, and X2, Y2. Once values are assigned to the myLine object, the line's StrokeThickness and Color are set.

```
myLine.X1 = p1.X;
myLine.Y1 = p1.Y;
myLine.X2 = p2.X;
myLine.Y2 = p2.Y;
myLine.StrokeThickness = 1;
SolidColorBrush stroke = new SolidColorBrush();
stroke.Color = Colors.Black;
myLine.Stroke = stroke;
```

Prior to adding the line to the canvas, a function called doAngle() is called with the code doAngle();. This function uses the start point and endpoint of the myLine object to determine the length of the vector created by the line. You should recognize the next couple of lines of code from the previous example—this is where the vector created by the line is converted into an angle.

The testLineAngle object is our sanity check—this object will be rotated the number of degrees calculated by our code, and the angle of the line should match the angle of the myLine object, assuming the code is functioning correctly. The values are converted to integers for display as they are output to the canvas.

```
void doAngle()
{
    vectorLength.X = myLine.X2 - myLine.X1;
    vectorLength.Y - myLine.Y2 - myLine.Y1;
    double radians = Math.Atan2(vectorLength.Y, vectorLength.X);
    angle = Convert.ToInt16(180 / Math.PI * radians);
    testLineAngle.Angle = angle;
    msgBlock.Text = "Vector X,Y: " +
                    Convert.ToInt16(vectorLength.X) + ", " +
                    Convert.ToInt16(vectorLength.Y) +
                    "\nAngle: " + angle;
}
```

Now that the initial state of the line has been used to determine the angle and the screen output is current, the line is added to the LayoutRoot Canvas:

```
LayoutRoot.Children.Add(myLine);
```

Next, the maximum limits for the sliders are set. The sliders will be used to allow a user to change the starting and ending points of the myLine object, and the application will not allow either point's x value to be greater than the width of the canvas, or either point's y value to be greater than the height of the canvas.

```
p1XSlider.Maximum = p2XSlider.Maximum = LayoutRoot.Width;
p1YSlider.Maximum = p2YSlider.Maximum = LayoutRoot.Height;
```

Each of the four sliders is then preset to the default value for the endpoints of myLine, and the text that displays the current value for each slider is updated:

```
p1XSlider.Value = myLine.X1;
p1YSlider.Value = myLine.Y1;
p2XSlider.Value = myLine.X2;
p2YSlider.Value = myLine.Y2;
msgP1XSlider.Text = "Point 1 X: " + (Int16)myLine.X1;
msgP1YSlider.Text = "Point 1 Y: " + (Int16)myLine.Y1;
msgP2XSlider.Text = "Point 2 X: " + (Int16)myLine.X2;
msgP2YSlider.Text = "Point 2 Y: " + (Int16)myLine.Y2;
```

With all of the preliminary setup out of the way, the application then sets up an event listener for each slider's ValueChanged event. This event will be raised when a slider is manipulated by a user.

```
p1XSlider.ValueChanged += new RoutedPropertyChangedEventHandler➡
                          <double>(p1XSlider_ValueChanged);
p1YSlider.ValueChanged += new RoutedPropertyChangedEventHandler➡
                          <double>(p1YSlider_ValueChanged);
p2XSlider.ValueChanged += new RoutedPropertyChangedEventHandler➡
                          <double>(p2XSlider_ValueChanged);
p2YSlider.ValueChanged += new RoutedPropertyChangedEventHandler➡
                          <double>(p2YSlider_ValueChanged);
```

The event handler code for each of the four sliders is fairly similar. The value of the slider is used to update the corresponding point of the myLine object. The text that shows the slider's value to the user is updated, and the doAngle() function is called to update the angle output on the screen.

```
private void p1XSlider_ValueChanged(object sender,
                        RoutedPropertyChangedEventArgs<double> e)
{
    myLine.X1 = p1XSlider.Value;
    msgP1XSlider.Text = "Point 1 X: " +
                        Convert.ToInt16(p1XSlider.Value);
    doAngle();
}
```

The p1 y slider event handler is shown in the following listing. Notice that functionally it is identical except that it references a different point of the myLine object, and outputs text to a different TextBlock.

```
private void p1YSlider_ValueChanged(object sender,
                        RoutedPropertyChangedEventArgs<double> e)
{
    myLine.Y1 = p1YSlider.Value;
    msgP1YSlider.Text = "Point 1 Y: " +
                        Convert.ToInt16(p1YSlider.Value);
    doAngle();
}
```

The sliders for p2 follow the same pattern. When the program runs, you can use the sliders to adjust the endpoints of the line object, and the code will calculate the length of the vector that is created by the line.

The vector length is used to calculate the angle of the line, which is then applied to the line object near the bottom of the screen. Aside from slight differences due to the conversion to integer data type and the imprecision that introduces, you should see that the code is doing what it is supposed to, as shown in Figure 5-14. Pretty cool, huh?

You've seen a pretty broad variety of ways to manipulate objects using vectors. You know how to make objects move using vectors, and you know how to make objects rotate by using vectors. Let's take a look at how you can separate the acceleration vector of an object from the directional vector.

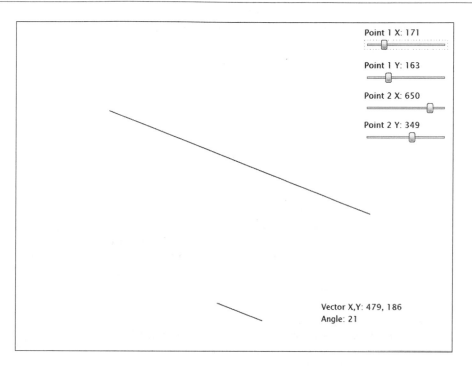

Figure 5-14. The vectorAngle project allows you to modify the endpoints of a line as it calculates the angle in real time.

Separating acceleration from direction

It's very likely that as you begin building out your own applications, you will find yourself in a situation where you will want to be able to separate the direction an object is traveling from the direction it is pointing. A great example of this type of motion would be the kind found in old arcade games like Asteroids. We're going to take a look at how to code this type of movement up.

1. To code along with this example, open the **vectorShip** project. This project contains the familiar Page.xaml file, which contains two additional canvases: contentCanvas and starCanvas. There is also a Border object to create a white border around the game board, as well as a TextBlock that will be used to provide some user feedback.

   There are two other user controls in this project. One is called star.xaml, which contains a simple 2✕2 ellipse that will be used to generate a random star field. The other is called rocketship.xaml, and contains a 45✕45 spaceship and a timer called gameLoop that will be used to make the spaceship move.

2. Start coding in the Page.xaml.cs file by declaring an instance of the rocket called myRocket and a Random data type called rng that will be used to generate random numbers. These two variables are placed before the Page() constructor:

```
private rocketship myRocket = new rocketship();
private Random rng = new Random();
```

3. Inside the Page() constructor, add code to position the ship at the center of the application:

```
Canvas.SetLeft(myRocket, (LayoutRoot.Width / 2) - myRocket.Width / 2);
Canvas.SetTop(myRocket, (LayoutRoot.Height / 2) - myRocket.Height / 2);
contentCanvas.Children.Add(myRocket);
```

4. After the closing curly brace of the Page() function, create a new function called buildStars() that accepts an integer argument:

```
private void buildStars(int numStars)
{

}
```

5. Inside the function, add the following code. The integer passed to the function is used to control a loop that draws stars in the background. For each iteration of the loop, the function creates a new star object, which is randomly positioned. Once the position has been set, a random color is generated for the star and assigned to the starEllipse Fill property. The star is then added to the starCanvas.

```
for (int i = 0; i < numStars; i++)
{
    star newStar = new star();
    Point position = new Point(rng.NextDouble() * Width,
                               rng.NextDouble() * Height);
    Canvas.SetLeft(newStar, position.X);
    Canvas.SetTop(newStar, position.Y);
    byte[] colors = new byte[3];
    rng.NextBytes(colors);
    Color c = Color.FromArgb(255, colors[0], colors[1], colors[2]);
    newStar.starEllipse.Fill = new SolidColorBrush(c);
    starCanvas.Children.Add(newStar);
}
```

6. Call the function from inside the Page() constructor, passing an integer that determines how many stars are created:

```
buildStars(150);
```

7. Press F5 to compile and run the program. The application will display the ship over a star field that contains 150 stars positioned and filled at random. The next step is to add the code to the rocketship.xaml.cs code-behind file that will be used to control the rocket, so open that file for editing.

8. Before the rocketship() constructor, declare the variables that this object will be using. The variables include a publicly accessible Point that will control the direction in which the ship is pointing, and two doubles for the application's width and height. There are also three private variables. One controls the direction in which the ship is accelerating, one controls the thrust, and one is for holding an angle-to-radians conversion.

```
public Point vector = new Point();
public double appWidth;
public double appHeight;
```

```
private Point acceleration = new Point();
private double thrust = .5;
private double radians;
```

9. Inside the rocketship() constructor, initialize the directional variable with a value of 0 for both components:

```
vector.X = vector.Y = 0;
```

10. Follow that up with code that adds an event handler for the Completed event of the gameLoop timer, and starts the timer:

```
gameLoop.Completed += new EventHandler(gameLoop_Completed);
gameLoop.Begin();
```

11. Create the gameLoop_Completed() event handler function after the closing curly brace of the rocketship() constructor:

```
private void gameLoop_Completed(object sender, EventArgs e)
{

}
```

12. Inside the function, add the following two lines of code that will change the ship's position by adding the vector.X and vector.Y components to the left and top properties of the ship:

```
Canvas.SetLeft(this, Canvas.GetLeft(this) + vector.X);
Canvas.SetTop(this, Canvas.GetTop(this) + vector.Y);
```

13. Follow that up with some boundary-checking code. If the ship moves completely off-canvas in any direction, it is wrapped to the opposite side of the canvas.

```
if (Canvas.GetTop(this) < -this.Height)
{
    Canvas.SetTop(this, this.appHeight);
}

if (Canvas.GetLeft(this) < -this.Width)
{
    Canvas.SetLeft(this, this.appWidth);
}

if (Canvas.GetTop(this) > this.appHeight)
{
    Canvas.SetTop(this, -this.Height);
}
if (Canvas.GetLeft(this) > this.appWidth)
{
    Canvas.SetLeft(this, -this.Width);
}
```

14. After the boundary checks, restart the timer to keep the movement going:

```
gameLoop.Begin();
```

15. Next, we'll add functions that will be used to control the ship's movement based on user input. Create a new, publicly accessible function called doThrust(). This function will convert the angle the rocket is currently rotated to radians. The radian value is then used to calculate acceleration along the x and y axes. The ship's movement vector is then updated by adding the acceleration vector.

```
public void doThrust()
{
    radians = rotateRocket.Angle * Math.PI / 180;
    acceleration.X = Math.Cos(radians) * thrust;
    acceleration.Y = Math.Sin(radians) * thrust;
    vector.X += acceleration.X;
    vector.Y += acceleration.Y;
}
```

16. Next, add two functions to control the rotation of the ship. These functions will be called based on user keyboard input. One will decrement the ship's angle of rotation to turn it counter-clockwise; the other will increment the ship's angle of rotation, causing the ship to rotate in a clockwise direction. The functions are passed an integer to determine the amount of change in the rotational value.

```
public void rotateLeft(int amount)
{
    this.rotateRocket.Angle -= amount;
}

public void rotateRight(int amount)
{
    this.rotateRocket.Angle += amount;
}
```

17. The last function we will need to add to this code-behind file will be used to stop the ship when the down arrow is pressed. Create a function called doBrakes(), and make it publicly accessible. This function simply sets both the acceleration and movement vectors to 0.

```
public void doBrakes()
{
    acceleration.X = 0;
    acceleration.Y = 0;
    vector.X = 0;
    vector.Y = 0;
}
```

We just did a whole lot of coding, but you won't see a lot of benefit from it just yet. If you run the program at this point, you'll see the same result as you did the last time—the ship will sit, quietly centered on the screen, over a star field. We'll change all that by making use of the code we just added.

18. Open the `Page.xaml.cs` file for editing. Since we're doing boundary checking in the rocket control, we'll need to initialize the `appHeight` and `appWidth` variables we set up in the code-behind for the rocket. Add the two following bold code lines to the `Page()` constructor:

```
Canvas.SetLeft(myRocket, (LayoutRoot.Width / 2) - myRocket.Width / 2);
Canvas.SetTop(myRocket, (LayoutRoot.Height / 2) - myRocket.Height / 2);
myRocket.appWidth = LayoutRoot.Width;
myRocket.appHeight = LayoutRoot.Height;
contentCanvas.Children.Add(myRocket);
```

19. Add another variable declaration above the `Page()` constructor. This one will be used to control the speed at which the ship rotates as the arrow keys are pressed.

```
private int rotateSpeed = 5;
```

20. Inside the `Page()` constructor, add an event handler for the `KeyDown` event:

```
this.KeyDown += new KeyEventHandler(LayoutRoot_KeyDown);
```

21. Create the `LayoutRoot_KeyDown()` event handler function:

```
private void LayoutRoot_KeyDown(object sender, KeyEventArgs e)
{

}
```

22. Inside the `KeyDown()` event handler, start by creating a `switch()` statement to listen for the arrow keys:

```
switch (e.Key)
{
    case Key.Up:
        break;

    case Key.Down:
        break;

    case Key.Left:
        break;

    case Key.Right:
        break;
}
```

23. Now we will make use of the functions created inside the rocketship's code-behind file. Inside this event handler, add code to listen for all four of the arrow keys. When the up arrow is pressed, the ship should thrust in the direction it is pointing. This is done by calling the `doThrust()` method you added to the ship's code-behind. The code will update the on-screen text to show the current x and y movement vectors of the ship as well.

```
case Key.Up:
    myRocket.doThrust();
    msgVel.Text = "Velocity        X: " +
                    String.Format("{0:0.00}",
                    myRocket.vector.X) + "        Y: " +
                    String.Format("{0:0.00}", myRocket.vector.Y);
    break;
```

24. Next, we'll handle the down key. In the event the down arrow is pressed, the rocket will come to a stop. This is done by calling the doBrakes() method for the ship before updating the on-screen text to show the movement vectors once again.

```
case Key.Down:
    myRocket.doBrakes();
    msgVel.Text = "Velocity        X: " +
                    String.Format("{0:0.00}",
                    myRocket.vector.X) + "        Y: " +
                    String.Format("{0:0.00}", myRocket.vector.Y);
    break;
```

25. When the left arrow key is pressed, the ship should rotate in a counterclockwise direction. The rotate speed of the ship was declared in the Page.xaml.cs code-behind. In order to rotate the ship, the rotateLeft() method is called and passed the rotateSpeed variable as an argument:

```
case Key.Left:
    myRocket.rotateLeft(rotateSpeed);
    break;
```

26. Finally, add the code to handle the right arrow key. This code calls the rotateRight() method of the rocket object, and like the rotateLeft() method, also passes the rotateSpeed variable.

```
case Key.Right:
    myRocket.rotateRight(rotateSpeed);
    break;
```

Press F5 to compile and run the program. Click the application to get focus for input. Press the left arrow key and the ship will rotate counterclockwise 5 degrees. Pressing the right arrow key will rotate the ship clockwise 5 degrees. Pressing the up arrow key causes the ship to thrust and move forward. The more you press the up arrow, the faster the ship will travel.

Notice that as the ship travels in one direction, you are still free to use the left and right arrow keys to rotate the ship so that it points in any direction you like. Pressing the up arrow key when the ship is pointed in a direction other than that in which it is traveling will create some thrust in that direction. However, to fully change the ship's direction, you need to use the thrust key enough times to overcome the current inertia of the ship. Figure 5-15 shows a screenshot of the application in action. The **vectorShipCompleted** project includes all of the code for this project.

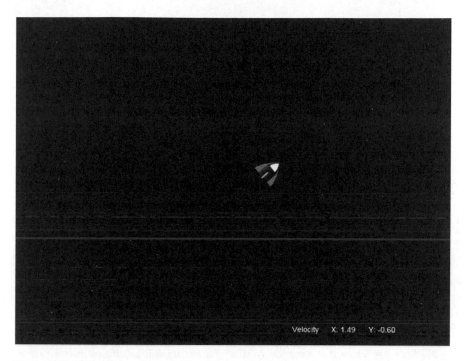

Velocity   X: 1.49   Y: -0.60

Figure 5-15. The completed vectorShip project, which illustrates how to separate acceleration from direction

Firing a weapon from the ship

To take this application one step further, let's add the ability to fire a missile from the ship. We already know in what direction the ship is pointing—it should be relatively easy to fire a missile, right?

1. Open the **vectorShipMissile** project to code along with this example. The project is identical to the completed ship project from the last example, except that it contains one additional user control: a missile that the ship will fire. There was also a small change to the doThrust() function in the rocketship.xaml.cs code-behind. Some checks were added to keep the thrust within a –2 to +2 range. This was done to keep the ship from out-accelerating the missile.

```
public void doThrust()
{
    radians = rotateRocket.Angle * Math.PI / 180;
    acceleration.X = Math.Cos(radians) * thrust;
    acceleration.Y = Math.Sin(radians) * thrust;

    vector.X += acceleration.X;
    vector.Y += acceleration.Y;
```

```
    if (vector.X > 2) vector.X = 2;
    if (vector.X < -2) vector.X = -2;
    if (vector.Y > 2) vector.Y = 2;
    if (vector.Y < -2) vector.Y = -2;
}
```

2. The `missile.xaml` file contains the missile shape and a storyboard called `missileTimer` that will be used to make the missile move. While the XAML itself isn't unusual, take a look at the file and notice the orientation and position of the missile. The missile's root canvas is 45×45, which matches the size of the canvas for the ship. The missile is placed vertically, centered just outside of this canvas. If you imagine the ship residing within the 45×45 canvas, as shown in Figure 5-16, you can see where the missile is in relation to the ship.

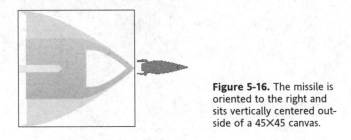

Figure 5-16. The missile is oriented to the right and sits vertically centered outside of a 45×45 canvas.

When the user presses a key that fires the missile, the missile will be drawn in front of the ship. If the missile were contained in a smaller canvas and positioned at the center of the ship when fired, it would appear to come out off-center, as the ship would continue to drift in one direction while the missile fired out in another. Placing the missile centered in front of the ship avoids this problem.

3. The majority of the code necessary to fire a missile goes into the `missile.xaml.cs` code-behind, so go ahead and open that file. Begin by declaring two variables. One will contain the acceleration vector for the missile, and the other will contain a thrust value. This code goes before the `missile()` constructor:

```
public Point acceleration = new Point();
private double thrust = 5;
```

4. Inside of the `missile()` constructor, add the following code to set the missile's `Visibility` property to Collapsed. This will keep the missile hidden until fired. In addition, add an event handler for the `Completed` event on the `missileTimer` storyboard:

```
this.Visibility = Visibility.Collapsed;
missileTimer.Completed += new EventHandler(missileTimer_Completed);
```

5. Create the event handler function for the `Completed` event:

```
private void missileTimer_Completed(object sender, EventArgs e)
{

}
```

6. Inside the event handler function, add the following code to update the position of the missile on the canvas, and then restart the timer to keep it moving. The position of the missile is updated by adding the acceleration vector components to the appropriate position properties of the missile. Remember that this event handler won't execute until the timer for the missile is started once it has been fired.

```
Canvas.SetLeft(this, Canvas.GetLeft(this) + acceleration.X);
Canvas.SetTop(this, Canvas.GetTop(this) + acceleration.Y);
missileTimer.Begin();
```

7. The last thing we'll add to this file is a public method that will be called when the rocket is fired. The public fireMissile() method will be passed the rotational angle of the ship, as well as the ship's left and top position on the canvas:

```
public void fireMissile(double rotation, double left, double top)
{
}
```

8. Inside the function, the following code will match the missile's angle of rotation with that of the ship, and calculate the acceleration vectors. The missile is positioned at the same x,y coordinate as the ship. It is then made visible, and the timer to control the movement is started.

```
this.missileRotate.Angle = rotation;
double radians = this.missileRotate.Angle * Math.PI / 180;
this.acceleration.X = Math.Cos(radians) * this.thrust;
this.acceleration.Y = Math.Sin(radians) * this.thrust;

Canvas.SetTop(this, top);
Canvas.SetLeft(this, left);

this.Visibility = Visibility.Visible;
this.missileTimer.Begin();
```

9. Now all we need to do is add a bit of code to the Page.xaml.cs file before we can test out our missile firing. Start by declaring an instance of the missile object:

```
private missile myMissile = new missile();
```

10. Inside the Page() constructor, insert code to add the missile to the contentCanvas. The missile object is added before the rocketship object so that the ship will be "on top" of the missile if the two cross paths.

```
public Page()
{
    InitializeComponent();

    buildStars(150);

    contentCanvas.Children.Add(myMissile);
```

```
Canvas.SetLeft(myRocket, (LayoutRoot.Width / 2)
                           - myRocket.Width / 2);
Canvas.SetTop(myRocket, (LayoutRoot.Height / 2)
                           - myRocket.Height / 2);
myRocket.appWidth = LayoutRoot.Width;
myRocket.appHeight = LayoutRoot.Height;
contentCanvas.Children.Add(myRocket);

this.KeyDown += new KeyEventHandler(LayoutRoot_KeyDown);
}
```

11. All that's left now is to hook up a key to cause the missile to fire. We'll be using the Enter key, so add the case for Key.Enter to the switch() statement inside the LayoutRoot_KeyDown() event handler, as shown. Remember that the fireMissile() method inside the missile.xaml. cs file is expecting three arguments of type double. When called, the method is passed the rocket's rotational value, and the rocket's left and top properties. The method then rotates and positions the missile appropriately before starting the timer.

```
switch (e.Key)
{
    case Key.Enter:
        myMissile.fireMissile(myRocket.rotateRocket.Angle,
                              Canvas.GetLeft(myRocket),
                              Canvas.GetTop(myRocket));
        break;

    case Key.Up:
        myRocket.doThrust();
        msgVel.Text = "Velocity      X: " +
                        String.Format("{0:0.00}",
                        myRocket.vector.X) + "      Y: " +
                        String.Format("{0:0.00}", myRocket.vector.Y);
        break;

    case Key.Down:
        myRocket.doBrakes();
        msgVel.Text = "Velocity      X: " +
                        String.Format("{0:0.00}",
                        myRocket.vector.X) + "      Y: " +
                        String.Format("{0:0.00}", myRocket.vector.Y);
        break;

    case Key.Left:
        myRocket.rotateLeft(rotateSpeed);
        break;

    case Key.Right:
        myRocket.rotateRight(rotateSpeed);
        break;
}
```

That should be all it takes. Press F5 to compile and run the program. Click the app to gain focus, and then use the left and right arrow keys to spin the rocket, the up arrow key to thrust, and the Enter key to fire. Figure 5-17 shows a missile being fired from the ship.

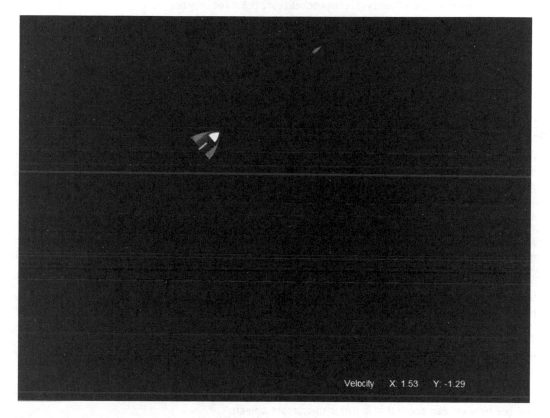

Figure 5-17. The ship fires a missile in the direction it is pointing.

As written, the code only really allows a single missile to be fired, and there is no collision detection being done, so the missile won't hit the ship.

If you'd like to change the code so the ship can fire multiple missiles, remove the object declaration and initialization code:

```
private missile myMissile = new missile();
contentCanvas.Children.Add(myMissile);
```

The code can be moved inside the case that handles the Enter key event. By adding the following code, the application will create a new instance of the missile each time the Enter key is pressed, and add it to the canvas. Be aware of the fact that this code only *adds* missiles—no cleanup is being done when a missile is off-screen, so this will eventually bog down the application's performance if left as-is.

```
case Key.Enter:
    missile newMissile = new missile();
    contentCanvas.Children.Add(newMissile);
    newMissile.fireMissile(myRocket.rotateRocket.Angle,
                            Canvas.GetLeft(myRocket),
                            Canvas.GetTop(myRocket));
    break;
```

All of the code described in this example can be found in **vectorShipMissileCompleted**.

Summary

We started out this chapter talking about the coordinate system in Silverlight. We're all familiar with the Cartesian coordinate system, but the coordinates used in Silverlight don't quite work the same way. In order to move an object toward the bottom of an application, you use an increasing y value. To move an object up, you use a decreasing y value.

With a firm grip on the coordinate system, we spent some time digging into vectors, and you learned about how they can be used to describe direction and distance for an object. One-dimensional vectors move along a single axis, while two-dimensional vectors move along two axes. To change the direction of a vector, one or both of a vector's components can be multiplied by −1.

Vectors can be used strictly in the code-behind, with frame-by-frame based animations, or with storyboard animations to create a wide variety of experiences and effects.

The line that represents a vector is related to an angle. To convert from vector to angle, use the `Math.Atan2()` function, passing the y component and then the x component. The function will return an angle in radians.

That wraps up our discussion on vectors. In the next chapter, we're going to dig into a little more math and see how we can apply that in order to animate objects.

Chapter 6

USING TRIGONOMETRY FOR ANIMATION

The word *trigonometry* is enough to strike fear into people's hearts. This is usually the part where everyone regrets having slept through their math classes, but not to worry—you've done a bit of trig already. It's true. In the last chapter when we were working with vectors, I slipped a little bit in. That wasn't so bad, was it? Good. Now we're going to take a deeper dive and explore what math can do for us when it comes to animating.

What is trigonometry?

Put simply, trigonometry is the study of how the angles and lengths of sides of triangles relate to one another. The word *trigonometry* means "three-angle measure," and was originally developed to help study astronomy. Today, the use of trigonometry is critical in science, technology, and programming Silverlight! That doesn't sound too scary, does it?

We're going to take a nice, long look at trigonometry and trigonometric functions, and what they can do for us in Silverlight. However, since trig is about measuring angles, it makes sense to start with a deeper look at the topic of angles.

Angles

We touched on an important topic briefly in Chapter 5—degrees vs. radians for angular measurement. You're going to be seeing radians, or converting between radians and degrees, a lot in this chapter, so it's probably a good time to get a better idea of what they're all about. This is important, because while Blend/XAML will take angular measurements in degrees, any rotations you do via trigonometric functions will give you radians, and you will get unexpected results if you forget to convert between the two units.

Conversion, as you have already seen, is simple:

$$radians = degrees \times \pi / 180$$

$$degrees = radians \times 180 / \pi$$

One of the things I have found to be useful is to include two generalized functions in my code to handle the conversion between degrees and radians on the fly. Internally, all of the calculations are always done with radians, but to apply a rotation to an object or display the degrees on the screen, there will be a need to convert. The following two functions will do the necessary conversions when passed an appropriate value:

```
double DegreesToRadians(double Degrees)
{
    return Degrees * Math.PI / 180;
}
double RadiansToDegrees(double Radians)
{
    return Radians * 180 / Math.PI;
}
```

The functions can be called like this:

```
DegreesToRadians(90);
```

where the value 90 is 90 degrees. This function returns 1.5707963267949 radians. If we then turn that around to test our RadiansToDegrees() function, we get the following:

```
RadiansToDegrees(1.5707963267949);
```

This returns a value of 90 and some tiny fraction of another degree. You can see that the mathematic conversions are pretty accurate, and that both of our functions are working as we would expect.

Let's try to demystify the radian a little bit. I mentioned earlier that 1 radian is equal to 57.2958 degrees. Where does that 57 come from? The mathematical explanation is that the radian is the subtended angle of an arc that is equal in length to the radius of the circle. Wow, that sounds pretty complex! It's a little easier to understand in pictures, so take a look at Figure 6-1, and it should make a little more sense.

From the figure, you can see that an arc whose length is equal to the radius of a circle will create an angle that is exactly 1 radian. But how do we figure out that measurement?

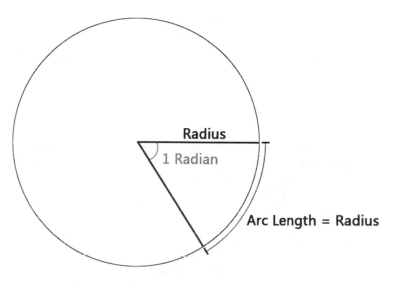

Figure 6-1. The radian is the subtended angle of an arc that is equal in length to the radius of the circle.

To get to the bottom of the specifics of the measurement, we'll work backward. We can work through an example angle where the measure in radians is known. We'll use a "straight" angle, which is 180 degrees. In Figure 6-2, an arc has been drawn that traces the angle, resulting in a semicircle. Because we know the radius, we can determine the length of the arc. The circumference of a circle is equal to 2 × pi × r, where r is the radius. In our example, if the radius is 1, the total circumference would be 6.283185[. . .].

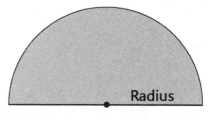

Figure 6-2. Measuring a "straight" angle of 180 degrees

Because our arc is a semicircle, it is equivalent to half that value, or simply pi × r. Since the radius of this particular circle is 1, that means that 180 degrees = pi radians. To determine the measure of each radian, we divide 180 degrees by pi, and we get 1 radian = 57.2958 degrees. Since 180 degrees equals pi radians, 360 degrees must be 2pi radians. Figure 6-3 shows some common angle measurements in both degrees and radians to help get you oriented.

So other than being a little overwhelming, what does all this mean to the way you code an animation? You need to be thinking in radians, but remember that Silverlight objects are rotated in degrees. Using the two code functions shown previously will save you a lot of trouble. All you'll really need to remember is that any number your code produces as the result of a trigonometric function will be expressed as a radian, and before you apply that rotation to an object, you need to convert it. Let's look at how to do that.

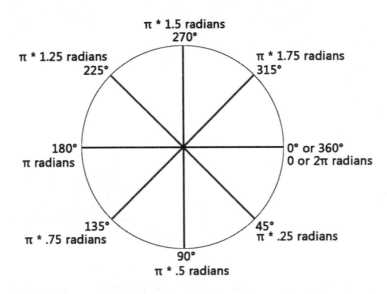

Figure 6-3. Some common angle measurements shown in both degrees and radians

The following code creates a rectangle object named MyRect that is 250×100 pixels. It is filled with red and has a black stroke. The corners of the rectangle are rounded by 7 pixels in both the x and y axes. It also has a Rotate transform called MyRectRotate, which rotates the rectangle 45 degrees.

```
<Rectangle x:Name="MyRect" Height="100" Fill="#FFFF0000"
           Stroke="#FF000000" RadiusY="7" RadiusX="7"
           RenderTransformOrigin="0.5,0.5" Width="250"
           Canvas.Left="194" Canvas.Top="132">
    <Rectangle.RenderTransform>
        <TransformGroup>
            <RotateTransform x:Name="MyRectRotate" Angle="45"/>
        </TransformGroup>
    </Rectangle.RenderTransform>
</Rectangle>
```

Let's assume that we have created a program to rotate the rectangle and our program has produced a rotational value of pi × .5, or 1.5707963267949 (90 degrees). Typically, the value will be stored in a variable, but for the purposes of clarity in this example, we'll use the value itself. To rotate our rectangle with code, we call the named Rotate transform, and then the property we wish to access (in this case, Angle). We can then assign a value based on what is returned from our conversion function:

```
MyRectRotate.Angle = RadiansToDegrees(1.5707963267949);
```

Our rectangle obliges by rotating to 90 degrees.

Now that you have a little more background on using radians as a unit of measure, it's time for a little refresher on triangles.

Triangles

Triangles are classified in one of two ways: either by their sides or by their angles. When categorized by their sides, they can be scalene, isosceles, or equilateral, as shown in Figure 6-4. A scalene triangle has no sides that are equal, or congruent. An isosceles triangle has two congruent sides, and in an equilateral triangle, all three sides (and therefore angles) are congruent. Triangles are typically annotated with letters at each angle, and referred to by their letters. The triangles shown in Figure 6-4 would be referred to as ABC, DEF, and GHI.

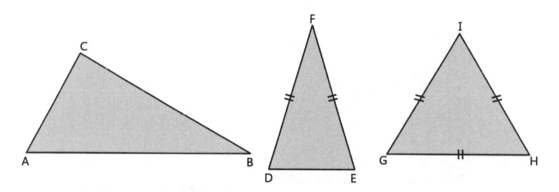

Figure 6-4. When categorized by their sides, triangles fall into one of three categories: scalene, isosceles, or equilateral.

In Figure 6-4, the isosceles triangle has two equal sides, referred to as DF and EF. Because the two sides are equal, angles D and E are also equal. In equilateral triangle GHI, all three sides are equal, as are all three angles.

The other way of categorizing triangles is by their angles, which results in four categories: acute, obtuse, equiangular, and right, as shown in Figure 6-5. Acute triangles contain one angle that is less than 90 degrees. Obtuse triangles have one angle that is greater than 90 degrees. Equiangular triangles have three equal angles (which also makes them equilateral). Finally, the right triangle contains one angle that is exactly 90 degrees. Notice that in each type of triangle, the three angles add up to exactly 180 degrees.

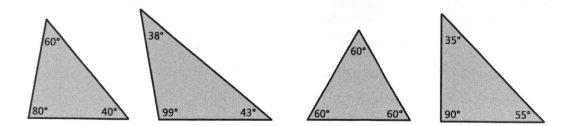

Figure 6-5. From left to right, the triangles are categorized as acute, obtuse, equiangular, and right.

The triangles we will be concerning ourselves with for trigonometry are right triangles, because as it turns out, the sides and angles of right triangles have very specific relationships, which are relatively easy to calculate with just a few basic formulas, called trigonometric functions.

Let's take a look at the relationships and how they are calculated. Right triangles like the one shown in Figure 6-6 are typically represented by a small box that is drawn in the right angle. We will need a meaningful way to refer to the sides of the triangle. A right triangle has two angles that are not right angles, one of which will be our angle of interest. This angle is labeled with the Greek symbol theta (θ), and referred to as angle q. The sides of the triangle can then be labeled based on their relationship to angle q.

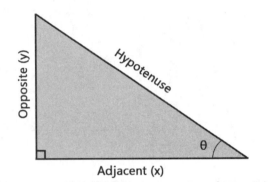

Figure 6-6. A right triangle with the sides meaningfully labeled

The side opposite the right angle is called the hypotenuse. This side will always be referred to as the hypotenuse regardless of which of the two non-right angles are selected. The other two sides are referred to as being "opposite to" or "adjacent to" angle q. The side of the triangle that touches angle q is the adjacent side, while the side farthest from angle q is the opposite.

Now that our sides have meaningful names, we can explore their relationships through trigonometric functions. For the purposes of working through these functions, let's assume that angle q measures 35 degrees.

Sine (Sin)

An angle's sine is the ratio of the angle's opposite side to the hypotenuse. To calculate the sine of an angle with code, we use the built-in sine function of C#:

```
Math.Sin(AngleInRadians);
```

So in code, assuming our conversion functions are in place, we would use the following:

```
Math.Sin(DegreesToRadians(35));
```

And we get 0.573576436351046.

This does not seem like a meaningful number at first glance, does it? This number describes the relationship of the opposite side of the triangle to the hypotenuse. What we have determined is that sine(35°) = 0.573576436351046 = opposite / hypotenuse. We now know that for *any* right triangle that has a 35-degree angle, the ratio of the opposite side to the hypotenuse will be 0.573576436351046.

I know you're waiting for me to explain how this helps us. Let's assume the hypotenuse of our triangle is 15 feet long. How long is the opposite side?

sine(35°) = opposite / hypotenuse

In order to solve for the opposite side, we multiply both sides of this equation by the hypotenuse. This effectively negates the hypotenuse in the right side of the equation (see Figure 6-7).

sine(35°) × hypotenuse = opposite / hypotenuse × hypotenuse

0.573576436351046 × hypotenuse = opposite / hypotenuse × hypotenuse

0.573576436351046 × hypotenuse = opposite

0.573576436351046 × 15 = opposite

opposite = 8.60'

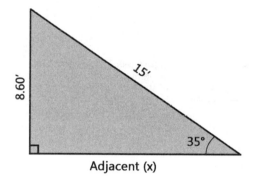

Figure 6-7. The sine of our angle multiplied by the length of the hypotenuse gives us the length of the opposite side.

So there you have it—we just used the sine function to figure out how long the opposite side of a triangle is. We'll put this into a Silverlight context in a bit—right now, we're going to move on to the cosine function.

Cosine (Cos)

The cosine function is the ratio of the angle's adjacent side to the hypotenuse. To calculate the cosine of an angle with code, use the built-in cosine function of C# (see Figure 6-8):

```
Math.Cos(AngleInRadians);
```

Once again, assuming our degrees/radians conversion functions are in place, we would use the following:

```
Math.Cos(DegreesToRadians(35));
```

This gives us 0.819152044288992, a number that describes the relationship of the adjacent side of our triangle to the hypotenuse:

cosine(35°) = 0.819152044288992 = adjacent / hypotenuse

Now we can calculate the adjacent side of the triangle. Start by multiplying both sides of the equation by the hypotenuse:

0.819152044288992 × hypotenuse = adjacent / hypotenuse × hypotenuse

This leaves us with the following:

0.819152044288992 × hypotenuse = adjacent

0.819152044288992 × 15 = adjacent

adjacent = 12.28'

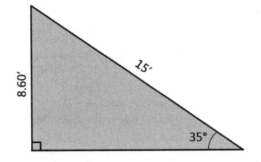

Figure 6-8. The cosine of our angle multiplied by the length of the hypotenuse gives us the length of the adjacent side.

You're becoming a regular math whiz, aren't you? You used trigonometry to calculate the lengths of two unknown sides on a right triangle! We can check our work by using yet another trigonometric function, called tangent.

Tangent (Tan)

The tangent of an angle describes the ratio between the opposite and adjacent sides of a triangle. To calculate tangent using code, use the tangent function of C#:

```
Math.Tan(AngleInRadians);
```

Utilizing our conversion functions, that looks like this:

```
Math.Tan(DegreesToRadians(35));
```

Which gives us the result 0.70020753820971.

Let's check our calculations by plugging some numbers into our ratio:

tangent = opposite / adjacent

tangent = 8.60 / 12.28

tangent = 0.70032573289902

That's pretty close! I'm willing to call it pretty accurate given that the final sine and cosine values were rounded off for readability.

Arcsine (Asin) and arccosine (Acos)

Arcsine and arccosine are just like sine and cosine, only rather than feeding in an angle and getting back a ratio, you provide the ratio and get back an angle.

Arcsine is utilized with the following code:

```
Math.Asin(RatioInRadians);
```

Recall that the sine of 35 degrees is 0.573576436351046. Using arcsine, the code looks like this:

```
Math.Asin(0.573576436351046);
```

Remember that the results are returned in radians, so we'll need to convert back to degrees:

```
RadiansToDegrees(Math.Asin(0.573576436351046));
```

And the result that's produced is (drum roll, please) . . . 35 degrees!

To use arccosine, the C# code is the following:

```
Math.Acos(RatioInRadians);
```

If we plug in the ratio from the preceding cosine example and wrap it up in our RadiansToDegrees() converter, it looks like this:

```
RadiansToDegrees(Math.Acos(0.819152044288992));
```

And once again, the result is 35 degrees.

Arctangent (Atan)

Arctangent is similar to arcsine and arccosine—you hand the function the ratio, and it will return the angle. Arctangent is utilized like this:

```
Math.Atan(RatioInRadians);
```

The full code wrapped in the RadiansToDegrees() converter would therefore look like the following:

```
RadiansToDegrees(Math.Atan(0.70032573289902));
```

This code returns 35.0045438660122.

The Math.Atan() function will return the arctangent of the number provided as a numeric value that is between –pi/2 and pi/2 radians, or in terms you can probably visualize a little more easily, –90 degrees to 90 degrees, as illustrated in Figure 6-9.

Looking at Figure 6-9 should leave you with a big question. How are you supposed to rotate objects all the way around if the tangent function only provides a set of values that covers 180 degrees? The simple answer is to use Math. Atan2(y, x) to do the calculations.

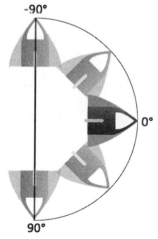

Figure 6-9. The Math.Atan() function returns values between 90 and –90 degrees

215

Math.Atan2(y, x) takes two arguments: the measurement of the opposite side and the measurement of the adjacent side. Notice the specific order of the arguments being passed—the opposite side comes first. If we insert the values we calculated earlier, and wrap the Atan2() function in our RadiansToDegrees() converter method, it looks like this:

```
RadiansToDegrees(Math.Atan2(0.573576436351046, 0.819152044288992));
```

And the result we get is 35.

Atan() also returned a result of 35 when the tangent of our triangle was input. So what's the difference between Atan() and Atan2()? Atan2() returns angles as a numeric value between –pi and pi radians, or –180 to 180 degrees. Figure 6-10 should help you visualize the rotation a little more clearly.

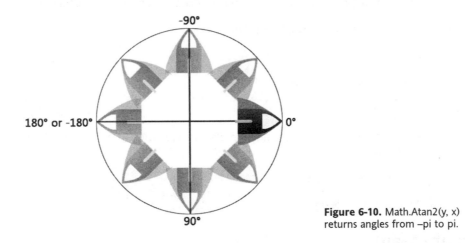

Figure 6-10. Math.Atan2(y, x) returns angles from –pi to pi.

Now we have access to a full range of 360-degree rotation! Since Silverlight will allow you to rotate to either a positive or negative value, the value returned from the Atan2() function can be converted to degrees and applied to an object.

Converting between degrees and radians

Let's code up a couple of examples to take a look at a few of the concepts we've covered so far. We'll begin with a project that will start getting you used to the idea of converting between radians and degrees.

1. Open the **DegreeRadianRotation** project to code along. The project contains two circles, each with a radius of 100 pixels, as well as a couple of TextBlock labels so we can place some feedback on the screen.

2. Start in the Page.xaml.cs file by creating the DegreesToRadians() and RadiansToDegrees() functions:

```
public partial class Page : UserControl
{
    public Page()
    {
        InitializeComponent();
    }
```

```
double RadiansToDegrees(double Radians)
{
    double Degrees = Radians * 180 / Math.PI;
    return Degrees;
}
double DegreesToRadians(double Degrees)
{
    double Radians = Degrees * Math.PI / 180;
    return Radians;
}
}
```

We're going to create two lines—one radius for each of the circles in the application. One will be rotated in degrees, and the other in radians. The rotation of each circle's radius is based off of the sine and cosine functions, which will be passed a changing angle.

3. We will need to track two angles and two rotations speeds—one expressed as degrees and the other as radians. To position the radius correctly, two Point variables are created in order to store the center of our circle elements. Add the following set of variables just before the Page() constructor. Notice that the RadianSpeed variable, which will be used to calculate the radian-based rotation, is .01745. This is the equivalent of 1 degree.

```
public partial class Page : UserControl
{
    double SinAngle = 0;
    double SinAngle2 = 0;
    double RotateSpeed = 1;
    double RadianSpeed = .01745;
    Line SineRadius = new Line();
    Point CircleCenter = new Point();
    Line SineRadius2 = new Line();
    Point Circle2Center = new Point();
[...]
```

4. We need to do a bit of initial setup to get our radii to draw on the screen. Inside the Page() constructor, just below the code that says InitializeComponent();, add the following code. These two blocks create the lines that are the radii for our circles. Both have a stroke that is 2 pixels wide. The first one has a blue color applied, and the second is colored red. Once the strokes have been defined, the lines are added to the canvas.

```
SineRadius.StrokeThickness = 2;
SolidColorBrush SineStroke = new SolidColorBrush();
SineStroke.Color = Color.FromArgb(100, 59, 130, 255);
SineRadius.Stroke = SineStroke;
LayoutRoot.Children.Add(SineRadius);
SineRadius2.StrokeThickness = 2;
SolidColorBrush SineStroke2 = new SolidColorBrush();
SineStroke2.Color = Color.FromArgb(255, 255, 0, 0);
SineRadius2.Stroke = SineStroke2;
LayoutRoot.Children.Add(SineRadius2);
```

5. Immediately following that code, we'll add some code to initialize our variables with the center values of each circle. Remember that a line is defined by two pairs of points. A circle's radius goes from the center of the circle to some point along the circle's edge. Since we have not yet calculated the location of our radius lines, we'll hide them by setting the start and finish x locations to the center x point, and both the start and finish y locations to the center y point.

```
CircleCenter.X = (double)Circle.GetValue(Canvas.LeftProperty)
                        + Circle.Width / 2;
CircleCenter.Y = (double)Circle.GetValue(Canvas.TopProperty)
                        + Circle.Height / 2;
SineRadius.X1 = SineRadius.X2 = CircleCenter.X;
SineRadius.Y1 = SineRadius.Y2 = CircleCenter.Y;
Circle2Center.X = (double)Circle2.GetValue(Canvas.LeftProperty)
                        + Circle2.Width / 2;
Circle2Center.Y = (double)Circle2.GetValue(Canvas.TopProperty)
                        + Circle2.Height / 2;
SineRadius2.X1 = SineRadius2.X2 = Circle2Center.X;
SineRadius2.Y1 = SineRadius2.Y2 = Circle2Center.Y;
```

6. This project already contains a timer called MoveTimer, so add a Completed event handler, and then get the timer going:

```
MoveTimer.Completed += new EventHandler(MoveTimer_Completed);
MoveTimer.Begin();
```

7. Depending upon whether you're letting Visual Studio create the event handler function for you, you may also need to add the following handler code after the closing curly brace of the Page() constructor. If this code isn't in your program, you need to add it.

```
void MoveTimer_Completed(object sender, EventArgs e)
{
}
```

At this point, the program will compile and run, but nothing will happen. We'll need to code up the good stuff. We'll start with the radius that will track degrees for us. Our angle incrementer would count 358, 359, 360, 0, 1, etc. We know that 360 degrees is equivalent to 0 degrees, and we don't want to calculate the location of the radius line twice, so we'll put our check in at 360.

8. The following code acts to reset our angle. If the angle is 360, the endpoint of the line is drawn according to the calculation shown—this draws the line at the correct location (359 degrees) before the angle is actually incremented to 360 degrees. The angle is then reset to 0 degrees, effectively skipping 360.

The x location of the line coordinate pair is calculated based on the cosine of the angle passed, and the y location is calculated based on the sine function. Add this code inside the moveTimer_Completed() event handler function:

```
// uses degrees
if (SinAngle == 360)
{
    SineRadius.X2 = CircleCenter.X
                    + Math.Cos(DegreesToRadians(SinAngle))
                    * Circle.Width / 2;
```

```
        SineRadius.Y2 = CircleCenter.Y
                        + Math.Sin(DegreesToRadians(SinAngle))
                        * Circle.Width / 2;
        SinAngle = 0;
}
```

9. Still working inside the event handler, add an `else` clause to the `if` statement that will do the majority of the work. This one starts out similarly to the `if` statement—by calculating the coordinates for the endpoint of the line. The angle is then incremented by 1 degree, the text on the screen is updated to show the current value of the angle, and the timer is restarted.

```
else
{
        SineRadius.X2 = CircleCenter.X
                        + Math.Cos(DegreesToRadians(SinAngle))
                        * Circle.Width / 2;
        SineRadius.Y2 = CircleCenter.Y
                        + Math.Sin(DegreesToRadians(SinAngle))
                        * Circle.Width / 2;
        SinAngle += RotateSpeed;
        MsgDegrees.Text = "Degrees: " + SinAngle;
        MoveTimer.Begin();
}
```

You can compile and run the program now if you'd like to take a look. The radius will draw in for the circle on the left, and will be calculated in real time as the angle is altered. This causes the endpoint of the radius to move around the outside of the circle, and the radius line to sweep through the rotation.

Since the timer is already being used to create the motion for the radius on the left, we'll cheat a bit and piggyback the version that will use radians. Even though the second radius is being calculated in radians, it still moves the same distance over the same period of time, so this will work well.

10. Type in the following code right after the closing curly brace of the `else` clause. Notice that this works exactly the same, except that the calculations are not converting the angle to radians first. Since the angle is already expressed in radian values, there is no reason to convert. Radians have a tendency to be a little lengthy on the screen, so the output is formatted to display only two decimal places, though the actual number is not changed. The final step is to increment the angle being used for the radius using radians by the RadianSpeed variable.

```
//uses radians
SineRadius2.X2 = Circle2Center.X
                 + Math.Cos(SinAngle2)
                 * Circle.Width / 2;
SineRadius2.Y2 = Circle2Center.Y
                 + Math.Sin(SinAngle2)
                 * Circle.Width / 2;
MsgRadians.Text = "Radians: " + String.Format("{0:0.00}", SinAngle2);
SinAngle2 += RadianSpeed;
```

Now when you compile and run, you'll see both radii sweeping around their rotations. Note that the circles drawn in the interface are purely for the reference of the person viewing the app. The circles around which the radii are traveling can be arbitrarily moved in the code by altering the center points and radius values. If you are so inclined, you can easily change the app to make one or both of the radii move counterclockwise, as shown in Figure 6-11.

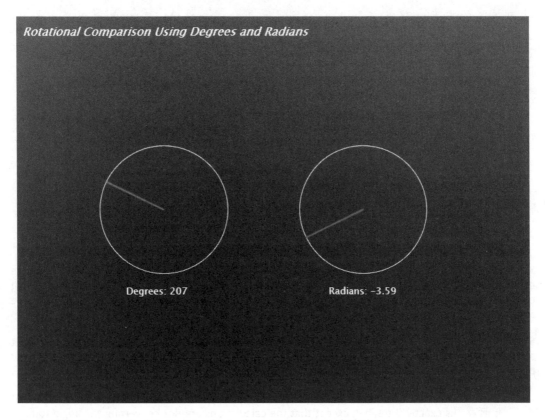

Figure 6-11. One or both of the radii can be made to rotate counterclockwise.

To change the radian-based radius, simply change the code that increments the angle so that it decrements the angle instead:

```
SinAngle2 -= RadianSpeed;
```

To change the degree-based radius, it is necessary to change the code that increments the angle, as well as the conditional if statement that checks to see if the end value has been reached:

```
// uses degrees
if (SinAngle == -360)
{
    SineRadius.X2 = CircleCenter.X
                 + Math.Cos(DegreesToRadians(SinAngle))
                 * Circle.Width / 2;
```

```
            SineRadius.Y2 = CircleCenter.Y
                            + Math.Sin(DegreesToRadians(SinAngle))
                            * Circle.Width / 2;
            SinAngle = 0;
    }
    else
    {
            SineRadius.X2 = CircleCenter.X
                            + Math.Cos(DegreesToRadians(SinAngle))
                            * Circle.Width / 2;
            SineRadius.Y2 = CircleCenter.Y
                            + Math.Sin(DegreesToRadians(SinAngle))
                            * Circle.Width / 2;
            SinAngle -= RotateSpeed;
            MsgDegrees.Text = "Degrees: " + SinAngle;
            MoveTimer.Begin();
    }
```

The final code for this project is in the **DegreeRadianRotationCompleted** project.

As you can see from the example, working with angles as a degree value or a radian value will give the same results, but sticking to radians keeps the code a little cleaner and more straightforward, since no conversions are taking place. This example was fairly basic—you can probably imagine that a complex application with a lot of conversions could get a little tricky to keep track of. This is why it's best to stick with radians in the code as much as possible, as we will be doing moving forward.

How does this relate to work you've done in Silverlight?

So you're sitting there looking at all the trigonometry and related functions and wondering how in the world right triangles and circles have anything to do with anything you've done in Silverlight. Let's take an example vector like the one shown in Figure 6-12.

Figure 6-12. An example vector

Looks familiar, right? A vector is the radius of a circle when it comes to doing calculations, and the start point of a vector (or more accurately, the coordinates of an object traveling along the vector) is the origin. Figure 6-13 shows the same vector with a circle drawn for reference.

If we drop a line from the endpoint of the vector to the y coordinate of the vector's start, and continue that line back to the origin of the circle, we'll have a right triangle like the one shown in Figure 6-14. All of a sudden, we can use what we've learned to figure out all kinds of useful information about the triangle.

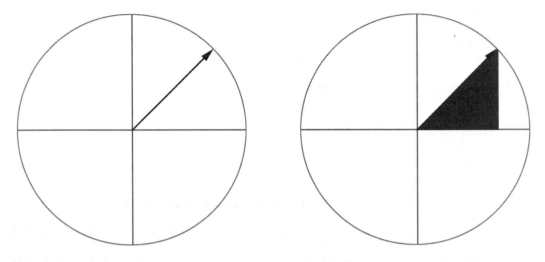

Figure 6-13. A vector is the radius of a circle.　　　**Figure 6-14.** A vector forms a right triangle.

Think back to the spaceship example from Chapter 5. Our spaceship is traveling along a vector, and we turn the spaceship and hit the thrust button. Figure 6-15 shows the triangle and calculations that are used in this case.

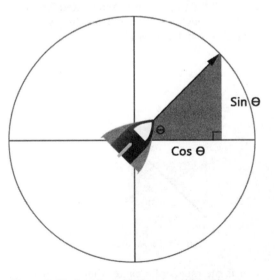

Figure 6-15. A vector with the spaceship and trigonometric functions overlaid

If I now throw the following code at you, you'll probably have a much better understanding of what is happening. Angle q is converted to radians, and then the Cos() and Sin() functions are used to determine the acceleration along the x and y axes:

```
Radians = RotateRocket.Angle * Math.PI / 180;
Acceleration.X = Math.Cos(Radians) * Thrust;
Acceleration.Y = Math.Sin(Radians) * Thrust;
```

One thing you *don't* see in the calculations is the length of the hypotenuse (or vector). The calculations are based on a *unit circle*, which is a circle whose radius is 1. The cosine calculation determines how far the ship moves horizontally when it moves one unit in the specified direction. The sine calculation determines the vertical distance per unit. The thrust variable is what will turn "units" into a meaningful measurement like "pixels" within our application. Starting to see how everything ties together here?

Free-form rotation

Next up, let's take a look at a real-world example of how we can put the Math.Atan2() function to work for us. We're going to create an application that allows us to rotate an object by dragging a handle with the mouse. To code along, open the **ImageRotate** project. This project contains a Page. xaml file that has a simple blue gradient fill, and a user control called RotateItem.

1. Open the RotateItem.xaml file and take a look at how the file is structured. There is a root Canvas called ItemCanvas, which contains an Image element and a yellow Ellipse element. The image does not currently have a source assigned—we will be doing this programmatically. The Ellipse element is named Handle and will be used as a handle to rotate the entire container canvas. Note that the container canvas has a named Rotate transform available.

```
<Canvas x:Name="ItemCanvas" Width="320" Height="240" Canvas.Left="77"
        Canvas.Top="57" Background="#FFFFFFFF"
        RenderTransformOrigin="0.5,0.5">
    <Canvas.RenderTransform>
        <TransformGroup>
            <RotateTransform x:Name="RotateItemCanvas" Angle="0"/>
        </TransformGroup>
    </Canvas.RenderTransform>
    <Image x:Name="Image" Width="300" Height="220"
           Canvas.Left="10" Canvas.Top="10"
           Source="" Stretch="Fill"/>
    <Ellipse x:Name="Handle" Width="15" Height="15"
             Fill="#FFEAFF00" Stroke="#FF000000"
             Canvas.Left="313" Canvas.Top="233"/>
</Canvas>
```

2. This time, all of the work is going to be done inside the user control to make the control reusable, so open the RotateImage.xaml.cs file.

3. Since we're creating a handle that will be used to rotate an object, we'll need a flag to determine if the mouse has been captured.

   We're also going to use three Point variables. The first, MousePosition, is used to get the current mouse position. The next, LastPosition, is used to store the last position of the mouse pointer. The last, CanvasCenter, is a public variable that will be assigned a value when the object is instantiated, and is used to provide easy access to the center coordinate of the canvas container.

The final three variables we need are all of type double. We will be storing a `CurrentAngle` calculation, a `LastAngle` calculation, and the difference between the two as `AngleDelta`.

The code for all of the variables is shown in the following listing. This code should be added before the Page() constructor.

```
private bool IsMouseCaptured;
private Point MousePosition;
private Point LastPosition;
public Point CanvasCenter;
private double LastAngle;
private double CurrentAngle;
private double AngleDelta;
```

4. Following the InitializeComponent() call in the RotateItem() constructor, add event handlers for MouseLeftButtonDown and MouseLeftButton up on the element named Handle:

```
Handle.MouseLeftButtonDown +=
        new MouseButtonEventHandler(Handle_MouseLeftButtonDown);
Handle.MouseLeftButtonUp +=
        new MouseButtonEventHandler(Handle_MouseLeftButtonUp);
```

5. Inside the event handler function for the MouseLeftButtonDown event, add the code shown in the following listing. This code should look somewhat familiar to you. We are creating a FrameworkElement object named Item, on which the mouse is captured. The cursor is changed to a hand, our Boolean flag that is used to keep track of a drag operation is set to true, and the LastPosition variable is initialized with the current position of the mouse.

```
void Handle_MouseLeftButtonDown(object sender, MouseButtonEventArgs e)
{
    FrameworkElement Item = sender as FrameworkElement;
    Item.CaptureMouse();
    Item.Cursor = Cursors.Hand;
    IsMouseCaptured = true;
    LastPosition = e.GetPosition(null);
}
```

6. The code for the MouseLeftButtonUp event handler function is used to once again create a FrameworkElement object named Item, from which the mouse capture is released. The Boolean flag is changed to false, indicating that the mouse is no longer being captured, and the cursor for the item that was clicked is reset to the default.

```
void Handle_MouseLeftButtonUp(object sender, MouseButtonEventArgs e)
{
    FrameworkElement Item = sender as FrameworkElement;
    Item.ReleaseMouseCapture();
    IsMouseCaptured = false;
    Item.Cursor = null;
}
```

7. We will also need to add our function to convert radian values to degrees, because we are rotating an object. The Rotate transform angle value for an object in Silverlight is expressed in degrees.

```
double RadiansToDegrees(double Radians)
{
    return Radians * 180 / Math.PI;
}
```

8. Now for the good stuff. The handle will point in the direction of the mouse as the mouse moves. Since this is a move operation, we'll need to add an event handler for MouseMove. This code goes inside the RotateItem() constructor with the other handlers:

```
Handle.MouseMove += new MouseEventHandler(Handle_MouseMove);
```

9. Inside the event handler function for MouseMove, we'll do the work of figuring out how much the image should be rotated based on the current location of the mouse pointer. The first thing the event handler does is get the current position of the mouse and store it in the MousePosition variable.

Then, if the mouse is being dragged, LastAngle is calculated by passing the coordinates that result when the center coordinates of the canvas being rotated are subtracted from the last pointer position to the Atan2() method. Notice that they are passed y and then x.

Next, CurrentAngle is calculated using the same method, but by subtracting the canvas center position from the current mouse position.

The difference between the two angles is determined, and the Rotate transform angle of the Canvas object is incremented by the difference after it's converted to degrees.

The LastPosition variable is then updated to the current mouse position for the next time the mouse moves.

```
void Handle_MouseMove(object sender, MouseEventArgs e)
{
    MousePosition = e.GetPosition(null);
    if (IsMouseCaptured)
    {
        LastAngle = Math.Atan2(LastPosition.Y - CanvasCenter.Y,
                               LastPosition.X - CanvasCenter.X);
        CurrentAngle = Math.Atan2(MousePosition.Y - CanvasCenter.Y,
                               MousePosition.X - CanvasCenter.X);
        AngleDelta = CurrentAngle - LastAngle;
        RotateItemCanvas.Angle += RadiansToDegrees(AngleDelta);
        LastPosition = MousePosition;
    }
}
```

Now all we need to do is add some code to the Page.xaml.cs file to instantiate our RotateItem object and see what kind of results we get.

10. We will be assigning images to Image elements, so we'll need to add a library reference to the list of references at the top of the page:

```
using System;
using System.Collections.Generic;
using System.Linq;
using System.Net;
using System.Windows;
using System.Windows.Controls;
using System.Windows.Documents;
using System.Windows.Input;
using System.Windows.Media;
using System.Windows.Media.Animation;
using System.Windows.Shapes;
using System.Windows.Media.Imaging;
```

The System.Windows.Media.Imaging library makes it possible for us to work with bitmaps.

11. Before the Page() constructor, create a new instance of the RotateItem object called Picture1.

```
RotateItem Picture1 = new RotateItem();
```

12. Inside the Page() constructor, assign the source of the Picture1 object's Image element, as shown in the following code listing. I've already added two sample JPGs to the project for you to work with. The code tells Silverlight where the Marigold.jpg image is relative to the application.

The left and top properties of the Picture1 object are then set to 100 to position it near the top-left corner of the root canvas. Next, the public CanvasCenter property for the object is assigned a value. The angle of the object is preset to –15 degrees so it looks interesting when it loads, and the object is added to the LayoutRoot Canvas.

```
public Page()
{
    InitializeComponent();
    Picture1.Image.Source =
            new BitmapImage(new Uri("Marigold.jpg", UriKind.Relative));
    Picture1.SetValue(Canvas.LeftProperty, 100.00);
    Picture1.SetValue(Canvas.TopProperty, 100.00);
    Picture1.CanvasCenter.X =
            (double)Picture1.GetValue(Canvas.LeftProperty)
            + Picture1.Width / 2;
    Picture1.CanvasCenter.Y =
            (double)Picture1.GetValue(Canvas.TopProperty)
            + Picture1.Height / 2;
    Picture1.RotateItemCanvas.Angle = -15;
    LayoutRoot.Children.Add(Picture1);
}
```

Compile and run the application. You should get something similar to Figure 6-16. Dragging the yellow handle with the mouse will rotate the image. Notice how the handle always points to the location of the mouse pointer.

Figure 6-16. The ImageRotate project creates images with rotate handles.

When the program runs, the code that does the rotation is essentially saying "Here are the coordinates of the mouse. Draw a line from the center of the canvas to these coordinates, calculate the angle that forms, and then calculate the angle difference between this angle and the last angle." This code runs constantly as the mouse moves, calculating the angle offsets in real time. In the application, the movements can be very small, but Figure 6-17 shows larger-scale movement to illustrate the code functionality.

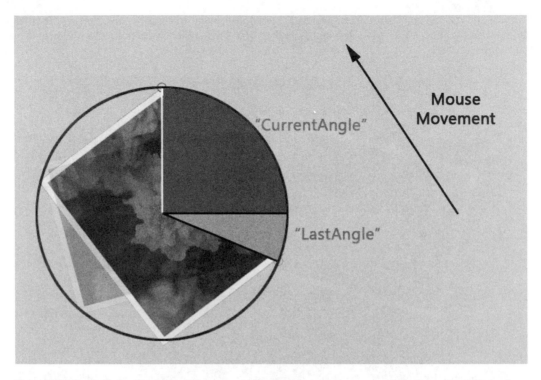

Figure 6-17. As the mouse is dragged, the code constantly calculates the new angle based on the distance from the center of the canvas to the mouse position.

Since the RotateItem user control is completely self-contained, it takes about a minute to add another instance of the object. You can add the following code to get a second image in the application.

13. Start by declaring a second object, named Picture2:

```
RotateItem Picture2 = new RotateItem();
```

14. Next, set the initial properties for the new object as per the following code listing. Be sure to reference the new object (Picture2) when setting the CanvasCenter property, or the rotation will give unexpected results.

```
Picture2.Image.Source =
        new BitmapImage(new Uri("PurpleFlower.jpg", UriKind.Relative));
Picture2.SetValue(Canvas.LeftProperty, 400.00);
Picture2.SetValue(Canvas.TopProperty, 300.00);
Picture2.CanvasCenter.X =
        (double)Picture2.GetValue(Canvas.LeftProperty)
        + Picture2.Width / 2;
Picture2.CanvasCenter.Y =
        (double)Picture2.GetValue(Canvas.TopProperty)
        + Picture2.Height / 2;
Picture2.RotateItemCanvas.Angle = -15;
LayoutRoot.Children.Add(Picture2);
```

If you compile and run the project at this point, you'll see both of the images drawn, and each can be rotated independently. If you'd like to use your own images, add them to the project by right-clicking the project name in Visual Studio's Solution Explorer, and then select Add ➤ New Item from the menu, as shown in Figure 6-18. They will then be available for use in the same way as the original two. The code shown in this example is available in the **ImageRotateCompleted** project.

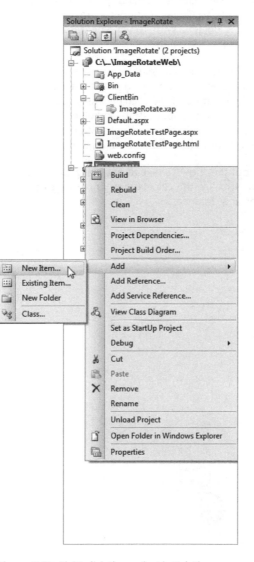

Figure 6-18. Right-click the project in Solution Explorer and select Add ➤ New Item to add your own images to the project.

A little help with the visualization

We've gone through triangles, angles, and a lot of math, and perhaps you're kind of getting it, but not sure how it all pulls together.

At http://www.kirupa.com/developer/actionscript/trigonometry.htm, I came across an application originally written by Trevor McCauley that does a great job of illustrating the calculations involving right triangles for moving objects. With Trevor's permission, I've included a Silverlight version in the projects for Chapter 6 as **RightTriangle**.

The application, shown in Figure 6-19, contains a red ball object that is rotating in a circular path. As the ball rotates, a red right triangle is drawn, with annotations for the Math.Sin() and Math.Cos() calculations based on the hypotenuse of the triangle. The angle of the ball object is tracked via a small blue circular path in the center of the application, and all of the associated calculations are displayed on the screen. There is also a Pause button on the screen that allows you to temporarily suspend the action of the application to take a closer look at the number.

This application is not about the "how," so we're not going to dig into the code; it's more for illustrative purposes to help you visualize the calculations you're performing, and how triangles and circles relate to rotational angles and distances.

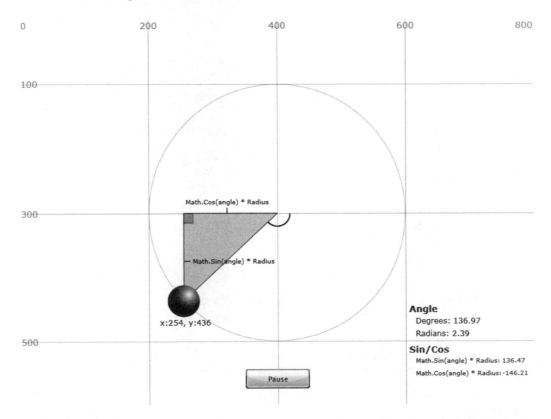

Figure 6-19. The RightTriangle application illustrates the right triangles created by trigonometric functions on a moving object.

Sine curves

Sine curves, or waves, like the one shown in Figure 6-20, are probably something with which you are already familiar. The sine curve is related to the sine function we used earlier—each of the points along the length of the wave is a result of feeding an angle into the function.

The horizontal points are the values of the angle being used, ranging from 0 to 2pi radians (0 to 360 degrees), while the vertical points are the resulting sine values for the angle at that particular point. To help you visualize the association between sine, cosine, and their related curves, I have included an application called **unitCircleSin**.

The application, shown in Figure 6-21, draws a real-time graph of both sine and cosine curves as they relate to the angle of rotation. You can turn off either curve with the check boxes on the interface. You will also see red lines within the circle that show the right angles created by the rotating radii. Notice that the values for sine and cosine fluctuate between 1 and –1.

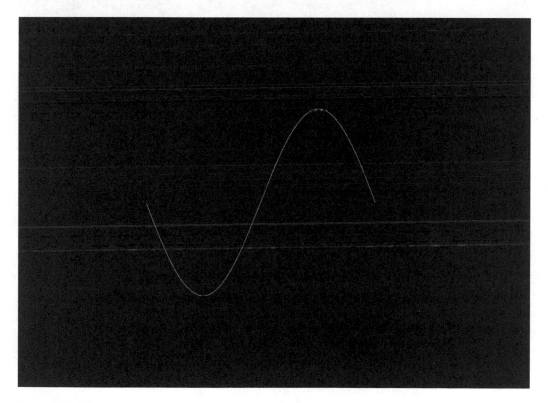

Figure 6-20. A basic sine curve

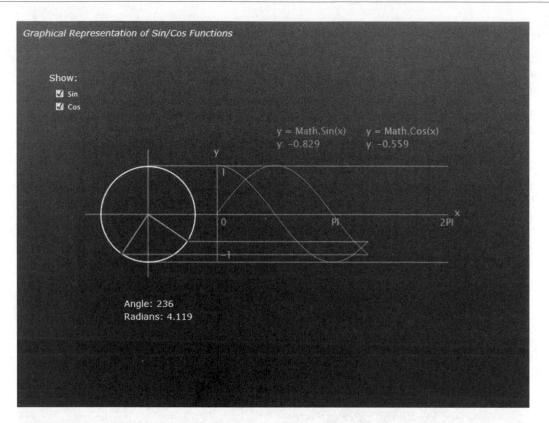

Figure 6-21. Graphing sine/cosine curves

This application is another intended to illustrate some of the concepts we've been discussing, so we won't dig into the code, but feel free to explore it on your own.

What we will be building is a sine wave generator application, which will allow a user to modify the amplitude or frequency of a sine wave by manipulating sliders in the interface. As a slider's value changes, the waveform will also change, being redrawn in real time.

In case you're not familiar with the terms, Dictionary.com defines amplitude as "the absolute value of the maximum displacement from a zero value during one period of an oscillation." Think of amplitude as the overall height of our waveform. Frequency is "the number of cycles or completed alternations per unit time of a wave or oscillation." As such, frequency will determine the density of waves along our curve. Figure 6-22 illustrates both of these definitions against a waveform for you.

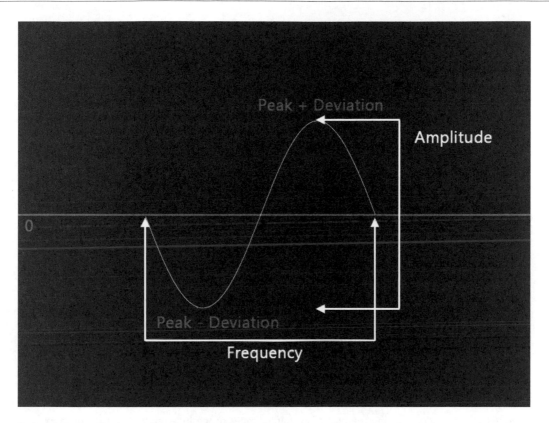

Figure 6-22. Amplitude and frequency of a sine waveform

To code along, open the **SineWaveGenerator** project. The Page.xaml file for the project contains the usual LayoutRoot Canvas, which is filled with a gradient brush. There is also a Border object used to make a thin white border for the application. To handle the drawing of the waveform, there is a Polyline object. For input, there are two sliders and associated TextBlock labels. There is also a TextBlock label for the application title.

1. All of the code for this project is contained within the Page.xaml.cs file, so open that file for editing. We'll begin by adding the variables we'll need to draw the waveform. The first is Angle, which is used to calculate the angle that our sine graph is based upon. Next is a PointCollection, which is literally a collection of points. We will calculate each point for the waveform, add it to the PointCollection, and then assign the PointCollection to the Polyline to draw the waveform. The NextPoint variable is used to store the next point being calculated along the graph of the waveform. Finally, we need variables for the amplitude and frequency of the waveform. Place these variables before the Page() constructor.

```
double Angle = 0;
PointCollection PC = new PointCollection();
Point NextPoint = new Point();
double Amplitude = 145;
double Frequency = .5;
```

2. The first thing we need to do is to write a function that creates the waveform. The application is 800 pixels wide, so the calculations will run from 0 to 799. The first line of code within the `for` loop in the following listing increments the angle by 2 degrees converted to radians, and multiplied by the frequency. Smaller angle increments will result in more waves fitting on the screen, while greater increments will produce fewer waves.

Next, the coordinates for the next point of the waveform are calculated. The wave fills the screen, so the x coordinate is equal to the value of the variable i, while the y coordinate is equal to the sine of the current angle times the amplitude of the wave. By subtracting this number from the height of the application divided by two, the wave will be centered vertically.

Once the coordinate has been determined, it is added to the `PointCollection`, which is then assigned to the Polyline object.

This code goes after the closing curly brace of the Page() constructor:

```
void DrawSine()
{
    for (int i = 0; i < this.Width; i++)
    {
        Angle += (Math.PI / 180 * 2) * Frequency;
        NextPoint.X = i;
        NextPoint.Y = this.Height / 2 - (Math.Sin(Angle) * Amplitude);
        PC.Add(NextPoint);
        Poly.Points = PC;
    }
}
```

3. As you can see, drawing the curve is a fairly simple procedure. All we need to do now is call the `DrawSine()` function from inside the `Page()` constructor. The complete code listing at this point is shown following:

```
namespace SineWaveGenerator
{
    public partial class Page : UserControl
    {
        double Angle = 0;
        PointCollection PC = new PointCollection();
        Point NextPoint = new Point();
        double Amplitude = 145;
        double Frequency = .5;
        public Page()
        {
            InitializeComponent();
            DrawSine();
        }
```

```
void DrawSine()
{
    for (int i = 0; i < this.Width; i++)
    {
        Angle += (Math.PI / 180 * 2) * Frequency;
        NextPoint.X = i;
        NextPoint.Y = this.Height / 2
                    - (Math.Sin(Angle) * Amplitude);
        PC.Add(NextPoint);
        Poly.Points = PC;
    }
}
}
}
```

When you run the program, you should get a sine wave drawn on the screen like the one shown in Figure 6-23.

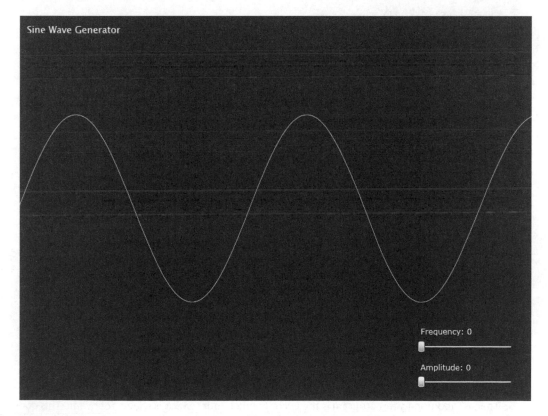

Figure 6-23. The default sine wave generated by the program

235

4. Let's hook up the sliders for frequency and amplitude. Inside the Page() constructor, just below the InitializeComponent() call, add the following code. This code sets minimum and maximum values for each of the sliders, and also "presets" them to the values already assigned to the Frequency and Amplitude variables. The label for each slider is also updated to show the current value of the slider.

```
FrequencySlider.Minimum = 0;
FrequencySlider.Maximum = 5;
FrequencySlider.Value = Frequency;
MsgFrequency.Text = "Frequency: " + FrequencySlider.Value;
AmplitudeSlider.Minimum = 0;
AmplitudeSlider.Maximum = 175;
AmplitudeSlider.Value = Amplitude;
MsgAmplitude.Text = "Amplitude: " + AmplitudeSlider.Value;
```

5. After that code, add event handlers for the ValueChanged event on each slider. Watch this code—both event listeners are calling the same event handler—slider_ValueChanged. This cuts down on some code duplication.

```
FrequencySlider.ValueChanged +=
    new RoutedPropertyChangedEventHandler<double>(slider_ValueChanged);
AmplitudeSlider.ValueChanged +=
    new RoutedPropertyChangedEventHandler<double>(slider_ValueChanged);
```

Your Page() constructor should now look like the following listing:

```
public Page()
{
    InitializeComponent();
    FrequencySlider.Minimum = 0;
    FrequencySlider.Maximum = 5;
    FrequencySlider.Value = Frequency;
    MsgFrequency.Text = "Frequency: " + FrequencySlider.Value;
    AmplitudeSlider.Minimum = 0;
    AmplitudeSlider.Maximum = 175;
    AmplitudeSlider.Value = Amplitude;
    MsgAmplitude.Text = "Amplitude: " + AmplitudeSlider.Value;
    FrequencySlider.ValueChanged +=
       new RoutedPropertyChangedEventHandler<double>➥
       (slider_ValueChanged);
    AmplitudeSlider.ValueChanged +=
       new RoutedPropertyChangedEventHandler<double>➥
       (slider_ValueChanged);
    DrawSine();
}
```

6. The last addition to this program is the event handler code, which is shown following. This code will execute any time a slider's value changes. The code clears the current PointCollection, effectively deleting the prior waveform. It then sets the Frequency and Amplitude variables to the values represented on the slider controls, and updates the text labels for each slider to show the current value. Finally, the DrawSine() function is called to draw the new sine wave.

```
void slider_ValueChanged(object sender,
    RoutedPropertyChangedEventArgs<double> e)
{
    PC.Clear();
    Frequency = FrequencySlider.Value;
    Amplitude = AmplitudeSlider.Value;
    MsgAmplitude.Text = "Amplitude: "
                        + String.Format("{0:0.00}",
                            AmplitudeSlider.Value);
    MsgFrequency.Text = "Frequency: "
                        + String.Format("{0:0.00}",
                            FrequencySlider.Value);
    DrawSine();
}
```

Now when you run the program, you can manipulate the sliders, and the waveform drawn in the application will change accordingly. The **SineWaveGeneratorCompleted** project contains the finalized code for the project.

Oscillation

You're probably playing with the project and thinking it's pretty nice, but wondering how in the world this will help you do what you're trying to do in Silverlight. What happens if you remove the x component from the wave? That's right! You get smooth up-and-down oscillating movement.

1. Open the **SimpleOscillation** project to code along with this example. We're going to make a slight change to the instantiation of the Silverlight user control here, so open up the SimpleOscillationTestPage.html file and scroll down to the object tag shown here:

```
<object data="data:application/x-silverlight,"
            type="application/x-silverlight-2-b2"
            width="100%" height="100%">
    <param name="source" value="ClientBin/SimpleOscillation.xap"/>
    <param name="onerror" value="onSilverlightError" />
    <param name="background" value="white" />
    <a href="http://go.microsoft.com/fwlink/?LinkID=115261"
        style="text-decoration: none;">
        <img src="http://go.microsoft.com/fwlink/?LinkId=108181"
            alt="Get Microsoft Silverlight"
            style="border-style: none"/>
    </a>
</object>
```

2. Just beneath the <param name="background" value="white" /> line, add the following line:

```
<param name="maxframerate" value="30" />
```

As the number of objects we're moving programmatically increases, this change will help Silverlight maintain a refresh speed of 30 frames per second (FPS) to keep our motion as smooth as possible. This should help maintain a more consistent experience from machine to machine.

3. In the Page.xaml.cs file, create an object instance for the Ball object, as well as variables to hold Angle, CenterY, Range, and Speed values. The code in the following listing goes before the Page() constructor:

```
Ball RedBall = new Ball();
double Angle = 0;
double CenterY;
double Range = 200;
double Speed = .1;
```

4. Inside the Page() constructor, instantiate the RedBall object at the horizontal center of the application:

```
Canvas.SetLeft(RedBall, (LayoutRoot.Width / 2) - (RedBall.Width / 2));
LayoutRoot.Children.Add(RedBall);
```

5. Initialize the CenterY variable with the vertical center of the application:

```
CenterY = LayoutRoot.Height / 2;
```

6. There is a storyboard timer called Timer already in the Page.xaml file. Add an event handler for the Completed event on the timer, and then call the timer's Begin() method:

```
Timer.Completed += new EventHandler(Timer_Completed);
Timer.Begin();
```

7. Inside the event handler function for the timer's Completed event, add the following code. This code will move the ball using a sine calculation to determine a y range of values before incrementing the angle and restarting the timer to continue the animation.

```
void Timer_Completed(object sender, EventArgs e)
{
    Canvas.SetTop(RedBall, CenterY + Math.Sin(Angle) * Range);
    Angle += Speed;
    Timer.Begin();
}
```

Run the application. The ball object will move up and down smoothly. Remember that the result of the Math.Sin(Angle) calculation will be a value between –1 and 1. This value is multiplied by the Range to determine the offset for the ball from the CenterY location.

If you would like to change the distance the ball travels, simply modify the Range variable and run the program again. Changing the CenterY variable will change the y location around which the ball is oscillating. Changing the Speed variable will alter the rate at which the Angle changes, which will speed up or slow down the oscillating motion.

The code shown in the previous example is available in the **SimpleOscillationCompleted** project.

A practical use for oscillation

The movement of the ball is pretty smooth, but let's take a look at a more practical application.

1. Open the **GuitarStrings** project to code along with this example. The project contains a guitar body object and a guitar string object. We're going to add six strings to the guitar, and make them vibrate as the mouse passes over each string.

2. We'll start coding up the GuitarString.xaml.cs file by declaring some variables. Much like the ball, the guitar string object has variables for Angle, Range, and Speed. There is also a variable called ResetRange, which is used to keep track of the Range setting for each string (the use of this variable will become more clear in a few moments), as well as a TopX variable. Both Range and TopX are public variables, so they are accessible from the main program. This code goes just before the GuitarString() constructor:

```
private double Angle = 0;
public double Range = 3;
private double ResetRange;
private double Speed = 2;
public double TopX;
```

3. Inside the GuitarString() constructor, ResetRange is used to store the Range value that is set when the GuitarString object is instantiated from the main code. The GuitarString object has a storyboard timer in it called Vibrate that is used to make the string move, and an event handler is added to the Completed event for this storyboard.

```
public GuitarString()
{
    InitializeComponent();
    ResetRange = Range;
    this.Vibrate.Completed += new EventHandler(Vibrate_Completed);
}
```

4. Each string handles its own oscillation movements inside the Completed event handler. When the storyboard completes, a quick check is done to see if the Range value is greater than 0. If so, the string is moved with our familiar oscillation code, and the timer is restarted. Notice that the Range value is dampened with each pass. Real guitar strings do not vibrate endlessly, and neither should ours. By dampening the range, we can make the string vibrate widely when first hit, and then fade down to no motion over time.

If the Range has dampened down to 0 or lower, the Vibrate movement is stopped, the angle is reset, and the Range value is reset to the original value in order to prepare for the next time the string needs to move. This code goes inside the event handler, which is placed outside of the Page() constructor:

```
void Vibrate_Completed(object sender, EventArgs e)
{
    if (Range > 0)
    {
        this.SetValue(Canvas.TopProperty, TopX
                      + Math.Sin(Angle) * Range);
        Angle += Speed;
        Range -= .025;
        Vibrate.Begin();
    }
```

```
    else
    {
        Vibrate.Stop();
        Angle = 0;
        Range = ResetRange;
    }
}
```

5. That's all we need to do for the strings. Now we need to work on our interface a bit, so open the Page.xaml.cs file for editing. We already know we're going to need an instance of the guitar body object, as well as six instances of the string object. In addition, we will use the mouse to determine if a string has been plucked, so we need a Point object to store the current mouse position, as well as one to store the last mouse position. All of these variable declarations are placed just before the Page() constructor:

```
Guitar MyGuitar = new Guitar();
GuitarString String6 = new GuitarString();
GuitarString String5 = new GuitarString();
GuitarString String4 = new GuitarString();
GuitarString String3 = new GuitarString();
GuitarString String2 = new GuitarString();
GuitarString String1 = new GuitarString();
Point MousePosition;
Point LastMousePosition;
```

6. Inside the Page() constructor, instantiate all of the objects. Normally, guitar strings are attached to both the bridge and the tuning pegs at the top of the neck, and vibrate in the middle. We are going to cheat a little bit and have the whole string vibrate, so we're going to get close up on the guitar body. As such, our guitar is scaled up to 450% and positioned appropriately before being added to the LayoutRoot Canvas.

Next come the strings. Each has its left and top property set. Notice that the TopX public variable is set along with the top property in order to create the point of origin for the oscillating movement that was created in the guitar string object. The thickness of guitar strings varies, and since our string object is made with a line stroke, we can adjust the stroke to create strings of varied thickness. We also define a range—the thicker strings of a guitar vibrate more widely than the thinner ones. After each string is set up, it is added to the LayoutRoot Canvas.

The next-to-last line of this section sets the y component of the LastMousePosition variable to be equal to the height of the application. This avoids having the strings play inadvertently when the application is loaded if the mouse is being moved toward the top of the application.

The last line sets up the MouseMove() event handler for the LayoutRoot Canvas. The event handler function for MouseMove() is where all the action takes place for the application.

```
public Page()
{
    InitializeComponent();
    MyGuitar.GuitarScale.ScaleX = MyGuitar.GuitarScale.ScaleY = 4.5;
    MyGuitar.SetValue(Canvas.LeftProperty, 600.00);
    MyGuitar.SetValue(Canvas.TopProperty, 250.00);
```

```
        LayoutRoot.Children.Add(MyGuitar);
        String6.SetValue(Canvas.LeftProperty, -10.00);
        String6.SetValue(Canvas.TopProperty, 265.00);
        String6.TopX = 265;
        String6.Range = 5;
        LayoutRoot.Children.Add(String6);
        String5.SetValue(Canvas.LeftProperty, -10.00);
        String5.SetValue(Canvas.TopProperty, 280.00);
        String5.TopX = 280;
        String6.Range = 4;
        LayoutRoot.Children.Add(String5);
        String4.SetValue(Canvas.LeftProperty, -10.00);
        String4.SetValue(Canvas.TopProperty, 296.00);
        String4.StringLine.StrokeThickness = 3;
        String4.TopX = 296;
        String4.Range = 4;
        LayoutRoot.Children.Add(String4);
        String3.SetValue(Canvas.LeftProperty, -10.00);
        String3.SetValue(Canvas.TopProperty, 312.00);
        String3.StringLine.StrokeThickness = 3;
        String3.TopX = 312;
        String3.Range = 3;
        LayoutRoot.Children.Add(String3);
        String2.SetValue(Canvas.LeftProperty, -10.00);
        String2.SetValue(Canvas.TopProperty, 328.00);
        String2.StringLine.StrokeThickness = 2;
        String2.TopX = 328;
        String2.Range = 3;
        LayoutRoot.Children.Add(String2);
        String1.SetValue(Canvas.LeftProperty, -10.00);
        String1.SetValue(Canvas.TopProperty, 344.00);
        String1.StringLine.StrokeThickness = 2;
        String1.TopX = 344;
        String1.Range = 3;
        LayoutRoot.Children.Add(String1);
        LastMousePosition.Y = LayoutRoot.Height;
        LayoutRoot.MouseMove += new MouseEventHandler(Page_MouseMove);
    }
```

7. The MouseMove() event handler code is shown in the following listing. The idea here is to only strum a string when the mouse is moved toward the bottom of the application. To do this, we start by getting the current position of the mouse. We can then check the current mouse position against the last mouse position to determine which way the mouse is moving, and if it has encountered the y position where a string is located.

The first check says, "If the mouse is located at 344y or greater, and the last mouse position was less than 344y (meaning it was above the string), then play that string's Vibrate storyboard." Each of the other five strings is checked the same way, with the appropriate y value inserted for the tests.

```
void Page_MouseMove(object sender, MouseEventArgs e)
{
    MousePosition = e.GetPosition(null);
    if (MousePosition.Y > 344 && LastMousePosition.Y < 344)
    {
        String1.Vibrate.Begin();
    }
    if (MousePosition.Y > 328 && LastMousePosition.Y < 328)
    {
        String2.Vibrate.Begin();
    }
    if (MousePosition.Y > 312 && LastMousePosition.Y < 312)
    {
        String3.Vibrate.Begin();
    }
    if (MousePosition.Y > 296 && LastMousePosition.Y < 296)
    {
        String4.Vibrate.Begin();
    }
    if (MousePosition.Y > 280 && LastMousePosition.Y < 280)
    {
        String5.Vibrate.Begin();
    }
    if (MousePosition.Y > 265 && LastMousePosition.Y < 265)
    {
        String6.Vibrate.Begin();
    }
    LastMousePosition = MousePosition;
}
```

When the application is run, the guitar and strings are drawn in the application, as shown in Figure 6-24. When the mouse is positioned above the strings and moved downward, the strings will vibrate as they are encountered, and continue to oscillate until the range dampening cuts the motion down enough to reset the string for the next pass.

Ideally, a range of y values would be provided to test for each string hit, as it is possible to move the mouse over a string without a hit being registered. In addition, a string should not be reset until the vibration has dampened enough to drop below the threshold set in the user control, so you cannot continuously strum the strings.

The **GuitarStringsCompleted** project contains the final version of the code for this project.

Figure 6-24. The guitar strings oscillate as the mouse is moved across them.

Horizontal oscillation

Just as you can create smooth up-and-down oscillation using a sine wave, smooth left-to-right movement can be achieved with cosine. Remember that sine is the y component of our triangle calculations, and cosine is the x component.

1. Open the **SimpleOscillationsCompleted** project.

2. Look in the Page.xaml.cs file for the line of code that creates the motion:

   ```
   Canvas.SetTop(RedBall, CenterY + Math.Sin(Angle) * Range);
   ```

3. Update that line of code to the following, in order to make the ball move from left to right:

   ```
   Canvas.SetLeft(RedBall, CenterY + Math.Cos(Angle) * Range);
   ```

4. As demonstrated in the application that generated the sine and cosine wave graphs earlier, it generally won't make any difference if you're using sine or cosine—either will generate a range of values between –1 and 1 multiplied by whatever distance range you choose. For example, the following code gives the same result as the code in step 3:

   ```
   Canvas.SetLeft(RedBall, CenterY + Math.Sin(Angle) * Range);
   ```

5. Once the ball oscillates horizontally, a few lines of code can be added to the project in order to add some linear motion along the y axis to the ball as well. Start with a variable before the `Page()` constructor to track the y position:

```
double PosY = 0;
```

6. Inside the `Timer_Completed()` event handler, add two lines of code. The first positions the ball to the current y position, and the second increments the y position:

```
Canvas.SetTop(RedBall, PosY);
PosY += 1;
```

Press F5 to run the project. As the project runs, the ball oscillates horizontally as it moves from the top of the application toward the bottom. Having linear motion combined with oscillating movement opens up some possibilities.

Falling snow

To code along with this project, open the **Snowflakes** project. The project contains a snowflake object with both Scale and Rotate transforms. The `Page.xaml` file contains the LayoutRoot Canvas with a black/gray gradient fill, and a storyboard timer called Snowfall. This project has a lot going on, so let's get started!

When run, the completed project will create a number of snowflakes that are positioned randomly about the application. Each flake will be scaled randomly, have a randomly generated y velocity, and a random transparency. The snowflakes will fall slowly, drifting back and forth. When a snowflake reaches the bottom of the application, it will be placed back at the top, in order to keep a continuous snowfall going.

1. Start by coding up the `Snowflake.xaml.cs` file. We'll start off with a variable to maintain the flake's position. Next are four variables related to the drifting motion of the flake. These should look similar to our previous examples: angle, range, position (or point of origin), and speed. Next comes a variable for the speed at which a flake will fall. Finally, we have a public variable used to hold the height of the main application, as well as a variable that will be used to generate random numbers.

```
private Point Position;
private double DriftAngle;
private double DriftRange;
private double DriftPosition;
private double DriftSpeed = .1;
private double Speed;
public double AppHeight;
private Random Rand = new Random();
```

2. This time, we're going to modify the `Snowflake()` constructor in order to pass variables as each flake is initialized by the main application. Normally, the code looks like this:

```
public Snowflake()
{
    InitializeComponent();
}
```

We want to change ours to accept three double values. Our main application will generate random numbers for the position and opacity and pass them to the Snowflake object as it is instantiated.

```
public Snowflake(double Left, double Top, double Opacity)
{
    InitializeComponent();
}
```

The Snowflake object will also do some self-configuration. The code shown in the following few steps is placed after the InitializeComponent() method.

3. The first line of the following code generates a random number between 0 and 5 for the flake. If the number generated is less than 1, then it is made 1. This will ensure that all of the flakes in the application actually fall.

```
Speed = Rand.Next(5);
1f (Speed < 1)
{
    Speed = 1;
}
```

4. Next, the point of origin for the flake's drift is assigned using the left position passed when the flake was instantiated. In addition, a range of up to 50 pixels is generated, and a random starting angle for the drift is selected. The random angle is important—this adds some variance to where in the drift motion each flake starts. Without it, all of the snowflakes would drift in unison, which would not look very natural.

```
DriftPosition = Left;
DriftRange = Rand.Next(50);
DriftAngle = Rand.Next(270);
```

5. Next, a scale value between .25 and 1 is generated for the flake. Once the scale value has been generated, it is assigned to both the x and y scale values for the flake in order to keep the scaling symmetrical.

```
ScaleFlake.ScaleX = ScaleFlake.ScaleY =
                (double)Rand.Next(25, 100) / 100.0;
```

6. The last bit of code in the Snowflake() constructor positions the flake, sets the opacity, and stores the position for when the flake is moving:

```
Canvas.SetLeft(this, Left);
Canvas.SetTop(this, Top);
this.Opacity = Opacity;
Position.X = Left;
Position.Y = Top;
```

7. Now we need to add a function that is called from the main code in order to move each flake when needed. This is a public method called MoveFlake() that is placed after the Snowflake() constructor. The function begins by updating the X and Y Position variables for the snowflake. The Y variable simply moves the flake down the screen. The X variable calculates the horizontal oscillation value that causes the snowflake to drift. Following this is a test to see if the flake has moved below the bottom of the application. If so, the flake is moved to the top of the application. Finally, the actual position of the flake is updated, and the angle used to determine the drift oscillation is incremented. This is a fairly simple bit of code that does a whole lot of work for us.

```
public void MoveFlake()
{
    Position.Y += Speed;
    Position.X = DriftPosition + Math.Cos(DriftAngle) * DriftRange;
    if (Position.Y > AppHeight)
    {
        Position.Y = -this.Height;
    }
    Canvas.SetLeft(this, Position.X);
    Canvas.SetTop(this, Position.Y);
    DriftAngle += DriftSpeed;
}
```

8. Now that the snowflake code-behind is all set, move to the Page.xaml.cs file. This is where we'll go about generating our snowflakes and getting them moving.

9. Before the Page() constructor, start by declaring three Lists. In C#, a List is similar to an Array, only it provides some methods that save time and code later (as you will see). The first List will contain all of our snowflake objects. The second List will be used to hold the starting x and y positions of each snowflake, and the third will hold the opacity values generated for each flake:

```
List<Snowflake> Flake;
List<Point> XYStart;
List<double> OpacityValue;
```

10. After the Lists are declared, declare an integer to give us control over how many flakes will be on the screen, and a random number generator for use in initializing the flakes:

```
int MaxFlakes = 250;
Random Rand = new Random();
```

11. With the variable declarations in place, move to the Page() constructor. The following code comes after the InitializeComponent() method. We'll start by initializing our Lists according to the length specified by the MaxFlakes variable:

```
Flake = new List<Snowflake>(MaxFlakes);
XYStart = new List<Point>(MaxFlakes);
OpacityValue = new List<double>(MaxFlakes);
```

12. Next, add a loop to generate the necessary number of x and y starting positions, and opacity values:

```
for (int i = 0; i < MaxFlakes; i++)
{
    Point newPoint = new Point(Rand.Next((int)LayoutRoot.Width),
                    Rand.Next((int)LayoutRoot.Height));
    XYStart.Add(newPoint);
    OpacityValue.Add(Rand.NextDouble());
}
```

13. With that in place, we'll call the InitFlakes() function (which we'll code up momentarily), add an event handler for the Completed event on the Snowfall storyboard, and start the storyboard:

```
InitFlakes();
Snowfall.Completed += new EventHandler(Snowfall_Completed);
Snowfall.Begin();
```

14. The InitFlakes() function referenced previously is shown in the following listing. Place this code after the Page() constructor. The sole purpose of this function is to create snowflakes based on the values that were just generated for starting positions and opacity values. This is done by once again running a quick loop.

The code instantiates a new flake using the corresponding x and y starting positions, and opacity. The newly instantiated flake is then added to the List of flakes. The flake instance has its public appHeight variable assigned in order to track the application height, and is then added to the LayoutRoot Canvas:

```
void InitFlakes()
{
    for (int i = 0; i < MaxFlakes; i++)
    {
        Snowflake flake = new Snowflake(XYStart[i].X,
                        XYStart[i].Y, OpacityValue[i]);
        Flake.Add(flake);
        flake.AppHeight = LayoutRoot.Height;
        LayoutRoot.Children.Add(flake);
    }
}
```

15. The last bit of code to add before compiling and running the application is the event handler code for the Completed event on the Snowfall storyboard. This code is very straightforward—for every flake in the Flake List, the MoveFlake() method is called. All of the flakes will have their on-screen positions updated, and then the Snowfall timer will be restarted.

```
void Snowfall_Completed(object sender, EventArgs e)
{
    foreach (Snowflake flake in Flake)
    {
        flake.MoveFlake();
    }
    Snowfall.Begin();
}
```

When the application runs, the snowflake object is instantiated 250 times randomly around the screen. Each flake is randomly scaled and drifts randomly, as shown in Figure 6-25.

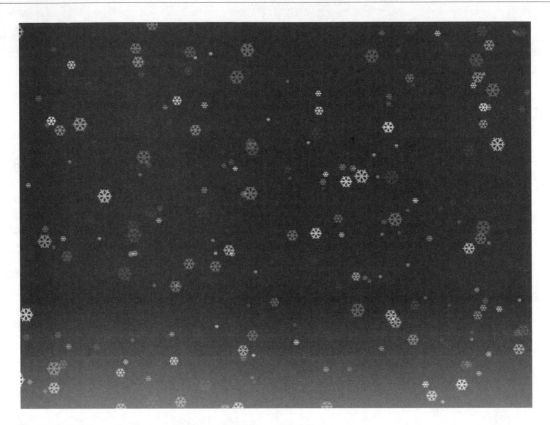

Figure 6-25. The application creates flakes that drift as they fall.

We can add a little polish to the application by making each flake spin as it falls. This can be accomplished with just three lines of code inside the Snowflake.xaml.cs file.

16. Add a variable declaration to hold the spin value for each flake:

```
private double Spin;
```

17. Inside the Snowflake() constructor, add the following line of code that generates a random spin speed between 0 and 5. It's OK if some of the flakes do not spin as they fall.

```
Spin = Rand.Next(5);
```

18. The final line of code goes into the public MoveFlake() method, and simply increments the rotational angle of the flake by the generated Spin value:

```
RotateFlake.Angle += Spin;
```

Now the flakes will spin a bit as they are falling, which makes the application a little more interesting to look at.

Flashing and blinking

You've seen how a sine or cosine calculation can be used to make an object oscillate. You've also seen how to combine linear motion with the oscillations to create interesting applications, like one that creates falling snowflakes. Try to think outside the box a little bit when working with sine and cosine, though.

You know that generated sine and cosine values are between −1 and 1. You can apply these values to other properties on an object to get interesting effects. For example, applying a sine calculation to the scale of an object would result in the object appearing to pulse. You can also attach such a calculation to the Opacity property of an object to make an object blink or fade in and out. Let's take a look at how to do that.

1. To code along with this example, open the **Flashing** project. The project contains a city street scene in the Page.xaml file, as well as a storyboard timer called Timer. In addition, it has a Barricade user control, which is a typical construction-type barricade with two orange lights on top. The lights on the barricade are made of four parts—two "on" versions that have white gradients, and two "off" versions that are flat orange. The on and off states for the lights are positioned directly on top of one another, and nothing has been hidden or made transparent.

2. The purpose of this application will be to make the lights blink off and on, opposite one another. When one light is on, the other will be off, and vice versa. All of the code for this application will be placed in the Page.xaml.cs file, so open that file for editing.

3. Begin by declaring an instance of the Barricade object, and adding variables to handle the angle and speed of the flashing effect. Add the following code before the Page() constructor:

```
Barricade MyBarricade = new Barricade();
Double Angle = 0;
Double FlashSpeed = .1;
```

4. Inside the Page() constructor, add the following code after the InitializeComponent() method. The first few lines position the Barricade object instance and add it to the LayoutRoot Canvas:

```
MyBarricade.SetValue(Canvas.LeftProperty, 175.00);
MyBarricade.SetValue(Canvas.TopProperty, 300.00);
LayoutRoot.Children.Add(MyBarricade);
```

5. Next, an event handler is attached to the Completed event for the Timer storyboard, and the storyboard is started:

```
Timer.Completed += new EventHandler(Timer_Completed);
Timer.Begin();
```

6. Add the Timer_Completed() event handler function. Inside the function, add the following code that calculates the opacity of the left and right barricade lights. Since Silverlight's Opacity values run from 0 to 1 (0 to 100%), no extra work has to be done to the calculations. The first light has Opacity set to the direct result of the Math.Sin(Angle) calculation, and the second light simply uses the inverse value. The Angle variable is incremented, and the storyboard is restarted to keep the animation going.

```
void Timer_Completed(object sender, EventArgs e)
{
    MyBarricade.LightLeft.Opacity = Math.Sin(Angle);
    MyBarricade.LightRight.Opacity = -Math.Sin(Angle);
    Angle += FlashSpeed;
    Timer.Begin();
}
```

When the application runs, you'll see the street scene and the barricade flashing, as shown in Figure 6-26. If you wanted the lights to blink in unison, you could change the code so that both opacity values were assigned the result of the sine calculation. The finalized version of this project is available as **FlashingCompleted**.

Figure 6-26. The barricade's flashing lights are driven by a sine calculation.

Combining oscillations and rotations

Of course, you can get much fancier with the way you're applying the calculations to various properties on objects. Let's code up something a little more complex. The next project, which will create some falling leaves, will combine many of the concepts we've covered. The leaves will be randomized much like the snowflakes, but as they fall and drift, they will rotate as well. We'll also randomize the fill for the leaves to give the application a little more of a natural feel. We'll use the concept of vector-based movement, and sine calculations for the drifting. We'll also tie a sine calculation into the rotational angle of each leaf object so that the leaves will float as they fall.

1. To code along with this example, open the **FallingLeaves** project. This project contains the Page.xaml file, which is a simple canvas with a background fill color, and our storyboard timer, called Autumn. There is also a Leaf.xaml user control, which is a simple alder leaf shape with a gradient fill. The Leaf object has a Rotate transform called RotateLeaf and a Scale transform called ScaleLeaf.

2. We'll code up the Leaf.xaml.cs file first. Begin by declaring variables before the Leaf() constructor. Add a public double to store the application height:

```
public double AppHeight;
```

3. Next, add the following private variables. We'll need a Point to store the starting position, a double for the speed at which the leaf will fall, and then four doubles to control the leaf drift. They include the angle, range of drift, drift origin, and drifting speed. Finish up with a random number generator.

```
private Point Position;
private double Speed;
private double DriftAngle;
private double DriftRange;
private double DriftPosition;
private double DriftSpeed = .1;
private static Random Rand = new Random();
```

Currently, the constructor for the Leaf object looks like the following code:

```
public Leaf()
{
    InitializeComponent();
}
```

4. As we did with the snowflake, we're going to modify the code so that we can pass variables to the Leaf object for use in initializing. Edit the code so it looks like the following:

```
public Leaf(double Left, double Top)
```

5. Next, we'll add code after the IntializeComponent() call inside the Leaf() constructor. We'll start by generating a random number for scale between .25 and .50 (25% and 50%).

```
ScaleLeaf.ScaleX = ScaleLeaf.ScaleY = (double)Rand.Next(25, 50) / 100;
```

6. Next, add the following code to generate a random value between 0 and 5 for the speed. We'll test for a value of 0, and change the value to 1 if we find it. Since this will be our y velocity, this will ensure that our leaf will fall.

```
Speed = Rand.Next(5);
if (Speed < 1) Speed = 1;
```

7. Add the next few lines to generate random numbers that will be used to make the leaf drift. The first is the side-to-side range for the leaf, the second is a starting angle seed, and the last determines the x coordinate point of origin for the drifting based on the values passed to the constructor.

```
DriftRange = Rand.Next(100);
DriftAngle = Rand.Next(270);
DriftPosition = Left;
```

8. Now add the following code, which sets the initial left and top positions for the leaf and stores them in the Position variable:

```
Canvas.SetLeft(this, Left);
Canvas.SetTop(this, Top);
Position.X = Left;
Position.Y = Top;
```

9. Now we're going to generate some random colors for the leaf's fill. The fill is a gradient with two stops, GradientStop1 and GradientStop2. For the first stop, we will generate a number between 185 and 255, and use that as the red component of the Argb color:

```
double randomColorValue = Rand.Next(185, 255);
Color C = Color.FromArgb(255, (byte)randomColorValue, 0, 0);
GradientStop1.Color = C;
```

10. The second color stop is based on the first. The value generated for the first color stop is divided in half, and used as the green component of the Argb color. The red component remains the same as it was in the first stop. This has a tendency to produce a more yellow- or orange-tinted color.

```
double C2 = randomColorValue * .5;
Color C3 = Color.FromArgb(255, (byte)randomColorValue, (byte)C2, 0);
GradientStop2.Color = C3;
```

11. That does it for the constructor. Next, add the following function to move the leaf. Start by incrementing the Position.Y variable by the Speed, and then calculate the drift for Position.X with our tried-and-true oscillation code. Increment the DriftAngle for the next pass.

A quick check is done to see if the leaf has moved beyond the bottom of the application. If so, it is relocated back at the top. Finally, the leaf is moved to the new position.

```
public void MoveLeaf()
{
    Position.Y += Speed;
    Position.X = DriftPosition + Math.Cos(DriftAngle) * DriftRange;
    DriftAngle += DriftSpeed;
    if (Position.Y > AppHeight) Position.Y = -this.Width;
    Canvas.SetLeft(this, Position.X);
    Canvas.SetTop(this, Position.Y);
}
```

That's all we need for the leaf for the time being. It won't yet be rotating—we want to generate the leaves and make sure everything is working correctly before adding additional code to this object.

12. Next, we'll move to Page.xaml.cs, so open that file for editing.

13. Before the Page() constructor, declare List objects to hold our leaves and starting x,y positions. We'll also need variables to determine the maximum number of leaves to draw in the application, and an integer called ReverseCounter that will be used to flip some of the leaves along the x axis to add some randomness to the application. Finally, we have a random number generator.

```
List<Leaf> Leaves;
List<Point> XYStart;
int MaxLeaves = 150;
int ReverseCounter = 0;
Random Rand = new Random();
```

14. Inside the Page() constructor, add the code shown in the following listing after the InitializeComponent() method. This code assigns a length to the List used in this project. The XYStart positions are then populated via a quick for loop. We finish up by calling the InitLeaves() function, setting up an event listener for the Completed event of our Autumn storyboard timer, and starting the storyboard:

```
Leaves = new List<Leaf>(MaxLeaves);
XYStart = new List<Point>(MaxLeaves);
for (int i = 0; i < MaxLeaves; i++)
{
    Point newPoint = new Point(Rand.Next(-136, (int)LayoutRoot.Width),
                    Rand.Next(-60, (int)LayoutRoot.Height));
    XYStart.Add(newPoint);
}
InitLeaves();
Autumn.Completed += new EventHandler(Autumn_Completed);
Autumn.Begin();
```

15. Next, write the InitLeaves() function. The function runs a loop that creates and positions each new leaf at the corresponding positions stored in the XYStart List. The leaf is then added to the Leaves List. The leaf's AppHeight variable is set to the application height. A test of the ReverseCounter value is done. If it is found to be 2, the leaf is scaled to −1x to flip it along the x axis. The ReverseCounter variable is incremented, and tested to keep within a range of 0 to 2. Finally, the leaf is added to the LayoutRoot Canvas.

```
void InitLeaves()
{
    for (int i = 0; i < MaxLeaves; i++)
    {
        Leaf leaf = new Leaf(XYStart[i].X, XYStart[i].Y);
                Leaves.Add(leaf);
        leaf.AppHeight = LayoutRoot.Height;
        if (ReverseCounter == 2) leaf.ScaleLeaf.ScaleX *= -1;
        ReverseCounter++;
        if (ReverseCounter > 2) ReverseCounter = 0;

        LayoutRoot.Children.Add(leaf);
    }
}
```

16. The last bit of code we need before we can test is the event handler code for Autumn_Completed. As with the snowflake example, this code goes through the Leaf objects in the Leaves List and calls the MoveLeaf() function for each one before restarting the Autumn storyboard that moves all of the leaves in the application.

```
void Autumn_Completed(object sender, EventArgs e)
{
    foreach (Leaf leaf in Leaves) leaf.MoveLeaf();
    Autumn.Begin();
}
```

At this point, the application should compile and run, and looks like Figure 6-27. We have 250 leaves on the screen, some are flipped, and there are a variety of colors. The leaves drift from side to side as they fall.

Changes to the MaxLeaves variable will change the number of leaves that appear in the application. If you would like more leaves to flip, you can adjust the test done against the ReverseCounter variable in the InitLeaves() function. If you feel it's something you may need to change often, you can set up a variable to make updating the number easy.

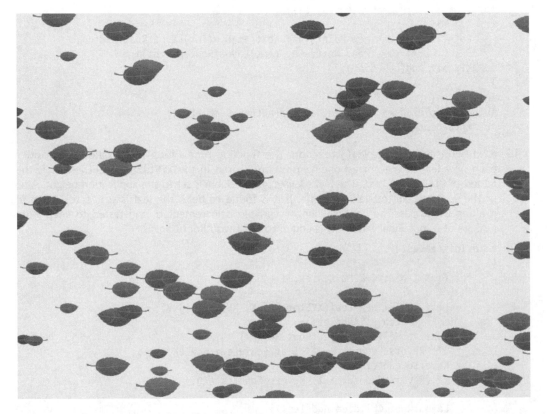

Figure 6-27. The nearly completed FallingLeaves project in action

Now that we know our application is in good shape and runs, we'll add the code that makes the leaves rock back and forth with the drifting as they fall. The nice thing about this addition is that we already have the values we need. The drifting oscillation has an angle associated with it, and we'll use that to determine an angle for the spin.

17. Inside the Leaf.xaml.cs file, find your MoveLeaf() function. Add the following line of code. Recall that the Leaf object has a Rotate transform called RotateLeaf. This code uses the angle of drift and existing drift range to determine a rotational value for the leaf as it falls. By multiplying the value by .5, the angle is dampened and makes the rotations a little less extreme.

```
RotateLeaf.Angle = (Math.Sin(DriftAngle) * DriftRange * .5);
```

Now when you run the application, the leaves will have a little more natural motion to them, as shown in Figure 6-28. Since the rotation is tied to the drifting oscillation, the leaf will rotate in the direction in which it is traveling. The code described in this example is available in the **FallingLeavesCompleted** project.

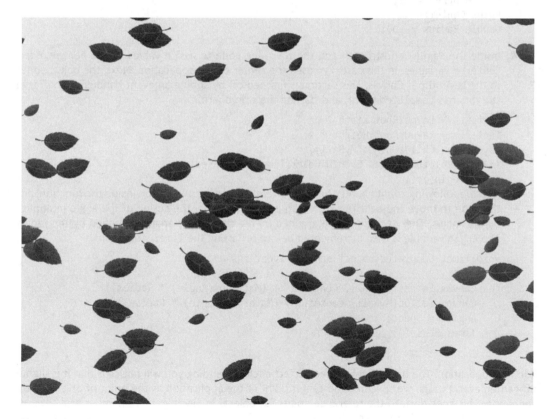

Figure 6-28. The final version of the FallingLeaves application

Circular movement

The next example we're going to look at will use the sine and cosine of an angle to create circular motion for an object. This type of motion uses an angle and a radius to calculate the sine and cosine values that determine the x,y position of an object for the given angle.

1. Open the **CircularMovement** project to code along with this example. The project contains a background canvas that contains a gradient fill, a storyboard named Timer, and a Ball user control.

2. All of the code for this project is placed in the Page.xaml.cs file, so open that file for editing.

3. Add the variable declarations shown in the following listing. This code declares an instance of the Ball object, and then our familiar Angle, Speed, and Radius values. We'll also be using a center point in this project.

```
Ball MyBall = new Ball();
double Angle = 0;
double Speed = .1;
Point Center;
double Radius = 100;
```

4. Inside the Page() constructor, add the following code to assign values to the Center.X and Center.Y variables. In this case, I've used the center of the application. Next, the ball is added to the LayoutRoot Canvas. This section is finished off by adding an event handler to the Timer storyboard's Completed event, and starting the storyboard.

```
Center.X = LayoutRoot.Width / 2;
Center.Y = LayoutRoot.Height / 2;
LayoutRoot.Children.Add(MyBall);
Timer.Completed += new EventHandler(Timer_Completed);
Timer.Begin();
```

5. Add the following event handler function after the Page() constructor. Inside the function, add the code to move the ball. The x position is determined by the cosine of the angle multiplied by the radius. The y position is determined by the sine of the angle multiplied by the radius. The Angle variable is then incremented before restarting the Timer storyboard.

```
void Timer_Completed(object sender, EventArgs e)
{
    Canvas.SetLeft(MyBall, Center.X + (Math.Cos(Angle) * Radius));
    Canvas.SetTop(MyBall, Center.Y + (Math.Sin(Angle) * Radius));
    Angle += Speed;
    Timer.Begin();
}
```

Run the application. The ball will rotate in a perfect circle. One thing you will notice is that it is slightly off-center, even though we specified the center point of the application as the point of origin for the animation. This goes back to the reference points for objects in Silverlight—remember that they are positioned by their top-left corner.

6. We can correct this fairly easily by adding an adjustment to the Center variable. Adjust the variable assignments as shown:

```
Center.X = LayoutRoot.Width / 2 - MyBall.Width / 2;
Center.Y = LayoutRoot.Height / 2 - MyBall.Height / 2;
```

Now when the application runs, the ball will animate correctly around the center point of the application, as illustrated by Figure 6-29.

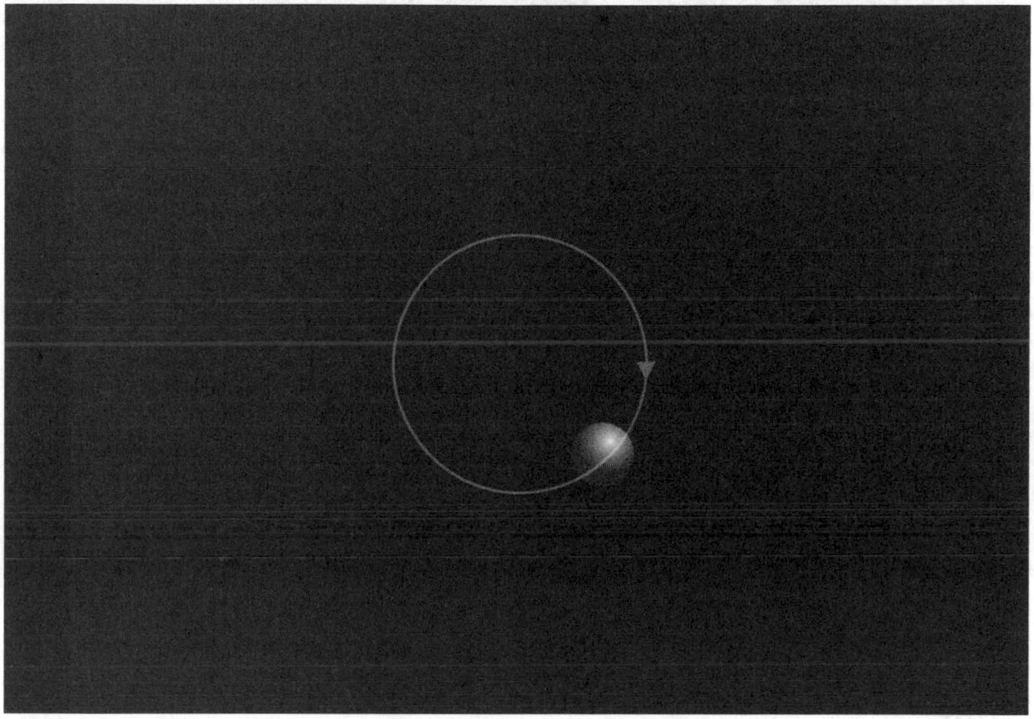

Figure 6-29. Circular movement created by using sine and cosine calculations

To create elliptical motion rather than circular, simply separate the x and y components of the motion by using different radius values for the x and y calculations. This is easy to do.

7. Start by changing the Radius from a double to a Point data type.

```
Point Radius;
```

8. Inside the Page() constructor, assign some values for the x and y radius:

```
Radius.X = 300;
Radius.Y = 100;
```

9. Inside the event handler function, use the new radius values:

```
Canvas.SetLeft(MyBall, Center.X + (Math.Cos(Angle) * Radius.X));
Canvas.SetTop(MyBall, Center.Y + (Math.Sin(Angle) * Radius.Y));
```

Now when you run the project, the ball will follow an elliptical path, as illustrated in Figure 6-30. The **CircularMovementCompleted** project contains both the circular and elliptical motion code described here. There are comments in the project explaining how to edit the code to change between the types of motion.

Figure 6-30. Elliptical motion created with sine and cosine

Orbiting

Let's take a look at an application of this concept that is fun to see in action. The project we're going to build will draw a moon object on the screen, and we will use the techniques that were just covered to make a small space capsule orbit the moon.

1. Open up the **MoonOrbit** project to code along with this example.

2. The Page.xaml file for this project has a black background and a storyboard timer. We're going to want to make the moon draggable, so I've already added the necessary drag-and-drop code to the Moon.xaml.cs file for you. As soon as the moon is added to the application, it will be draggable. All of the code for this project will go into the Page.xaml.cs file, so open this file for editing.

3. As always, we'll start by declaring our variables before the Page() constructor. Create an instance of the Moon object and the SpaceCapsule object. Following this, we will need doubles for Angle and Speed, and Points for radius and position. The Radius variable will be used to determine the elliptical path of the capsule. The Position variable will store the center point of the Moon object.

```
Moon MyMoon = new Moon();
SpaceCapsule MyCapsule = new SpaceCapsule();
double Angle = 0;
double Speed = .1;
Point Radius;
Point Position;
```

4. Inside the Page() constructor, add code to set the initial values for Position.X and Position.Y. These values are then used to set the moon's location on the Layout Canvas. Once positioned, the Moon object is added to the canvas. Next, the SpaceCapsule object is added to the canvas. We do not need to specify a position since we will be doing that through our sine and cosine operations. The Radius.X and Radius.Y values that will give the capsule an elliptical orbit are set. Finally, the Completed event handler for the storyboard is coded, and the storyboard is started. The completed Page() constructor is shown in the following listing:

```
public Page()
{
    InitializeComponent();
    Position.X = LayoutRoot.Width / 2 - MyMoon.Width / 2;
    Position.Y = LayoutRoot.Height / 2 - MyMoon.Height / 2;
    Canvas.SetTop(MyMoon, Position.Y);
    Canvas.SetLeft(MyMoon, Position.X);
    LayoutRoot.Children.Add(MyMoon);
    LayoutRoot.Children.Add(MyCapsule);
    Radius.X = 300;
    Radius.Y = 25;
    Timer.Completed += new EventHandler(Timer_Completed);
    Timer.Begin();
}
```

5. Create the event handler function. Inside the function, begin by updating the values stored in the Position variable. If the moon object is dragged around the screen, we want to make sure we're keeping track of the current center point in order to maintain proper rotation. Following this, the capsule is positioned using code similar to some you've already seen. Next, the Angle variable is incremented, and the Timer storyboard is restarted to keep the motion going. The event handler code is shown following:

```
void Timer_Completed(object sender, EventArgs e)
{
    Position.X = Canvas.GetLeft(MyMoon) + MyMoon.Width / 2;
    Position.Y = Canvas.GetTop(MyMoon) + MyMoon.Height / 2;
    Canvas.SetLeft(MyCapsule, (Position.X - MyCapsule.Width / 2)
                    + (Math.Cos(Angle) * Radius.X));
    Canvas.SetTop(MyCapsule, (Position.Y - MyCapsule.Height / 2)
                    + (Math.Sin(Angle) * Radius.Y));
    Angle += Speed;
    Timer.Begin();
}
```

If you run the project at this point, you'll see the objects drawn on the screen and the capsule go zipping along as expected. You can even drag the moon around and the capsule will maintain its position. One slight problem is that the capsule never passes behind the moon. We can fix this by augmenting the Completed event handler code a bit.

6. Right after the line of code that increments the angle, add the following line of code. Remember that our numbers are being specified in radians, and that 180 degrees is equal to pi radians. 2pi radians is equal to 360 degrees (or 0 degrees). This code will reset our angle when it reaches a threshold so that we're always working with in the 0-to-2pi range.

```
if (Angle > 6.28) Angle = 0;
```

7. Next, add the following `if...else` statement to the very top of the event handler code. This code will check to see if the angle value is greater than pi. If so, the Moon object's Z-index is set to 1, and the capsule's Z-index is set to 0. This will cause the capsule to be drawn behind the moon. If the angle is less than pi, the moon's Z-index will be set to 0, and the space capsule's Z-index will be set to 1. This will cause the capsule to draw in front of the moon.

```
if (Angle > 3.14)
{
    Canvas.SetZIndex(MyMoon, 1);
    Canvas.SetZIndex(MyCapsule, 0);
}
else
{
    Canvas.SetZIndex(MyMoon, 0);
    Canvas.SetZIndex(MyCapsule, 1);
}
```

As the capsule moves along its elliptical path, the motion is based on angles from 0 to 360 degrees, or 0 to 2pi radians. We know that as the capsule passes 180 degrees (pi radians), it should no longer appear in front of the moon. We also know that after it passes 360 degrees (2pi radians), the capsule should be drawn in front of the moon. This code handles that for us.

When you run the program, you should see something similar to Figure 6-31, with the capsule obediently moving behind the moon with each revolution. If you would like to change the speed of the capsule's flight, modify the Speed variable.

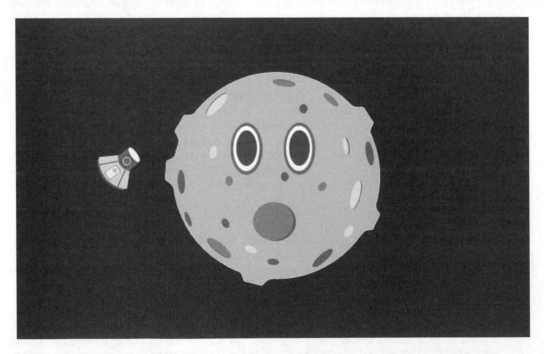

Figure 6-31. The space capsule orbits the moon along an elliptical path.

The Pythagorean theorem

The final topic we're going to cover in this chapter is the Pythagorean theorem. The theorem deals once again with the measurement of triangles, and looks like this:

$$a^2 + b^2 = c^2$$

Let's take another look at our right triangle, shown in Figure 6-32.

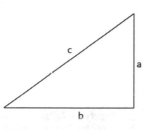

Figure 6-32. A triangle with sides labeled

An illustration of the theorem is shown in Figure 6-33. If you calculate the area of the squares on each leg of the triangle and add them together, you will get the area of the square on the hypotenuse.

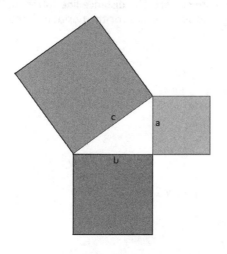

Figure 6-33. An illustration of the Pythagorean theorem. The area of side a^2 plus the area of side b^2 is equal to the area of side c^2.

I know at this point your vision may be getting blurry and your mind weary, and you may be wondering how a triangle and square roots will be of any value to you in Silverlight. However, the Pythagorean theorem can be used to determine distances between two points, which can be applied in many interesting ways. Take a look at Figure 6-34. Here we have two objects, each one with its own set of coordinates.

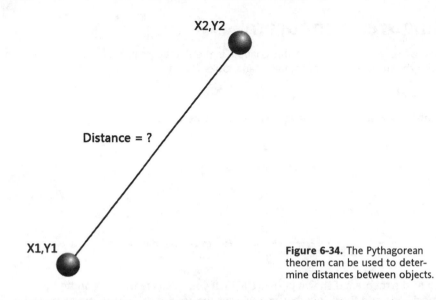

Figure 6-34. The Pythagorean theorem can be used to determine distances between objects.

If this chapter has done its job, you should be seeing right triangles when you close your eyes. If you think you see a right triangle in Figure 6-34, you are correct. The distance line forms the hypotenuse of a right triangle. If we fill in the triangle's legs and some values for the position of the two objects, we get something like what is shown in Figure 6-35.

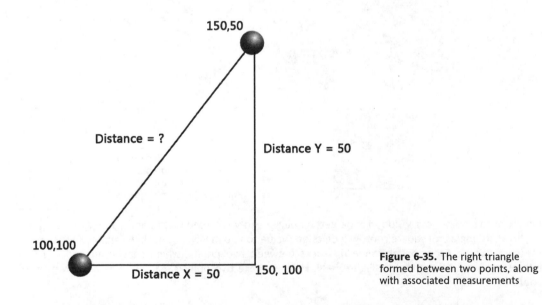

Figure 6-35. The right triangle formed between two points, along with associated measurements

As you can see, once we know two points, we can determine the third, as well as the distances of the two legs of the triangle. Distance X and Distance Y in the figure are typically coded as DX and DY, or can be stored as a Point data type, D.X and D.Y.

The calculation for distance, then, would look like the following:

```
DX = X2 - X1;
DY = Y2 - Y1;
Distance = Math.Sqrt(DX * DX + DY * DY);
```

This code determines the x and y distances, squares them, sums them, and calculates the square root. If we plug in the numbers from Figure 6-35, we get the following:

```
Distance = Math.Sqrt(50 * 50 + 50 * 50);
Distance = Math.Sqrt(2500 + 2500);
Distance = Math.Sqrt(5000);
Distance = 70.71[...]
```

Distance between objects

Now, I suspect you would like to see this in action, and I am happy to oblige.

1. Open the **PythagoreanTheorem** project to code along with this example. The project contains the root canvas, which has a simple dark gray fill color. There is a TextBlock in the top-left corner that we will use to provide output so we can see the results of our calculations. The project also contains a single user object—a red ball. The ball will be draggable, and I have already included that code with the user control for you.

2. All of the code for this example will go into the Page.xaml.cs file, so open that file for editing.

3. Start by adding the variables we'll be using before the Page() constructor. Create two instances of the Ball control, and two Point objects that we will use to store the center points of the balls. We'll also use a Point object to store the x and y distances between the points, and a double to store the resulting distance calculation.

```
Ball Ball1 = new Ball();
Ball Ball2 = new Ball();
Point Ball1Center;
Point Ball2Center;
Point D;
double Distance;
```

4. Inside the Page() constructor, add the following code that positions each ball before adding it to the root canvas. We won't need a storyboard timer for this project—instead we'll do our calculations when the mouse is moving. Create an event handler for the MouseMove event on the LayoutRoot Canvas:

```
Canvas.SetLeft(Ball1, 0);
Canvas.SetTop(Ball1, 0);
Canvas.SetLeft(Ball2, LayoutRoot.Width - Ball2.Width);
Canvas.SetTop(Ball2, LayoutRoot.Height - Ball2.Height);
LayoutRoot.Children.Add(Ball1);
LayoutRoot.Children.Add(Ball2);
LayoutRoot.MouseMove += new MouseEventHandler(LayoutRoot_MouseMove);
```

5. Create the LayoutRoot_MouseMove() function. Inside the function, add some code to do the distance calculation. Start by calculating the centers for Ball1 and Ball2.

Next come the calculations to determine the x distance and y distance. Once we have those, we can calculate the distance between Ball1 and Ball2. Finally, the value of the Distance variable is output to the TextBlock.

```
void LayoutRoot_MouseMove(object sender, MouseEventArgs e)
{
    Ball1Center.X = Canvas.GetLeft(Ball1) + Ball1.Width / 2;
    Ball1Center.Y = Canvas.GetTop(Ball1) + Ball1.Height / 2;
    Ball2Center.X = Canvas.GetLeft(Ball2) + Ball2.Width / 2;
    Ball2Center.Y = Canvas.GetTop(Ball2) + Ball2.Height / 2;
    D.X = Ball2Center.X - Ball1Center.X;
    D.Y = Ball2Center.Y - Ball1Center.Y;
    Distance = Math.Sqrt(D.X * D.X + D.Y * D.Y);
    MsgBlock.Text = "Distance: " + String.Format("{0:0}", Distance);
}
```

Compile and run the application—you should see an application like the one shown in Figure 6-36. Use the mouse to drag the balls around the canvas, and see how the distance value is affected. Either ball can be moved around without affecting the accuracy of the calculation. Since we used the center point value for each ball object, placing the balls perfectly on top of one another will reduce the distance to 0.

The completed version of this project is available as **PythagoreanTheoremCompleted**.

Figure 6-36. The Pythagorean theorem in action

So you're sitting there thinking this is kind of neat, but not really sure what you're going to do with it. Once again, there are plenty of options, and I'm going to show you one right now.

A more practical use for the Pythagorean theorem

1. Open the **HotAndCold** project to code along with this example. In this project, we'll place a sun, moon, and space capsule object on the canvas. If the space capsule is dragged toward the sun, it will become hotter (redder), and if it is moved toward the moon, it will become cooler (bluer).

The project already contains the user controls for the sun, the moon, and the capsule. I have also already added the code to each to allow drag-and-drop. The XAML for the capsule is a little unique. The file contains both the blue "cold" capsule and the red "warm" capsule, both positioned over one another. As we drag objects around the screen, we will manipulate the transparency of the CapsuleWarm Canvas.

2. All of the code for this project will be added to the Page.xaml.cs file, so open Page.xaml.cs for editing.

3. Before the Page() constructor, add the following code to declare instances of the Sun, Moon, and SpaceCapsule objects:

```
Sun MySun = new Sun();
Moon MyMoon = new Moon();
SpaceCapsule MyCapsule = new SpaceCapsule();
```

4. Continue by creating four Point variables—one each for the center positions of the Sun, Moon, and SpaceCapsule objects, and one to hold the x and y distances for our calculation:

```
Point D;
Point SunCenter;
Point MoonCenter;
Point CapsuleCenter;
```

5. The last few variables that need to be added are for determining some distances using the Pythagorean theorem:

```
double Distance;
Point TotalD;
double Multiplier;
```

6. Inside the Page() constructor, position the moon, sun, and capsule and add all three objects to the canvas:

```
Canvas.SetLeft(MyMoon, 675);
Canvas.SetTop(MyMoon, 475);
Canvas.SetLeft(MySun, 10);
Canvas.SetTop(MySun, 10);
Canvas.SetLeft(MyCapsule, 330);
Canvas.SetTop(MyCapsule, 230);
LayoutRoot.Children.Add(MyMoon);
LayoutRoot.Children.Add(MySun);
LayoutRoot.Children.Add(MyCapsule);
```

7. Once again, we'll use the MouseMove event to trigger our calculations, so add an event handler for LayoutRoot.MouseMove. We need to do our calculation after the objects have been added to the canvas to set the correct value for the capsule so it looks correct before any mouse input is received. The CalcDistance() function will be where we perform our calculations:

```
LayoutRoot.MouseMove += new MouseEventHandler(LayoutRoot_MouseMove);
CalcDistance();
```

8. Because we will create a function to handle the calculations, there is no reason to repeat them in the MouseMove event handler. However, as the mouse moves around the application canvas, we still want to do our magic. Code up the event handler function. Inside the MouseMove event handler, add code to call the CalcDistance() function:

```
void LayoutRoot_MouseMove(object sender, MouseEventArgs e)
{
    CalcDistance();
}
```

9. Next comes the CalcDistance() function, shown in the following listing. The function starts by calculating the center positions for each object on the canvas. The distance between the sun and the moon is then determined. Dividing 100 by the multiplier and then dividing the resulting number by 100 converts the number to a value that will be used to determine a final opacity value. The next few lines of code calculate the distance between the moon and the capsule. To finish up, the opacity of the CapsuleWarm Canvas in the capsule object is set to the Distance multiplied by the Multiplier variable.

```
void CalcDistance()
{
    SunCenter.X = Canvas.GetLeft(MySun) + MySun.Width / 2;
    SunCenter.Y = Canvas.GetTop(MySun) + MySun.Height / 2;
    MoonCenter.X = Canvas.GetLeft(MyMoon) + MyMoon.Width / 2;
    MoonCenter.Y = Canvas.GetTop(MyMoon) + MyMoon.Height / 2;
    CapsuleCenter.X = Canvas.GetLeft(MyCapsule) + MyCapsule.Width / 2;
    CapsuleCenter.Y = Canvas.GetTop(MyCapsule) + MyCapsule.Height / 2;
    // calculate scaling for Opacity calculations
    TotalD.X = MoonCenter.X - SunCenter.X;
    TotalD.Y = MoonCenter.Y - SunCenter.Y;

    Multiplier = Convert.ToInt16(Math.Sqrt(TotalD.X
                * TotalD.X + TotalD.Y * TotalD.Y));
    Multiplier = (100 / Multiplier) / 100;
    // distance between the moon and the capsule
    D.X = MoonCenter.X - CapsuleCenter.X;
    D.Y = MoonCenter.Y - CapsuleCenter.Y;
    Distance = Convert.ToInt16(Math.Sqrt(D.X * D.X + D.Y * D.Y));
    MyCapsule.CapsuleWarm.Opacity = Distance * Multiplier;
}
```

By the code, the calculations may look a little confusing, so let's plug in some numbers to see what's happening. If the sun is 700 pixels from the moon, the calculated multiplier is 0.001428.

The distance between the moon and the capsule is then determined. If the capsule is 200 pixels from the moon, we get an opacity value of 200 × 0.001428, or .2857[. . .]. As an opacity value, this results in the warm capsule canvas being 28% opaque. The farther the capsule is from the moon, the higher the value, and the redder the capsule will appear.

Go ahead and run the application to see how it works. You should be able to drag the objects around the screen, and the capsule will change according to the proximity of the objects to one another. Figure 6-37 shows the final version of the application, for which the code is available in **HotAndColdCompleted**.

Figure 6-37. As the ship moves closer to the sun, it becomes redder in color.

Summary

Wow, nice work! Your brain may feel heavy, and it looks like your left eyelid is twitching a little bit, but you did it! You went 12 rounds with trigonometry and came out on top. This chapter will probably be one to which you find yourself referring often. It may take a while before some of the ideas, like converting between radians and degrees, become automatic, but you've laid a solid foundation for all the great work you have yet to do. Let's recap some of the ideas we discussed.

Trigonometry is the study of how the angles and lengths of sides of triangles relate to one another. When measuring angles, especially in Silverlight, we're accustomed to using a measurement of degrees. However, the trigonometric functions produce angles measured in radians. To convert between degrees and radians, use the following formulas:

radians = degrees × π / 180

degrees = radians × 180 / π

To make the job of converting between angle types easier, it's helpful to add conversion functions to your programs. Since Silverlight objects are rotated in degrees, it's a safe bet you'll need to convert between the two angle types at some point.

We talked about several trigonometric functions—let's review what they do.

Sine is used to determine the y length of a right triangle for a given angle, while cosine is used to determine the x length. After working with them a bit, the sine/y and cosine/x associations will become a little more natural for you.

Arctangent—specifically, the Atan2() method—can be used to determine an angle from two lengths. This trigonometric function uses an origin and given point to create a right triangle, and returns the value of the angle **q**.

We took some time to explore how sine and cosine can be used to create oscillating, circular, and elliptical motions for objects. We also explored how movements created with sine and cosine calculations can be combined with linear motions to create interesting effects such as snowfall or drifting leaves. Remember that the calculations for sine or cosine can be used for more than just movement. The resulting values of these operations can be applied to an object's scale for pulsing motion, or opacity for flashing motion. Altering the speed of change for the angle in the calculation will change the rate at which the object pulses or flashes.

The Pythagorean theorem says that by taking the square root of the squared and summed lengths of the two legs of a right triangle, we will get the squared value of the length of the hypotenuse. This theorem is expressed as follows:

$a^2 + b^2 = c^2$

The Pythagorean theorem can be used to determine the distance between two objects. By determining how far apart objects are, we can create animations that cause objects to react to one another in interesting ways.

In Chapter 7, we'll take a look at how we can simulate 3D in a 2D environment. This opens the door for creating some interesting animations, such as orbiting planets, and horizontal or vertical carousel navigation systems.

Chapter 7

SIMULATING 3D IN 2D

In this chapter, we're going to apply some of the concepts from Chapter 6 to emulate 3D object rotations. While Silverlight doesn't yet support true 3D, you can add a little pop to your applications by implementing the concepts we'll talk about here.

3D

As you are aware, the coordinate system in Silverlight has only x and y axes, where x is the horizontal axis and y is the vertical. To imagine a 3D coordinate system like the one shown in Figure 7-1, a z axis line is drawn straight into your computer screen.

We're not going to be coding up a true 3D coordinate system—instead, we'll fake the visual cues that make people see objects as being farther away using some of the trigonometry you learned in Chapter 6.

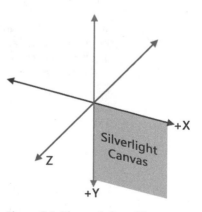

Figure 7-1. The z axis for a 3D coordinate system in Silverlight would run perpendicular to your monitor.

Z axis rotation

We'll start out with an easy one: z axis rotation. Any object you rotate around the z axis on the screen would be moving in a circular or elliptical pattern, as shown in Figure 7-2.

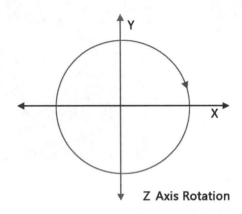

Z Axis Rotation

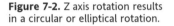

Figure 7-2. Z axis rotation results in a circular or elliptical rotation.

As such, z axis 3D movement isn't really emulating any 3D motion. It will still become part of your toolbox, however, so it's worth taking a look at. You saw how to create circular movements in Chapter 6, but let's do a quick review project that puts our terms in a context that works for 3D. In this example, we will build a project that moves a ball around the z axis.

1. Open the **ZAxis3D** project. This project contains a gradient-filled Ball object, and the main page. The Page.xaml file also contains a storyboard timer named MoveBall.

2. If you were building an application that supported multiple objects traveling in circular or elliptical paths, you might choose to place some of the code in the object's code-behind files. However, for this project, we'll just take a look at the one ball, so all of our code will go into the Page.xaml.cs file. Open Page.xaml.cs for editing.

3. Start by declaring an instance of the Ball object:

```
Ball MyBall = new Ball();
```

4. Next, declare the variables we'll be using for the movement. Origin will be the origin point for the motion, and Radius will determine the radius of the circle the ball will travel. Angle and Speed will be used to determine our sine and cosine calculations, and Position will determine where on the canvas the ball will be placed.

```
Point Origin;
double Radius = 150;
double Angle = 0;
double Speed = .1;
Point Position;
```

5. Inside the Page() constructor, add the following code to initialize the Origin variable. We're adjusting the location of the point of origin for the size of the ball by subtracting half of the ball's height or width from the center point on the canvas. This adjustment accounts for the fact that objects are identified by the point at the top left of the object rather than the center.

```
Origin.X = LayoutRoot.Width / 2 - MyBall.Width / 2;
Origin.Y = LayoutRoot.Height / 2 - MyBall.Height / 2;
```

6. Continue adding code inside the Page() constructor. The following three lines will place the ball object at the Origin position calculated in step 5, and add it to the LayoutRoot Canvas.

```
Canvas.SetLeft(MyBall, Origin.X);
Canvas.SetTop(MyBall, Origin.Y);
LayoutRoot.Children.Add(MyBall);
```

At this point, you can compile and run the application if you'd like. The main canvas will be drawn, and the ball will be positioned at the center of the canvas. When you're done looking at the application, close the browser window and return to the Page.xaml.cs file.

7. The next thing we need to do is make the ball move. The following two lines also go into the Page() constructor. They set up an event listener for the Completed event of the MoveBall storyboard, and start the storyboard.

```
MoveBall.Completed += new EventHandler(MoveBall_Completed);
MoveBall.Begin();
```

8. The code block shown here is the complete code for the MoveBall_Completed() event handler. The code calculates a new x and y position for the ball based on the cosine and sine of the Angle. The ball's position is then updated on the canvas before incrementing the Angle and restarting the MoveBall storyboard.

```
void MoveBall_Completed(object sender, EventArgs e)
{
    Position.X = Radius * Math.Cos(Angle);
    Position.Y = Radius * Math.Sin(Angle);
    Canvas.SetLeft(MyBall, Position.X + Origin.X);
    Canvas.SetTop(MyBall, Position.Y + Origin.Y);

    Angle += Speed;
    MoveBall.Begin();
}
```

That's all there is to it—compile and run the application, and the ball will move in a circular pattern around the center of the canvas. With a couple of small changes, the path the ball follows can be made elliptical.

9. Change the Radius data type to Point:

```
Point Radius;
```

10. Inside the Page() constructor, initialize Radius.X and Radius.Y with some values:

```
Radius.X = 300;
Radius.Y = 50;
```

11. Finally, in the MoveBall_Completed() event handler, change the Position calculations to use the Radius values:

```
Position.X = Radius.X * Math.Cos(Angle);
Position.Y = Radius.Y * Math.Sin(Angle);
```

Take some time and look at the **ZAxis3DCompleted** project, shown in Figure 7-3. It contains the code shown here in the example, but I also added a few sliders so you can manipulate some of the values in real time as the application runs.

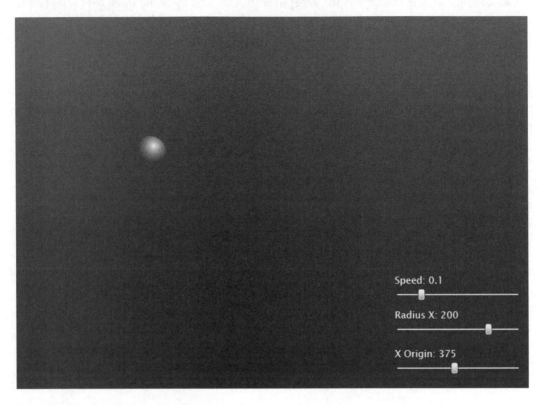

Speed: 0.1

Radius X: 200

X Origin: 375

Figure 7-3. The ZAxis3DCompleted project

A model of the inner solar system

So you've built this project and put some thought into it, but maybe you're not entirely sure where something like this can be applied in your own applications. As an example, let's build a real-world, working model of the orbits of the inner planets in our solar system. We will write the program in a way that supports elliptical orbits—the inner planets travel in more circular orbits than the outer planets, but you may choose to augment the program with elliptical orbits at a later time.

1. Open the **InnerSolarSystem** project. The project contains the sun and four planet objects: Mercury, Venus, Earth, and Mars (the planets are not to scale). We will be coding up each planet's code-behind file in order, starting at the center of the solar system and moving outward. There is also a timer storyboard called MovePlanets.

2. Open the Page.xaml.cs file for editing. Since we're starting from the center and working our way out, we'll begin with the sun. Declare an instance of the Sun object just above the Page() constructor:

```
Sun MySun = new Sun();
```

3. Inside the `Page()` constructor, add the following code to position the sun and add it to the main canvas:

```
Canvas.SetLeft(MySun, 395.00);
Canvas.SetTop(MySun, 300.00);
LayoutRoot.Children.Add(MySun);
```

4. If you compile and run the application, you will see the sun object near the center of the black canvas. Next, we'll add Mercury, the planet closest to the sun. Still working in `Page.xaml.cs`, create an instance of the Mercury user control:

```
Mercury MyMercury = new Mercury();
```

5. Inside of the `Page()` constructor, add the Mercury object to the main canvas. Notice here that we're not positioning the planet. We'll be calculating its location mathematically, so it's not necessary to specify a starting location. It will automatically be added at 0,0.

```
LayoutRoot.Children.Add(MyMercury);
```

6. We'll add a little code to make the planet move. Open the `Mercury.xaml.cs` file for editing.

7. Before the `Mercury()` constructor, declare the following variables. We'll declare doubles for Angle and Speed, and Points for Center and Radius. The smaller a planet's orbit, the faster the planet travels. As such, Mercury will be our fastest-moving planet, and the speed of all of our other planets will be determined using Mercury's speed as a base.

```
private double Angle = 0;
private double Speed = .05;
private Point Center;
private Point Radius;
```

8. Inside the `Mercury()` constructor, initialize the Radius and Center variables as shown in the following code. The values being used were determined by me from a reference image. Notice that we are once again adjusting the location of the center point to accommodate the way Silverlight references objects by their top-left coordinate.

```
public Mercury()
{
    InitializeComponent();
    Radius.Y = 79.5;
    Radius.X = 78;
    Center.X = 410 - this.Width / 2;
    Center.Y = 328.50 - this.Height / 2;
}
```

9. The last bit of code we need for Mercury will be used to move the object. The following public method is used to update Mercury's position on the screen based on the calculated Angle value. Each time the method is called, the Angle is decremented to move the planet in a counter-clockwise direction.

```
public void MoveMercury()
{
    Canvas.SetLeft(this, Center.X + (Math.Cos(Angle) * Radius.X));
    Canvas.SetTop(this, Center.Y + (Math.Sin(Angle) * Radius.Y));
    Angle -= Speed;
}
```

10. In order to make Mercury orbit the sun, we'll need to add a little more code to the main code-behind, so return to the Page.xaml.cs file. In the Page() constructor, add the following code to attach a Completed event listener to the MovePlanets storyboard, and start the storyboard:

```
MovePlanets.Completed += new EventHandler(MovePlanets_Completed);
MovePlanets.Begin();
```

11. The event handler code for the MovePlanets_Completed() event is shown following. This code calls the MoveMercury() method of the MyMercury object, which will update the location of the planet on the main canvas. The storyboard timer is then restarted.

```
void MovePlanets_Completed(object sender, EventArgs e)
{
    MyMercury.MoveMercury();
    MovePlanets.Begin();
}
```

Compile and run the program. Mercury should be orbiting the sun, as shown in Figure 7-4.

Figure 7-4. Mercury orbiting the sun

12. The next planet is Venus. In the Page.xaml.cs file, declare an instance of the Venus user control:

```
Venus MyVenus = new Venus();
```

13. Add MyVenus to the main canvas:

```
LayoutRoot.Children.Add(MyVenus);
```

14. Open the Venus.xaml.cs file for editing. Add the following variable declarations just above the Venus() constructor. Notice the Speed value here. The average speed of the planet Mercury is 48km/sec. For MyMecury, we used a Speed value of .05, and we need to make the other planets move relative to MyMercury's speed. The average speed of the planet Venus is 35km/sec. To determine the speed of MyVenus in relation to MyMercury, we take 35 / 48 × .05.

```
private double Angle = 0;
private double Speed = .036;
private Point Center;
private Point Radius;
```

15. Next, add the following bold code to the Venus() constructor to initialize the Radius and Center variables:

```
public Venus()
{
    InitializeComponent();
    Radius.Y = 140;
    Radius.X = 140;
    Center.X = 414 - this.Width / 2;
    Center.Y = 315 - this.Height / 2;
}
```

16. Finish up the Venus code-behind by adding the MoveVenus() method. The code inside the method is identical to that used for Mercury.

```
public void MoveVenus()
{
    Canvas.SetLeft(this, Center.X + (Math.Cos(Angle) * Radius.X));
    Canvas.SetTop(this, Center.Y + (Math.Sin(Angle) * Radius.Y));
    Angle -= Speed;
}
```

17. In the Page.xaml.cs file, locate the MovePlanets_Completed() event handler code. Add a call to the MoveVenus() method on the MyVenus object:

```
MyVenus.MoveVenus();
```

Compile and run the application. Both Mercury and Venus should be in view, as shown in Figure 7-5. Notice that Venus is moving more slowly than Mercury as both planets orbit the sun.

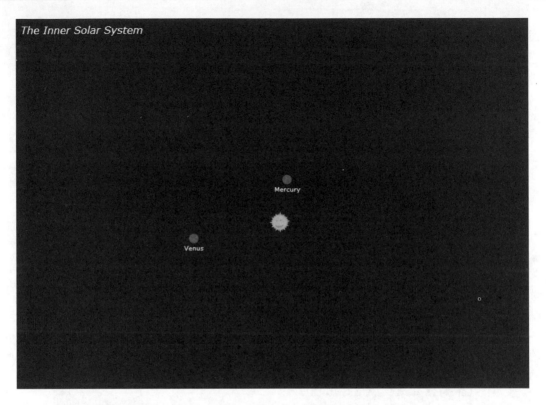

The Inner Solar System

Figure 7-5. The InnerSolarSystem project with both Venus and Mercury in view

18. The last two planets follow the same pattern, so we'll advance the pace a bit. In the `Page.xaml.cs` file, create an instance of the Earth user control, and inside of the `Page()` constructor, add it to the main canvas:

```
Earth MyEarth = new Earth();
LayoutRoot.Children.Add(MyEarth);
```

19. In the `Earth.xaml.cs` file, declare the necessary variables. The planet Earth orbits the sun at about 30km/sec, so to determine MyEarth's speed, we take 30 / 48 × .05.

```
private double Angle = 0;
private double Speed = .0312;
private Point Center;
private Point Radius;
```

20. Inside the `Earth()` constructor, initialize the Radius and Center variables by adding the code shown in bold in the following listing:

```
public Earth()
{
    InitializeComponent();
    Radius.Y = 189;
    Radius.X = 189;
```

```
    Center.X = 414 - this.Width / 2;
    Center.Y = 318 - this.Height / 2;
}
```

21. Create the MoveEarth() method:

```
public void MoveEarth()
{
    Canvas.SetLeft(this, Center.X + (Math.Cos(Angle) * Radius.X));
    Canvas.SetTop(this, Center.Y + (Math.Sin(Angle) * Radius.Y));
    Angle -= Speed;
}
```

22. In the Page.xaml.cs file, call the MyEarth.MoveEarth() method to add the Earth object to the storyboard's Completed event handler:

```
MyEarth.MoveEarth();
```

23. Running the application at this point will show our first three planets orbiting the sun, which means we have only one more to code up!

Still in the Page.xaml.cs file, create an instance of the Mars user control, and add it to the main canvas of the application:

```
Mars MyMars = new Mars();
LayoutRoot.Children.Add(MyMars);
```

24. In the Mars.xaml.cs file, declare the requisite variables. The planet Mars orbits the sun at about 24km/sec. In relation to MyMercury's orbital speed, we get 24 / 48 × .05.

```
private double Angle = 0;
private double Speed = .0250;
private Point Center;
private Point Radius;
```

25. Add the following bold code to the Mars() constructor to initialize the Radius and Center values:

```
public Mars()
{
    InitializeComponent();
    Radius.Y = 281;
    Radius.X = 281;
    Center.X = 391 - this.Width / 2;
    Center.Y = 305 - this.Height / 2;
}
```

26. Create the MoveMars() method as shown:

```
public void MoveMars()
{
    Canvas.SetLeft(this, Center.X + (Math.Cos(Angle) * Radius.X));
    Canvas.SetTop(this, Center.Y + (Math.Sin(Angle) * Radius.Y));
    Angle -= Speed;
}
```

27. In the `Page.xaml.cs` file, locate the `MovePlanets_Completed()` event handler, and add a call to `MyMars.MoveMars()`:

```
MyMars.MoveMars();
```

Compile and run the program, and you'll see all four planets orbiting the sun. The **InnerSolarSystemCompleted** project, shown in Figure 7-6, contains the code covered in this example. I also added a check box that allows you to toggle the orbits of the planets, which are ellipses that were manually added.

Think about some of the ways this program could be augmented. Certainly, adding more planets is an option. What about adding moons? How would you go about doing that? Can you figure out a way to "seed" the starting angle for each planet so it starts at a random location along its orbit? Is it possible to calculate each planet's distance from the sun?

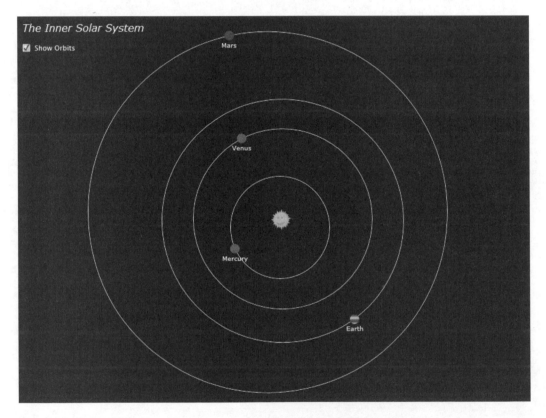

Figure 7-6. The completed InnerSolarSystem project with orbits visible

Y axis rotation

In this section, we're going to look at how we can go about emulating movement of an object around the y axis, as illustrated in Figure 7-7.

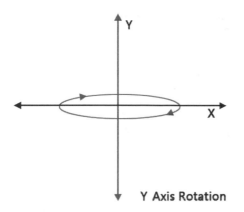

Figure 7-7. Y axis rotation causes an object to move up and down, front to back.

One of the biggest visual clues we have to tell how far we are from an object is scale. Objects closer to us are larger, and those farther away are smaller, as illustrated by Figure 7-8. Our brains are pretty good at comparing the relative sizes of objects we know, such as houses, trees, and vehicles, in order to estimate how large an object may be.

Generally speaking, the farther away an object is, the harder it is to see—our view becomes obscured by haze, and distant objects are not as well defined. Next, you're going to learn how to exploit scale and translucency in order to make objects appear to be moving either toward or away from the viewer.

Figure 7-8. Objects appear to get more distant as they are scaled down and made more translucent.

Let's code up another example. This time, we'll write some code that emulates motion around the y axis.

1. Open the **YAxis3D** project. This project contains a simple layout Canvas, our trusty Ball user control, and a storyboard timer called MoveBall.

2. All of the code for this project will go into the Page.xaml.cs file, so open that file for editing.

3. Above the Page() constructor, declare an instance of the Ball object as well as the variables shown. Origin will be used as the origin for the rotation. As with the previous examples, Radius determines the distance the ball will travel. Angle and Speed handle the rotation for us. Distance and Perspective are not things you have seen yet. These two variables work together to create a modifier for scaling the object during rotation. Position is used to place the ball on the canvas.

```
Ball MyBall = new Ball();
Point Origin;
Point Radius;
double Angle = 0;
double Speed = .1;
double Distance;
double Perspective = 400;
Point Position;
```

4. Inside the Page() constructor, add the following code to initialize the Origin variable, and place the ball object at that location before adding it to the main canvas. As with the previous examples, the Origin variable is adjusted to align to the center point of the ball rather than the top left.

```
Origin.X = LayoutRoot.Width / 2 - MyBall.Width / 2;
Origin.Y = LayoutRoot.Height / 2 - MyBall.Height / 2;
Canvas.SetLeft(MyBall, Origin.X);
Canvas.SetTop(MyBall, Origin.Y);
LayoutRoot.Children.Add(MyBall);
```

5. Continuing with variable initialization, set the Y Position variable to match the Origin.Y value. This is where the ball is currently located.

```
Position.Y = Origin.Y;
```

6. Assign values to the Radius variable. This will control the height and width of the movement.

```
Radius.X = 200;
Radius.Y = 50;
```

7. Finish up the constructor code by adding a Completed event listener to the MoveBall storyboard and starting the storyboard:

```
MoveBall.Completed += new EventHandler(MoveBall_Completed);
MoveBall.Begin();
```

8. Add the code to the MoveBall_Completed() event handler. The first two lines calculate the position of the ball. The third line calculates the scale modifier based on the y position of the ball and the Perspective variable. The next line adjusts the scale of the ball based on the Distance calculation. The position of the ball on the canvas is then updated before increment-ing the Angle value and restarting the storyboard.

```
void MoveBall_Completed(object sender, EventArgs e)
{
    Position.X = Radius.X * Math.Cos(Angle);
    Position.Y = Radius.Y * Math.Sin(Angle);
    Distance = 1 / (1 - (Position.Y / Perspective));
    MyBall.BallScale.ScaleX = MyBall.BallScale.ScaleY = Distance;

    Canvas.SetLeft(MyBall, Position.X + Origin.X);
    Canvas.SetTop(MyBall, Position.Y + Origin.Y);
    Angle += Speed;
    MoveBall.Begin();
}
```

9. Compile and run the application. The ball will follow a circular path that appears to be 3D. There's one small addition we can make to help with the illusion. Inside the MoveBall_Completed() function, adjust the Opacity property of the ball along with the scale. Now the ball will also fade out as it scales down on the back side of the rotational movement.

```
MyBall.Opacity = MyBall.BallScale.ScaleX =
                 MyBall.BallScale.ScaleY = Distance;
```

10. Try some different values and see what happens when you run the program. One of the things you'll notice is that the Perspective variable, when used in conjunction with a decreasing x Radius, will act similarly to the depth of field on a camera, "flattening" the motion. Here are a couple of values with which you can experiment:

   a. Radius.X: 200; Radius.Y: 0

   b. Elliptical path: Radius.X: 200; Radius.Y: 200; Perspective: 1000

All of the code for this example is in the **YAxis3DCompleted** project. I also added a few sliders and a check box to the project, as shown in Figure 7-9. The sliders will allow you to change the Speed, Radius, and Perspective values as the application is running. The check box allows you to toggle the transparency so you can see what effect that has on the object.

Now, I bet some of you reading this are thinking that the motion looks a bit like what you might use on a carousel-style interface, and you'd be right. Getting from here to there requires a few extra steps, but it's not as hard as it might seem. In the next exercise, we're going to take a detailed look at how to create a horizontal carousel. We'll create a carousel that uses proxy containers for the carousel items, to which you can add whatever functionality you'd like (images, movies, etc.).

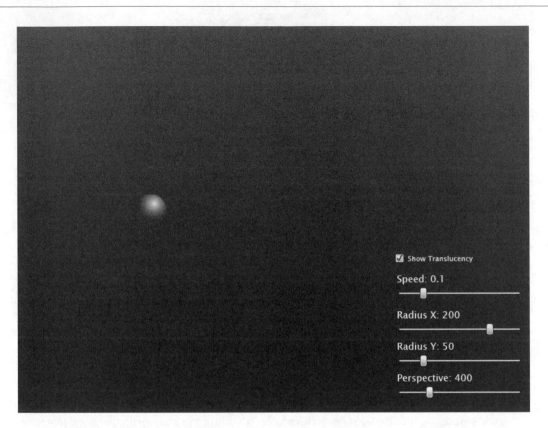

Figure 7-9. The YAxis3DCompleted project includes some sliders to change values in real time.

A horizontal carousel

This time, you're going to do almost all of the work. I've set up a base project so you can follow along, but to really understand how everything fits together, it will be of more value to you to work through the project from the very beginning.

1. Open the **HorizontalCarousel** project. The project currently contains only the main page XAML, which consists of a gradient background and a storyboard timer called Spin.

2. Right-click the HorizontalCarousel C# project name in Visual Studio's Solution Explorer and select Add ➤ New Item, as shown in Figure 7-10.

3. When the Add New Item dialog opens, select Silverlight User Control. Type in the name CarouselItem and click the Add button. Visual Studio will create the new object for you and add it to Solution Explorer. This object will become the basis for each carousel item added to the application.

4. Edit the CarouselItem.xaml file—you can do this either directly in Visual Studio or by right-clicking CarouselItem.xaml in Solution Explorer and selecting Open in Expression Blend from the pop-up menu.

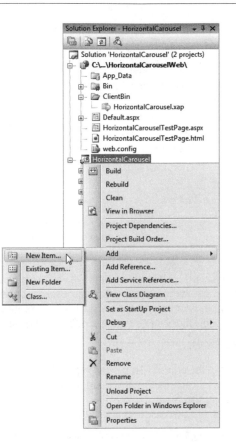

Figure 7-10. Adding a new item through
Visual Studio's Solution Explorer

5. Change the size of the user control to 150×100—change both the user control and LayoutRoot
Canvas dimensions. Add a white rectangle with a black stroke that is 150×100 with rounded
corners—both the RadiusX and RadiusY properties should be 5. Name this rectangle
RectBackground. In addition, add two TextBlocks. These will be used to identify which item is
which. Center the first TextBlock near the top of the rectangle and add the text Carousel Item.
Name the TextBlock MsgItem. Center the second TextBlock beneath the first, add the text 00,
and name it MsgNumber. Also, add a transform group to the LayoutRoot Canvas. Name the
ScaleTransform ItemScale. The XAML that goes inside the user control for this object is shown
in the following listing. Figure 7-11 shows the object.

```
<Canvas x:Name="LayoutRoot" RenderTransformOrigin="0.5,0.5"
        Width="150" Height="100">
    <Canvas.RenderTransform>
        <TransformGroup>
            <ScaleTransform x:Name="ItemScale" ScaleX="1" ScaleY="1"/>
        </TransformGroup>
    </Canvas.RenderTransform>
```

```
<Rectangle Height="100" Width="150" Fill="#FFFFFFFF"
           RadiusX="5" RadiusY="5"
           x:Name="RectBackground" Stroke="#FF000000"/>
<TextBlock Text="Carousel Item" TextWrapping="Wrap"
           Canvas.Left="25.769" Canvas.Top="10"
           x:Name="MsgItem"/>
<TextBlock Text="00" TextWrapping="Wrap"
           Canvas.Top="50" Canvas.Left="65.726"
           x:Name="MsgNumber"/>
```
`</Canvas>`

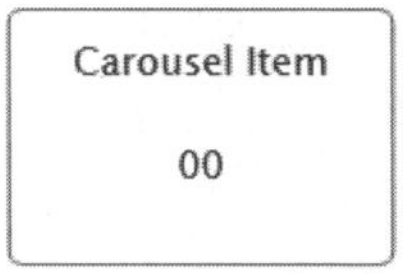

Figure 7-11. This figure shows what the carousel item should look like.

6. Open the `CarouselItem.xaml.cs` file for editing. We will be using code to distribute the carousel items along an elliptical path when creating the carousel. In order to position each item appropriately, we need to store a unique angle for each carousel item. Above the `CarouselItem()` constructor, add the following code to create a publicly accessible `Angle` variable:

```
public double Angle = 0;
```

7. Open the `Page.xaml` file for editing. This is the main application page. One thing I have found useful when working with carousels is to create a canvas to contain the carousel rather than generating it directly on the main canvas. This makes the carousel much more manageable later—move the canvas and the carousel goes with it.

   Add a canvas container to `Page.xaml`. Enter the following code two lines up from the bottom of the XAML, just before the closing `</Canvas>` tag. Notice that this canvas is identical in size to one of the carousel items. This will make adjustments for centering later very easy.

```
<Canvas Height="100" Width="150" x:Name="CarouselCanvas"/>
```

8. Now we'll start coding up the carousel. Open the `Page.xaml.cs` file for editing, and add the following variable declarations just before the `Page()` constructor. Each element added to the carousel will be stored in a `List` called `Items`. The `NumItems` variable allows easy modification to the number of elements in the carousel. By now, you should be familiar with the functionality provided by `Radius`, `Position`, `Speed`, `Distance`, and `Perspective`.

```
List<CarouselItem> Items;
int NumItems = 8;
Point Radius;
Point Position;
double Speed = .0125;
double Distance;
double Perspective = 300;
```

9. Inside the `Page()` constructor, add code to define a length for the `Items` `List` in the carousel. The length of the list is determined by the `NumItems` variable initialized in step 8.

```
Items = new List<CarouselItem>(NumItems);
```

10. Add code to initialize the Radius variable. Using a negative value for the radius will make the carousel appear to be tipped forward.

```
Radius.X = 300;
Radius.Y = -50;
```

11. Position the canvas that will contain the carousel:

```
Canvas.SetLeft(CarouselCanvas, LayoutRoot.Width / 2
                - CarouselCanvas.Width / 2);
Canvas.SetTop(CarouselCanvas, LayoutRoot.Height / 2
                - CarouselCanvas.Height / 2);
```

12. Next, we will build a function called BuildCarousel() that will be used to populate the carousel. The process of defining each element is done inside of a for loop. The basic structure for the function is shown in the following code listing:

```
private void BuildCarousel()
{
    for (int i = 0; i < NumItems; i++)
    {
    }
}
```

13. Begin filling in the for loop with the following code. Here, we create an instance of CarouselItem() called item. Once the instance has been defined, we populate one of the TextBlocks with the element number. This is strictly for reference for this carousel—if you had a set of images or videos in your carousel, this is where you would assign the Source property.

```
CarouselItem item = new CarouselItem();
item.MsgNumber.Text = String.Format("{0:00}", i);
```

14. Next, each item has a value assigned to its public Angle variable. The Angle is then used to calculate the Position variable:

```
item.Angle = i * ((Math.PI * 2) / NumItems);
Position.X = Math.Cos(item.Angle) * Radius.X;
Position.Y = Math.Sin(item.Angle) * Radius.Y;
```

15. Once Position has been calculated, place the element at the value stored in the variable:

```
Canvas.SetLeft(item, Position.X);
Canvas.SetTop(item, Position.Y);
```

16. The Distance variable is calculated to determine a modifier value that will be used for scaling the elements and adjusting their opacity. With Distance calculated, the Opacity and ItemScale are adjusted.

```
Distance = 1 / (1 - (Position.Y / Perspective));
item.Opacity = item.ItemScale.ScaleX =
                item.ItemScale.ScaleY = Distance;
```

17. To finish out the function, add the item to the Items List and the CarouselCanvas:

```
Items.Add(item);
CarouselCanvas.Children.Add(item);
```

18. The function that was just created needs to be called from the Page() constructor in order to create the carousel when the application is loaded. Add the following code as the last line in the Page() constructor:

```
BuildCarousel();
```

Compile and run the application. When the browser opens, you should see an application similar to the one shown in Figure 7-12. The application calls the BuildCarousel() function, which adds eight elements to the CarouselCanvas. The elements are evenly distributed based on the Angle and Radius variables that were defined.

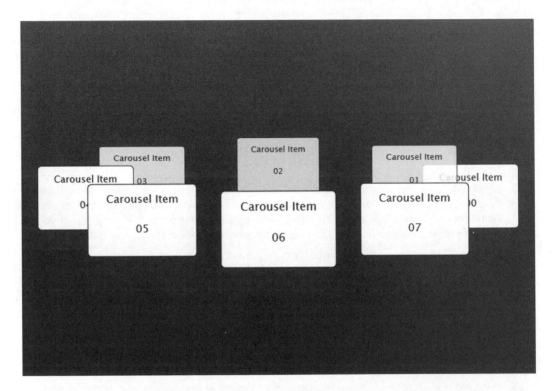

Figure 7-12. The carousel is populated and drawn on the screen.

19. Now we need to make it move. If you're thinking this is done by manipulating the angle of each object, you're right! To start, we'll need to add a bit of code at the bottom of the Page() constructor. The two lines shown following attach an event listener to the Completed event of the Spin storyboard, and start the storyboard. Notice that the event handler being called is named MoveCarousel().

```
Spin.Completed += new EventHandler(MoveCarousel);
Spin.Begin();
```

20. The MoveCarousel() event handler takes advantage of the foreach loop, which will step through each element in a List like the one we're using. The basic structure for the event handler is shown in the following listing:

```
private void MoveCarousel(object sender, EventArgs e)
{
    foreach (CarouselItem item in Items)
    {
    }
}
```

21. Inside the foreach loop, add the following code. This code decrements the angle for each element, recalculates the position, and repositions the object on the CarouselCanvas.

```
item.Angle -= Speed;
Position.X = Math.Cos(item.Angle) * Radius.X;
Position.Y = Math.Sin(item.Angle) * Radius.Y;
Canvas.SetLeft(item, Position.X);
Canvas.SetTop(item, Position.Y);
```

22. As the objects rotate, the Z-index needs to be adjusted—the items in the front need to appear in front of the items in the back. To do this, the Z-index is tied to an item's y position. A test is done against the y Radius value to determine if it is greater than or equal to 0. If so, the distance is calculated and the Z-index of the item adjusted. If the y radius is less than 0, the distance calculation is performed opposite the first method. This ensures that the carousel will draw correctly regardless of the y Radius value. Be careful when you type in this code—the difference between the two distance calculations is very small, but makes a big difference in the end result.

```
if (Radius.Y >= 0)
{
    Distance = 1 * (1 - (Position.Y / Perspective));
    Canvas.SetZIndex(item, -(int)Position.Y);
}
else
{
    Distance = 1 / (1 - (Position.Y / Perspective));
    Canvas.SetZIndex(item, (int)Position.Y);
}
```

23. With the Distance variable having been recalculated based on the y position of the carousel item, the scale and transparency of the object can be updated:

```
item.Opacity = item.ItemScale.ScaleX
             = item.ItemScale.ScaleY = Distance;
```

24. That's all for the foreach loop, but we still need to restart the storyboard. Just after the closing curly brace (}) for the foreach loop, add the following code to restart the storyboard:

```
Spin.Begin();
```

Now when you compile and run the program, the carousel will load, draw, and begin spinning from right to left (clockwise when viewed from above). If you wanted the carousel to spin in the opposite direction, you would increment the Angle variable in step 21 rather than decrement it. We still need to augment our functionality a little bit—the carousel isn't going to be very useful unless it's interactive. Let's begin adding to the carousel by creating some mouse events for the carousel items.

25. Inside the `BuildCarousel()` function, add event listeners for MouseEnter and MouseLeave. Since we're creating our carousel items inside of a loop, we only need to add the following two lines to create event listeners for every item on the carousel:

```
item.MouseEnter += new MouseEventHandler(item_MouseEnter);
item.MouseLeave += new MouseEventHandler(item_MouseLeave);
```

26. Inside the `MouseEnter()` event handler, add code to stop the carousel from spinning:

```
void item_MouseEnter(object sender, MouseEventArgs e)
{
    Spin.Stop();
}
```

27. When the mouse pointer leaves an item, we want to restart the carousel spinning. The item_MouseLeave() event handler code is shown here:

```
void item_MouseLeave(object sender, MouseEventArgs e)
{
    Spin.Begin();
}
```

Now when you run the application, placing the mouse over any of the items on the carousel will cause the carousel to stop spinning. Moving the mouse off of the item will start the carousel back up. Chances are you will at some point need to further augment the functionality to access the properties of each carousel item.

For example, if the carousel contained images, when a user clicked on one of the images, you might want to display the image on another panel elsewhere in the application. The basis for retrieving information from the carousel items is the same regardless of the type of property you're trying to get, so we'll add some basic functionality to access which item has been clicked.

28. Open the `Page.xaml` file for editing. Just below the code that defines the CarouselCanvas element, add the following code to create a TextBlock named MsgSelected:

```
<TextBlock x:Name="MsgSelected" Text="You clicked: 00"
           TextWrapping="Wrap" Foreground="#FFFFFFFF"/>
```

29. Back in the `BuildCarousel()` function in the `Page.xaml.cs` file, add a MouseLeftButtonUp event listener.

```
item.MouseLeftButtonUp +=
    new MouseButtonEventHandler(item_MouseLeftButtonUp);
```

30. Since we know that the items being clicked are of the type CarouselItem, the code inside the event handler captures the sender as a CarouselItem. We then have access to all of the objects, properties, and so on that are part of the CarouselItem, so it's easy to assign the value of the MsgNumber TextBlock in the selected item to the TextBlock we just added to the main page.

```
void item_MouseLeftButtonUp(object sender, MouseButtonEventArgs e)
{
    CarouselItem WhichItem = sender as CarouselItem;
    MsgSelected.Text = "You clicked: " + WhichItem.MsgNumber.Text;
}
```

Compile and run the application. Each time you click an item in the carousel, the text in the TextBlock at the top left of the screen should update, as shown in Figure 7-13.

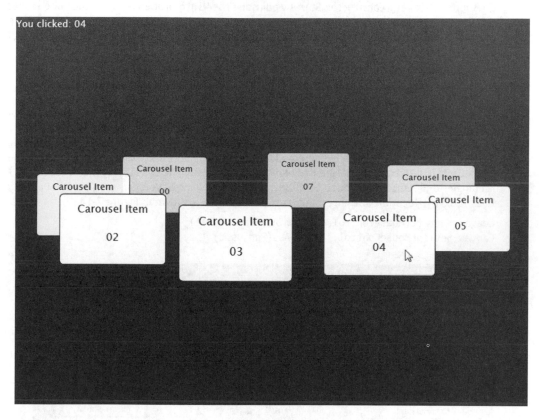

Figure 7-13. The carousel with some click functionality in place

The last bit of functionality we will be adding to the carousel will allow the mouse to control the speed and direction of spin. A lot of carousel controls have a tendency to be a little twitchy when it comes to control, so I'll show you a way to make the carousel behave the way we want, and you can change it as you see fit.

The functionality we will add is to place a rectangle in the CarouselCanvas object and hook up a MouseMove event to the rectangle. As the mouse moves, we will determine the offset from the center of the canvas, and use that calculation to spin the carousel in one direction or the other, allowing the speed to change as the mouse moves farther from center.

31. Open the Page.xaml file for editing. Add a rectangle called MouseControl inside of the CarouselCanvas container. The rectangle size will be manipulated via code, so a 100×100 rectangle is fine. Save the Page.xaml file.

```
<Canvas Height="100" Width="150" x:Name="CarouselCanvas">
    <Rectangle Height="100" Width="100" Fill="#FFFFFFFF"
        x:Name="MouseControl" Opacity="0"/>
</Canvas>
```

291

32. Open the Page.xaml.cs file for editing. Since the MouseControl rectangle has already been added to the XAML, we will make some adjustments to its size and location. The following code goes into the Page() constructor. Start by adjusting the Width property—here, the code makes the MouseControl element twice as wide as the Radius.X value and adds the Width of the CarouselCanvas to account for the top-left positioning Silverlight uses. Otherwise, our control would stop at the left side of the rightmost carousel item. The height of 100 is fine as-is. If you need a taller control for mouse input, you can modify the Height property to suit your needs.

```
MouseControl.Width = Math.Abs(Radius.X * 2) + CarouselCanvas.Width;
```

33. Next, we will position the MouseControl element. The element is moved left the equivalent of the Radius.X value. The top is moved down twice as far as the Radius.Y value. Note that while these values work well for the settings on this carousel, they may not work for every carousel. As the y radius is increased or decreased, you may need to adjust the top location for the MouseControl. An easy way to see where it's located is to set the Opacity of the MouseControl rectangle to .5. Once it has been positioned where you want it, you can then set the Opacity back to 0. The location of the rectangle for this example is shown in Figure 7-14.

```
Canvas.SetLeft(MouseControl, -(Math.Abs(Radius.X)));
Canvas.SetTop(MouseControl, (Math.Abs(Radius.Y) * 2));
```

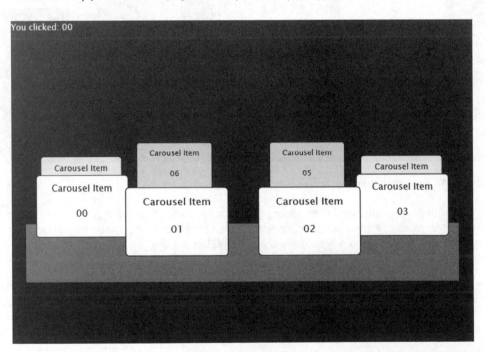

Figure 7-14. The location of the MouseControl rectangle for the carousel project

34. Finish up the work in the Page() constructor by adding an event listener for the MouseMove event on the MouseControl element:

```
MouseControl.MouseMove +=
        new MouseEventHandler(MouseControl_MouseMove);
```

35. The following code shows the MouseControl_MouseMove() event handler function. This code adds the functionality illustrated in Figure 7-15. The farther the mouse pointer moves from the center of the control rectangle, the faster the carousel will spin in the direction the mouse is moving. As the pointer approaches the center of the rectangle, the movement of the carousel slows or stops, eventually changing direction as the pointer crosses the center point.

This code gets the current position of the mouse pointer, and then calculates an offset from the center of the control rectangle. The speed is then calculated by dividing the offset by 10,000. The divisor you use depends upon the initial speed of your carousel, so you will likely need to modify that value based on your carousel design. The fewer decimal places represented in your Speed variable, the lower the divisor you will use. The function finishes up by checking the Speed value and limiting it to a maximum of two times the original speed.

```
void MouseControl_MouseMove(object sender, MouseEventArgs e)
{
    Point MousePoint = e.GetPosition(MouseControl);
    double OffsetCalc = MousePoint.X - (MouseControl.Width / 2);
    Speed = -OffsetCalc / 10000;
    if (Speed < 0 && Speed < -0.0250) Speed = -0.0250;
    else if (Speed > 0 && Speed > 0.0250) Speed = 0.0250;
}
```

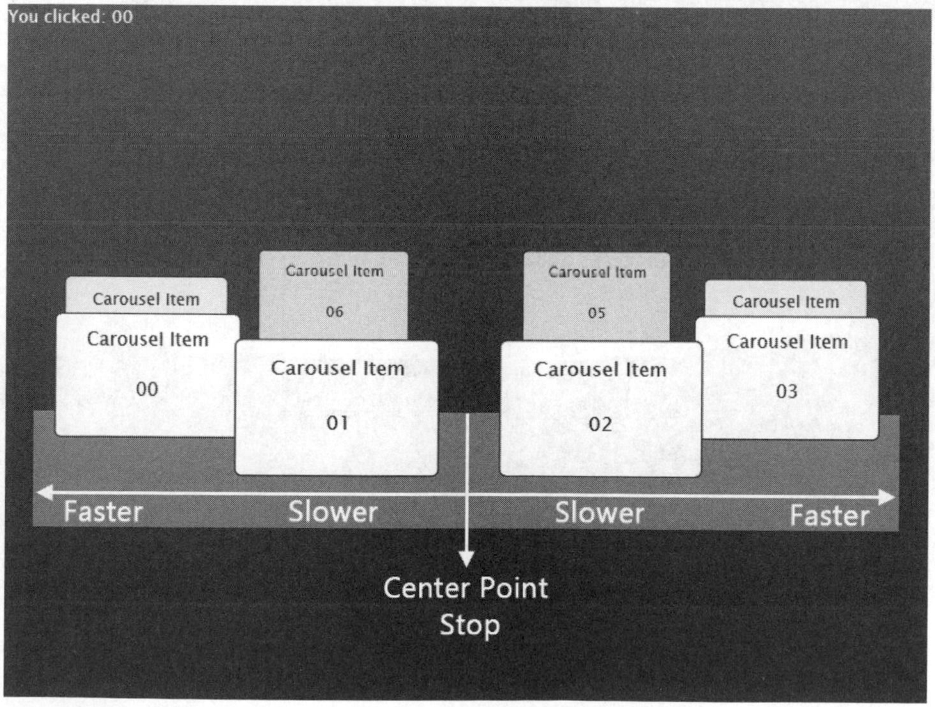

Figure 7-15. The mouse control for the carousel application

Now the application is pretty much complete. You can compile and run it to see the results. Moving the mouse just below the carousel will change the speed and/or direction of spin. Placing the mouse over an item on the carousel stops the movement, while moving the pointer off an object restarts the movement. Clicking an item in the carousel reports back which item was selected. While I am certain there are some further code optimizations that can be made, the end result of this application is worth mentioning—6.5K. Of course, the application size would grow as content were added to the carousel items, but we packed a lot of functionality into just about 130 lines of code.

All of the code described in this example is included in the **HorizontalCarouselCompleted** project. I also added an extra project for you to compile and run: **HorizontalCarouselHelper**. This project, shown in Figure 7-16, contains sliders that allow you to control the x and y origin, x and y radius, perspective, speed, and number of items for the demonstration carousel. You may find the application helpful in determining what settings you want to use for your own carousel applications before you dig in and start building. Take a good look at the code for the helper application—it illustrates how to move a carousel in two axes—the x to tilt, and the y for the rotation of the carousel.

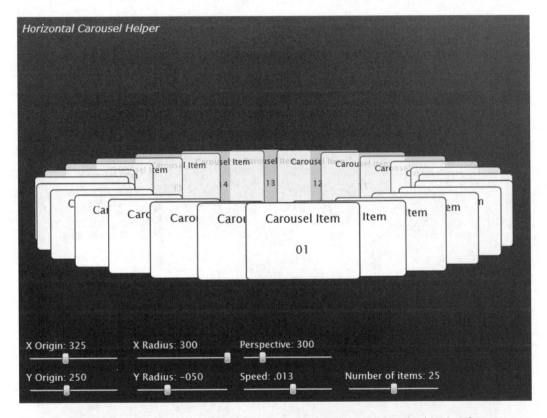

Figure 7-16. The HorizontalCarouselHelper application may help you determine optimal settings for your carousel application before you build.

Can you figure out how to add reflections to each object added on the carousel? What about rotating it with buttons rather than the mouse control? Would it work to put 30 items on a carousel, each item containing a frame from an animation, and then spin the carousel fast enough to see the motion from the individual frames?

X axis rotation

In this section, we'll finish out our look at emulating 3D movement in a 2D environment by looking at x axis rotation, which is illustrated in Figure 7-17.

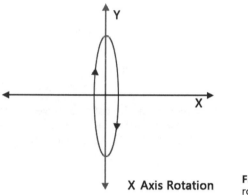

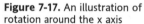
X Axis Rotation

Figure 7-17. An illustration of rotation around the x axis

As with y axis rotations, scale and transparency will once again be our clues as to the location of the object within the context of 3D space. The technique for doing an x axis rotation is the same as it is for a y axis rotation, but is applied slightly differently.

1. Open the **XAxis3D** project to code along with this example. The project contains the main page canvas, as well as the Ball object we have been using.

2. All of the code for this example will once again go into the Page.xaml.cs file, so open that file for editing.

3. Add an instance of the Ball user control and the variables necessary to code up this example. You should be pretty familiar with each of the variables by now.

```
Ball MyBall = new Ball();
Point Origin;
Point Radius;
double Angle = 0;
double Speed = .1;
double Distance;
double Perspective = 400;
Point Position;
```

4. Inside the Page() constructor, initialize the Origin variables, and position the instance of the Ball object before adding it to the main canvas:

```
Origin.X = LayoutRoot.Width / 2 - MyBall.Width / 2;
Origin.Y = LayoutRoot.Height / 2 - MyBall.Height / 2;
Canvas.SetLeft(MyBall, Origin.X);
Canvas.SetTop(MyBall, Origin.Y);
LayoutRoot.Children.Add(MyBall);
```

5. Set the x and y Radius values:

```
Radius.X = 50;
Radius.Y = 200;
```

6. Finish up the constructor by adding a Completed event listener to the MoveBall storyboard and starting the storyboard:

```
MoveBall.Completed += new EventHandler(MoveBall_Completed);
MoveBall.Begin();
```

7. Inside the MoveBall_Completed() event handler, place the code to move the ball. This code is very nearly identical to that used to simulate y axis rotations in the previous section of the chapter. The only difference is that when calculating the Distance, Position.X is used rather than Position.Y.

```
void MoveBall_Completed(object sender, EventArgs e)
{
    Position.X = Radius.X * Math.Cos(Angle);
    Position.Y = Radius.Y * Math.Sin(Angle);
    Distance = 1 / (1 - (Position.X / Perspective));
    MyBall.Opacity = MyBall.BallScale.ScaleX
                   = MyBall.BallScale.ScaleY = Distance;
    Canvas.SetLeft(MyBall, Position.X + Origin.X);
    Canvas.SetTop(MyBall, Position.Y + Origin.Y);
    Angle += Speed;
    MoveBall.Begin();
}
```

Compile and run the application, and the ball will travel in an elliptical path around the x axis. The code shown in this example is included in the **XAxis3DCompleted** project. The project, shown in Figure 7-18, has been augmented with sliders and a check box that allow you to modify the program's values in real time.

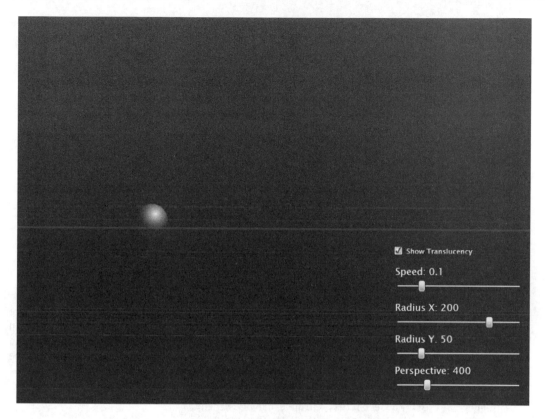

Figure 7-18. The XAxis3DCompleted project includes some sliders to change values in real time.

A vertical carousel

Let's go ahead and apply this to a real-world situation. Since we created a horizontal carousel for the y axis rotation, we'll create a vertical, Rolodex-style carousel for our x axis example. Because the majority of the code for the vertical carousel is similar to that of the horizontal carousel, we'll start out a little farther along in the project.

1. Open the **VerticalCarousel** project. This project contains the main canvas, along with the CarouselCanvas, rectangle MouseControl object, and messaging TextBlock. The CarouselItem object is also already present in the project, and has had the publicly accessible Angle variable added.

2. All of the code we will be adding will go into the Page.xaml.cs file, so open that file for editing.

3. Begin by declaring a List to contain all of the CarouselItem objects that will be used in the application. Once again, declare a variable to control the number of elements in the carousel, as well as Radius, Position, Speed, Distance, and Perspective variables.

```
List<CarouselItem> Items;
int NumItems = 8;
Point Radius;
Point Position;
double Speed = .0125;
double Distance;
double Perspective = 300;
```

4. Inside the Page() constructor, add the following code to initialize the List of CarouselItem objects:

```
Items = new List<CarouselItem>(NumItems);
```

5. Assign values for the Radius.X and Radius.Y variables:

```
Radius.X = -25;
Radius.Y = 225;
```

6. Code up the resizing and positioning for the MouseControl rectangle element. The code here differs slightly from that used in the horizontal carousel. It is height-adjusted rather than width-adjusted, and the positioning calculation is a little different—recall that you may need to customize this a little depending upon the style of your carousel. Figure 7-19 shows where the MouseControl element is located for the vertical carousel.

```
MouseControl.Height = Math.Abs(Radius.Y * 2) + CarouselCanvas.Height;
Canvas.SetLeft(MouseControl, CarouselCanvas.Width);
Canvas.SetTop(MouseControl, -(Math.Abs(Radius.Y)));
MouseControl.MouseMove +=
        new MouseEventHandler(MouseControl_MouseMove);
```

7. Continue coding the Page() constructor by positioning the CarouselCanvas:

```
Canvas.SetLeft(CarouselCanvas, LayoutRoot.Width / 2
                - CarouselCanvas.Width / 2);
Canvas.SetTop(CarouselCanvas, LayoutRoot.Height / 2
                - CarouselCanvas.Height / 2);
```

8. Finish up the constructor by calling the BuildCarousel() function (which we have yet to code), adding an event listener to the Completed event for the Spin storyboard, and starting the storyboard:

```
BuildCarousel();
Spin.Completed +=new EventHandler(MoveCarousel);
Spin.Begin();
```

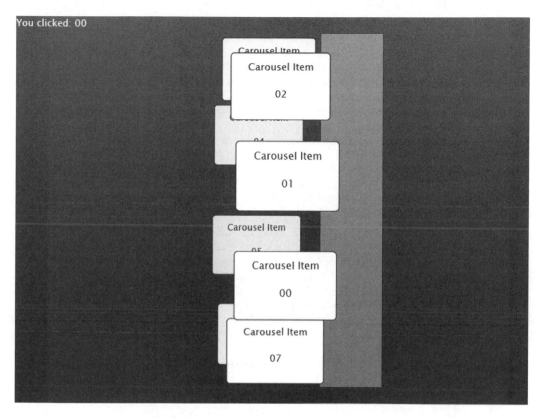

Figure 7-19. The MouseControl rectangle for the vertical carousel

9. We're working top-down through the code this time. We have three functions to build: MouseControl_MouseMove(), BuildCarousel(), and MoveCarousel(). We'll also be adding three more event listeners for the mouse events on the carousel items. We'll start with the BuildCarousel() function. This code is nearly identical to that used in the horizontal carousel, with one exception—the Distance calculation is based on the Position.X variable rather than Position.Y.

```
private void BuildCarousel()
{
    for (int i = 0; i < NumItems; i++)
    {
        CarouselItem item = new CarouselItem();
        item.MsgNumber.Text = String.Format("{0:00}", i);
        item.Angle = i * ((Math.PI * 2) / NumItems);
        Position.X = Math.Cos(item.Angle) * Radius.X;
        Position.Y = Math.Sin(item.Angle) * Radius.Y;
        Canvas.SetLeft(item, Position.X);
        Canvas.SetTop(item, Position.Y);
```

```
              item.MouseEnter += new MouseEventHandler(item_MouseEnter);
              item.MouseLeave += new MouseEventHandler(item_MouseLeave);
              item.MouseLeftButtonUp +=
                      new MouseButtonEventHandler(item_MouseLeftButtonUp);
              Distance = 1 / (1 - (Position.X / Perspective));
              item.Opacity = item.ItemScale.ScaleX
                          = item.ItemScale.ScaleY = Distance;
              Items.Add(item);
              CarouselCanvas.Children.Add(item);
          }
      }
```

10. Next, we'll tackle the three event handlers that were attached in step 9. The event handler code is identical to the code used in the horizontal carousel:

```
void item_MouseLeftButtonUp(object sender, MouseButtonEventArgs e)
{
    CarouselItem WhichItem = sender as CarouselItem;
    MsgSelected.Text = "You clicked: " + WhichItem.MsgNumber.Text;
}
void item_MouseLeave(object sender, MouseEventArgs e)
{
    Spin.Begin();
}
void item_MouseEnter(object sender, MouseEventArgs e)
{
    Spin.Stop();
}
```

11. Let's code up the MouseControl_MouseMove() event handler. The differences between this and the horizontal carousel are related to using y values rather than x. The Speed calculation is modified slightly to account for the vertical orientation of the carousel.

```
void MouseControl_MouseMove(object sender, MouseEventArgs e)
{
    Point MousePoint = e.GetPosition(MouseControl);
    double OffsetCalc = MousePoint.Y - (MouseControl.Height / 2);
    Speed = OffsetCalc / 10000;
    if (Speed < 0 && Speed < -0.0250) Speed = -0.0250;
    else if (Speed > 0 && Speed > 0.0250) Speed = 0.0250;
}
```

12. We'll finish off by adding the MoveCarousel() function shown following. The difference in code between the vertical and horizontal carousels comes in the test that is done against the Radius.X value, not the Radius.Y value.

```
private void MoveCarousel(object sender, EventArgs e)
{
    foreach (CarouselItem item in Items)
    {
        item.Angle -= Speed;
        Position.X = Math.Cos(item.Angle) * Radius.X;
        Position.Y = Math.Sin(item.Angle) * Radius.Y;
        Canvas.SetLeft(item, Position.X);
        Canvas.SetTop(item, Position.Y);
        if (Radius.X >= 0)
        {
            Distance = 1 * (1 - (Position.X / Perspective));
            Canvas.SetZIndex(item, -(int)Position.X);
        }
        else
        {
            Distance = 1 / (1 - (Position.X / Perspective));
            Canvas.SetZIndex(item, (int)Position.X);
        }
        item.Opacity = item.ItemScale.ScaleX
                     = item.ItemScale.ScaleY = Distance;
    }
    Spin.Begin();
}
```

When you compile and run, the application will look like the one shown in Figure 7-20. You can move the mouse up or down just to the right of the carousel to alter the speed/direction of rotation. Placing the pointer over an element stops the carousel, and moving the pointer off of an element will restart the carousel. Clicking an item will display the selected item number in the TextBlock at the top left of the screen.

As with the horizontal carousel, you can configure the application to meet your needs by adjusting the x or y radius values, perspective, or spin speed. All of the code covered in this example is available in the **VerticalCarouselCompleted** project.

As with the horizontal carousel, I included an extra project called **VerticalCarouselHelper**, which is shown in Figure 7-21. The program allows you to adjust many of the carousel parameters in real time in order to help you with some of the planning on your carousel application projects.

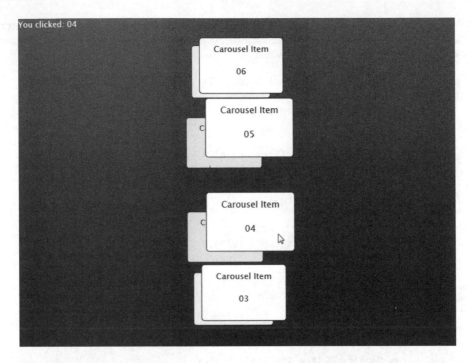

Figure 7-20. The vertical carousel application

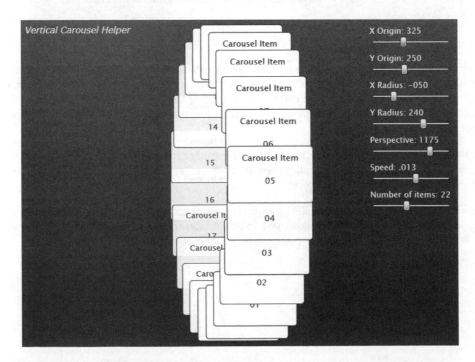

Figure 7-21. The vertical carousel helper application

Summary

In this chapter, we talked about how we can use some of the techniques from Chapter 6 to make objects appear as though they are moving in a 3D environment on our 2D canvas. We can trick our brains into seeing objects as 3D by using scale and transparency (distant objects are smaller and visually obscured, while close objects are large and well defined) in conjunction with Z-index.

Rotations around the z axis are really nothing more than circular or elliptical movements. You saw how several z axis rotations could be combined to create a simulation of the inner solar system.

In order to simulate a y axis rotation, an object must have its Scale and Opacity properties tied to its location on the path it is traveling. This will cause the object to scale down and become more transparent as it "moves away." As the object "moves forward," the object will become larger and more opaque. We explored y axis rotations by creating a horizontal carousel.

Our example of x axis rotation worked much like that for y axis rotation, except that the y radius we were using was larger than the x radius. As with y axis rotations, the Scale and Opacity properties for x axis rotation are tied to an object's location along the path it is traveling. To simulate a 3D x axis rotation, we built a vertically oriented carousel.

In Chapter 8, we're going to take a look at different methods we can use for collision detection in Silverlight. We'll create projects that demonstrate a few different scenarios, and hopefully give you a few ideas that you can apply in your own projects.

Chapter 8

COLLISIONS

So far, you've learned how to make objects move in a variety of interesting ways. They are missing one crucial component, however: interaction. In this chapter, we're going to talk about how to tell when objects have collided, and what to do with them when a collision has occurred.

We will look at how to determine if a collision has occurred along a single axis, along multiple axes, and against an angled surface. We'll also take a look at how to implement a pixel-level collision test using the built-in HitTest() method. The linear, angular, and angled-surface projects are based on projects created by Keith Peters.

The basics of detecting collisions

There are different techniques available for detecting collisions, but we're going to stick to simple methods that use bounding circles or rectangles. Why circles? Most of the objects you will deal with can fit into a circle fairly well, circles are not expensive from a processing perspective, and they are easy to detect collisions on. Take the spaceship we used earlier as an example. Figure 8-1 shows the ship inside of a bounding circle.

If we want to determine whether the ship in Figure 8-1 has collided with the sun in Figure 8-2, it's as simple as determining the distance between the two objects, and if the distance is less than the sum of the two radii, a collision has occurred. Figure 8-3 illustrates this concept.

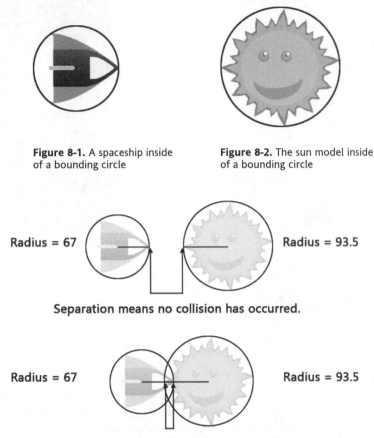

Figure 8-1. A spaceship inside of a bounding circle

Figure 8-2. The sun model inside of a bounding circle

Radius = 67   Radius = 93.5

Separation means no collision has occurred.

Radius = 67   Radius = 93.5

Overlap means collision has occurred.

Figure 8-3. If the distance between two objects is less than the sum of their bounding circle radii, a collision has occurred.

It sounds simple in theory, right? Let's see what it looks like in code.

Linear collisions

A linear collision is one that occurs along a single axis. In this case, we'll be coding up a collision along the x axis between two ball objects.

1. Open the **LinearCollisions** project to code along with this example. One thing I've done in this (and other collision projects) that is a little unusual is give the ball a center point of sorts. Take a good look at the Ball.xaml file so you can see what I mean.

The default size for the Ball user control is 50✕50. The LayoutRoot element was made to be 1✕1, and the BallShape is 50✕50, but offset –25,–25. If you select the LayoutRoot element in Blend, you will see that it serves as the center point for the ball. This means when it is referenced in code as Canvas.GetLeft or Canvas.GetTop, we are returned the LayoutRoot left or top point, which is the center of the ball. When resized from code, the actual BallShape is resized rather than scaled, and when a size is needed for something like a collision or bounds check, the BallShape is referenced directly. While it takes a few extra lines of code to account for this, the math seems to behave a little better than it does when scaling is used on an object. You may find an alternative method that works better for you.

2. Each ball has public variables for mass and velocity. Start by declaring a List that will contain all of the instances of the Ball object, two instances of the Ball object, and a random number object. This code goes just before the Page() constructor:

```
private List<Ball> allBalls;
private Ball Ball1 = new Ball();
private Ball Ball2 = new Ball();
private Random Rand = new Random();
```

3. Inside the Page() constructor, following the InitializeComponent() call, initialize the List:

```
allBalls = new List<Ball>();
```

4. Next, we'll add the two ball instances. Start by generating a random x velocity for the ball. Since this is a linear collision, there is no need for y velocity.

```
Ball1.Velocity.X = Rand.Next(1, 16) - 8;
```

5. Now we'll define the ball. In step 1, I talked about how the Ball object in this project is different than ones we've used before. This code covers our needs for an object defined this way. It starts by changing the BallShape height and width, and assigning a mass to the ball based on its width. The last two lines adjust the position of the BallShape relative to the LayoutRoot (center point). This is done to simply keep the center point at the center.

```
Ball1.BallShape.Width = Ball1.BallShape.Height = 75;
Ball1.Mass = Ball1.BallShape.Width / 50;
Canvas.SetLeft(Ball1.BallShape, -Ball1.BallShape.Width / 2);
Canvas.SetTop(Ball1.BallShape, -Ball1.BallShape.Height / 2);
```

6. Next, the ball object is positioned on the main canvas. This ball is positioned at the left side of the canvas. We can't place the ball at 0 because while the user control is 50 pixels wide, the ball shape is 75, and offset. To accommodate this change, the location is adjusted by finding the difference between the widths and dividing it in two. The ball top position is then set before adding the ball to the main canvas and the allBalls List:

```
Canvas.SetLeft(Ball1, (Ball1.BallShape.Width - Ball1.Width) / 2);
Canvas.SetTop(Ball1, 275);
LayoutRoot.Children.Add(Ball1);
allBalls.Add(Ball1);
```

7. Add a second ball with the following code. This one is smaller—25 pixels in diameter, and positioned at the right side of the canvas:

```
Ball2.Velocity.X = Rand.Next(1, 16) - 8;
Ball2.BallShape.Width = Ball2.BallShape.Height = 25;
Ball2.Mass = Ball2.BallShape.Width / 50;
Canvas.SetLeft(Ball2.BallShape, -Ball2.BallShape.Width / 2);
Canvas.SetTop(Ball2.BallShape, -Ball2.BallShape.Height / 2);
```

```
Canvas.SetLeft(Ball2, LayoutRoot.Width - Ball2.BallShape.Width
            + (Ball2.BallShape.Width - Ball2.Width) / 2);
Canvas.SetTop(Ball2, 275);
LayoutRoot.Children.Add(Ball2);
allBalls.Add(Ball2);
```

8. OK, the two balls are on the main canvas. Create an event handler for the Completed event on the Move storyboard, and start the storyboard:

```
Move.Completed += new EventHandler(Move_Completed);
Move.Begin();
```

9. Add the event handler function that will be called when the Completed event is raised:

```
void Move_Completed(object sender, EventArgs e)
{
}
```

10. Inside of the event handler function, place a for loop that steps through each ball in the allBalls List:

```
for (int i = 0; i < allBalls.Count; i++)
{
}
```

11. Inside the loop, add the following two lines of code. The first line creates a Ball object from the current ball in the List, and the second line moves the ball according to the random x velocity that was generated when the ball was initialized.

```
Ball currentBall = allBalls[i];
Canvas.SetLeft(currentBall, Canvas.GetLeft(currentBall)
            + currentBall.Velocity.X);
```

12. After the closing curly brace of the for loop, restart the timer:

```
Move.Begin();
```

13. You can run the program at this point if you'd like. The two balls will move, but they will eventually both travel off the screen since there is no boundary checking in place. Let's add some boundary checks. Inside the for loop in the Move_Completed() function, add the following code. This code tests the left and right application boundaries. Notice that there are references to the width of the specific BallShape being checked.

```
if (Canvas.GetLeft(currentBall) -
    (currentBall.BallShape.Width - currentBall.Width)
    / 2 < 0)
{
    currentBall.Velocity.X *= -1;
}
else if (Canvas.GetLeft(currentBall) >
        LayoutRoot.Width - (currentBall.Width
        + (currentBall.BallShape.Width
        - currentBall.Width) / 2))
```

```
{
    currentBall.Velocity.X *= -1;
}
```

14. The code you just added will keep the balls on the main canvas when the program runs. Now that the balls move and collide with the walls, we need to get them to collide with each other. The first thing you need to do is create a new function called CheckCollision() that accepts two passed arguments of type Ball.

```
private void CheckCollision(Ball firstBall, Ball secondBall)
{
}
```

15. At the beginning of the function, add the following three lines of code. The first two lines calculate the distance between the centers of the two objects, and the third line determines the distance at which a collision occurs.

```
double DX = Canvas.GetLeft(secondBall) - Canvas.GetLeft(firstBall);
double Distance = Math.Sqrt(DX * DX);
double CollisionDistance =
    firstBall.BallShape.Width / 2
    + secondBall.BallShape.Width / 2;
```

16. Following those three lines, test to see if there's been a collision. If the distance between the two objects is less than the collision distance, a collision has occurred. Inside this if statement is where the code goes to handle the collision reaction.

```
if (Distance < CollisionDistance)
{
}
```

17. Inside the if statement, begin the collision code by determining the total velocity. While it looks like the two velocity values are being subtracted, one of the two balls will be moving with a negative x velocity, and subtracting a negative number results in a positive result. For example, if firstBall had an x velocity of 3, and secondBall had an x velocity of –2, you would get 3 – –2, which is 5.

```
double VXTotal = firstBall.Velocity.X - secondBall.Velocity.X;
```

18. Next is the following exciting formula that calculates the velocity of firstBall. Without going into the type of detail that only someone with a PhD in physics can provide, here's what you need to know: this is the formula for the conservation of momentum along a single axis. When two objects collide as they do in this program, this formula will give you the velocity of the first object.

```
firstBall.Velocity.X = ((firstBall.Mass - secondBall.Mass) *
        firstBall.Velocity.X + 2 *
        secondBall.Mass *
        secondBall.Velocity.X) /
        (firstBall.Mass + secondBall.Mass);
```

19. Following that code, we have the far less intimidating-looking calculation for the velocity of the second object. Remember that one of the two objects will be moving with a negative velocity, so this line will provide the remaining velocity.

```
secondBall.Velocity.X = VXTotal + firstBall.Velocity.X;
```

20. Finally, update the position of each of the objects that was passed to the function:

```
Canvas.SetLeft(firstBall, Canvas.GetLeft(firstBall)
                + firstBall.Velocity.X);
Canvas.SetLeft(secondBall, Canvas.GetLeft(secondBall)
                + secondBall.Velocity.X);
```

21. With the collision code in place, all we need to do is call the function and hand it a couple of objects. Inside the `if` statement in the `Move_Completed()` function, add the following `for` loop after the boundary-checking code. Like the main `for` loop, this loop counts through the ball objects in the `allBalls` `List`, but notice that it is indexing one ball ahead of the main loop (j = I + 1) . The current ball object and the next ball in the list are then passed to the `CheckCollision()` function that was just created.

```
for (int j = i + 1; j < allBalls.Count; j++)
    CheckCollision(currentBall, allBalls[j]);
```

If you now compile and run the program, you will see two balls moving toward each other, as shown in Figure 8-4. When the balls collide, their mass and velocity are taken into account as they rebound in opposite directions.

Figure 8-4. Two balls of varying size and mass colliding along a single axis

22. One thing you may see when a fast collision occurs near a boundary is that one of the ball objects may get "stuck" along the boundary. This occurs when the object's velocity carries it beyond the boundary check. Fortunately, it's easily corrected with a few lines of code that limit the boundary checking so that it only occurs if a ball is moving toward a wall. Inside the Move_Completed() function, after the line of code that gets a reference to the current ball (Ball currentBall = allBalls[i];), add the following code. This code sets up a Boolean flag to determine whether or not the current ball has negative velocity.

```
bool hasNegativeVelocity;
if (currentBall.Velocity.X < 0)
    hasNegativeVelocity = true;
else
    hasNegativeVelocity = false;
```

23. Next, update the first boundary check to also check for negative velocity. The new code is shown in bold in the following listing. This will only check the collision for the left boundary if the ball object is moving to the left.

```
if (Canvas.GetLeft(currentBall) -
            (currentBall.BallShape.Width - currentBall.Width)
            / 2 < 0 && hasNegativeVelocity)
```

24. Make a similar change to the code that checks for the right boundary. This time, you want to check the boundary only if the ball is moving to the right.

```
else if (Canvas.GetLeft(currentBall) >
        LayoutRoot.Width - (currentBall.Width
        + (currentBall.BallShape.Width
        - currentBall.Width) / 2) && !hasNegativeVelocity)
```

Since we used a List to contain the ball objects, adding another ball into the mix is fairly easy. See if you can figure that out on your own for practice. Add a Ball3 object that has a width and height of 40, and starts at the center of the main canvas when the application runs. If you get stuck, use the **LinearCollisionsCompleted** project for help.

Now that you have some experience with linear collisions, it's time to step up to angular collisions.

Angular collisions

An angular collision is one that occurs along two axes. Since the collision occurs along two axes, the code that handles the reaction for an angular collision is quite a bit more complex than the code for a linear collision. The basic process we will be coding up is shown in the following six images, starting with the angular collision shown in Figure 8-5. The arrows represent the direction of travel; the lighter line between the center points is the angle of collision.

The process for calculating the collision begins by finding the angle of collision between the two balls and rotating the entire collision counterclockwise by that same angle. The result of this rotation would look like Figure 8-6.

Figure 8-5. A collision occurring along two axes

Figure 8-7 shows the same collision, with each ball's travel vector split into its respective x and y velocities. The original travel vectors are represented by the ghosted out arrows.

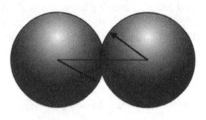

Figure 8-6. The same collision rotated counterclockwise. The rotation is the opposite of the angle between the two objects.

Figure 8-7. The x and y velocity of each vector is drawn with a black arrow. The original velocity is represented by a ghosted arrow.

By removing the original travel vectors and y velocities, you are left with a linear collision along the x axis, as shown in Figure 8-8.

After the collision occurs, the x velocities would be altered, while the y velocities would remain the same. The post-collision velocities and travel vector are shown in Figure 8-9.

Figure 8-8. The x velocities create a linear collision.

Figure 8-9. After the collision, the y velocities remain unchanged, while the x velocities are new.

The final step in the process is to rotate the collision in the clockwise direction to its original position. As you can see in Figure 8-10, the balls now have a different direction of travel.

New Direction   Original Direction

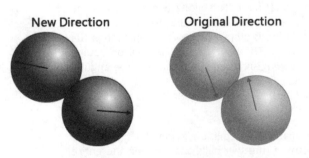

Figure 8-10. The collision, rotated back to the original angle

As you probably figured, it takes a fair amount of code to perform this operation. It's not overly complex, but the code is not something you would be likely to just look at and understand. With that in mind, let's write it up. In this example, you will be coding angular collisions between multiple ball objects.

1. Open the **AngularCollisions** project to code along with this example. The project contains essentially the same code as the **LinearCollisions** project, except that each ball is given both an x and y velocity, and there is some additional bounds checking for the top and bottom of the application. For this example, the bounds checking was moved to its own function: CheckBounds(). Compile and run the program to test it out—two balls are placed on the screen and given random velocities. They will bounce off of the application boundaries, but not each other. Take a few moments to examine the differences between this project and the **LinearCollisions** project.

2. Inside the CheckCollision() function is an empty if statement that tests whether or not a collision has occurred. Begin coding inside that if statement by determining the angle of the collision, as well as the sine and cosine of the angle.

```
double Angle = Math.Atan2(DY, DX);
double Sine = Math.Sin(Angle);
double Cosine = Math.Cos(Angle);
```

3. Next, rotate the coordinates of the positions. X0,Y0 will be the coordinates of firstBall and X1,Y1 are the coordinates of secondBall. The rotation of the collision is occurring around firstBall, which is why X0 and Y0 are both 0.

```
double X0 = 0;
double Y0 = 0;
double X1 = DX * Cosine + DY * Sine;
double Y1 = DY * Cosine - DX * Sine;
```

4. To rotate the velocity of firstBall, add the code shown here:

```
double VX0 = firstBall.Velocity.X * Cosine
             + firstBall.Velocity.Y * Sine;
double VY0 = firstBall.Velocity.Y * Cosine
             - firstBall.Velocity.X * Sine;
```

5. Follow that with the code that rotates the velocity of secondBall:

```
double VX1 = secondBall.Velocity.X * Cosine
             + secondBall.Velocity.Y * Sine;
double VY1 = secondBall.Velocity.Y * Cosine
             - secondBall.Velocity.X * Sine;
```

6. Resolve the collision. This code is very similar to the collision code used in the **LinearCollision** project, except that it is using the rotated values calculated in steps 4 and 5.

```
double VXTotal = VX0 - VX1;
VX0 = ((firstBall.Mass - secondBall.Mass) *
      VX0 + 2 * secondBall.Mass * VX1) /
      (firstBall.Mass + secondBall.Mass);
VX1 = VXTotal + VX0;
```

7. Now that the collision has been resolved, rotate the positions back:

```
double X0Final = X0 * Cosine - Y0 * Sine;
double Y0Final = Y0 * Cosine + X0 * Sine;
double X1Final = X1 * Cosine - Y1 * Sine;
double Y1Final = Y1 * Cosine + X1 * Sine;
```

8. Update the positions of `firstBall` and `secondBall` on the main canvas:

```
Canvas.SetLeft(secondBall, Canvas.GetLeft(firstBall) + X1Final);
Canvas.SetTop(secondBall, Canvas.GetTop(firstBall) + Y1Final);
Canvas.SetLeft(firstBall, Canvas.GetLeft(firstBall) + X0Final);
Canvas.SetTop(firstBall, Canvas.GetTop(firstBall) + Y0Final);
```

9. Rotate the `firstBall` and `secondBall` object's velocities back:

```
firstBall.Velocity.X = VX0 * Cosine - VY0 * Sine;
firstBall.Velocity.Y = VY0 * Cosine + VX0 * Sine;
secondBall.Velocity.X = VX1 * Cosine - VY1 * Sine;
secondBall.Velocity.Y = VY1 * Cosine + VX1 * Sine;
```

Since that was a fair amount of code, here's the whole `if` statement shown in one listing:

```
if (Distance < CollisionDistance)
{
    double Angle = Math.Atan2(DY, DX);
    double Sine = Math.Sin(Angle);
    double Cosine = Math.Cos(Angle);
    double X0 = 0;
    double Y0 = 0;
    double X1 = DX * Cosine + DY * Sine;
    double Y1 = DY * Cosine - DX * Sine;
    double VX0 = firstBall.Velocity.X * Cosine +
                 firstBall.Velocity.Y * Sine;
    double VY0 = firstBall.Velocity.Y * Cosine -
                 firstBall.Velocity.X * Sine;
    double VX1 = secondBall.Velocity.X * Cosine +
                 secondBall.Velocity.Y * Sine;
    double VY1 = secondBall.Velocity.Y * Cosine -
                 secondBall.Velocity.X * Sine;
    double VXTotal = VX0 - VX1;
    VX0 = ((firstBall.Mass - secondBall.Mass) *
            VX0 + 2 * secondBall.Mass * VX1) /
            (firstBall.Mass + secondBall.Mass);
    VX1 = VXTotal + VX0;
    double X0Final = X0 * Cosine - Y0 * Sine;
    double Y0Final = Y0 * Cosine + X0 * Sine;
    double X1Final = X1 * Cosine - Y1 * Sine;
    double Y1Final = Y1 * Cosine + X1 * Sine;
    Canvas.SetLeft(secondBall, Canvas.GetLeft(firstBall) + X1Final);
    Canvas.SetTop(secondBall, Canvas.GetTop(firstBall) + Y1Final);
```

```
Canvas.SetLeft(firstBall, Canvas.GetLeft(firstBall) + XOFinal);
Canvas.SetTop(firstBall, Canvas.GetTop(firstBall) + YOFinal);

firstBall.Velocity.X = VX0 * Cosine - VY0 * Sine;
firstBall.Velocity.Y = VY0 * Cosine + VX0 * Sine;
secondBall.Velocity.X = VX1 * Cosine - VY1 * Sine;
secondBall.Velocity.Y = VY1 * Cosine + VX1 * Sine;
    }
```

Press F5 to compile and run the project, and wait for a collision to occur. If it doesn't look like the two balls will hit, press F5 in the browser to reload the application with new starting velocities. Eventually, the two objects will collide, and bounce off of each other according to their mass and velocity.

Go ahead and add another ball or two to the project. Vary their size a little bit, and then run the project and see how it behaves. Generally speaking, you will get accurate, good-quality collisions, but one thing you may notice is that as an object travels faster, the collision will become less accurate.

The reason for this is in the way the positions are updated and the collisions are checked. The balls are moved, the collisions are checked, the balls are moved again, the collisions are checked again, and so on. If a ball has an x velocity of –7 and is 3 pixels from the object with which it is going to collide, the next time the ball is moved, it will overlap the object by 4 pixels. This becomes a bigger issue when there are many more objects on screen—one object may end up "trapping" another. This occurs when one object makes it inside the bounds of another when the two objects are moved. The collision checking will then determine that a collision has occurred between those two objects, but the objects will often be unable to separate and will remain stuck together.

10. To account for this issue, add the following bit of code to the collision reaction code, just after the line that calculates the updated x velocity of the secondBall object (VX1 = VXTotal + VX0;). This code sums the absolute values of both objects' x velocities, figures out the amount that the two objects are overlapping, and then adjusts each object based on a portion of the total overlap determined by their contribution to the total velocity. This will result in very clean collisions even at higher velocity.

```
double AbsVel = Math.Abs(VX0) + Math.Abs(VX1);
double Overlap = (firstBall.BallShape.Width / 2 +
                secondBall.BallShape.Width / 2) -
                Math.Abs(X0 - X1);
X0 += VX0 / AbsVel * Overlap;
X1 += VX1 / AbsVel * Overlap;
```

The finished code from this example is available in the **AngularCollisionsCompleted** project.

Angular collisions with forces

Collisions become even more interesting when you start applying other forces such as gravity to them. I've included an extra project for you to look at called **BallDropCompleted** that uses the same collision engine described in the previous example.

When the application starts, two balls are generated, and then an additional ball of a random size and color is created every second until the user-specified number is reached. As the balls move around the main canvas, they are pulled downward by the force of gravity, bouncing and colliding as they fall until they eventually come to rest, as shown in Figure 8-11.

Figure 8-11. The BallDropCompleted project applies gravity and multiaxis collisions to a user-specified number of balls.

Collisions with angled surfaces

Earlier in the book, you saw how the law of reflection is used to create collisions with horizontal or vertical surfaces. The angle of incidence is equal to the angle of reflection, which means an object will bounce off of a flat surface at the same angle in which it hit the surface.

But what about angled surfaces? Bouncing objects off of angled surfaces is very similar to performing angular collisions, except that the angle of the collision is determined by the angle of the surface being hit. When a collision with an angled surface occurs, the coordinate system is rotated, the collision is resolved, and then the system is rotated back. Let's take a look at an example.

1. Open the **AngledSurfaceCollision** project to code along with this example. This project contains a ball object and a line object, both of which have been adjusted as described earlier in this chapter to have the LayoutRoot Canvas act as a center point. The line object user control is 1×1, as is the LayoutRoot within the control. The actual visual reference line inside the LineObject control is called ReferenceLine, and is 400 pixels wide, offset –200 along the x to position the center point.

2. Press F5 to compile and run the project. I've already placed the gravity and boundary checking in place, as well as the basic motion loop, so you should see the ball drop and bounce.

3. I've already declared an instance of the line object for you, but you'll need to add it to the main canvas. Inside the Page() constructor, add the following code. This will center the line object on the main canvas, rotate the line 25 degrees, and add the line to the main canvas.

```
Canvas.SetLeft(theLine, LayoutRoot.Width / 2);
Canvas.SetTop(theLine, LayoutRoot.Height / 2);
theLine.rotateLine.Angle = 25;
LayoutRoot.Children.Add(theLine);
```

4. The line is now drawn on the main canvas, but it won't do anything—the ball will still fall straight through and hit the floor. We'll need to add the collision code to the MoveBall() function. Since we'll be rotating the coordinate system again, we'll need variables for Angle, Cosine, and Sine. In the previous example, Angle was the angle between the two colliding objects—here, the value is taken directly from the line object's Rotate transform value.

```
double Angle = theLine.rotateLine.Angle * Math.PI / 180;
double Cosine = Math.Cos(Angle);
double Sine = Math.Sin(Angle);
```

5. Next, figure out the distance between the ball and the line:

```
double DX = Canvas.GetLeft(whichBall) - Canvas.GetLeft(theLine);
double DY = Canvas.GetTop(whichBall) - Canvas.GetTop(theLine);
```

6. Add the following code to rotate the coordinates:

```
double X1 = DX * Cosine + DY * Sine;
double Y1 = DY * Cosine - DX * Sine;
```

7. Follow that by rotating the velocities:

```
double VX1 = Cosine * whichBall.Velocity.X
            + Sine * whichBall.Velocity.Y;
double VY1 = Cosine * whichBall.Velocity.Y
            - Sine * whichBall.Velocity.X;
```

8. Now that the velocities have been rotated, we can perform the bounce:

```
if (Y1 > -(whichBall.Height / 2))
{
    Y1 = -(whichBall.Height / 2);
    VY1 *= Restitution;
}
```

9. Rotate back the coordinates:

```
double X = Cosine * X1 - Sine * Y1;
double Y = Cosine * Y1 + Sine * X1;
```

10. Rotate back the velocities:

```
whichBall.Velocity.X = Cosine * VX1 - Sine * VY1;
whichBall.Velocity.Y = Cosine * VY1 + Sine * VX1;
```

11. Finish by updating the position of the ball on the main canvas:

```
Canvas.SetLeft(whichBall, Canvas.GetLeft(theLine) + X);
Canvas.SetTop(whichBall, Canvas.GetTop(theLine) + Y);
```

Press F5 to compile and run the program. The ball drops, hits the line, and bounces. When it reaches the edge of the line, it keeps rolling as if the line were still there. What happened? Technically speaking, the line *is* still there. The code defines a line mathematically, and that line continues all the way across the application. The line that's drawn in the interface is nothing more than a visual reference and really doesn't have any effect on the behavior of the ball as it bounces, even though it looks like it does.

The solution to this problem is to introduce some boundary checking for the line into the application.

We can't use the position of the reference line within the line object, because the position of that object is relative to its container and will never change as the application runs.

We also cannot use the center point of the object +/– the radius to locate the endpoints, because that will only be accurate when the line is completely horizontal. The more the line rotates, the closer in the left and right bounds become, and the less accurate the location +/– radius method will become.

However, we do know the position of the line, the rotation of the line, and the radius formed by the line, so we can determine the left and right bounds fairly easily.

12. Open the LineObject.xaml.cs file for editing. Before the LineObject() constructor, declare three variables that will be used to store the center point of the line, the radius, and the angle of rotation:

```
private Point Center;
private double Radius;
private double Angle;
```

13. We'll also need publicly accessible variables to hold the boundary values that we calculate:

```
public double BoundX1;
public double BoundX2;
```

14. Create a publicly accessible function called SetBounds(). We'll be placing code that calculates the boundaries of the line inside this function. When the line object is instanced, this function will be called.

```
public void SetBounds()
{
}
```

15. Inside the function, place code to initialize the variables that were declared:

```
Center.X = Canvas.GetLeft(this);
Center.Y = Canvas.GetTop(this);
Radius = this.ReferenceLine.Width / 2;
Angle = this.rotateLine.Angle * Math.PI / 180;
```

16. Follow that up with the code to calculate the left and right boundaries of the line:

```
BoundX1 = Center.X + Math.Cos(Angle) * -Radius;
BoundX2 = Center.X + Math.Cos(Angle) * Radius;
```

17. In the Page.xaml.cs file, the code inside the Page() constructor that initializes the line needs to be updated to call the new function. The newly added line is shown in bold in the following code. Notice that the line comes *after* the angle for the line is set.

```
Canvas.SetLeft(theLine, LayoutRoot.Width / 2);
Canvas.SetTop(theLine, LayoutRoot.Height / 2);
theLine.rotateLine.Angle = 25;
theLine.SetBounds();
LayoutRoot.Children.Add(theLine);
```

18. Now that we have boundaries for the line, we can apply them by wrapping our collision reaction code in an if statement that checks to see if the ball is within the bounds of the line. The updated collision reaction code from the MoveBall() function follows—add only the lines shown in bold:

```
if (Canvas.GetLeft(whichBall) > theLine.BoundX1 &&
    Canvas.GetLeft(whichBall) < theLine.BoundX2)
{
    double Angle = theLine.rotateLine.Angle * Math.PI / 180;
    double Cosine = Math.Cos(Angle);
    double Sine = Math.Sin(Angle);
    double DX = Canvas.GetLeft(whichBall) - Canvas.GetLeft(theLine);
    double DY = Canvas.GetTop(whichBall) - Canvas.GetTop(theLine);
    double X1 = DX * Cosine + DY * Sine;
    double Y1 = DY * Cosine - DX * Sine;
    double VX1 = Cosine * whichBall.Velocity.X
                + Sine * whichBall.Velocity.Y;
    double VY1 = Cosine * whichBall.Velocity.Y
                - Sine * whichBall.Velocity.X;
    if (Y1 > -(whichBall.Height / 2))
    {
        Y1 = -(whichBall.Height / 2);
        VY1 *= Restitution;
    }
    double X = Cosine * X1 - Sine * Y1;
    double Y = Cosine * Y1 + Sine * X1;
    whichBall.Velocity.X = Cosine * VX1 - Sine * VY1;
    whichBall.Velocity.Y = Cosine * VY1 + Sine * VX1;
    Canvas.SetLeft(whichBall, Canvas.GetLeft(theLine) + X);
    Canvas.SetTop(whichBall, Canvas.GetTop(theLine) + Y);
}
```

Press F5 to compile and run the program again. This time, the ball drops, hits the line, bounces, and drops off the line as you would expect it to. However, after hitting the edge of the application and rolling back toward the line, the ball moves inside the right boundary, and then "jumps" as the code calculates the collision again. This issue is easily corrected.

19. Locate the if statement that performs the collision reaction calculation—it looks like this: if (Y1 > -(whichBall.Height / 2)). Change it so that it includes an && (and) function like the code shown following.

The Y1 < VY1 tests the rotated position of the ball to see if it is less than the velocity of the ball. When above the line, the ball's rotated y position is negative, so it will be less than the ball's y velocity, which is positive as the ball drops. Once below the line and inside the line's boundaries, the ball's rotated y position becomes positive, and is greater than the ball's y velocity, so no collision takes place.

```
if (Y1 > -(whichBall.Height / 2) && Y1 < VY1)
```

Now when you compile and run the program, the ball will roll under the line as expected. Play around with the angle of the line a little bit and see what kind of effect it has on the ball bouncing. Take a few minutes and add a slider to the application that allows you to change the angle of the line while the application is running. If you get stuck, I've included the code in the **AngledSurfaceCollisionCompleted** project, shown in Figure 8-12.

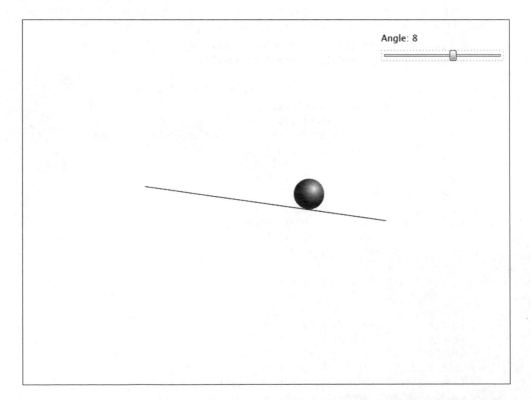

Figure 8-12. The slider in the project allows you to control the angle of the surface with which the ball collides.

From where you're currently at in the project, it takes just a few steps to add multiple lines for the ball to collide with to the application.

20. Before the Page() constructor, add a new List called Lines. This List will be used to hold each line added to the application.

```
private List<LineObject> Lines;
```

21. Remove the declaration for the theLine object:

```
private LineObject theLine = new LineObject();
```

22. Add the following four LineObject declarations:

```
private LineObject Line1 = new LineObject();
private LineObject Line2 = new LineObject();
private LineObject Line3 = new LineObject();
private LineObject Line4 = new LineObject();
```

23. Inside the Page() constructor, remove the initialization code for the LineObject that was removed:

```
Canvas.SetLeft(theLine, LayoutRoot.Width / 2);
Canvas.SetTop(theLine, LayoutRoot.Height / 2);
theLine.rotateLine.Angle = 0;
theLine.SetBounds();
LayoutRoot.Children.Add(theLine);
```

24. Add the initialization code to the Page() constructor for the Lines List, and the four LineObjects you declared:

```
Lines = new List<LineObject>();
Canvas.SetLeft(Line1, 200);
Canvas.SetTop(Line1, 100);
Line1.rotateLine.Angle = 10;
Line1.SetBounds();
Lines.Add(Line1);
LayoutRoot.Children.Add(Line1);
Canvas.SetLeft(Line2, 500);
Canvas.SetTop(Line2, 200);
Line2.rotateLine.Angle = -20;
Line2.SetBounds();
Lines.Add(Line2);
LayoutRoot.Children.Add(Line2);
Canvas.SetLeft(Line3, 200);
Canvas.SetTop(Line3, 300);
Line3.rotateLine.Angle = 20;
Line3.SetBounds();
Lines.Add(Line3);
LayoutRoot.Children.Add(Line3);
Canvas.SetLeft(Line4, 500);
Canvas.SetTop(Line4, 450);
```

```
Line4.rotateLine.Angle = -12;
Line4.SetBounds();
Lines.Add(Line4);
LayoutRoot.Children.Add(Line4);
```

25. Change the MoveBall() function so it accepts a LineObject argument, and replace the references inside the function to theLine with whichLine. The altered lines are shown in bold in the following code:

```
private void MoveBall(Ball whichBall, LineObject whichLine)
{
    if (Canvas.GetLeft(whichBall) > whichLine.BoundX1 &&
        Canvas.GetLeft(whichBall) < whichLine.BoundX2)
    {
        double Angle = whichLine.rotateLine.Angle * Math.PI / 180;
        double Cosine = Math.Cos(Angle);
        double Sine = Math.Sin(Angle);
        double DX = Canvas.GetLeft(whichBall)
                    - Canvas.GetLeft(whichLine);
        double DY = Canvas.GetTop(whichBall)
                    - Canvas.GetTop(whichLine);
        double X1 = DX * Cosine + DY * Sine;
        double Y1 = DY * Cosine - DX * Sine;
        double VX1 = Cosine * whichBall.Velocity.X
                    + Sine * whichBall.Velocity.Y;
        double VY1 = Cosine * whichBall.Velocity.Y
                    - Sine * whichBall.Velocity.X;
        if (Y1 > -(whichBall.Height / 2) && Y1 < VY1)
        {
            Y1 = -(whichBall.Height / 2);
            VY1 *= Restitution;
        }
        double X = Cosine * X1 - Sine * Y1;
        double Y = Cosine * Y1 + Sine * X1;
        whichBall.Velocity.X = Cosine * VX1 - Sine * VY1;
        whichBall.Velocity.Y = Cosine * VY1 + Sine * VX1;
        Canvas.SetLeft(whichBall, Canvas.GetLeft(whichLine) + X);
        Canvas.SetTop(whichBall, Canvas.GetTop(whichLine) + Y);
    }
}
```

26. Inside the Move_Completed() event handler function, replace MoveBall(aBall); with the following code. This code will step through each LineObject in the List of lines and do collision checking.

```
foreach (LineObject lo in Lines)
{
    MoveBall(aBall, lo);
}
```

Press F5 to compile and run the program. The ball will now roll and bounce along multiple lines, as shown in Figure 8-13.

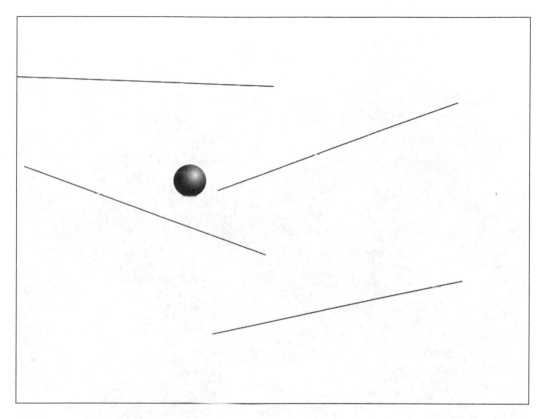

Figure 8-13. The ball rolls and bounces along multiple lines.

If you want to change the length of a line at the time of instantiation, all you need to do is change the Width property of the ReferenceLine element, and adjust the position of the ReferenceLine element so that LayoutRoot remains the center point for the object. The following code shows a typical instantiation block for a line element, with the two lines of code that resize the individual line element in bold:

```
Canvas.SetLeft(Line1, 200);
Canvas.SetTop(Line1, 100);
Line1.ReferenceLine.Width = 250;
Canvas.SetLeft(Line1.ReferenceLine, -(Line1.ReferenceLine.Width / 2));
Line1.rotateLine.Angle = 10;
Line1.SetBounds();
Lines.Add(Line1);
LayoutRoot.Children.Add(Line1);
```

I've included code showing how to play around with some of the line properties in the **MultipleAngledSurfaces** project, which is shown in Figure 8-14. This project also turns the line that the ball is in contact with orange.

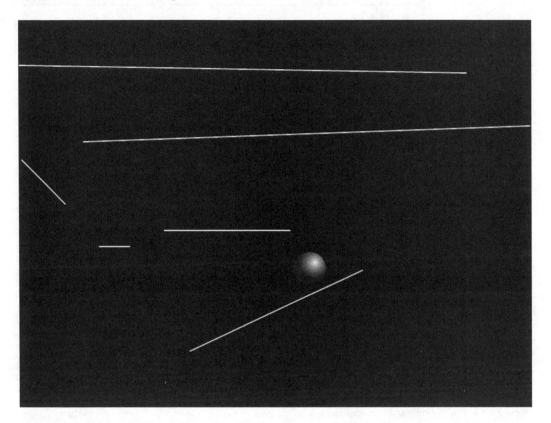

Figure 8-14. A ball colliding with multiple lines of different sizes and angles

We've talked about how to do collision detection using circles to detect the collision. Silverlight also provides a pixel-by-pixel comparison method, called HitTest(), which we'll look at in the following section and example.

HitTest

You have already seen how Silverlight describes objects with a bounding box, no matter what their shape. The box is defined by the top-left point, and width and height properties, as illustrated in Figure 8-15. While the method for collision detection described earlier in this chapter works pretty well, take a look at Figure 8-16. If the space capsule were traveling in the direction indicated by the arrow, this would produce a hit using circles as collision objects, because the distance between the two objects is less than the sum of their radii.

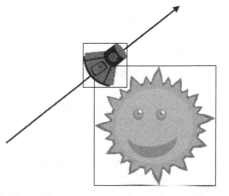
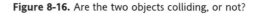

Figure 8-15. The bounding boxes for the sun and space capsule objects

Figure 8-16. Are the two objects colliding, or not?

If you think this is a possibility and you need a method of collision testing that is more precise than the methods described previously, you will want to consider the built-in HitTest() method in Silverlight. HitTest() is expensive from a processing perspective, so you will want to optimize the collision checking code to avoid doing the test unless necessary.

Andy Beaulieu came up with a pretty good solution, and we will build a streamlined version of his example in the following example. The concept is to do a "precheck" by comparing the two objects' bounding boxes—if they don't overlap, there's no reason to spend the cycles checking each pixel for a collision. If the bounding boxes *do* overlap, there might be a collision, so we'll check pixel by pixel to see if, in fact, a collision has occurred.

The one important thing you need to know is that a good collision test is dependent upon an outline of the object. In some cases, like the sun and space capsule, there are many paths that make up the object. What you want is just a single path that outlines the shape, as shown in Figures 8-17 and 8-18. For the space capsule, I just traced around the edges with the Path tool, filled the path with a transparent color, and saved it as CapsuleOutline. For the sun object, I was able to combine several of the existing paths into the SunOutline element.

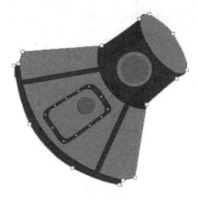

Figure 8-17. The outline path for the space capsule object

Figure 8-18. The outline path for the sun object

1. Open the **HitTestBuild** project to code along with this example. The project contains an instance of the space capsule and an instance of the sun, each of which has drag-and-drop code already in place. Both objects have been initialized and placed on the main canvas—you will see them if you run the application.

2. Open the `Page.xaml.cs` file for editing. Start by creating a new function called `UserControlBounds()` that accepts a `FrameworkElement` and returns a `Rectangle`:

```
public Rect UserControlBounds(FrameworkElement control)
{
}
```

3. Inside the function, begin by creating a `Point` object that gets the left and top properties of the passed object:

```
Point ptTopLeft = new Point(Convert.ToDouble
            (control.GetValue(Canvas.LeftProperty)),
            Convert.ToDouble(control.
            GetValue(Canvas.TopProperty)));
```

4. Follow that up with a `Point` object that gets the bottom-right corner of the object that was passed:

```
Point ptBottomRight = new Point(Convert.ToDouble
            (control.GetValue(Canvas.LeftProperty)) +
            control.Width, Convert.ToDouble(control.
            GetValue(Canvas.TopProperty)) + control.Height);
```

5. Finish the function by returning the rectangle object to the calling code:

```
return new Rect(ptTopLeft, ptBottomRight);
```

6. Next, create a function called `CheckCollision()` that accepts four `FrameworkElement` objects and returns a Boolean. Inside this function, we'll test to see if a collision occurred. If it did, the function will return true; otherwise, it will return false.

```
private bool CheckCollision(FrameworkElement control1,
                    FrameworkElement controlElem1,
                    FrameworkElement control2,
                    FrameworkElement controlElem2)
{
}
```

7. Inside the function, begin by declaring two rectangles, rect1 and rect2, which are defined by the results of passing two of the elements passed into this function on to the `UserControlBounds()` function created earlier:

```
Rect rect1 = UserControlBounds(control1);
Rect rect2 = UserControlBounds(control2);
```

8. Test to see if the rect1 and rect2 objects intersect:

```
rect1.Intersect(rect2);
if (rect1 != Rect.Empty)
{
}
```

9. If the results of the intersection test were true, declare a new Point that will be used for the pixel testing:

```
Point ptCheck = new Point();
```

10. The following block of code steps through each point in the rect1 object, which contains the overlapping area between the two rectangles, and checks to see if it contains any of the pixels in the first object. If so, the same point is tested against the second object. If pixels from the second object are found, a collision has occurred, and a value of true is returned.

```
for (int x = Convert.ToInt32(rect1.X); x <
            Convert.ToInt32(rect1.X + rect1.Width); x++)
{
    for (int y = Convert.ToInt32(rect1.Y); y <
                Convert.ToInt32(rect1.Y + rect1.Height); y++)
    {
        ptCheck.X = x;
        ptCheck.Y = y;
        List<UIElement> hits = (List<UIElement>)control1.➥
                            HitTest(ptCheck);
        if (hits.Contains(controlElem1))
        {
            // we have a hit on the first control elem, now
            // see if the second elem has a similar hit
            List<UIElement> hits2 = (List<UIElement>)control2.➥
                                HitTest(ptCheck);
            if (hits2.Contains(controlElem2))
            {
                return true;
            }
        }
    }
}
```

11. If no collision has been found, the function can return false, so add the following code after the closing curly brace of the if statement:

```
return false;
```

The completed function is shown in the following listing for clarity:

```
private bool CheckCollision(FrameworkElement control1,
                    FrameworkElement controlElem1,
                    FrameworkElement control2,
                    FrameworkElement controlElem2)
```

```
    {
        // first see if sprite rectangles collide
        Rect rect1 = UserControlBounds(control1);
        Rect rect2 = UserControlBounds(control2);
        rect1.Intersect(rect2);
        if (rect1 != Rect.Empty)
        {
            Point ptCheck = new Point();
            // now we do a more accurate pixel hit test
            for (int x = Convert.ToInt32(rect1.X); x <
                        Convert.ToInt32(rect1.X + rect1.Width); x++)
            {
                for (int y = Convert.ToInt32(rect1.Y); y <
                            Convert.ToInt32(rect1.Y + rect1.Height); y++)
                {
                    ptCheck.X = x;
                    ptCheck.Y = y;
                    List<UIElement> hits = (List<UIElement>)control1.➥
                                        HitTest(ptCheck);
                    if (hits.Contains(controlElem1))
                    {
                        // we have a hit on the first control elem,
                        // now see if the second elem has a similar hit
                        List<UIElement> hits2 = (List<UIElement>) ➥
                                                control2.HitTest(ptCheck);
                        if (hits2.Contains(controlElem2))
                        {
                            return true;
                        }
                    }
                }
            }
        }
        return false;
    }
```

12. Now all we need to do is make use of that code! At the bottom of the Page() constructor, create a new event handler for LayoutRoot.MouseMove:

```
LayoutRoot.MouseMove += new MouseEventHandler(LayoutRoot_MouseMove);
```

13. Create the MouseMove() event handler function:

```
void LayoutRoot_MouseMove(object sender, MouseEventArgs e)
{
}
```

14. Inside the function, set up pointers to the "outline" paths of the two objects being compared:

```
Path capsuleHit = myCapsule.FindName("CapsuleOutline") as Path;
Path sunHit = mySun.FindName("SunOutline") as Path;
```

15. I added Dragging Boolean flags to each object so they could be tested. As the mouse is moving, we will test to see if a collision has occurred, but only if one of the objects is being dragged.

```
if (mySun.Dragging || myCapsule.Dragging)
{
}
```

16. All that's left is to pass the CheckCollision() function the two collision paths and the two objects, and update the output message based on the result of the check.

```
if (CheckCollision(myCapsule, capsuleHit, mySun, sunHit))
    MsgBlock.Text = "Hit: true";
else
    MsgBlock.Text = "Hit: false";
```

Press F5 to compile and run the program. Drag the two objects around and see how the application responds. As you can see from Figure 8-19, using rectangles alone for collision detection would create a positive hit when in fact the objects have not collided, whereas the function shown in this example is very accurate, as illustrated in Figure 8-20.

Figure 8-19. Rectangle-based collision detection would indicate a collision had occurred.

As long as you keep in mind that this method can be expensive and write your code in a way that avoids doing the pixel-level check unless absolutely necessary, you should be able to apply this technique in your applications rather easily. The code for this example is in the **HitTestCompleted** project.

Hit: true

Figure 8-20. A very precise pixel-by-pixel collision test

Summary

In this chapter, we looked at some ways to detect collisions and make objects react when a collision has occurred. One of the most common methods for collision detection involves using bounding circles for objects. By checking the distance between objects and testing to see if the distance is less than the sum of the two radii, we can quickly tell if the two objects are hitting.

Linear collisions occur along a single axis and are the easiest to resolve. Angular collisions occur along two axes, and are resolved by rotating the coordinates and velocities of the objects involved, resolving the collision as though it were a linear collision, and then rotating the coordinates and velocities back.

Collisions with angled surfaces work in a similar manner. The coordinates and velocity are rotated an amount equal to the opposite angle of the surface being hit. This rotation results in a horizontal surface, upon which a collision can be resolved by applying the law of reflection, which states that the angle of incidence is equal to the angle of reflection.

The HitTest() method in Silverlight can be used to get very accurate pixel-level collision checking. Make certain when using this method that the collision-checking code is only called upon when needed, as it can be expensive to process.

In Chapter 9, we'll take a look at how we can implement forward and inverse kinematics in Silverlight.

Chapter 9

KINEMATICS

In this chapter, we're going to discuss how we can go about implementing basic forward and inverse kinematic chains/systems in Silverlight. Both techniques have been used pretty extensively in 3D animation to create objects with articulated, constrained joints that walk, interact, and so on. The concept is based upon a group (or chain) of objects. Given that chain of objects, kinematics is a method of determining an object's rotation and position based on the object next to it.

In the case of **forward** kinematics, the location and rotation of the first object in the chain determines the position of other objects in the chain. For **inverse** kinematics, the position and rotation of the last object in the chain propagates backward through the chain.

To illustrate the concepts, stand on one leg and hold your other leg out in front of you. Viewing the leg you're holding out from a forward kinematics perspective, the position of your thigh, calf, and foot all depend upon the position of your hip. If your hip moves, so do all the parts of the chain.

If we view the leg you're holding out from an inverse kinematic perspective, we consider that the position of your foot will determine where your calf and thigh will end up. Consider what would happen if someone were to come along and give the foot you're holding out a good yank—your leg would straighten out or rotate in the direction it was being pulled.

The basis for both the forward and inverse kinematic projects with which we'll be working was developed by Keith Peters and adapted into Silverlight with his permission. The techniques were custom-developed, and while they may not be the "official" methods for creating kinematic chains, they are easy to set up and they work really well, which is why they're here. If you'd like to learn more about inverse kinematics, a good place to start is the Wikipedia entry at http://en.wikipedia.org/wiki/Inverse_kinematics.

Forward kinematics

Let's start out easy with a simple kinematic chain. Open the **ForwardKinematics** project to code along with this example. The project contains two sliders that we will be using to control the angle of our segments, and a segment object called KinematicSegment, which is shown in Figure 9-1. The KinematicSegment object has a Rotate transform called RotateSegment that we will be using to manipulate the angle of rotation for the segment.

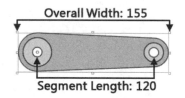
Overall Width: 155

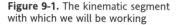
Segment Length: 120

Figure 9-1. The kinematic segment with which we will be working

Notice in the segment object that the point around which the object will rotate is positioned over the hole on the left side of the object. While the overall width of the segment object is 155 pixels, the length of the segment for our project is 120. This keeps the joints aligned, as opposed to laying them from end to end.

In this project, we'll be setting up a basic forward kinematic chain consisting of two segments. You'll get the opportunity to see how the motion of each segment relates to the other.

1. With the project open, open the Page.xaml.cs file for editing.

2. Before the Page() constructor, declare an instance of the KinematicSegment object called Seg0:

```
KinematicSegment Seg0 = new KinematicSegment();
```

3. Inside the Page() constructor, add the following code to set limits on the first slider control, attach an event handler to the ValueChanged event for the slider, and update the on-screen text:

```
Slider0.Minimum = -90;
Slider0.Maximum = 90;
Slider0.Value = 0;
Slider0.ValueChanged +=
    new RoutedPropertyChangedEventHandler<double>➥
    (Slider0_ValueChanged);
MsgSlider0.Text = "Seg. 0 Angle: "
                + String.Format("{0:0}", Slider0.Value);
```

4. Since we added an event handler for the slider, we need to add an event handler function. The following code shows the `Slider0_ValueChanged()` function. For the time being, it simply updates the text label for the slider on the screen.

```
void Slider0_ValueChanged(object sender,
                          RoutedPropertyChangedEventArgs<double> e)
{
    MsgSlider0.Text = "Seg. 0 Angle: "
                      + String.Format("{0:0}", Slider0.Value);
}
```

5. Back inside the `Page()` constructor, add code to position the `Seg0` object and add it to the main canvas:

```
Canvas.SetLeft(Seg0, 100);
Canvas.SetTop(Seg0, LayoutRoot.Height/2);
LayoutRoot.Children.Add(Seg0);
```

6. Next, create a function called `MoveSegments()`. Inside this function, we will place the code to move the segment as the slider is manipulated. You can see that it simply adjusts the segment's angle of rotation to match the value of the slider.

```
private void MoveSegments()
{
    Seg0.RotateSegment.Angle = Slider0.Value;
}
```

7. In order to call the `MoveSegments()` function, place the following code inside the `Slider0_ValueChanged()` event handler function:

```
MoveSegments();
```

At this point, the program will compile and run, but doesn't do much—you can manipulate the slider for Seg0 and watch the value change as the segment rotates. As you can see, the range of the slider determines the constraints of motion for the segment. Let's add another segment to the project and see what the kinematics will do for us.

8. Back above the `Page()` constructor, add a second instance of the `KinematicSegment` object, as well as a double that will be used to store the length of the segment:

```
KinematicSegment Seg1 = new KinematicSegment();
double segmentLength = 120;
```

9. Add code inside the `Page()` constructor to add the new segment to the main canvas:

```
LayoutRoot.Children.Add(Seg1);
```

10. Also inside the `Page()` constructor, add the code to define the behavior for the second slider. Here, we're setting a slider range of –90 to 90, presetting the value to 0, creating a `ValueChanged` event handler, and updating the on-screen messaging.

```
Slider1.Minimum = -90;
Slider1.Maximum = 90;
Slider1.Value = 0;
```

```
Slider1.ValueChanged +=
    new RoutedPropertyChangedEventHandler<double>➥
    (Slider1_ValueChanged);
MsgSlider1.Text = "Seg. 1 Angle: "
                + String.Format("{0:0}", Slider1.Value);
```

11. Create the `Slider1_ValueChanged()` function. Like the event handler for the first slider, this function simply updates the on-screen text and then calls the MoveSegments() function.

```
void Slider1_ValueChanged(object sender,
                        RoutedPropertyChangedEventArgs<double> e)
{
    MsgSlider1.Text = "Seg. 1 Angle: "
                    + String.Format("{0:0}", Slider1.Value);
    MoveSegments();
}
```

12. Next, add the following code to the MoveSegments() function beneath the existing line of code. The code starts out by setting the angle of Seg1 based on its own angle of rotation and the angle of Seg0. It then uses the angle and location of Seg0 to position Seg1 on the canvas. Those last few lines of code should look somewhat familiar to you—they find a point on a circle based on a radius. In this case, Seg0 is the center point, and the radius is the length of the segment.

```
Seg1.RotateSegment.Angle = Seg0.RotateSegment.Angle + Slider1.Value;
double radians = Seg0.RotateSegment.Angle * Math.PI / 180;
Canvas.SetLeft(Seg1, Canvas.GetLeft(Seg0)
                + Math.Cos(radians)
                * segmentLength);
Canvas.SetTop(Seg1, Canvas.GetTop(Seg0)
                + Math.Sin(radians)
                * segmentLength);
```

13. With that code in place, we can add one more line at the bottom of the Page() constructor. Since we are positioning Seg1 via the code, it would draw at the top left of the main canvas until a slider is manipulated. Adding a call to MoveSegments() will adjust the position of Seg1 based on the position of Seg0. That way, when the application loads, we'll have a nice-looking presentation.

```
MoveSegments();
```

Press F5 to compile and run the program. You will see an app like the one shown in Figure 9-2. You can control the rotation of Seg1, and change the rotation of Seg0 to affect the rotation of Seg1. The effect is a kind of organic, arm-like motion. Adjusting the range of Slider1 will further constrain the motion for the forearm segment. Test out a range of –120 to 0 and see if that more closely emulates the range of motion for your arm. The code for this project can be found in the **ForwardKinematicsCompleted** project.

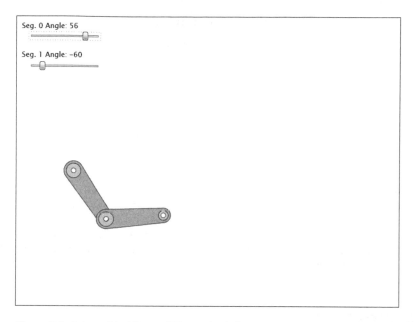

Figure 9-2. A two-object forward kinematic chain

Automating forward kinematics

Let's take a look at how we can go about automating this motion. Open up the **ForwardKinematics2** project to code along with this example. The project contains most of the code from the first project, but does not include the sliders or their associated code. It also does not include the code that moves the segments. It does contain a storyboard timer that will be used for the motion.

1. Open the Page.xaml.cs file for editing. We will be using oscillating movements to control Seg0, which means working with sine and cosine. To do this, we'll need to cycle through the angles of a circle and determine a new angle of rotation for the segment. Add the following two variable declarations prior to the Page() constructor to get started:

   ```
   double Cycle = 0;
   double Angle;
   ```

2. At the bottom of the Page() constructor, add an event handler for the Completed event on the Move storyboard, and begin the storyboard:

   ```
   Move.Completed += new EventHandler(Move_Completed);
   Move.Begin();
   ```

3. Add the Completed() event handler function shown in the following listing. The code will determine a new angle based on the sine value of the Cycle variable. Since the slider that constrained the motion has been removed, the * 90 in there simply defines the range. Since we're using sine, you should recognize that as creating motion between –90 and 90. Once that calculation is done, the Cycle variable is incremented, the MoveSegments() function is called, and the Move timer is restarted to keep the motion going.

```
void Move_Completed(object sender, EventArgs e)
{
    Angle = Math.Sin(Cycle) * 90;
    Cycle += .05;
    MoveSegments();
    Move.Begin();
}
```

4. Add the following two lines of code to the top of the MoveSegments() function. This code performs the movement on the segments by setting their angles based on the value calculated in step 3.

```
Seg0.RotateSegment.Angle = Angle;
Seg1.RotateSegment.Angle = Seg0.RotateSegment.Angle + Angle;
```

Compile and run the program. The rotational angles of the segments will run from –90 to 90, creating an interesting, if somewhat mechanical, motion for the arm. The **ForwardKinematics2Completed** project contains the code covered here.

Walking/running

Let's see what else we can do with forward kinematics. Open the **ForwardKinematics3** project to code along with the next example. This project contains two instances of the KinematicSegment object, with the first instance positioned at the center of the canvas. The second instance will be controlled from code.

1. Open the Page.xaml.cs file for editing. Before the Page() constructor, add the following three variables. We'll be automating the movement again, so we have a variable that defines the segment length as well as a variable to handle the changing angle upon which the motion is based. The final variable, Offset, will be used to offset the lower segment's angle from the upper segment's angle.

```
double SegmentLength = 120;
double Cycle = 0;
double Offset = -Math.PI / 2;
```

2. Take a look at the MoveSegments() function. Notice the function declaration was changed in order to accept three arguments—two segments and a cycle value:

```
private void MoveSegments(KinematicSegment SegA,
                          KinematicSegment SegB, double Cyc)
```

3. We'll move our angle calculations and constraints inside the MoveSegments() function. Start the function with the following code. Here, both angles have a range of 0 to 45. The 90 added to the end of the first line rotates AngleA 90 degrees from the original position, so SegA will be pointing down, not to the right. The 45 degrees added to the end of AngleB rotates that 45-degree range of motion 45 degrees past the range of motion for AngleA.

```
double AngleA = Math.Sin(Cyc) * 45 + 90;
double AngleB = Math.Cos(Cyc + Offset) * 45 + 45;
```

4. Next, add some code to apply the calculated rotations to the segment objects that were passed to the function:

```
SegA.RotateSegment.Angle = AngleA;
SegB.RotateSegment.Angle = AngleA + AngleB;
```

5. Finally, move the second segment in relation to the first to line them up:

```
double radians = SegA.RotateSegment.Angle * Math.PI / 180;
Canvas.SetLeft(SegB, Canvas.GetLeft(SegA)
                    + Math.Cos(radians)
                    * SegmentLength);
Canvas.SetTop(SegB, Canvas.GetTop(SegA)
                    + Math.Sin(radians)
                    * SegmentLength);
```

6. Inside the Move_Completed() function, add the following code before the Move storyboard is started. This code passes the MoveSegments() function you just wrote two segments, and the current Cycle value used to determine the rotation of the first segment.

```
MoveSegments(Seg0, Seg1, Cycle);
Cycle += .05;
```

Press F5 to compile and run the program. The contraints work with the motion of the segments to form what looks like a single leg walking, as shown in Figure 9-3.

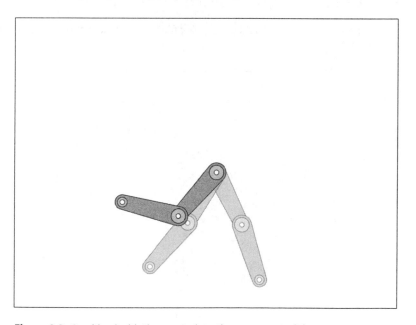

Figure 9-3. Combined with the constraints, the movement of the two segments looks like a leg walking.

7. Let's continue by adding two more segments that will form the second leg. Before the Page() constructor, declare two more instances of the KinematicSegment object:

```
KinematicSegment Seg2 = new KinematicSegment();
KinematicSegment Seg3 = new KinematicSegment();
```

8. Inside the Page() constructor, position the Seg2 object at the center of the main canvas, as was done for Seg0. Add Seg3 to the main canvas—don't worry about positioning since the code will take care of that for you.

```
Canvas.SetLeft(Seg2, LayoutRoot.Width / 2);
Canvas.SetTop(Seg2, LayoutRoot.Height / 2);
LayoutRoot.Children.Add(Seg2);
LayoutRoot.Children.Add(Seg3);
```

9. Inside the Move_Completed() function, add a line of code to move the newly added segments:

```
MoveSegments(Seg2, Seg3, Cycle);
```

10. If you run the program, it will look as though there is just a single pair of segments on the screen. All four are there, but they are moving at the same rate, in the same position. In order to offset the angle of the second leg, modify the line of code you just added. By adding pi to the Cycle passed to the MoveSegments() function, the second pair of segments will be offset from the first by 180 degrees.

```
MoveSegments(Seg2, Seg3, Cycle + Math.PI);
```

Now when you run the program, you should get a pair of legs that look as though it's walking, like the one shown in Figure 9-4.

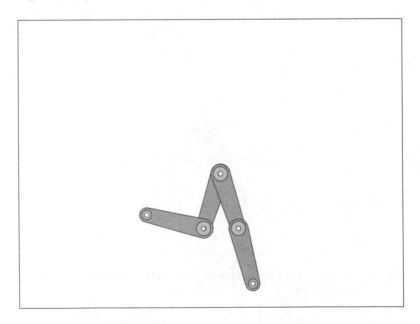

Figure 9-4. A set of walking legs

The **ForwardKinematics3Completed** project contains all of the code covered in the tutorial. I also added several sliders that allow you to change the speed and constraints as the application runs.

Multiple forward kinematic chains

As you can probably imagine, there's some pretty neat stuff you can do with longer chains of objects. The next example of forward kinematics is going to be a little more complex. We're going to write a user control that will create a series of tentacles based on a forward kinematic chain. Once we're done, a few lines of code will allow you to create some pretty interesting effects.

1. Open the **Tentacles** project to code along with this example. The project contains the KinematicSegment user control, from which our tentacles will be constructed. I've also added a Tentacle user control to the project. The main canvas also contains the Move storyboard, but other than that, the project is pretty much empty.

2. Open the KinematicSegment.xaml.cs file for editing. Because the Tentacle object will be building the kinematic chain from the KinematicSegment user control, we need to push some of the functionality to the individual segments. We're going to make the segments responsible for tracking their own angles rather than doing it globally as we did with the walk cycle. To do this, add the following variable declarations before the KinematicSegment() constructor. These variables should all be familiar to you from earlier examples.

```
public double Angle;
public double Cycle;
public double Range;
public double SegmentLength;
```

3. After the KinematicSegment() constructor, add the following function. This function will be called from the Tentacle user control to update the angles of the segments in the kinematic chain.

```
public void UpdateAngle()
{
    this.Angle = Math.Sin(this.Cycle) * Range;
}
```

4. Save the KinematicSegment.xaml.cs file and open Tentacle.xaml.cs for editing. This file is where most of the heavy lifting will be done. We'll be modifying the control to accept arguments and build a kinematic chain, and create a function to move the chain.

5. Start by declaring the following variables before the Tentacle() constructor. These variables determine the speed and range constraint of the base segment in the tentacle. The Multiplier variable is used to help vary the Range variable, and TentacleRotation determines the initial orientation of the tentacle when it's added to the main canvas. The List is used to store all of the segments in the tentacle. Since all of the variables are used only in the user control, they are scoped as private.

```
private double Speed;
private double Range;
private double Multiplier;
private double TentacleRotation;
private List<KinematicSegment> Segments;
```

6. The Tentacle() constructor needs to be modified to accept five arguments. When a tentacle is instantiated on the main canvas, we will pass in the number of segments desired for the tentacle, the speed, the range, the multiplier, and the angle of rotation. Inside the constructor, the passed values are assigned to the local variables, and the segments List is initialized. We then call two functions (which we will create momentarily): CreateSegments() and MoveSegments(). When completed, your constructor should look like the following listing:

```
public Tentacle(int elements,
                double tentacleSpeed,
                double tentacleRange,
                double tentacleMult,
                double rotateTentacle)
{

    InitializeComponent();

    Speed = tentacleSpeed;
    Range = tentacleRange;
    Multiplier = tentacleMult;
    TentacleRotation = rotateTentacle;

    Segments = new List<KinematicSegment>();

    CreateSegments(elements);
    MoveSegments();
}
```

7. After the Tentacle() constructor, create the CreateSegments() function. The function should accept a single integer argument that represents the number of segments in the kinematic chain. You can see in step 6 that when CreateSegments() is called, it is passed the number of elements:

```
private void CreateSegments(int num)
{

}
```

8. Inside the CreateSegments() function, add the following for loop:

```
for (int i = 0; i < num; i++)
{
}
```

9. Inside the for loop, add the following code. This code creates a new instance of the KinematicSegment object, and scales it based on its position in the chain.

```
KinematicSegment nextSegment = new KinematicSegment();

nextSegment.ScaleSegment.ScaleX =
    nextSegment.ScaleSegment.ScaleY = 1 - (i * .1);
nextSegment.SegmentLength = 120 * nextSegment.ScaleSegment.ScaleX;
nextSegment.Range = Range - (i * Multiplier);
nextSegment.Cycle = 0;
```

The segmentLength variable for that instance of the segment is then updated to reflect the appropriate size based on scale. The Range for the segment is based upon the passed variable minus the Multiplier multiplied by the segment's position in the chain. This has the effect of diminishing the angle of rotation of each successive piece of the chain. However, if the multiplier is set large enough across a number of segments, the angle of rotation will eventually cross a threshold and become negative. For instance, a Range of 45 with a Multiplier of 10 across 10 segments results in range values of 45, 35, 25, 15, 5, –5, –15, –25, –35, and –45. This will result in a snaking chain. You'll probably need to spend a little time experimenting with the Range and Multiplier to get a good feel for it.

The newly created segment's Cycle is then set to 0.

10. Following that code, add the following if statement. Here, the code simply positions the first segment in the Tentacle.xaml Canvas. Since all of the other segments are positioned programmatically, they can just be added to the root, which is handled by the else clause.

```
if (i == 0)
{
    Canvas.SetLeft(nextSegment, 0);
    Canvas.SetTop(nextSegment, LayoutRoot.Height / 2);
    LayoutRoot.Children.Add(nextSegment);
}
else
{
    LayoutRoot.Children.Add(nextSegment);
}
```

11. After the else clause in step 10, add the following line of code. This places the new segment in the segments List.

```
segments.Add(nextSegment);
```

12. Next up is the MoveSegments() function. The code to create the function looks like this:

```
public void MoveSegments()
{
}
```

13. Now start typing inside those curly braces. The first line of this function sets the rotational angle and segment instance Angle variable to the rotation value that was passed into the Tentacle() constructor. Remember that in a forward kinematic chain, the first segment drives the rotation and location of every other segment. This simply sets up that angle of rotation on the first segment.

```
Segments[0].RotateSegment.Angle =
    Segments[0].Angle + TentacleRotation;
```

14. Follow that up with a counter to keep track of the current segment:

```
int currentSegmentIndex = 0;
```

15. Next, we'll need a loop to step through all of the segments in the chain:

```
foreach (var segment in Segments)
{

}
```

16. Inside the `foreach` loop, place the following `if` statement—here we're just testing to make sure that we're making changes to every segment in the chain except for the first one, which has already been handled with the code shown in step 13.

```
if (currentSegmentIndex > 0)
{

}
```

17. Inside the `if` statement, begin by declaring an instance of the `KinematicSegment` object that is the previous segment in the chain:

```
KinematicSegment previousSegment = Segments[currentSegmentIndex - 1];
```

18. Next, set the rotation of the current segment to the sum of the previous segment's rotation angle and the current segment's Angle variable:

```
segment.RotateSegment.Angle =
    previousSegment.RotateSegment.Angle + segment.Angle;
```

19. Next, add the intimidating-looking lines of code shown following. This code is not new, however—it's the same code you used in the walking example, modified to work inside of the `if` statement. The angle of rotation (in radians) of the previous segment is calculated, and then the current segment is positioned based on that angle.

```
double radians = previousSegment.RotateSegment.Angle * Math.PI / 180;
Canvas.SetLeft(segment, Canvas.GetLeft(previousSegment) +
    Math.Cos(radians) * previousSegment.SegmentLength);
Canvas.SetTop(segment, Canvas.GetTop(previousSegment) +
    Math.Sin(radians) * previousSegment.SegmentLength);
```

20. That's it for the `if` statement. After the closing curly brace, add the following code. Now that the segment has been positioned, we will need to call the `UpdateAngle()` method to update the segment's Angle variable, and then increment the segment's Cycle variable. This is the code that keeps each segment rotating. Finish up by incrementing the `currentSegmentIndex` variable.

```
segment.UpdateAngle();
segment.Cycle += Speed;
currentSegmentIndex++;
```

That was a pretty good chunk of coding—here's what the completed Tentacle() class looks like:

```
public partial class Tentacle : UserControl
{
    public double Speed;
    public double Range;
    public double Multiplier;
    public double TentacleRotation;

    private List<KinematicSegment> Segments;
```

```csharp
public Tentacle(int elements,
                double tentacleSpeed,
                double tentacleRange,
                double tentacleMult,
                double rotateTentacle)
{
    InitializeComponent();

    Speed = tentacleSpeed;
    Range = tentacleRange;
    Multiplier = tentacleMult;
    TentacleRotation = rotateTentacle;

    Segments = new List<KinematicSegment>();

    CreateSegments(elements);
    MoveSegments();
}

private void CreateSegments(int num)
{
    for (int i = 0; i < num; i++)
    {
        KinematicSegment nextSegment = new KinematicSegment();

        nextSegment.ScaleSegment.ScaleX =
            nextSegment.ScaleSegment.ScaleY = 1 - (i * .1);
        nextSegment.SegmentLength =
            120 * nextSegment.ScaleSegment.ScaleX;
        nextSegment.Range = Range - (i * Multiplier);
        nextSegment.Cycle = 0;

        if (i == 0)
        {
            Canvas.SetLeft(nextSegment, 0);
            Canvas.SetTop(nextSegment, LayoutRoot.Height / 2);
            LayoutRoot.Children.Add(nextSegment);
        }
        else LayoutRoot.Children.Add(nextSegment);
        segments.Add(nextSegment);
    }
}

    public void MoveSegments()
    {
        Segments[0].RotateSegment.Angle =
            Segments[0].Angle + TentacleRotation;
        int currentSegmentIndex = 0;
```

```
            foreach (var segment in Segments)
            {
                if (currentSegmentIndex > 0)
                {
                    KinematicSegment previousSegment =
                        Segments[currentSegmentIndex - 1];

                    segment.RotateSegment.Angle =
                        previousSegment.RotateSegment.Angle
                        + segment.Angle;
                    double radians =
                        previousSegment.RotateSegment.Angle
                        * Math.PI / 180;
                    Canvas.SetLeft(segment,
                                Canvas.GetLeft(previousSegment)
                                + Math.Cos(radians)
                                * previousSegment.SegmentLength);
                    Canvas.SetTop(segment,
                                Canvas.GetTop(previousSegment)
                                + Math.Sin(radians)
                                * previousSegment.SegmentLength);
                }

                segment.UpdateAngle();
                segment.Cycle += Speed;
                currentSegmentIndex++;
            }
        }
    }
```

21. Now it's time to test out the code. Open the Page.xaml.cs file for editing. Before the Page() constructor, declare a new instance of the Tentacle object:

    `Tentacle myTentacle;`

22. Inside the Page() constructor, type myTentacle = new Tentacle(. An IntelliSense window like the one shown in Figure 9-5 will pop up, showing you all of the variables you need to pass to the Tentacle() class. For a first pass, type 10, .02, 45, 25, 0 to create a tentacle with ten segments, a speed of .02, and a root segment range of 45 degrees. Each successive segment will then have a range of 25 degrees less (remember what I mentioned earlier about creating a snaking shape?). The rotation of the base segment is 0, meaning this tentacle will point to the right.

```
myTentacle = new Tentacle(
            Tentacle.Tentacle (int elements, double tentadeSpeed, double tentadeRange, double tentadeMult, double rotateTentacle)
```

Figure 9-5. IntelliSense leads the way when calling the Tentacle control.

23. Next, set the position of the tentacle and add it to the main canvas:

```
Canvas.SetLeft(myTentacle, 0);
Canvas.SetTop(myTentacle, LayoutRoot.Height / 2);

LayoutRoot.Children.Add(myTentacle);
```

24. To make the tentacle move, we still need to use the timer on the main page. Add a Completed event handler, and start the timer.

```
Move.Completed += new EventHandler(Move_Completed);
Move.Begin();
```

25. Add the Move_Completed event handler function after the Page() constructor. The function is fairly simple—it calls the MoveSegments() method on the tentacle and restarts the timer.

```
void Move_Completed(object sender, EventArgs e)
{
    myTentacle.MoveSegments();
    Move.Begin();
}
```

Press F5 to compile and run the program. You will be greeted with a moving, curling tentacle like the one shown in Figure 9-6.

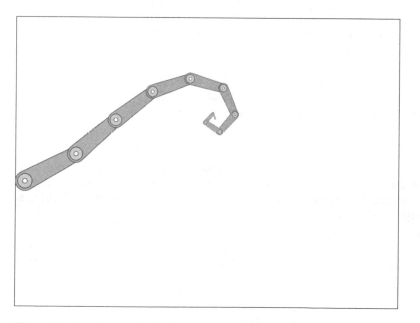

Figure 9-6. A moving, curling tentacle

26. Now that we know the code works, we can change it so that we can create a group of tentacles on demand. Go ahead and remove or comment out all the code you just added to the Page.xaml.cs file. We'll change the code so that the tentacles are generated more randomly. Before the Page() constructor, declare the following two variables. The first is a List of Tentacle objects, and the second is for generating random numbers.

```
List<Tentacle> Tentacles;
Random Rand = new Random();
```

27. After the Page() constructor, add a function called CreateTentacles() that accepts an integer argument named howMany. The passed integer will be used to determine how many tentacles should be drawn on the screen.

```
private void CreateTentacles(int howMany)
{
    for (int i = 0; i < howMany; i++)
    {

    }
}
```

28. Inside the for loop, generate some random numbers. We'll randomize almost the whole process. Start with a random number for the number of segments. That's followed by declaring a speed variable, setting it to 0, and then generating a random number between −.04 and .04. The while loop is there to avoid tentacles that don't move. Next come variables for the base segment's range, a random multiplier, and random initial rotation that should generally keep the tentacles pointing downward.

```
int rngSegments = Rand.Next(6, 10);
double rngSpeed = 0;
while (rngSpeed == 0) rngSpeed = Rand.Next(-4, 4) / 100.0;
double rngRange = Rand.Next(5, 60);
double rngMult = Rand.Next(5, 50);
double rngRotate = Rand.Next(0, 180);
```

29. Next, add the following code to instance the Tentacle object based on the random numbers that were just generated. The new instance of the Tentacle is then scaled randomly between .5 and .8 before being positioned and added to the main canvas. The last line adds the new Tentacle object to the List of Tentacles.

```
Tentacle nextTentacle =
    new Tentacle(rngSegments, rngSpeed, rngRange, rngMult, rngRotate);
nextTentacle.ScaleTentacle.ScaleX = nextTentacle.ScaleTentacle.ScaleY =
    Rand.Next(5, 8) / 10.0;
Canvas.SetLeft(nextTentacle, LayoutRoot.Width / 2 - 50);
Canvas.SetTop(nextTentacle, 150);
LayoutRoot.Children.Add(nextTentacle);
Tentacles.Add(nextTentacle);
```

30. To call the newly created function, we'll add code to the Page() constructor. Start by initializing the Tentacles List. Next, call the new function and pass it the number of tentacles you'd like created:

```
Tentacles = new List<Tentacle>();
CreateTentacles(6);
```

31. The tentacles still need to be made to move, so add the `Completed` event handler to the `Move` storyboard, and start the storyboard:

```
Move.Completed += new EventHandler(Move_Completed);
Move.Begin();
```

32. The event handler function looks like the following listing. A foreach loop steps through each tentacle in the `List` and calls the `MoveSegments()` method for that tentacle. The function closes out by restarting the timer.

```
private void Move_Completed(object sender, EventArgs e)
{
    foreach (Tentacle tent in Tentacles)
    {
        tent.MoveSegments();
    }
    Move.Begin();
}
```

Press F5 to compile and run the program. You will get something similar to Figure 9-7. Each time you reload the browser, a new and unique set of waving tentacles is created. Spend some time playing around with the constraint ranges and see what kind of results you can come up with. There are certainly enough variables to experiment with! Due to the random scaling, you may also want to add some code to adjust the location of each tentacle on the screen so they line up a little better.

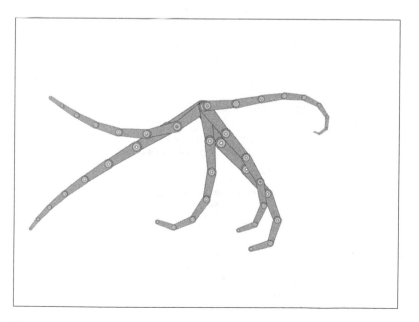

Figure 9-7. A group of waving tentacles

Inverse kinematics

We've gotten a pretty good look at how we can apply forward kinematics to a chain of objects and the type of motion it will create. Now we're going to take a look at inverse kinematics, where the free end of a kinematic chain determines what the rest of the objects in the chain do.

A good example of this would be to imagine a section of chain laying on a surface. If you grab one end of the chain and pull, the links will follow. If you pull just a bit, only the links close to the link you're pulling will move, and the rest will remain stationary. Pulling the first link farther will result in more links being affected, until the entire chain is eventually in motion. This type of behavior is inverse kinematic **dragging** behavior. Another type of behavior, **reaching**, would be demonstrated if the other end of the chain—the base—were nailed to a board, and the free end were reaching.

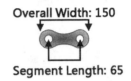

Figure 9-8. The kinematic segment we'll be using to demonstrate inverse kinematics

We'll take a look at both behavior types, but first take a look at the segment shown in Figure 9-8. The chain link shown in the image will be the segment shape and length we will use for the inverse kinematic examples.

Reaching

Next, we will create a simple example that demonstrates a single segment that reaches for the mouse. You will be able to see the effect that having one end of an object pinned as it reaches for the mouse has on the motion for that object.

1. Open the **InverseKinematics** project. The project contains the chain link KinematicSegment user control, which is instanced a single time and placed on the main canvas. Open the Page.xaml.cs file for editing.

2. For this example, we'll have the segment reach for the mouse. At the bottom of the Page() constructor, add a MouseMove event handler:

   ```
   LayoutRoot.MouseMove += new MouseEventHandler(LayoutRoot_MouseMove);
   ```

3. Add the event handler code shown following. The function includes some code that should look familiar to you. It begins by getting the current position of the mouse. It then finds the x and y distances between the link and the mouse point, and uses Atan2() to determine the angle. This is similar to the way the picture rotation worked in Chapter 6. Finally, the segment's angle of rotation is updated by converting the calculated angle variable from radians to degrees.

   ```
   private void LayoutRoot_MouseMove(object sender, MouseEventArgs e)
   {
       Point mousePoint = e.GetPosition(null);

       double dx = mousePoint.X - Canvas.GetLeft(MySegment);
       double dy = mousePoint.Y - Canvas.GetTop(MySegment);
       double angle = Math.Atan2(dy, dx);
       MySegment.RotateSegment.Angle = angle * 180 / Math.PI;
   }
   ```

Press F5 to compile and run the project. As you move the mouse, the segment will turn to reach for the mouse location. The code for this example is in the **InverseKinematicsCompleted** project.

Dragging

The other way I mentioned using inverse kinematics is by dragging. In this example, you will see how dragging a kinematic chain is much like dragging a length of real chain—each link in the chain will follow the link before it.

1. Open the **InverseKinematics2** project. This base project is identical to the one used in the first example, except that it includes an integer variable to store the length of the segment (65) for use in calculations. Once again, open the Page.xaml.cs file for editing.

2. Like the first example, this method also uses the MouseMove event to move the segment. Inside the Page() constructor, add the event handler:

```
LayoutRoot.MouseMove += new MouseEventHandler(LayoutRoot_MouseMove);
```

3. Create the event handler function:

```
private void LayoutRoot_MouseMove(object sender, MouseEventArgs e)
{

}
```

4. Start the event handler just as you did with the previous example. Get the mouse location, determine the angle between the points, and rotate the segment:

```
Point mousePoint = e.GetPosition(null);

double dx = mousePoint.X - Canvas.GetLeft(MySegment);
double dy = mousePoint.Y - Canvas.GetTop(MySegment);
double angle = Math.Atan2(dy, dx);
MySegment.RotateSegment.Angle = angle * 180 / Math.PI;
```

5. Add two more lines to position the segment based on the position of the mouse and the length of the segment.

```
Canvas.SetLeft(MySegment, mousePoint.X
                    - Math.Cos(angle) * SegmentLength);
Canvas.SetTop(MySegment, mousePoint.Y
                    - Math.Sin(angle) * SegmentLength);
```

Press F5 to compile and run the project. As you move the mouse around the screen, the segment rotates and follows, and you didn't even need to add any dragging code to the segment object!

6. Let's keep working in this project to add another segment. Before the Page() constructor, declare a second instance of the KinematicSegment object:

```
private KinematicSegment MySegment2 = new KinematicSegment();
```

7. Inside the Page() constructor, add the second segment to the main canvas. Don't worry about the position—the code will handle that.

```
LayoutRoot.Children.Add(MySegment2);
```

8. Inside the MouseMove event handler function, after the code that positions mySegment, add the following code to calculate the position for the second segment and position it in relation to the first. Since the variables are already declared, we just reuse them here for the second set of calculations. The positioning of the second segment is based upon the location of the first.

```
dx = Canvas.GetLeft(MySegment) - Canvas.GetLeft(MySegment2);
dy = Canvas.GetTop(MySegment) - Canvas.GetTop(MySegment2);
angle = Math.Atan2(dy, dx);
MySegment2.RotateSegment.Angle = angle * 180 / Math.PI;
Canvas.SetLeft(MySegment2, Canvas.GetLeft(MySegment)
                            - Math.Cos(angle) * SegmentLength);
Canvas.SetTop(MySegment2, Canvas.GetTop(MySegment)
                            - Math.Sin(angle) * SegmentLength);
```

Press F5 again to test the project. When it first loads, the second segment will be up in the corner of the application, but when you move the mouse over the canvas, it will position itself correctly as part of the chain. Drag the mouse around a little bit and test the motion out. One of the interesting things about this type of motion is that you can use the first segment to push the second one backward, or pull the first one and the second one will follow. The code for this project is in the **InverseKinematics2Completed** project.

Dragging longer chains

Now, you're probably thinking that this is pretty neat, and you'd like to do a really long chain to see how it works. So let's code it up.

1. Open the **InverseKinematics3** project. This is essentially an empty project that contains the same kinematic segment object with which we have been working.

2. Start by declaring variables above the Page() constructor. We'll be using a List to hold our segments, a Point to store the mouse location, and scale and length variables. For longer chains, you will likely want to scale the segment object down so it will fit on the canvas.

```
private List<KinematicSegment> IKChain;
private Point MousePoint = new Point();
private double LinkScale = .25;
private double SegmentLength = 65;
```

3. We're going to use a function to create the kinematic chain for us, so create a new function called CreateChain() that accepts an integer argument that represents the number of items in the chain. Inside the function, we will use a for loop to create the chain.

```
private void CreateChain(int numLinks)
{
    for (int i = 0; i < numLinks; i++)
    {
    }
}
```

4. Inside the for loop, add the following code, which will create the instances of the segment for the chain. Notice that the segments are created, scaled according to the variable we declared earlier, and then added to the main canvas and IKChain List. They are not positioned on the canvas. We'll add a bit of code to handle that later.

```
KinematicSegment nextSegment = new KinematicSegment();
nextSegment.ScaleSegment.ScaleX =
    nextSegment.ScaleSegment.ScaleY = LinkScale;

LayoutRoot.Children.Add(nextSegment);
IKChain.Add(nextSegment);
```

5. Inside the Page() constructor, add the following code to initialize the IKChain List, adjust the segmentLength variable based on the scale, and call the CreateChain() function:

```
IKChain = new List<KinematicSegment>();

SegmentLength *= LinkScale;

CreateChain(100);
```

6. If you run the program at this point, all 100 segments will be created, but they will all be piled on top of one another at the top left of the main canvas. We'll need to add some code to move the chain objects. We'll separate this behavior into its own function rather than tying it to the MouseMove event. Create a function called MoveSegment() that accepts a KinematicSegment, and two doubles as arguments.

```
private void MoveSegment(KinematicSegment Segment,
                         double XOffset,
                         double YOffset)
{

}
```

7. Inside the MoveSegment() function, add the following code. This will calculate the distance between segment and offsets passed to the function, and calculate the angle between them.

```
double dx = XOffset - Canvas.GetLeft(Segment);
double dy = YOffset - Canvas.GetTop(Segment);
double angle = Math.Atan2(dy, dx);
```

8. Next, add the following code, which should look familiar to you. This code sets the rotation and position of the passed segment.

```
Segment.RotateSegment.Angle = angle * 180 / Math.PI;
Canvas.SetLeft(Segment, XOffset - Math.Cos(angle) * SegmentLength);
Canvas.SetTop(Segment, YOffset - Math.Sin(angle) * SegmentLength);
```

9. Now that the movement and positioning code has been generalized, create a new function called MoveChain(). This function will be called as the mouse moves, and will be used to call out to the function that was just created in order to move the chain.

```
private void MoveChain()
{

}
```

10. Inside the MoveChain() function, add the following code to position the first object in the chain:

```
MoveSegment(IKChain[0], MousePoint.X, MousePoint.Y);
```

11. Follow that with the following for loop, which will position the rest of the objects in the chain:

```
for (int i = 1; i < IKChain.Count; i++)
{
    MoveSegment(IKChain[i],
                Canvas.GetLeft(IKChain[i - 1]),
                Canvas.GetTop(IKChain[i - 1]));
}
```

12. Inside the Page() constructor, add the following code. This will preset the MousePoint location to a position on the screen, and then call the MoveChain() function to position as many of the links as possible.

```
MousePoint.X = 700;
MousePoint.Y = 300;
MoveChain();
```

13. If you run the project at this point, the chain will draw in a diagonal line from the top left of the app down toward the right. Our chain is being created, added to the canvas, and positioned. All we need to do is add code to attach some mouse control to it. Add the following MouseMove event handler following the code you added in step 9.

```
LayoutRoot.MouseMove += new MouseEventHandler(LayoutRoot_MouseMove);
```

14. The LayoutRoot_MouseMove() event handler is shown following. Here, we're just grabbing the mouse position to update the MousePoint variable, and then calling MoveChain() to update the location of all the chain segments.

```
private void LayoutRoot_MouseMove(object sender, MouseEventArgs e)
{
    MousePoint = e.GetPosition(null);
    MoveChain();
}
```

Press F5 to run the project. Drag the mouse around the screen and notice how the chain follows (see Figure 9-9). You might need to drag it around a bit to see the rest of the links unfold from the pile near the top left, but you should be able to see how this behavior mimics the example I mentioned earlier in the chapter—moving the mouse just a bit moves just the few end links on the end of the chain. You need to move the mouse much further to move the links way down at the end of the chain. The completed version of this project is called **InverseKinematics3Completed**.

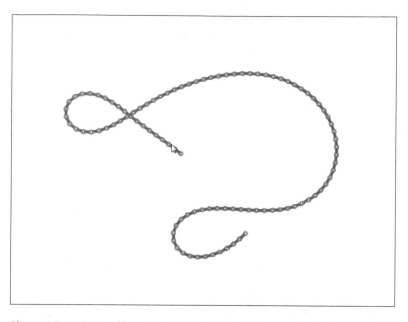

Figure 9-9. An inverse kinematic chain containing 100 segments. As the mouse is dragged, the chain follows.

Organic animations

One of the things I find really appealing about inverse kinematics is the organic-like quality you can apply to chains of objects—they start acting like little creatures inside a Silverlight application. In the next example, I'm going to show you a way to set up a Chinese dragon that will cruise around the application on its own, occasionally changing direction and speed. As you'll see, I went pretty easy on the code that changes the direction of the dragon, but I'm sure when you get the opportunity to modify the code for your own critters, you'll come up with some new and interesting ways to make them move.

1. Open the **IKDragon** project to code along with this example. The project may seem a little complex, but the concept is relatively straightforward. We'll create a head that roams freely about the canvas, and a series of body segments arranged in an inverse kinematic chain. As the head moves, the body segments will update their angle of rotation and position on the screen. Every 3 seconds, we'll have the head change direction.

   The project contains two timelines: Move, which will automate the head and body movements, and ChangeDirection, which we will use to change the direction of the head. The project also contains two user controls: the dragon's head and a body segment, both of which are shown in Figure 9-10. The head control has a public variable in it to store a velocity value.

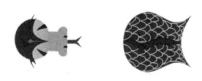

Figure 9-10. The dragon's head (left) and body (right)

2. Open the Page.xaml.cs file for editing. We'll start with the dragon's head, so create an instance of the DragonHead user control. We'll also need doubles for managing the scale of the objects and the length of the segment, and a random number generator to create some velocities for the head.

```
private DragonHead Head;
private double Scaling = .25;
private double SegmentLength = 90;
private Random Rand = new Random();
```

3. Add the following code inside the Page() constructor. This code initializes the Head object, and then scales the instance according to the scaling value set up in step 2. After that, random x and y velocities between 4 and 6 are generated. The while loop runs to make sure the y velocity does not match the x velocity. This will keep the head from moving in a straight line. If the velocities do match, a toned-down y velocity is generated. Finally, the head is positioned and added to the main canvas.

```
Head = new DragonHead();
Head.ScaleHead.ScaleX = Head.ScaleHead.ScaleY = Scaling;

Head.velocity.X = Rand.Next(4, 6);
Head.velocity.Y = Rand.Next(4, 6);

while (Head.velocity.Y == Head.velocity.X)
{
    Head.velocity.Y = Rand.Next(2, 4);
}
Canvas.SetLeft(Head, 600);
Canvas.SetTop(Head, 300);
LayoutRoot.Children.Add(Head);
```

4. You can compile and run the program if you'd like, and you'll see the dragon head drawn on the main canvas. The next step is to make it move, so inside the Page() constructor, create an event handler for the Move timer's Completed event, and start the timer.

```
Move.Completed += new EventHandler(Move_Completed);
Move.Begin();
```

5. After the Page() constructor, create the event handler function:

```
private void Move_Completed(object sender, EventArgs e)
{

}
```

6. Inside the function, start by calculating the angle of rotation from the head. Use the x and y velocity to calculate angle, and then apply the rotation to the head:

```
double Angle = Math.Atan2(Head.velocity.Y, Head.velocity.X);
Head.RotateHead.Angle = Angle * 180 / Math.PI;
```

7. Next, update the position of the head on the canvas:

```
Canvas.SetLeft(Head, Canvas.GetLeft(Head) + Head.velocity.X);
Canvas.SetTop(Head, Canvas.GetTop(Head) + Head.velocity.Y);
```

8. Check to see if the head has hit a boundary, and if so, change the direction of the velocity. Note here that while we're adjusting the boundaries for the scale, we're not taking into account the rotation of the head, so the head may duck off canvas or change direction prematurely when it reaches a boundary.

```
// check left and right bounds and reverse velocity if hit
if (Canvas.GetLeft(Head) < -(Head.Width * Scaling))
{
    Head.velocity.X *= -1;
}
else if (Canvas.GetLeft(Head)
        > LayoutRoot.Width - (Head.Width * Scaling))
{
    Head.velocity.X *= -1;
}

// check upper and lower bounds and reverse velocity if hit
if (Canvas.GetTop(Head) < -(Head.Height * Scaling))
{
    Head.velocity.Y *= -1;
}
else if (Canvas.GetTop(Head)
        > LayoutRoot.Height - (Head.Height * Scaling))
{
    Head.velocity.Y *= -1;
}
```

9. Finally, restart the timer.

```
Move.Begin();
```

10. Press F5 to test the application out. The head should be moving around the screen, changing direction when it reaches the edge of the main canvas. We want to change the direction more often than boundary collisions will occur, which is why there is a second timer. At the bottom of the Page() constructor, add the following code to create a Completed event handler for the ChangeDirection storyboard, and start the storyboard. ChangeDirection is a storyboard timer with a duration of 3 seconds.

```
ChangeDirection.Completed +=
    new EventHandler(ChangeDirection_Completed);
ChangeDirection.Begin();
```

11. Add the ChangeDirection_Completed() event handler function after the Page() constructor. This function will store the oldY velocity, and generate a new one. If the head is currently moving up, the new velocity will point it down. If the head is moving down, the new velocity will point it up. The code shown here is where you can spend some time to make the movement more interesting. The last line of the code restarts the storyboard so that this function will be called again in 3 seconds.

```
private void ChangeDirection_Completed(object sender, EventArgs e)
{
    double oldY = Head.velocity.Y;
    if (oldY > 0)
```

```
    {
        Head.velocity.Y = Rand.Next(4, 6) * -1;
    }

    if (oldY < 0)
    {
        Head.velocity.Y = Rand.Next(4, 6);
    }
    ChangeDirection.Begin();
}
```

12. Now when you run the program, the head will zigzag about the canvas. While the changes may look a little abrupt at the moment, having the body in there will smooth them out. Speaking of the body, we're all done with the head, so now we need to create our kinematic chain of body segments. Before the Page() constructor, add the following lines of code to your variable declaration section. This code declares a List of DragonBody objects and sets up a variable to store the number of body segments.

```
private List<DragonBody> BodySegments;
private int BodyParts = 25;
```

13. Inside the Page() constructor, initialize the List of BodySegments, and adjust the SegmentLength for scaling. The last line calls a function we will create next.

```
BodySegments = new List<DragonBody>();
SegmentLength *= Scaling;
CreateBody();
```

14. Create the CreateBody() function shown in the following code. The function contains a for loop that will be used to generate the body segment objects.

```
private void CreateBody()
{
    for (int i = 0; i < BodyParts; i++)
    {
    }
}
```

15. Type the following code inside the for loop. This should be pretty easy for you to figure out by now. A new instance of the body segment is created, scaled, positioned, and added to the List of segments and the main canvas.

```
DragonBody Segment = new DragonBody();
Segment.ScaleBody.ScaleX = Segment.ScaleBody.ScaleY = Scaling;
Canvas.SetTop(Segment, 0);
Canvas.SetLeft(Segment, 0);
BodySegments.Add(Segment);
LayoutRoot.Children.Add(Segment);
```

16. If you run the program again, you'll see that the body segments get generated in a pile at the top left of the main canvas, and the disembodied head is still running around loose. We'll add another function to handle the movement of the segments. As with the example earlier in this chapter, the movement is handled by a generalized method that accepts a DragonBody segment as well as two double arguments.

```
private void MoveSegment(DragonBody Segment,
                    double XOffset,
                    double YOffset)
{
}
```

17. The function begins by calculating the distance between the offset and the segment, and calculates an angle from that offset:

```
double dx = XOffset - Canvas.GetLeft(Segment);
double dy = YOffset - Canvas.GetTop(Segment);
double angle = Math.Atan2(dy, dx);
```

18. From there, the segment that was passed in can be rotated and positioned:

```
Segment.RotateBody.Angle = angle * 180 / Math.PI;
Canvas.SetLeft(Segment, XOffset - Math.Cos(angle) * SegmentLength);
Canvas.SetTop(Segment, YOffset - Math.Sin(angle) * SegmentLength);
```

19. With the function that handles the positioning of the segments in place, create a function called MoveBody() that will make the necessary calls to the MoveSegment() method:

```
private void MoveBody()
{

}
```

20. This function starts by calling the MoveSegment() function in order to position the first body segment in relation to the head:

```
MoveSegment(BodySegments[0],
            Canvas.GetLeft(Head),
            Canvas.GetTop(Head));
```

21. After the first body segment is positioned, the following loop will step through the remaining segments, calling the MoveSegment() function for each one in order to position it based upon the previous segment in the chain:

```
for (int i = 1; i < BodySegments.Count; i++)
{
    MoveSegment(BodySegments[i],
                Canvas.GetLeft(BodySegments[i - 1]),
                Canvas.GetTop(BodySegments[i - 1]));
}
```

22. At the bottom of the `Page()` constructor, add a call to the `MoveBody()` function you just wrote. This will preset the locations of as many of the body segments as possible before the timer starts.

```
MoveBody();
```

23. In the `Move_Completed()` event handler function, add the same line of code just before the closing `Move.Begin();` line. The first time we called the function, it set the body segments into their initial positions. This time, the function will be called each time the `Move` storyboard timer expires—this is where the body movement takes place as the application runs.

```
MoveBody();
```

Press F5 to compile and run the program. The dragon will work its way around the screen, changing vertical directions every 3 seconds (see Figure 9-11). Play around with some of the velocities and timing for the direction changes. See if you can come up with something that's interesting and organic-looking with regard to the movement.

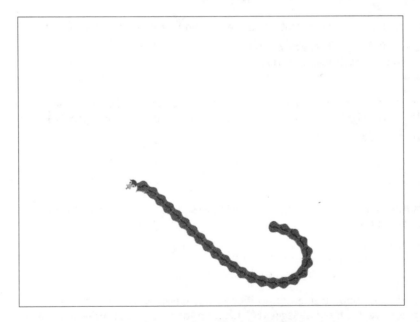

Figure 9-11. The Chinese dragon cruises around the application on its own.

Reaching with longer chains

Since we looked at how to go about making longer chains that can be dragged around on the canvas, we will also take a look at how to make a longer chain that reaches. Open the **InverseKinematics4** project to code along with this example. This project is similar to the **InverseKinematicsCompleted** project, except that the single segment in the application has been moved to the bottom center of the main canvas, and the code to move the segment has been removed. We'll modify the code to include a second segment and move both.

1. Open the Page.xaml.cs file for editing.

2. Before the Page() constructor, add the following variable declarations. This will create a second instance of the KinematicSegment object and declare a variable that will be used to position the second segment.

```
private KinematicSegment MySegment2 = new KinematicSegment();
private int SegmentLength = 65;
```

3. Inside the Page() constructor, position the new instance of the segment object and add it to the main canvas:

```
Canvas.SetLeft(MySegment2,
               LayoutRoot.Width / 2 - MySegment2.Width / 2);
Canvas.SetTop(MySegment2, LayoutRoot.Height - MySegment2.Height);
LayoutRoot.Children.Add(MySegment2);
```

4. In order to calculate the angle and rotation of any given segment, we're going to be using a generalized method once again. Create a method called RotateSegment() that accepts a KinematicSegment and two double arguments, and returns a double:

```
private double RotateSegment(KinematicSegment Segment,
                            double XOffset,
                            double YOffset)
{

}
```

5. Inside the RotateSegment() function, add the following code. This code determines the angle between the passed segment and offsets, rotates the passed segment, and returns the angle of rotation:

```
double dx = XOffset - Canvas.GetLeft(Segment);
double dy = YOffset - Canvas.GetTop(Segment);
double angle = Math.Atan2(dy, dx);
Segment.RotateSegment.Angle = angle * 180 / Math.PI;

return angle;
```

6. Now take a look at the LayoutRoot_MouseMove() function. After the code that determines the value of mousePoint, add the following code. This code uses the position of the mouse and length of the segment to determine where mySegment2 would hit the target coordinate based on the angle of rotation of the first segment.

```
double angle = RotateSegment(MySegment, mousePoint.X, mousePoint.Y);
double tx = mousePoint.X - Math.Cos(angle) * SegmentLength;
double ty = mousePoint.Y - Math.Sin(angle) * SegmentLength;
```

7. Next, a call is made to the RotateSegment() function, which passes mySegment2 and the calculated target positions. This will rotate mySegment2.

```
RotateSegment(MySegment2, tx, ty);
```

8. With all of the calculations done, mySegment is positioned based on the location of mySegment2:

```
Canvas.SetLeft(MySegment, Canvas.GetLeft(MySegment2) +
            Math.Cos(MySegment2.RotateSegment.Angle *
            Math.PI / 180) * SegmentLength);
Canvas.SetTop(MySegment, Canvas.GetTop(MySegment2) +
            Math.Sin(MySegment2.RotateSegment.Angle *
            Math.PI / 180) * SegmentLength);
```

Now, maybe you're looking at the code and scratching your head a little bit wondering what just happened, because we didn't move the left or top positions for MySegment2 in the move code, and it still seems to be moving around. Keep in mind that we're building an *inverse* chain here—MySegment2 is now the segment that is in contact with the floor. I've illustrated this functionality for you in Figure 9-12. The chain builds from the reaching position backward. The completed code for this example is in the **InverseKinematics4Completed** project.

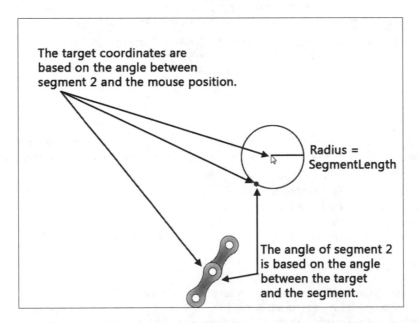

Figure 9-12. A graphical representation of a simple reaching inverse kinematic chain

Variable-length reaching chains

As you can probably imagine, coding up more than a couple of chain segments would get pretty tedious and require a fair amount of code. Much like we did with the dragging chain, we can add some functions that will make the work of moving a chain easier. To follow along with this example, open the **InverseKinematics5** project. This project is stubbed out with a good deal of code with which you should already be familiar. It contains a List to contain the segments, variables for the segment size and scaling, and a CreateChain() function to build the chain. When run, the project will create a chain with 25 links, but they won't yet move. We'll add code to the existing LayoutRoot_MouseMove() function to handle that for us:

1. Open the Page.xaml.cs file for editing. Even though the code to move the chain will go in the MouseMove event handler, we'll still need to create separate functions to handle the reaching and positioning of the segments. Create a new function called Reach(). The function will accept a KinematicSegment and two doubles as arguments, and return a Point.

```
private Point Reach(KinematicSegment seg, double x, double y)
{
}
```

2. Inside the function, place the code that handles the angle between the x and y values and the segment passed in:

```
double dx = x - Canvas.GetLeft(seg);
double dy = y - Canvas.GetTop(seg);
double angle = Math.Atan2(dy, dx);
seg.RotateSegment.Angle = angle * 180 / Math.PI;
```

3. In the last example, the target location was based around the mouse location and the segment. This time, we're using passed values. Add the following code, which calculates the target location based on the x and y values and the angle calculated in step 2:

```
Point tx = new Point();
tx.X = x - Math.Cos(angle) * segmentLength;
tx.Y = y - Math.Sin(angle) * segmentLength;
return tx;
```

4. Next, add a function that accepts two KinematicSegment objects. This is where the code goes that positions the segments, so call this function Position:

```
private void Position(KinematicSegment seg1, KinematicSegment seg2)
{
}
```

5. Inside this function, add the following code. This code calculates an angle based on the rotation of the first passed segment, and uses it in conjunction with the position of the first segment to position the second segment.

```
double angle = seg1.RotateSegment.Angle * Math.PI / 180;
Canvas.SetLeft(seg2, Canvas.GetLeft(seg1)
            + Math.Cos(angle) * segmentLength);
Canvas.SetTop(seg2, Canvas.GetTop(seg1)
            + Math.Sin(angle) * segmentLength);
```

6. Next, we'll be adding code to the LayoutRoot_MouseMove() function to make use of the functions we just added. Start by creating two Point objects:

```
Point target = new Point();
Point mousePoint = e.GetPosition(null);
```

7. The next line calculates the target points by calling the Reach() function and passing the first segment in the chain, as well as the x and y position of the mouse:

```
target = Reach(Segments[0], mousePoint.X, mousePoint.Y);
```

8. Add a for loop that repeats step 7 for the rest of the segments in the chain. Each time through, the target coordinates are updated and passed into the function for the next segment.

```
for (int i = 1; i < numLinks; i++)
{
    target = Reach(Segments[i], target.X, target.Y);
}
```

9. Finish up the function with the following for loop. This loop starts at the second loop in the chain (second segment closest to the mouse), and steps backward through the List of segments. For each iteration of the loop, the Position() function is passed the current segment and the next segment.

```
for (int i = numLinks - 1; i >= 1; i--)
{
    Position(Segments[i], Segments[i - 1]);
}
```

Press F5 to compile and run the project. Move the mouse around on the main canvas, and the chain will follow the mouse, as shown in Figure 9-13. Play around with the scaling and number of segments in the chain to get a feel for the application.

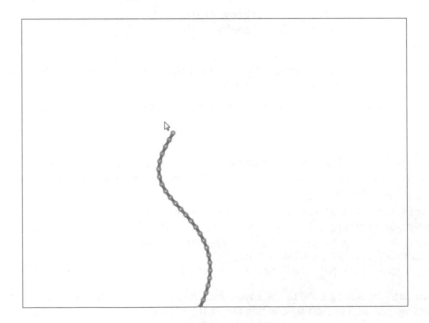

Figure 9-13. A longer reaching inverse kinematic chain

Reaching for objects

You can start getting some really interesting effects with reaching chains when they reach for something other than the mouse. We'll close out the examples in this chapter by building an underwater mine that appears to be tethered to the bottom of the application with a chain. This example will demonstrate how to reach for an object other than the mouse point.

1. Open the **UnderwaterMine** project to code along with the example. This project has a few parts to it. The Page.xaml file has the usual main canvas—this one has a blue gradient fill. There is also a storyboard timer called Move. It's not in use yet, but we'll be using it soon.

   I also added two user controls to the project. The first one is called KinematicSegment, but contains two different paths that form the chain shapes shown in Figure 9-14. By default, only the one on the left is visible in the control. The side view is hidden. There is also an underwater mine user control called Mine. This control contains the mine shape shown in Figure 9-15.

Figure 9-14. The two path shapes in the segment object

Figure 9-15. The shape inside the Mine user control

2. Take a couple of minutes and go through the code in the project. This is the same code used in the last example, with two minor differences. First, the chain has 23 links in it. I happen to know that's how many we will need to reach from the bottom of the app to the bottom of the mine object. The other difference is that the segments in the chain look different. If you compile and run the project, you'll see a bunch of links forming a chain that reaches for the mouse position just like the one shown in Figure 9-16.

3. Open the Page.xaml.cs file for editing. We'll start out by updating the chain. This is done by changing the CreateChain() function, which follows:

```
private void CreateChain()
{
    for (int i = 0; i < NumLinks; i++)
    {
        KinematicSegment nextSegment = new KinematicSegment();
        nextSegment.ScaleSegment.ScaleX =
            nextSegment.ScaleSegment.ScaleY = Scaling;

        Canvas.SetLeft(nextSegment,
                    LayoutRoot.Width / 2 - nextSegment.Width / 2);
        Canvas.SetTop(nextSegment,
                    LayoutRoot.Height - nextSegment.Height / 2);
        LayoutRoot.Children.Add(nextSegment);
        Segments.Add(nextSegment);
    }
}
```

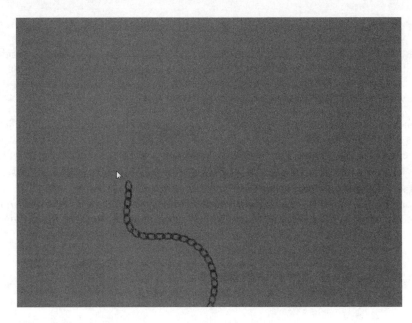

Figure 9-16. The chain of links reaches for the mouse position.

4. Update the function with the code shown following. This just sets up a simple alternating flag that changes the visibility of the links on every other iteration. A Boolean would have worked here just as easily. If you run the program again after making this change, you'll see that the chain looks more chain-like.

```
private void CreateChain()
{
    int alternateLinks = 1;
    for (int i = 0; i < NumLinks; i++)
    {
        KinematicSegment nextSegment = new KinematicSegment();
        nextSegment.ScaleSegment.ScaleX =
            nextSegment.ScaleSegment.ScaleY = Scaling;

        if (alternateLinks == 1)
        {
            nextSegment.LinkFront.Visibility = Visibility.Collapsed;
            nextSegment.LinkSide.Visibility = Visibility.Visible;
            alternateLinks = 0;
        }
        else
        {
            alternateLinks = 1;
        }
```

```
                Canvas.SetLeft(nextSegment,
                        LayoutRoot.Width / 2 - nextSegment.Width / 2);
                Canvas.SetTop(nextSegment,
                        LayoutRoot.Height - nextSegment.Height / 2);
            LayoutRoot.Children.Add(nextSegment);
            Segments.Add(nextSegment);
        }
    }
```

5. Next, we'll add the `Mine` object to the application. Before the `Page()` constructor, add the following declaration:

```
private Mine MyMine;
```

6. Inside the `Page()` constructor, add the following code to initialize the `Mine` object, position the top of the mine, and add it to the main canvas. We're not going to worry about positioning the left side of the `Mine` object—we'll be handling that with some code.

```
MyMine = new Mine();

Canvas.SetTop(MyMine, 150);
LayoutRoot.Children.Add(MyMine);
```

7. We will no longer be using the `MouseMove` event, so remove the following line of code from the `Page()` constructor:

```
LayoutRoot.MouseMove += new MouseEventHandler(LayoutRoot_MouseMove);
```

8. Next, we'll modify the `LayoutRoot_MouseMove()` event handler function, which follows:

```
private void LayoutRoot_MouseMove(object sender, MouseEventArgs e)
{
    Point target = new Point();
    Point mousePoint = e.GetPosition(null);
    target = reach(Segments[0], mousePoint.X, mousePoint.Y);

    for (int i = 1; i < NumLinks; i++)
    {
        target = Reach(Segments[i], target.X, target.Y);
    }
    for (int i = NumLinks - 1; i >= 1; i--)
    {
        Position(Segments[i], Segments[i - 1]);
    }
}
```

9. Begin by changing the name of the function to `MoveChain()`. Be sure to remove the parameters as well.

```
private void MoveChain()
```

10. Delete the line of code that gets the mouse position:

```
Point mousePoint = e.GetPosition(null);
```

11. At the moment, the target calculation uses the mouse coordinates as a location. Update that code to look like the following. It will now use the first element in the Segments List—the one closest to the target—to reach for the mine object. The + 50 and + 100 adjustments are to position the reaching point at the bottom center of the mine—since the object is scaled, I hard-coded these values, which is probably not a good habit to get into.

```
target = Reach(Segments[0],
                Canvas.GetLeft(MyMine) + 50,
                Canvas.GetTop(MyMine) + 100);
```

12. The target is all set up; now we just need to make it move. Inside the Page() constructor, create an event handler for the Completed event on the Move storyboard, and then start the storyboard:

```
Move.Completed += new EventHandler(Move_Completed);
Move.Begin();
```

13. Create the Move_Completed() event handler function. For the moment, all it needs to do is call MoveChain() to update the location of the chain, and restart the storyboard.

```
void Move_Completed(object sender, EventArgs e)
{
    MoveChain();
    Move.Begin();
}
```

14. If you run the project at this point, you'll see that the chain does indeed stretch toward the mine, but doesn't reach it, and nothing is moving. We're going to move the mine slowly back and forth along the x axis. With that in mind, add the following variables before the Page() constructor:

```
private double Angle = 0;
private double CenterX;
private double Range = 200;
private double Speed = .01;
```

15. Inside the Page() constructor, initialize the CenterX variable:

```
CenterX = LayoutRoot.Width / 2 - MyMine.Width / 2;
```

16. Add the following code to the Move_Completed() event hander function. This code should look familiar to you from the oscillation examples in Chapter 6.

```
Canvas.SetLeft(MyMine, CenterX + Math.Sin(Angle) * Range);

Angle += Speed;
```

17. Press F5 to compile and run the program. The mine will drift slowly back and forth as the chain follows.

18. There's one more addition we can make to the Move_Completed() function to add a little more realism to the project. In order to make the mine rotate slightly as it's drifting, add the following line of code. This will rotate the mine back and forth 25 degrees as it drifts. Now when you run the program, the mine tilts as it drifts, as shown in Figure 9-17.

```
MyMine.RotateMine.Angle = Math.Sin(Angle) * 25;
```

Figure 9-17. The mine drifts and rotates, and the chain follows.

The final version of the code for this example is in the **UnderwaterMineCompleted** project. I also added a gradient mask to the final project to give the effect a little more depth.

Now, given that an underwater mine is actually tethered to a chain, it probably makes more sense to do this one as a dragging chain rather than a reaching chain, so with that in mind, I'm going to leave you with two assignments. First, write the mine example using a dragging chain, and second, use either the reaching or dragging example, and turn the mine and chain into a user control so that you can instance the entire mine with just a couple of lines of code.

Summary

In this chapter, we talked about how to implement basic forward and inverse kinematic chains/systems in Silverlight. Forward kinematic chains are formed when the base of a chain drives the angle and position of the objects in the chain. An example of a forward kinematic chain would be moving your upper arm—your lower arm and hand would follow.

Inverse kinematic chains are formed when the free end of a chain dictates the angle and position of the objects in the chain. An example of an inverse kinematic chain would be if someone were to grab your hand and pull—your forearm, upper arm, and maybe even body would follow.

While the method of implementation discussed here may not be the "official" method for doing forward or inverse kinematics, they look and work extremely well, and don't put too much pressure on the processor.

In Chapter 10, we'll take a look at how to implement a basic particle system. Once that's in place, we'll look at some interesting ways to implement particle systems in Silverlight.

Chapter 10

PARTICLE SYSTEMS

In this chapter, we're going to take a look at how to build particle systems in Silverlight. Particle systems are often used to model so-called fuzzy objects—objects that do not have well-defined surfaces, such as smoke, fire, and water. Now, before you get too excited, you should know that we won't be doing those types of particle systems here. Instead, we're going to create a base system that you can augment based on other concepts you've learned in this book in order to move in that direction.

The first thing we need to address is the definition of a particle. A particle is generally defined as a small portion of something. For our purposes, we will define a particle as a single occurrence of an object. That might mean a car, a tire, a drop of water, a ball, or even a leaf or snowflake. That's right—the projects we did way back in Chapter 6 to make snow fall and leaves waft were particle system implementations.

The basic model for particle systems is that for each unit of time that passes, the application may create new particles based on some condition, assign a unique set of attributes to any new particles that are created, remove any particles based on some condition, and update the position of the particles on the screen. Typically, the destruction of particles occurs based on a life span for the particle, but as you will see, you can also use other conditions, such as if a particle goes off the canvas.

A basic particle system

Let's take a look at how we would go about building a basic particle system in Silverlight.

1. Open the **BasicParticleSystem** project. This project contains the base Page.xaml file with a timer storyboard and an object called Particle.xaml.

2. Open the Particle.xaml file and take a look at the XAML, which is shown following. The particle itself is a less-than-impressive gray ellipse with a black stroke, as shown in Figure 10-1. Items of note in the code are that both the Scale transform and ellipse shape are named to make them easily accessible from the code-behind.

Figure 10-1. The particle used in the BasicParticle-System project

```xaml
<UserControl x:Class="BasicParticleSystemCompleted.Particle"
    xmlns="http://schemas.microsoft.com/winfx/2006/xaml/presentation"
    xmlns:x="http://schemas.microsoft.com/winfx/2006/xaml"
    Width="75" Height="75">
    <Canvas x:Name="LayoutRoot" Width="75" Height="75"
            RenderTransformOrigin="0.5,0.5">
        <Canvas.RenderTransform>
            <TransformGroup>
                <ScaleTransform
                    x:Name="ParticleScale" ScaleX="1" ScaleY="1"/>
            </TransformGroup>
        </Canvas.RenderTransform>
        <Ellipse Height="75" Width="75"
            Canvas.Left="0" Canvas.Top="0" x:Name="ParticleShape"
            Fill="#FF5F615E" Stroke="#FF000000" StrokeThickness="3"/>
    </Canvas>
</UserControl>
```

3. Open the Page.xaml.cs file for editing. Just above the Page() constructor, add the following three lines of code. These will declare a List of type Particle named Particles. The List will be used to track the number of particles in our particle system. The NumParticles variable will be used to generate the particles. The Rand variable will allow us to use random numbers to vary the look of the particles as they are generated.

```csharp
private List<Particle> Particles;
private int NumParticles = 150;
private Random Rand = new Random();
```

4. Next, we'll create a function that will generate our particles. This code goes after the closing curly brace of the Page() constructor. Notice that we will be passing the function an integer that will be used to generate particles. Inside the function is a simple for loop that creates a new instance of the Particle object, assigns random locations to the left and top properties, adds the new particle to the Particles List, and draws the particle on the main canvas.

```csharp
private void CreateParticles(int HowMany)
{
    for (int i = 0; i < HowMany; i++)
```

```
    {
        Particle particle = new Particle();
        Canvas.SetLeft(particle, Rand.Next((int)LayoutRoot.Width));
        Canvas.SetTop(particle, Rand.Next((int)LayoutRoot.Width));

        Particles.Add(particle);
        LayoutRoot.Children.Add(particle);
    }
}
```

5. Inside the Page() constructor, we need to add a bit of code before we can use our List and create some particles. After the InitializeComponent() line, add the following two lines of code. The first line initializes our List so that its length equals the number of particles we'll be placing on the canvas. The second line calls the CreateParticles() function created in step 4, and passes the NumParticles variable to the function.

```
public Page()
{
    InitializeComponent();

    Particles = new List<Particle>(NumParticles);
    CreateParticles(NumParticles);
}
```

6. Test out the project by pressing F5 to compile and run. You should see something similar to what is shown in Figure 10-2. Just to test out the randomness of the particle placement, press F5 a few times in the browser to reload the application. The particles should redraw at different locations each time.

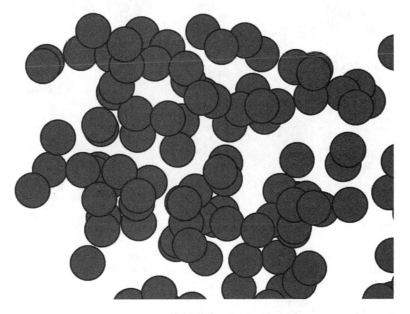

Figure 10-2. The CreateParticles() function at work

7. Let's add a little bit of randomness to the particles. Just before the Particles.Add(particle); line, add the following code. This will create an array of bytes, generate random numbers for each byte value in the array, and then use those values to change the colors of the particles.

```
byte[] colors = new byte[3];
Rand.NextBytes(colors);
Color c = Color.FromArgb(255, colors[0], colors[1], colors[2]);
particle.ParticleShape.Fill = new SolidColorBrush(c);
```

8. After the code added in step 7, and before the code that adds the particle to the List, add the following lines of code to mix up the scaling and opacity of the particles. The Rand.NextDouble() line generates a value between 0 and 1 for the Opacity property. The ScaleX and ScaleY properties are handled in the same way, except that we do a quick test to make sure the particles are at least 25% in scale.

```
particle.Opacity = Rand.NextDouble();
particle.ParticleScale.ScaleX = particle.ParticleScale.ScaleY =
    Rand.NextDouble();
if (particle.ParticleScale.ScaleX < .25) particle.ParticleScale.ScaleX
    = particle.ParticleScale.ScaleY = .25;
```

9. Compile and run the program. You will see something like what is shown in Figure 10-3.

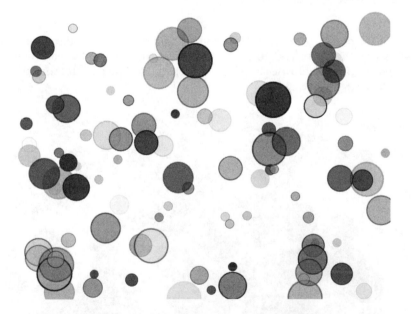

Figure 10-3. The particles now have random color, scale, and opacity.

10. So the particle generator is in place and does a pretty good job of randomizing our particles, but at this point, they're static. We need to make them move. Let's start by adding age and life span to each particle. Open the Particle.xaml.cs file and add the following lines of code before the Particle() constructor. These are two simple, publicly accessible properties that will be used to track a particle's age and life span.

```
public int Age { get; set; }
public int LifeSpan { get; set; }
```

11. Back in Page.xaml.cs, add the following two lines at the bottom of the Page() constructor. These lines of code will set up an event listener for our timer storyboard and start the storyboard running.

```
Move.Completed += new EventHandler(MoveParticles);
Move.Begin();
```

12. Inside the CreateParticles() function, add the following line, which will create a random life span between 0 and 120 frames for each particle as it is created. At 30 frames per second, that should be a maximum of 4 seconds that any given particle is on the screen.

```
particle.LifeSpan = Rand.Next(120);
```

13. The MoveParticles() event handler is shown following. This code uses the foreach loop to step through each particle in the Particles List, increment the age, and test to see if the particle has reached its life span. If so, the particle is removed from the main canvas.

```
private void MoveParticles(object sender, EventArgs e)
{
    foreach (Particle particle in Particles)
    {
        particle.Age += 1;

        if(particle.Age >= particle.LifeSpan) {
            LayoutRoot.Children.Remove(particle);
        }
    }
    Move.Begin();
}
```

14. Compile and run the project. The particles will be drawn, and after a second or so, will start disappearing from the screen until they're all gone.

15. Each time a particle dies, we'll create a new one. To do this, we'll first need to make a change to the MoveParticles() code, however. The foreach loop locks up the enumeration of our Particles List. When a particle dies, it's not enough to remove it from the main canvas; we should also pull it out of our List. Since the enumeration is locked, attempting to change the List length while the loop is running would cause an exception. Instead, we'll change that to a basic for loop. After the change, the MoveParticles() function should look like the following:

```
private void MoveParticles(object sender, EventArgs e)
{
    for (int i = 0; i < Particles.Count; i++)
    {
        Particles[i].Age += 1;
```

```
        if (Particles[i].Age >= Particles[i].LifeSpan)
        {
            LayoutRoot.Children.Remove(Particles[i]);
        }
    }
    Move.Begin();
}
```

16. Now we can add code inside the if logic to remove the dead particle from the List, and generate a new one on the screen. The relevant new code is shown in bold in the following listing:

```
private void MoveParticles(object sender, EventArgs e)
{
    for (int i = 0; i < Particles.Count; i++)
    {
        Particles[i].Age += 1;

        if (Particles[i].Age >= Particles[i].LifeSpan)
        {
            LayoutRoot.Children.Remove(Particles[i]);
            Particles.Remove(Particles[i]);
            CreateParticles(1);
        }
    }
    Move.Begin();
}
```

17. If you run the program at this point, your particles will draw on the screen, and as a particle dies, a new one will be generated to replace it. All that's left to do is to add a little code to make them move. Inside the Particle.xaml.cs file, add the following variable declaration before the Page() constructor:

```
public Point Velocity;
```

18. Inside the CreateParticle() function in the Page.xaml.cs file, add the following code to create random values for the x and y velocity values of each particle. Just to make sure none of the particles are standing still, test for 0 values and assign them a new value to keep them moving:

```
particle.Velocity.X = Rand.Next(-5, (int)5);
particle.Velocity.Y = Rand.Next(-5, (int)5);
if (particle.Velocity.X == 0) particle.Velocity.X = 2;
if (particle.Velocity.Y == 0) particle.Velocity.Y = 2;
```

19. Inside the MoveParticles() function, add the following two lines of code just before the line that increments the particle's age:

```
Canvas.SetLeft(Particles[i], Canvas.GetLeft(Particles[i]) +
                Particles[i].Velocity.X);
Canvas.SetTop(Particles[i], Canvas.GetTop(Particles[i]) +
                Particles[i].Velocity.Y);
```

Press F5 to compile and run the project. The particles will be drawn and move about the screen randomly. Each time a particle dies, another will be generated to take the place of the recently deceased. The final version of this code is available in the **BasicParticleSystemsCompleted** project.

If you were so inclined, you might consider adding a "dying" storyboard animation to the Particle. xaml file, perhaps one that quickly shrinks the particle to nothing. When the particle reaches its life span, the dying animation would be played, and upon completion, the particle would be removed from the Particles List and main canvas.

Emitters

Emitters are just what their name implies: objects that emit particles. The example project we just built didn't make use of a specific emitter for the particle, but emitters are relatively easy to implement. Let's take a look at how we can make use of an emitter.

1. Open the **ParticleEmitters** project. This project contains the same Page.xaml and particle as the last project did, but also includes an object called Emitter. The XAML for the Emitter object is shown following—it's nothing more than a 100×100 canvas with a gray background so you can see it on the screen. The reason why we want to be able to see it in this case is because the canvas is draggable. I've already added the dragging code to the Emitter.xaml. cs file, and the two lines of code necessary to instance the object on the main canvas. You can compile and run the project and see that the gray canvas can be dragged around the application.

```
<UserControl x:Class="ParticleEmitters.Emitter"
    xmlns="http://schemas.microsoft.com/winfx/2006/xaml/presentation"
    xmlns:x="http://schemas.microsoft.com/winfx/2006/xaml"
    Width="100" Height="100">
    <Canvas x:Name="LayoutRoot" Background="Gray"
        Width="100" Height="100"/>
</UserControl>
```

2. The majority of the code for this project is identical to that of the last project, so we'll move through it a little more quickly. Once again, the variable declarations that are placed above the Page() constructor in Page.xaml.cs are as follows:

```
private List<Particle> Particles;
private int NumParticles = 150;
private Random Rand = new Random();
```

3. Add the following four lines of code to the Page() constructor to give the Particles List a length, call the CreateParticles() function, and set up the Completed event listener on the storyboard timer before starting the timer:

```
Particles = new List<Particle>(NumParticles);
CreateParticles(NumParticles);

Move.Completed += new EventHandler(MoveParticles);
Move.Begin();
```

4. The CreateParticles() function should be added below the Page() constructor. Here, the code has changed a bit, so I've highlighted the changed lines in bold. The particle positions are now based on the center of the ParticleEmitter Canvas. We've also toned down the scaling a bit to keep the particles at a maximum of 25%. Most importantly, the last line of the function adds the particle to the ParticleEmitter.LayoutRoot Canvas. (This is different than the Page LayoutRoot Canvas.)

```
private void CreateParticles(int HowMany)
{
    for (int i = 0; i < HowMany; i++)
    {
        Particle particle = new Particle();
        Canvas.SetLeft(particle,
            ParticleEmitter.Width / 2 - particle.Width / 2);
        Canvas.SetTop(particle,
            ParticleEmitter.Height / 2 - particle.Height / 2);

        byte[] colors = new byte[3];
        Rand.NextBytes(colors);
        Color c = Color.FromArgb(255, colors[0], colors[1], colors[2]);
        particle.ParticleShape.Fill = new SolidColorBrush(c);

        particle.Opacity = Rand.NextDouble();
        particle.ParticleScale.ScaleX =
                particle.ParticleScale.ScaleY = Rand.NextDouble();
        if (particle.ParticleScale.ScaleX > .25)
            particle.ParticleScale.ScaleX =
            particle.ParticleScale.ScaleY = .25;

        particle.Velocity.X = Rand.Next(-5, (int)5);
        particle.Velocity.Y = Rand.Next(-5, (int)5);
        if (particle.Velocity.X == 0) particle.Velocity.X = 2;
        if (particle.Velocity.Y == 0) particle.Velocity.Y = 2;

        particle.LifeSpan = Rand.Next(120);

        Particles.Add(particle);
        ParticleEmitter.LayoutRoot.Children.Add(particle);
    }
}
```

5. Add the MoveParticles() event handler function. The code here has also been updated. The line that removes the dead particles needed to be updated to remove them from the ParticleEmitter object. Once again, the updated code is shown in bold.

```
private void MoveParticles(object sender, EventArgs e)
{
    for (int i = 0; i < Particles.Count; i++)
    {
        Canvas.SetLeft(Particles[i],
                    Canvas.GetLeft(Particles[i]) +
                    Particles[i].Velocity.X);
```

```
        Canvas.SetTop(Particles[i],
                    Canvas.GetTop(Particles[i]) +
                    Particles[i].Velocity.Y);

        Particles[i].Age += 1;

        if (Particles[i].Age >= Particles[i].LifeSpan)
        {
            ParticleEmitter.LayoutRoot.Children.Remove(Particles[i]);
            Particles.Remove(Particles[i]);
            CreateParticles(1);
        }
    }
    Move.Begin();
}
```

6. Press F5 to compile and run the program. You will see something similar to Figure 10-4. The gray emitter Canvas will appear in the upper-left corner and begin emitting particles. You can use the mouse to move the emitter around the main canvas.

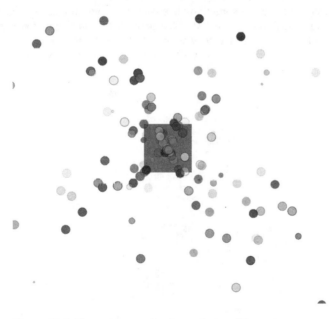

Figure 10-4. The emitter can be dragged around the main canvas.

7. There are two things we will add to this program to improve the functionality. The first will adjust the program so that when it starts, the number of particles will increase—the program won't begin with an initial burst of particles. Inside the Page() constructor, update the CreateParticles() call so that it creates only a single particle:

```
CreateParticles(1);
```

8. Now when the program runs, it will create only a single particle. As the program continues to run, we want to build up the number of visible particles, so inside the MoveParticles() function, add the following code as the very first line, before the for loop. Each time the storyboard completes, another particle will be added if the number of particles on the screen is not equal to the number of particles specified.

```
if (Particles.Count < NumParticles) CreateParticles(1);
```

9. Press F5 to run the program. The emitter now produces one particle at a time, building up to the specified 150. Close the browser when you're done checking out the program.

10. Let's make one more tweak to this program. We're going to add some gravity to pull the particles downward. You're going to be surprised how easy this is. At the top of the Page.xaml.cs file, add the following variable declaration for gravity:

```
private double Gravity = .6;
```

11. Inside the MoveParticles() event handler code, just *before* the closing curly brace of the for statement, add the following line of code:

```
Particles[i].Velocity.Y += Gravity;
```

12. Run the program again. You will see something like what is shown in Figure 10-5. Play around with the gravity setting a little bit and see what happens to the particles. If you want to play around with the spread of the particles as they are emitted, tweak the values in the line of code that sets the x velocity for each particle (particle.Velocity.X = Rand.Next(-5, (int)5);).

Figure 10-5. The particles are pulled downward by gravity.

The finished version of this code is available in **ParticleEmittersCompleted**. I added a particle count to the top-left corner and changed the emitter Canvas to have no background color. The emitter can still be dragged around on the screen, but the application looks a little cleaner.

One thing you will notice is that if you move the emitter Canvas, all of the particles move as well. If you want to be able to make trails with the particles, you'll like the next project.

Building a comet

For this project, we're going to build a comet that moves in an elliptical path, emitting particles as it travels. The particles in this project are emitted to the main canvas based on the location of the emitter. This means that as the emitter moves, the point of origin for the particles will move, but the particles will sprinkle around the main canvas, leaving a tail on the comet.

1. Open up the **ParticleComet** project to code along with this example. The project contains a few parts. There is the Page.xaml file, which contains a black background and the Move timer. We also have the Emitter object, which in this case is an ellipse with an orange center and a translucent red edge, like the one shown in Figure 10-6. Finally, there is the Particle object, which looks just like the emitter, but is smaller, as shown in Figure 10-7.

Figure 10-6. The particle emitter shape used in the ParticleComet project

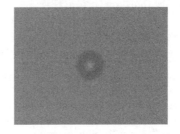

Figure 10-7. The particle shape used in the ParticleComet project

2. Take a look at the Emitter.xaml.cs code-behind file. This file already has some variables declared—you should recognize them as being the necessary components for making the emitter move in an elliptical path.

```
public double Angle = 0;
public double Speed = .1;
public Point Center;
public Point Radius;
```

3. Inside the Particle.xaml.cs file is our usual particle-related code:

```
public int Age { get; set; }
public int LifeSpan { get; set; }
public Point Velocity;
```

4. Let's start coding! Open up the Page.xaml.cs file. We'll start by getting the emitter moving. Declare an instance of the Emitter object before the Page() constructor:

```
private Emitter ParticleEmitter = new Emitter();
```

5. Inside the Page() constructor, add the code shown in the following listing. The code will set the Center and Radius values the Emitter will use for its elliptical movement. The Emitter is then positioned according to the cosine/sine calculations you learned about back in Chapter 6. To finish up, we set the Z-index property of the Emitter to 1 before adding it to the LayoutRoot Canvas. This will cause the particle emitter to draw on top of the particles as they are added to the LayoutRoot Canvas.

```
ParticleEmitter.Center.X = LayoutRoot.Width / 2 -
                           ParticleEmitter.Width / 2;
ParticleEmitter.Center.Y = LayoutRoot.Height / 2 -
                           ParticleEmitter.Height / 2;
ParticleEmitter.Radius.X = 300;
ParticleEmitter.Radius.Y = 100;
Canvas.SetLeft(ParticleEmitter,
               ParticleEmitter.Center.X +
               (Math.Cos(ParticleEmitter.Angle) *
               ParticleEmitter.Radius.X));
Canvas.SetTop(ParticleEmitter,
               ParticleEmitter.Center.Y +
               (Math.Sin(ParticleEmitter.Angle) *
               ParticleEmitter.Radius.Y));
Canvas.SetZIndex(ParticleEmitter, 1);
LayoutRoot.Children.Add(ParticleEmitter);
```

6. Finish coding up the Page() constructor with the following code. This sets an event listener on the Completed event for the Move storyboard before starting the storyboard. Notice that the event handler is still called MoveParticles—we'll be augmenting the function we used before, but we're starting with the emitter.

```
Move.Completed += new EventHandler(MoveParticles);
Move.Begin();
```

7. Create the MoveParticles() event handler as shown in the following listing. Remember that this code will run each time the timer storyboard expires. When that happens, the code here will update the position of the Emitter object on the main canvas, increment its Angle, and restart the timer.

```
private void MoveParticles(object sender, EventArgs e)
{
    Canvas.SetLeft(ParticleEmitter,
                   ParticleEmitter.Center.X +
                   (Math.Cos(ParticleEmitter.Angle) *
                   ParticleEmitter.Radius.X));
    Canvas.SetTop(ParticleEmitter,
                   ParticleEmitter.Center.Y +
                   (Math.Sin(ParticleEmitter.Angle) *
                   ParticleEmitter.Radius.Y));
    ParticleEmitter.Angle += ParticleEmitter.Speed;

    Move.Begin();
}
```

8. Press F5 to compile and run the project. The comet will be drawn on the screen and will travel an elliptical path, as shown in Figure 10-8.

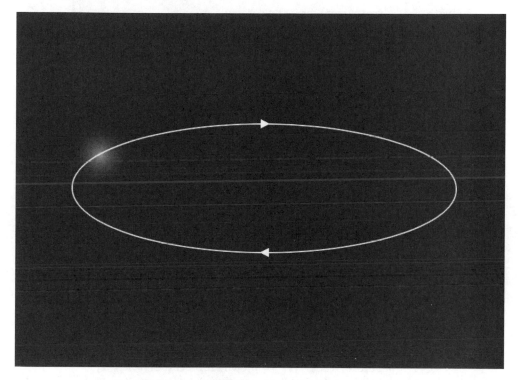

Figure 10-8. The comet travels an elliptical path.

9. Next, we'll add in the particles. Still working the Page.xaml.cs file, add the following declarations before the Page() constructor. We're going for a few more particles this time, and slightly less gravity, to give the particles a little more float.

```
private List<Particle> Particles;
private int NumParticles = 200;
private Random Rand = new Random();
private double Gravity = .4;
```

10. Before the Move.Completed event listener inside the Page() constructor, add the following two lines of code. This will initialize the List of particles with a length of 200, and call the CreateParticles() function to create a single particle:

```
Particles = new List<Particle>(NumParticles);
CreateParticles(1);
```

11. Next, code up the CreateParticles() function. Once again, we're passing an integer value to tell the function how many particles to generate. Notice that the positioning code positions the particle based on the location and size of the ParticleEmitter object. The Opacity and Scale properties are randomly generated, as are the Velocity and Lifespan. Once all that has been done, the Particle object is added to the Particles List and then added to the LayoutRoot

383

Canvas. Did you catch that? The particle is positioned based on the location of the *emitter* object, but added to the *main* canvas, not the emitter Canvas.

```
private void CreateParticles(int HowMany)
{
    for (int i = 0; i < HowMany; i++)
    {
        Particle particle = new Particle();
        Canvas.SetLeft(particle,
                    ParticleEmitter.Width / 2 -
                    particle.Width / 2 +
                    Canvas.GetLeft(ParticleEmitter));
        Canvas.SetTop(particle,
                    ParticleEmitter.Height / 2 -
                    particle.Height / 2 +
                    Canvas.GetTop(ParticleEmitter));

        particle.Opacity = Rand.NextDouble();
        particle.ParticleScale.ScaleX =
                particle.ParticleScale.ScaleY =
                Rand.NextDouble();
        if (particle.ParticleScale.ScaleX < .25)
                particle.ParticleScale.ScaleX =
                particle.ParticleScale.ScaleY = .25;

        particle.Velocity.X = Rand.Next(-3, (int)3);
        particle.Velocity.Y = Rand.Next(-2, (int)2);
        if (particle.Velocity.X == 0) particle.Velocity.X = 2;
        if (particle.Velocity.Y == 0) particle.Velocity.Y = 2;

        particle.LifeSpan = Rand.Next(120);

        Particles.Add(particle);
        LayoutRoot.Children.Add(particle);
    }
}
```

12. Next, you'll need to augment the MoveParticles() function with the following code. Add this code to the top of the MoveParticles() function. This code will check the particle count and add a particle if necessary. The code then drops into the familiar for loop that updates the position of the particles on the screen, increments the particles' ages, and then checks to see if any particles have died and removes them if they have. Finally, each particle has its y velocity modified by the Gravity variable.

```
if (Particles.Count < NumParticles) CreateParticles(1);

for (int i = 0; i < Particles.Count; i++)
{
    Canvas.SetLeft(Particles[i], Canvas.GetLeft(Particles[i]) +
                Particles[i].Velocity.X);
```

```
            Canvas.SetTop(Particles[i], Canvas.GetTop(Particles[i]) +
                        Particles[i].Velocity.Y);

            Particles[i].Age += 1;

            if (Particles[i].Age >= Particles[i].LifeSpan)
            {
                LayoutRoot.Children.Remove(Particles[i]);
                Particles.Remove(Particles[i]);
                CreateParticles(1);
            }
            Particles[i].Velocity.Y += Gravity;
    }
```

For reference, here is a listing of the completed MoveParticles() event handler after adding the code shown previously:

```
    private void MoveParticles(object sender, EventArgs e)
    {
        if (Particles.Count < NumParticles) CreateParticles(1);

        for (int i = 0; i < Particles.Count; i++)
        {
            Canvas.SetLeft(Particles[i], Canvas.GetLeft(Particles[i]) +
                        Particles[i].Velocity.X);
            Canvas.SetTop(Particles[i], Canvas.GetTop(Particles[i]) +
                        Particles[i].Velocity.Y);

            Particles[i].Age += 1;

            if (Particles[i].Age >= Particles[i].LifeSpan)
            {
                LayoutRoot.Children.Remove(Particles[i]);
                Particles.Remove(Particles[i]);
                CreateParticles(1);
            }
            Particles[i].Velocity.Y += Gravity;
        }

        Canvas.SetLeft(ParticleEmitter, ParticleEmitter.Center.X +
                    (Math.Cos(ParticleEmitter.Angle) *
                    ParticleEmitter.Radius.X));
        Canvas.SetTop(ParticleEmitter, ParticleEmitter.Center.Y +
                    (Math.Sin(ParticleEmitter.Angle) *
                    ParticleEmitter.Radius.Y));
        ParticleEmitter.Angle += ParticleEmitter.Speed;

        Move.Begin();
    }
```

13. Press F5 to compile and run the project. The comet will travel the elliptical path, leaving a trail of particles behind, as shown in Figure 10-9.

Figure 10-9. The comet now has a particle-based tail.

14. That looks pretty good, but we can push it a little farther. I put a storyboard called `Flicker` in the `Particle.xaml` file. It's shown in the following listing. The storyboard fades the particle out over .5 seconds, and then fades it back in over the next .5 seconds. The storyboard will then reverse automatically, and is set to repeat endlessly.

```
<UserControl.Resources>
    <Storyboard x:Name="Flicker"
        AutoReverse="True" RepeatBehavior="Forever">
        <DoubleAnimationUsingKeyFrames BeginTime="00:00:00"
            Storyboard.TargetName="Comet"
            Storyboard.TargetProperty="(UIElement.Opacity)">
            <SplineDoubleKeyFrame KeyTime="00:00:00.50" Value="0"/>
            <SplineDoubleKeyFrame KeyTime="00:00:01" Value="1"/>
        </DoubleAnimationUsingKeyFrames>
    </Storyboard>
</UserControl.Resources>
```

15. Inside the `CreateParticles()` function in the `Page.xaml.cs` file, just before the `Particles.Add(particle);` line, add the following two lines of code. The first line will generate a random `SpeedRatio` between 5 and 10 for the `Flicker` storyboard, and then begin the storyboard.

```
particle.Flicker.SpeedRatio = Rand.Next(5, 10);
particle.Flicker.Begin();
```

16. In the MoveParticles() function, you need to add some code that stops the storyboard before the particle is removed from the canvas and the Particles List. The following listing includes the for loop where the new line of code should be placed—the relevant line of code is shown in bold.

```
if (Particles[i].Age >= Particles[i].LifeSpan)
{
    Particles[i].Flicker.Stop();
    LayoutRoot.Children.Remove(Particles[i]);
    Particles.Remove(Particles[i]);
    CreateParticles(1);
}
```

Press F5 to run the project and check it out. Now as the comet moves, it leaves a trail of shimmering debris, as shown in Figure 10-10. The final code for this project is available in **ParticleCometCompleted**. See if you can figure out how to create a project that drops sparkling particles from the mouse when it is moving.

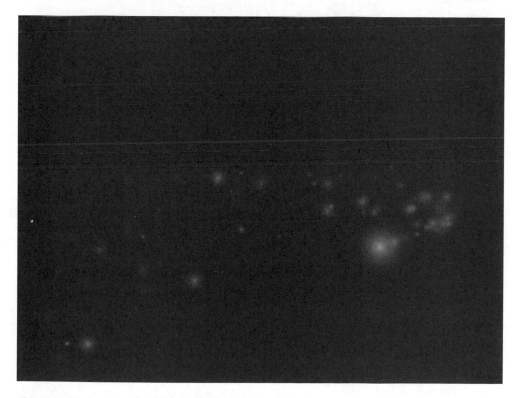

Figure 10-10. The comet leaves a trail of shimmering debris.

Explosions

The next type of particle system we'll take a look at is an explosion. We'll start out with a circular explosion—similar to the type you see in games or movies when a spaceship explodes. Debris will move out from the center point in a circular pattern, the diameter of which will increase along with the life span of the explosion. Open the **RingExplosions** project to code along with this example.

Since this particle system is built on the same base system as the earlier examples, I've already provided a lot of the code in the project for you. We'll just concentrate on adding the parts that make the explosion look the way we want.

1. Open the Page.xaml.cs file for editing. The particles in this explosion will form a ring that expands. As such, the particles will need to have their x and y velocities match. We could easily use a random number to generate the speed, but in this case, we'll set up a variable to control the speed. Add the following line of code to the variable declarations that precede the Page() constructor:

    ```
    private int ExplosionSpeed = 7;
    ```

2. Inside the CreateParticle() function, add code to set the velocity of the particles being created:

    ```
    particle.Velocity.X = ExplosionSpeed;
    particle.Velocity.Y = ExplosionSpeed;
    ```

3. If you're thinking ahead, you're figuring we're going to be using sine and cosine to pull off the magic with this particle system, and you're correct. Still inside the CreateParticle() function, add the following line of code to assign a random angle to each of the particles in the system:

    ```
    particle.Angle = Rand.Next(360);
    ```

4. Inside the MoveParticles() function, we'll need to convert our particle's angle to radians. Add the following code at the top of the for loop:

    ```
    double Radians = Particles[i].Angle / 180 * Math.PI;
    ```

5. Next, the position of the particle is based on the value calculated in step 4. The following two lines of code come after the code added in step 4, and will position the particle—you can see the calculations use sine and cosine to determine the correct location for the particle.

    ```
    Canvas.SetLeft(Particles[i], Canvas.GetLeft(Particles[i]) +
                Particles[i].Velocity.X * Math.Cos(Radians));
    Canvas.SetTop(Particles[i], Canvas.GetTop(Particles[i]) +
                Particles[i].Velocity.Y * Math.Sin(Radians));
    ```

Press F5 to compile and run the project. You will see an expanding ring explosion like the one shown in Figure 10-11. The finalized version of the code described in this example is available in the **RingExplosionsCompleted** project.

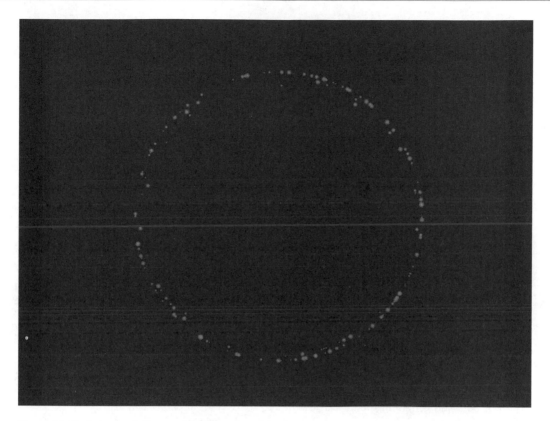

Figure 10-11. A ring explosion particle system

Random explosions

Of course, not every explosion is ring-shaped, so let's work through an example of a more randomized explosion. This time, we'll create an application that creates a random explosion at the location of a mouse click on the main canvas. To code along, open the **RandomExplosions** project. Once again, the main code for the particle system is in place, and we'll walk through what you need to add in to make the explosion happen.

1. Open the Page.xaml.cs file for editing. Since we'll be using the mouse pointer's location to place the explosion, we'll need a variable that holds the mouse location. Add the following line of code to the variable declarations just before the Page() constructor:

   ```
   private Point MousePoint;
   ```

2. Inside the CreateParticles() function, just after the Particle particle = new Particle(); declaration, add the following two lines of code to position the new particle at the mouse location:

   ```
   Canvas.SetLeft(particle, MousePoint.X);
   Canvas.SetTop(particle, MousePoint.Y);
   ```

3. In prior examples, we used NextDouble() to generate a random number between 0 and 1 for the particle scale. For this example, we want a scale value between 1 and 4. Add the following line of code just after the random Opacity value is set:

```
particle.ParticleScale.ScaleX =
        particle.ParticleScale.ScaleY =
        Rand.Next(1, (int)4);
```

4. After the code that tests the scale value, add the following two lines of code. This code determines the spread of the explosion.

```
particle.Velocity.X = Rand.Next(-7, (int)8);
particle.Velocity.Y = Rand.Next(-8, (int)1);
```

5. In the MoveParticles() function, add the following code just after the line that adjusts the velocity for gravity. This code will slowly fade the opacity out over the lifetime of the particle system.

```
Particles[i].Opacity -= .025;
```

6. The particle system itself is pretty much ready to go, but we need to make it show up when a user clicks on the main canvas. Inside the Page() constructor, add an event listener for the MouseLeftButtonUp event:

```
LayoutRoot.MouseLeftButtonUp +=
        new MouseButtonEventHandler(LayoutRoot_MouseLeftButtonUp);
```

7. Inside the event handler, we need to reset the explosion. This is done by clearing the root canvas of existing children (particles), clearing the Particles List, getting the current mouse position, and generating new particles.

```
void LayoutRoot_MouseLeftButtonUp(object sender,
                                  MouseButtonEventArgs e)
{
    LayoutRoot.Children.Clear();
    Particles.Clear();
    MousePoint = e.GetPosition(this);
    CreateParticles(NumParticles);
}
```

8. Press F5 to compile and run the project. Click somewhere on the canvas and an explosion will appear. The explosions look pretty good, but we can enhance the look a bit with just a couple more lines of code. Once again, I've added the Flicker storyboard to the Particle object. This storyboard fades the particle out over .5 seconds, and fades it back in over .5 seconds. However, unlike the comet, we don't want the particles flickering right away for the explosion; instead, the explosion should be allowed to happen, and then the particles will be made to flicker after a short delay. To accomplish this, the BeginTime property for the animation inside the Flicker storyboard was set to 3 seconds.

9. Inside the CreateParticles() function, add the following two lines of code to set a random SpeedRatio for the storyboard, and then start it:

```
particle.Flicker.SpeedRatio = Rand.Next(3, 10);
particle.Flicker.Begin();
```

10. Inside the MoveParticles() function, we need to stop the storyboard before removing the particle from the canvas. Add the following bold line of code to the particle age check:

```
if (Particles[i].Age >= Particles[i].LifeSpan)
{
    Particles[i].Flicker.Stop();
    ParticleCanvas.Children.Remove(Particles[i]);
    Particles.Remove(Particles[i]);
}
```

Compile and run the project. When you click, you will see a nice-looking random explosion, and the individual particles will start to flicker as they drop toward the bottom of the application, as shown in Figure 10-12. The **RandomExplosionsCompleted** project contains the code covered in this example. I added a color picker to the completed project that allows you to alter the outer color of the particles.

Figure 10-12. The individual particles in a random explosion start to flicker as they fade and drop.

Fountains

For our next particle system, we'll take a look at how to create a fountain, like the one shown in Figure 10-13. The particles are emitted from the top area of the tube, fly upward, and eventually fall back as they are affected by the force of gravity.

Figure 10-13. A particle fountain

The particle system for the fountain is similar to the one for the explosion, so rather than walk through all of the code, we'll hit on the important parts, and you can spend some time exploring the project for yourself. All of the code shown in this example is from the **ParticleFountain** project.

The variable declarations and Page() constructor should look pretty familiar to you by now. Inside the CreateParticles() function are a couple of changes. The first is where the particles are placed on the screen. The code uses the center point of the main canvas to determine the x position and the top of the emitter tube to determine the y position.

```
Canvas.SetLeft(particle, (LayoutRoot.Width / 2) - particle.Width / 2);
Canvas.SetTop(particle, Canvas.GetTop(EmitterTube));
```

A bit further down in the code, you can see where the x and y velocities are assigned via a random number generator. Notice that the y velocity for each particle will vary between –15 and –2. Remember that to move a particle up, you use a –y velocity; to move a particle downward, you use a +y velocity.

```
particle.Velocity.X = Rand.Next(-2, 3);
particle.Velocity.Y = Rand.Next(-15, (int)-2);
```

The rest of the code is pretty much what you've been working with in the last few examples. Even though it's a fairly simple particle system, a lot of flexibility can be programmed into it. Take a look at the **ParticleFountainCompleted** project, shown in Figure 10-14.

I've taken the base fountain and added particle count messaging and sliders to allow real-time control over the number of particles, gravity, y velocity, and x spread as the particles are emitted.

Particles: 150

Number of particles: 150.0

Gravity: 0.4

Y Velocity Max: -15.0

X Spread: 2.0

Figure 10-14. A particle fountain with some sliders to control the look and feel of the fountain

We're going to close out this chapter with a look at some really interesting ways to work with particles. The examples shown here are adapted from the originals done in Flash by Keith Peters, and used with his kind permission. We'll be seeing how each particle can be made to affect the particles around it.

Particles and gravity

For this example, we'll add some gravitational pull between particles. Like planets, the influence each particle has on any particles nearby is affected by distance. The farther away a particle is from another particle, the less influence it will have. Gravitational force is affected by mass—the larger something is, the greater the mass and the greater the gravitational pull. The equation for the force of gravity looks like this:

force = G $\times$ m1 $\times$ m2 / distance^2

This equation reads as follows: the gravitational force one object has on another equals the gravitational constant times the mass of both objects, divided by the square of the distance between them. That may seem relatively straightforward, except that the gravitational constant is not so easily figured out:

G = (6.6742 $\pm$ 0.0010) $\times$ 10^{-11} $\times$ m3 $\times$ kg^{-1} $\times$ s^{-2}

The easiest way to work around the gravitational constant for our particle systems is to ignore it. Since we're working with particles, and not sending manned spacecraft to Mars, the following formula will work:

force = m1 $\times$ m2 / distance^2

Let's check it out and see how it works. Open the **ParticleGravitation** project. This project has a bit of code in it that will place 30 instances of a particle object around the canvas, as shown in Figure 10-15. There's nothing fancy going on here—it's the same basic particle system we've been using all along. The particle object contains variables for velocity and mass.

Figure 10-15. The ParticleGravitation project randomly places 30 particles on the main canvas.

1. Inside the Page.xaml.cs file in the MoveParticles() function is a foreach loop that is used to move each particle. The particles currently don't go anywhere because they all have x and y velocities of 0. Gravity will be doing the work for us in this project. Just after the closing curly brace of the foreach loop, add the following nested for loop. The nested for loop will figure out the interactions between particles. The first for loop gets a particle (i), while the nested loop gets the next particle (i + 1). Those two particles are then passed to a function that will handle the gravity.

```
for (int i = 0; i < NumParticles - 1; i++)
{
    for (int j = i + 1; j < NumParticles; j++)
    {
        Gravitate(Particles[i], Particles[j]);
    }
}
```

2. Add the Gravitate() function shown following after the MoveParticles() function. This function begins by calculating the distance between the two particles being compared. The DistSQ calculation is used to get the distance squared, which goes into the total force calculation,

which you will see about midway through the code listing. Once that has been done, calculate the total acceleration along the x and y axes. Finally, the total force and total acceleration are divided up between the two particles based on their individual masses.

```
private void Gravitate(Particle Particle1, Particle Particle2)
{
    double DX = Canvas.GetLeft(Particle2) - Canvas.GetLeft(Particle1);
    double DY = Canvas.GetTop(Particle2) - Canvas.GetTop(Particle1);
    double DistSQ = DX * DX + DY * DY;
    double Distance = Math.Sqrt(DistSQ);
    double Force = Particle1.Mass * Particle2.Mass / DistSQ;
    double AX = Force * DX / Distance;
    double AY = Force * DY / Distance;
    Particle1.Velocity.X += AX / Particle1.Mass;
    Particle1.Velocity.Y += AY / Particle1.Mass;
    Particle2.Velocity.X -= AX / Particle2.Mass;
    Particle2.Velocity.Y -= AY / Particle2.Mass;
}
```

Press F5 to compile and run the project. The particles will start out motionless, but will slowly be attracted to one another. Some may begin to orbit each other. Many of the particles will get very close, and then speed off in opposite directions. This is called the "slingshot effect," and is expected behavior. This behavior models the way NASA sends spacecraft into deep space—as a spacecraft approaches a planet, it feels an increasing amount of the planet's gravitational pull, and starts traveling at an increased velocity. By aiming very close to a planet without hitting it, a spacecraft will accelerate beyond the planet's ability to capture it with gravitational pull, and gain the velocity necessary to travel through space without burning fuel.

In the particle system we built, the behavior seems unusual—we expect to see particles bouncing off of each other rather than flying off in opposite directions. For this, we'll need to add some collision detection and reaction code to our program.

3. Begin by creating a new function called CheckCollisions(), as shown:

```
private void CheckCollisions(Particle Particle1, Particle Particle2)
{
}
```

4. Inside the new CheckCollisions() function, add variables to determine the distance between two particles:

```
double DX = Canvas.GetLeft(Particle2) - Canvas.GetLeft(Particle1);
double DY = Canvas.GetTop(Particle2) - Canvas.GetTop(Particle1);
double Distance = Math.Sqrt(DX * DX + DY * DY);
```

5. Add an if statement to check if two particles are colliding based on their distance:

```
if (Distance < (Particle1.Width *
            Particle1.ParticleScale.ScaleX) / 2 +
            (Particle2.Width *
            Particle2.ParticleScale.ScaleX) / 2)
{
}
```

6. Calculate the angle between the two particles and split it into x and y components:

```
double Angle = Math.Atan2(DY, DX);
double Sine = Math.Sin(Angle);
double Cosine = Math.Cos(Angle);
```

7. Here's where this function gets fun. We're going to rotate the coordinate system and particle velocities to resolve the collision along a linear path, and then rotate the coordinate system and velocities back before updating the particle's positions on the main canvas. Begin by rotating Particle1's position. The rotation of the coordinate system occurs around Particle1, so these values are 0.

```
double X0 = 0;
double Y0 = 0;
```

8. Rotate the position of Particle2:

```
double X1 = DX * Cosine + DY * Sine;
double Y1 = DY * Cosine - DX * Sine;
```

9. Rotate both particles' velocities:

```
double VX0 = Particle1.Velocity.X * Cosine +
             Particle1.Velocity.Y * Sine;
double VY0 = Particle1.Velocity.Y * Cosine -
             Particle1.Velocity.X * Sine;

double VX1 = Particle2.Velocity.X * Cosine +
             Particle2.Velocity.Y * Sine;
double VY1 = Particle2.Velocity.Y * Cosine -
             Particle2.Velocity.X * Sine;
```

10. Calculate the reaction to the collision—here, the total velocity along the x axis is being calculated (remember that we rotated the coordinate system), and then divided up between particles:

```
double VXTotal = VX0 - VX1;
VX0 = ((Particle1.Mass - Particle2.Mass) * VX0 +
      2 * Particle2.Mass * VX1) /
      (Particle1.Mass + Particle2.Mass);
VX1 = VXTotal + VX0;
```

11. Update the position variables:

```
X0 += VX0;
X1 += VX1;
```

12. Now it's time to rotate everything back into proper position. Begin by calculating the particles' final positions prior to rotating them back:

```
double X0Final = X0 * Cosine - Y0 * Sine;
double Y0Final = Y0 * Cosine + X0 * Sine;
double X1Final = X1 * Cosine - Y1 * Sine;
double Y1Final = Y1 * Cosine + X1 * Sine;
```

13. Update the position of the particles on the screen. Since the coordinate system was rotated about Particle1, Particle1's original position is added to the calculated new position.

```
Canvas.SetLeft(Particle2, Canvas.GetLeft(Particle1) + X1Final);
Canvas.SetTop(Particle2, Canvas.GetTop(Particle1) + Y1Final);
Canvas.SetLeft(Particle1, Canvas.GetLeft(Particle1) + X0Final);
Canvas.SetTop(Particle1, Canvas.GetTop(Particle1) + Y0Final);
```

14. Finish up by rotating the velocities back. These are applied directly to the velocities in the particle objects.

```
Particle1.Velocity.X = VX0 * Cosine - VY0 * Sine;
Particle1.Velocity.Y = VY0 * Cosine + VX0 * Sine;
Particle2.Velocity.X = VX1 * Cosine - VY1 * Sine;
Particle2.Velocity.Y = VY1 * Cosine + VX1 * Sine;
```

15. Now all we need to do is call the newly added function from the MoveParticles() function. Add the following line of code inside the nested for loop, just before the line of code that calls the Gravitate() function:

```
CheckCollisions(Particles[i], Particles[j]);
```

Press F5 to compile and run the project. The particles will start out motionless, and become attracted to each other. This time, the collision code will kick in when the particles get close, and they will bounce off one another. We've included a variable for mass on each particle, but haven't really done anything with it, so let's finish out this example by adding a couple of lines of code to vary the scale and mass of the particles a bit.

16. Inside the CreateParticles() method, add the following line of code to assign a random scale between 1 and 5 to each particle as it is initialized:

```
nextParticle.ParticleScale.ScaleX =
    nextParticle.ParticleScale.ScaleY = Rand.Next(1, 5);
```

17. Still inside the CreateParticles() method, change the nextParticle.Mass = 1; line so that it uses a particle's scale as mass—the larger an object, the higher the mass.

```
nextParticle.Mass = nextParticle.ParticleScale.ScaleX;
```

Now when the program runs, the size and mass of the particles are randomized a bit, and it gives a pretty interesting effect as they bounce around off of one another. The code shown in this example is available in the **ParticleGravitationCompleted** project.

Particles and springs

In the next example, we'll take a look at how we can use springs as force between particles. Springs act similarly to gravity in that two particles influencing one another will be drawn toward each other. In the gravity example, particles farther apart decrease in acceleration. With springs, it's just the opposite—particles that are farther apart increase in acceleration. Open the **ParticleSprings** project to follow along with this example.

1. The base code for this project is very similar to the previous projects. If you compile and run the project, you will see 30 particles meandering aimlessly about the canvas. This was done by assigning random x and y velocities between –3 and 3. The other thing you may notice is that in the Page.xaml.cs file, there are two additional variables declared. The first determines the distance between two particles that will cause them to affect one another. If no distance were set, all of the particles would lump together. Instead, we will use this variable to make sure that only particles within 100 pixels of one another will affect each other. The second variable is SpringAmount, which is used to determine the springiness of the two particles' interaction.

```
private double MinDistance= 100;
private double SpringAmount = .001;
```

2. Add a new function beneath the MoveParticles() function, called Spring(). This function will determine the distance between the two particles passed to the function. If the distance between the particles is less than the value contained in the MinDistance variable, the acceleration along each axis is calculated based on the current distance and spring amount. That acceleration is then added to Particle1's velocity, and subtracted from Particle2's velocity. This is what pulls two particles together.

```
private void Spring(Particle Particle1, Particle Particle2)
{
    double DX = Canvas.GetLeft(Particle2) - Canvas.GetLeft(Particle1);
    double DY = Canvas.GetTop(Particle2) - Canvas.GetTop(Particle1);
    double Distance = Math.Sqrt(DX * DX + DY * DY);

    if (Distance < MinDistance)
    {
        double AX = DX * SpringAmount;
        double AY = DY * SpringAmount;

        Particle1.Velocity.X += AX;
        Particle1.Velocity.Y += AY;
        Particle2.Velocity.X -= AX;
        Particle2.Velocity.Y -= AY;
    }
}
```

3. Inside the nested for loop in the MoveParticles() function, add the following line of code to pass the current two particles to the function that was just created:

```
Spring(Particles[i], Particles[j]);
```

Press F5 to compile and run the project. The particles will now affect each other, form into little clumps, and break away to join other nearby clumps. If you increase the value used for SpringAmount, this behavior becomes even more pronounced. The final version of this code is available in the **ParticleSpringsCompleted** project.

Visualizing particle interactions

The last project we're going to build out in this chapter will illustrate a really cool way of visualizing particle interactions. This project is built on top of the spring-based particle system from the last example. In fact, if you compile and run the **NodeGarden** project, you will see that other than a slightly different look and feel, the behavior is the same. Particles of different sizes drift around the screen, affected by their proximity to other particles with springing behavior, as shown in Figure 10-16.

Figure 10-16. The basis for the NodeGarden project is a spring-based particle system.

1. Let's start by adding lines between particles that are influencing one another. For this, we will need a List of lines, which we will call Connections. Add the declaration in the usual area, just before the Page() constructor:

   ```
   private List<Line> Connections;
   ```

2. Inside the Page() constructor, initialize the Connections List:

   ```
   Connections = new List<Line>(NumParticles);
   ```

3. Next, we'll add some code to the MoveParticles() function. Each time the function runs, we'll clear the existing lines drawn between particles, so add the code shown in the following listing at the very top of the function:

   ```
   foreach (Line nextConnection in Connections)
   {
       LayoutRoot.Children.Remove(nextConnection);
   }
   Connections.Clear();
   ```

4. The code to draw the lines goes inside the `Spring()` function. Since we only care about the relationships for particles that are less than 100 pixels apart, place the following code inside the `if` statement that tests the distance between particles, at the very top.

```
Line nextConnection = new Line();
nextConnection.X1 = Canvas.GetLeft(Particle1) + Particle1.Width / 2;
nextConnection.Y1 = Canvas.GetTop(Particle1) + Particle1.Height / 2;
nextConnection.X2 = Canvas.GetLeft(Particle2) + Particle2.Width / 2;
nextConnection.Y2 = Canvas.GetTop(Particle2) + Particle2.Height / 2;

nextConnection.StrokeThickness = 2;
SolidColorBrush LineStroke = new SolidColorBrush();
LineStroke.Color = Colors.White;
nextConnection.Stroke = LineStroke;

Connections.Add(nextConnection);
LayoutRoot.Children.Add(nextConnection);
```

Press F5 to compile and run the program. You will see something like Figure 10-17. As two particles come within 100 pixels of each other, a 2-pixel-wide white line is drawn between them. When the distance between particles that are connected by a line increases beyond 100 pixels, the line is removed.

Even as-is, this project creates a pretty nice effect that is somewhat mesmerizing. But with one more line of code, you will feel like you can stare at it for hours on end.

Figure 10-17. Lines are drawn between particles within each other's area of influence.

5. The line of code you add next will alter the opacity of the line as the distance between particles changes. The closer the particles, the more opaque (brighter) the line will be. As they grow more distant, their influence on each other fades, as does the line indicating their connection. Add the following line of code to the code you added in step 4, after the line that sets the stroke color (LineStroke.Color = Colors.White;):

```
LineStroke.Opacity = 1 - Distance / MinDistance;
```

Now when you compile and run the program, you'll see connections like those shown in Figure 10-18. The closer two particles are, the brighter the line between them. The effect is almost like looking at moving constellations. Imagine this effect between drifting images or other objects. The final version of the code from this example is available in the **NodeGardenCompleted** project.

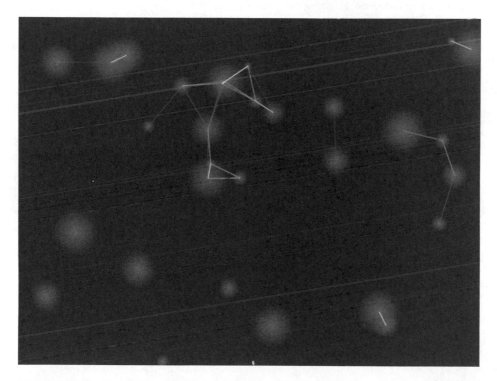

Figure 10-18. The lines between particles fade as the distance between the particles increases.

Summary

In this chapter, we talked about what a particle is and how to create a basic particle system. The model for a particle system is that as time passes, new particles may be created, old (dead) particles are removed, and the remaining particles have their positions updated on the main canvas.

Once you built a basic particle system, you learned about emitters and how to use them to create particles that emanate from a specific location in your application. You also learned about how gravity can be used to affect particles.

With all of that in place, we looked at some example particle systems. The comet example used an emitter that moved, but placed particles on the main canvas. Then we looked at how to go about creating ring-shaped and random explosions, as well as particle fountains.

We then talked about how forces can be applied between particles. You saw examples of how particles can gravitate toward one another, colliding and bouncing, and also how springing behavior can be used to create interesting, organic-looking bunches of particles. We then closed out the chapter by looking at a way to visualize the relationship between particles with lines, creating a nice-looking particle node garden based on springing behavior.

In the next chapter, you're going to learn how to create Silverlight-based virtual reality objects. You'll learn how the SLVR engine works, and how you can implement VR objects in your own Silverlight applications.

Chapter 11

SILVERLIGHT VR (SLVR) OBJECTS

In this chapter, we'll talk about how to use Silverlight to display virtual reality (VR) objects. Everybody's seen this type of object—the image loads, and as you use the mouse to drag inside the window, the object rotates with the mouse, allowing a more interactive experience with the object being displayed. You'll also see something you're not likely to find in any other book. I'm going to show you how to use Silverlight to travel through time. Yes, really.

There are two fundamental approaches to creating a VR object–based application. The first is to take a series of photos of the object from different angles, load the photos into the application, and then "flip" through them like a deck of cards.

The second is to take a series of photos, assemble them in columns and rows in a single image, and then use the application to translate the image inside of a clipped canvas. We'll be using the single-image method. Based on my experience building both types, it seems a little snappier; it's much easier to set up, update, and augment; and it has fewer moving parts to keep track of.

With that in mind, let's get started. The first thing we need to talk about is the images.

VR object images

Getting content to use in your Silverlight VR (SLVR)-based applications is likely to be the most time-consuming part of the process. When it comes to getting images, you basically have three options.

The first is to use a 3D program to render an object out. This may involve some expense and a learning curve if you don't know 3D, although you may be able to get a friend or neighbor to help out if you know someone who uses a 3D program.

The second method for getting content is to photograph your own object. This is not terribly difficult to do, but may require a bit of extra equipment like a turntable for the object, and some time to practice.

The third option is to use a company that specializes in doing the photography, such as PhotoSpherix (www.photospherix.com/), who was kind enough to supply the example object photos you'll be working with in this chapter.

Generally speaking, there are two types of VR objects: single-row (or single-plane) and multirow (multiplane). The general concept for creating either is the same. An object is set up on a rotating turntable, photographed, rotated some number of degrees, and photographed again. The process continues until the desired number of photos has been taken. Taking photos of an object that is rotated 10 degrees between shots means there are 35 shots per row for a full 360-degree rotation. The smaller the increment the object is rotated, the smoother the final action will be, but the larger the file, so there is a trade-off there. Figure 11-1 shows a few example frames from a single-plane object.

Figure 11-1. The first few frames of a single-plane VR object

For a multiplane object, the camera is typically placed directly overhead (0 degrees), and then tilted down in 10-degree increments as each row is completed. As you can probably imagine, this would be tricky to do for the average home user. Companies that specialize in this type of photography have specially made motorized camera rigs that make the process of taking the shots more exact. Figure 11-2 shows the first few frames of the first few rows of a multiplane VR object.

Figure 11-2. The first few frames of the first few rows of
a multiplane VR object

You may end up with quite a few images. As long as they are numbered sequentially from the top left across the first row, and then to the second row if you have one, and so on, you'll be fine. For example, one of the models with which we will be working has 120 source images (5 rows of 20 images), the files for which are named `mini_new-001.jpg` through `mini_new-120.jpg`.

What do I do with all these images?

For use as a SLVR object, we need to take a big pile of 21 images and make a single image. The best way to do this is to find a program that will create customizable **contact sheets**. Photoshop has a contact sheet script, found under File ➤ Automate ➤ Contact Sheet II, but I've found that it will occasionally place unexpected whitespace between images. Instead, take a few moments and download the freeware program IrfanView from www.irfanview.com/. Let's practice making an image using IrfanView.

1. Start the program. From the File menu, select Thumbnails, as shown in Figure 11-3.

2. The Thumbnails view window will open. Navigate to the inhabit_bed folder in the projects for Chapter 11. All 21 image thumbnails will be displayed in the right-hand pane. Click one to select it, and then press Ctrl+A to select all of the images.

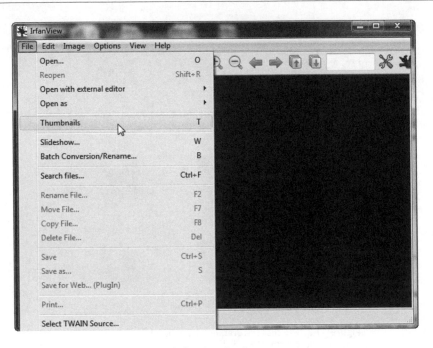

Figure 11-3. In IrfanView, select File ➤ Thumbnails.

3. Select File ➤ Create contact sheet from selected files, as shown in Figure 11-4.

Move selected files...	F7
Copy selected files...	F8
Delete selected files...	Del
Start slideshow with selected files	
Save selected files as current slideshow	
Append selected files to current slideshow	
Start batch dialog with selected files...	B
Transfer selected files by FTP...	
Save selected file names as TXT...	
JPG Lossless Operations	▶
Create contact sheet from selected files...	
Start Panorama dialog with selected files...	
Save selected thumbs as an image...	
Save selected thumbs as single images...	
Save selected thumbs as HTML file...	
Print selected files as single images (batch print)...	
Send selected files by EMail...	Shift+M
Open with external editor	▶

Figure 11-4. Creating a contact sheet in IrfanView

4. You'll get a somewhat intimidating-looking Create Contact Sheet dialog box. We only need to deal with the left side of the box, though, so it's not too bad. The first things we need to fill in are the width and height. There are 21 images in a single row. Each image is 600×600 pixels. For Width, enter 12600 (21 images × 600 pixels), and for Height, enter 600 (each image is 600 pixels tall).

5. In the Columns box, enter 21. For Rows, enter 1, since this is a single-plane VR object.

6. Leave the Stretch small images to maximal size box unchecked, and verify that Thumbnail spacing is 0 for both Horizontal and Vertical. The Horizontal and Vertical fields for Margins should also be 0. When you're finished, the panel should look like Figure 11-5.

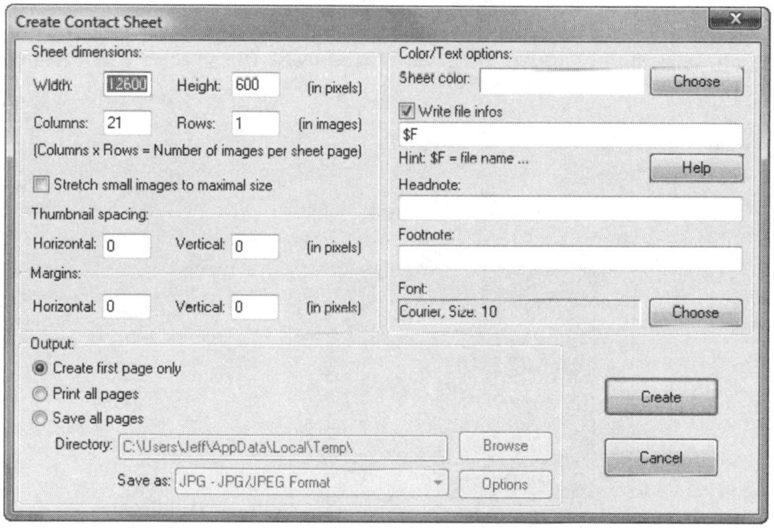

Figure 11-5. The Create Contact Sheet dialog box in IrfanView

7. Click the Create button. A clipboard window will open showing the contact sheet. Select File Save As to save the file. JPG is your best bet for an image of this size, so select JPG from the Save as type drop-down, and go for about 60% compression on the JPEG/GIF save options dialog. Click Save and you're done.

Depending upon your specific compression settings, the single file will end up somewhere between 250 and 300K, which isn't bad for an image that is 12600×600 pixels.

You create multiplane images the same way, except that for the contact sheet, you also specify the number of rows in your source photos. Unfortunately, IrfanView runs out of steam a little bit here with the high-resolution images, and doesn't support contact sheets that are taller than 1800 pixels at this resolution.

As a workaround, you can make multiple contact sheets of three rows each, and put them together in your favorite graphics program. It will still be quick and relatively painless, and you can't beat the price. You can try creating multirow contact sheets with the images in the mini folder if you'd like. There are 6 rows of 20 images, each of which is 600×600. Just in case you don't have a program like Photoshop readily accessible, I included the **Mini** contact sheet in the mini folder. The 12000×3600-pixel image is called MiniAll.jpg.

What do I do with this giant image?

So you got the photos of your object, or had a company like PhotoSpherix help you out; you converted the images into a big contact sheet image; and you're ready to plug them into Silverlight and watch some magic happen. This is where the SLVR user control comes in. The control is already built, but we're going to go through all of the code so you understand how it does what it does; that way you can add custom features if you like.

The first thing to take a look at is the user control. The architecture for the control is shown in Figure 11-6. Inside the user control is the main LayoutRoot Canvas, which contains a rectangle called MouseControl, and an Image object called ActiveImage. The default size for each of these objects is 320×240, but the control will resize them based on how it is set up. A very important aspect of this control is a clipping path applied to the ImageControl Canvas. This creates a window onto the image in the ActiveImage object.

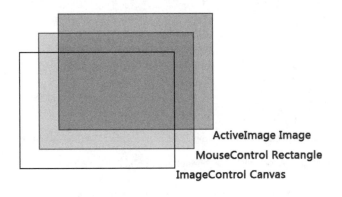

ActiveImage Image
MouseControl Rectangle
ImageControl Canvas

Figure 11-6. The basic architecture of the SLVR user control

When the SLVR user control is instanced, it is handed an image, which is placed in the ActiveImage object, behind the window of the ImageControl Canvas. This makes it so only a single frame of the image is visible. The image is then translated behind the window, as illustrated in Figure 11-7, based on input from the mouse on the MouseControl layer.

Let's go through the code in the SLVR.xaml.cs file. You'll get to add this control to a project after the walkthrough, so don't worry about coding anything up right now. If you would like to follow along, you can open the SLVR.xaml.cs file in the SLVR Control folder.

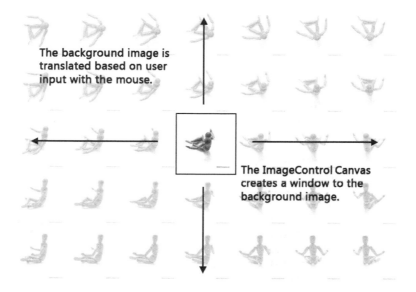

The background image is translated based on user input with the mouse.

The ImageControl Canvas creates a window to the background image.

Figure 11-7. The clipped ImageControl Canvas creates a window to the background image.

The first variable, MouseSensitivity, is used to determine how far the mouse will move before the visible image is changed. This allows you some control over the smoothness of the action in the application. The MouseCounter variable is used to keep track of how far the mouse has moved, and is the trigger for changing the image.

```
private Point MouseSensitivity;
private Point MouseCounter;
```

The FrameStep variable tells the application how large the images are. It is a Point data type because not all images are square, so it is used to store both the width and height of a single image frame.

```
private Point FrameStep;
```

The next four variables let the application know how many columns and rows there are in the source image, and whether or not the columns and rows should be wrapped when the beginning or end is reached.

```
private int Columns;
private int Rows;
private bool WrapColumns;
private bool WrapRows;
```

The FlipMouse variable is used to change the functionality of the application so that the view can move opposite the mouse. The standard behavior is to let the user feel as though they are moving the object. When FlipMouse is active, the motion is more akin to moving the camera around the object.

```
private bool FlipMouse;
```

The last four variables are used for drag-and-drop control:

```
private Point CurrentMouse;
private Point OldMouse;
private bool DragInProgress = false;
private Point DragStart;
```

Next is the SLVR() constructor. Here, the control accepts a bunch of variables upon initialization. Many of the private variables declared are initialized with the values passed here, and are named similarly. In fact, a lot of the code in the constructor is used to apply these values to the control.

```
public SLVR(double FrameWidth,
            double FrameHeight,
            int NumColumns,
            int NumRows,
            bool ColumnWrap,
            bool RowWrap,
            string ImageName,
            int DampenMouseMovement,
            bool FlipMouseControl)
```

After the InitializeComponent() method, the code for the control begins. These two lines adjust the width and height of the Image object in the control to the size of the full image.

```
ActiveImage.Width = FrameWidth * NumColumns;
ActiveImage.Height = FrameHeight * NumRows;
```

Next, the size of the steps used to translate the image, control width, and MouseControl rectangle width are adjusted to the passed FrameWidth value:

```
FrameStep.X = this.Width = this.MouseControl.Width = FrameWidth;
FrameStep.Y = this.Height = this.MouseControl.Height = FrameHeight;
```

Now the columns, rows, and wrapping behavior are assigned to the private variables in the control:

```
Columns = NumColumns;
Rows = NumRows;

WrapColumns = ColumnWrap;
WrapRows = RowWrap;
```

Next, the image specified by the user is loaded into the ActiveImage object in the control. This particular method for loading images requires the addition of the two resources at the top of the control:

```
using System.Windows.Resources;
using System.Windows.Media.Imaging;
```

The loading code looks like this:

```
StreamResourceInfo sr =
    Application.GetResourceStream(new Uri(ImageName,
                                          UriKind.Relative));
BitmapImage bmp = new BitmapImage();
bmp.SetSource(sr.Stream);
ActiveImage.Source = bmp;
```

Now the clipping region on the ImageControl Canvas is adjusted. The clip will always begin at 0,0, and will have a width of FrameWidth, and height of FrameHeight, so this is fairly easy to apply through code:

```
RectangleGeometry ImageClipRegion = new RectangleGeometry();
ImageClipRegion.Rect = new Rect(0, 0, FrameWidth, FrameHeight);
ImageControl.Clip = ImageClipRegion;
```

The next two lines of code try to find an image near the center of the single source image so that you're not always starting at 0,0. You'll see how to override this feature if necessary when the control is instanced.

```
TranslateImage.X = -(Math.Floor(Columns / 2) * FrameWidth);
TranslateImage.Y = -(Math.Floor(Rows / 2) * FrameHeight);
```

Since it's possible to have an image that contains only a single column or row, the control checks to see if this is the case, and if so, starts at the image in the beginning of the series:

```
if (Columns == 1) TranslateImage.Y = 0;
if (Rows == 1) TranslateImage.X = 0;
```

The next bit of code grabs the value of the passed Boolean FlipMouseControl:

```
FlipMouse = FlipMouseControl;
```

Next, the mouse sensitivity is adjusted based on the value passed when the control was instanced:

```
MouseSensitivity.X = DampenMouseMovement;
MouseSensitivity.Y = DampenMouseMovement;
MouseCounter.X = MouseCounter.Y = 0;
```

Finally, the event listeners used for dragging are set up:

```
MouseControl.MouseMove +=
    new MouseEventHandler(MouseControl_MouseMove);
MouseControl.MouseLeftButtonDown +=
    new MouseButtonEventHandler(MouseControl_MouseLeftButtonDown);
MouseControl.MouseLeftButtonUp +=
    new MouseButtonEventHandler(MouseControl_MouseLeftButtonUp);
```

The MouseLeftButtonDown() and MouseLeftButtonUp() functions are the standard drag functions we've used in other projects, so we won't be rehashing them here. The MouseMove() function is worth taking a look at, though—this is where the magic happens.

If a drag is occurring, the current position of the mouse is acquired and compared against the last position of the mouse. This is then used to increment the counters used to move the image:

```
CurrentMouse = e.GetPosition(this);

if (CurrentMouse.X < OldMouse.X) MouseCounter.X += 1;
if (CurrentMouse.X > OldMouse.X) MouseCounter.X += 1;
if (CurrentMouse.Y < OldMouse.Y) MouseCounter.Y += 1;
if (CurrentMouse.Y > OldMouse.Y) MouseCounter.Y += 1;
```

Next comes the if statement that does the work. The FlipMouse flag is checked. The only difference the flag makes is which way the image is moved, so the if and else clauses are exactly opposite when it comes to moving the ActiveImage object. This code is commented so you can see what each test checks for—the control needs to know in which direction the mouse is moving, and if it is time to switch the image. If so, the correct translation step is applied.

```
if (FlipMouse)
{
    // moving left, pixel counter exceeds dampening value
    if (CurrentMouse.X < OldMouse.X
        && MouseCounter.X >= MouseSensitivity.X)
    {
        TranslateImage.X += FrameStep.X;
        MouseCounter.X = 0;
    }

    // moving right, pixel counter exceeds dampening value
    if (CurrentMouse.X > OldMouse.X
        && MouseCounter.X >= MouseSensitivity.Y)
    {
        TranslateImage.X -= FrameStep.X;
        MouseCounter.X = 0;
    }

    // moving up, pixel counter exceeds dampening value
    if (CurrentMouse.Y < OldMouse.Y
        && MouseCounter.Y >= MouseSensitivity.Y)
    {
        TranslateImage.Y += FrameStep.Y;
        MouseCounter.Y = 0;
    }

    // moving down, pixel counter exceeds dampening value
    if (CurrentMouse.Y > OldMouse.Y
        && MouseCounter.Y >= MouseSensitivity.Y)
    {
        TranslateImage.Y -= FrameStep.Y;
        MouseCounter.Y = 0;
    }
}
```

```
    else
    {
        // moving left, pixel counter exceeds dampening value
        if (CurrentMouse.X < OldMouse.X
            && MouseCounter.X >= MouseSensitivity.X)
        {
            TranslateImage.X -= FrameStep.X;
            MouseCounter.X = 0;
        }

        // moving right, pixel counter exceeds dampening value
        if (CurrentMouse.X > OldMouse.X
            && MouseCounter.X >= MouseSensitivity.Y)
        {
            TranslateImage.X += FrameStep.X;
            MouseCounter.X = 0;
        }

        // moving up, pixel counter exceeds dampening value
        if (CurrentMouse.Y < OldMouse.Y
            && MouseCounter.Y >= MouseSensitivity.Y)
        {
            TranslateImage.Y -= FrameStep.Y;
            MouseCounter.Y = 0;
        }

        // moving down, pixel counter exceeds dampening value
        if (CurrentMouse.Y > OldMouse.Y
            && MouseCounter.Y >= MouseSensitivity.Y)
        {
            TranslateImage.Y += FrameStep.Y;
            MouseCounter.Y = 0;
        }
    }
```

The next block of code checks to see if the image needs to wrap left or right, top or bottom, and then takes the appropriate action to adjust the translation of the image:

```
// check wrap left and take appropriate action
if (WrapColumns && TranslateImage.X == -(Columns * FrameStep.X))
    TranslateImage.X = 0;
else if (!WrapColumns && TranslateImage.X
        < -((Columns - 1) * FrameStep.X))
    TranslateImage.X = -((Columns - 1) * FrameStep.X);

// check wrap right and take appropriate action
if (WrapColumns && TranslateImage.X > 0) TranslateImage.X =
    -(Columns * FrameStep.X) + FrameStep.X;
else if (!WrapColumns && TranslateImage.X > 0) TranslateImage.X = 0;
```

```
    // check wrap up and take appropriate action
    if (WrapRows && TranslateImage.Y == -((Rows - 1) * FrameStep.Y))
        TranslateImage.Y = 0;
    else if (!WrapRows && TranslateImage.Y < -((Rows - 1) * FrameStep.Y))
        TranslateImage.Y = -((Rows - 1) * FrameStep.Y);

    // check wrap down and take appropriate action
    if (WrapRows && TranslateImage.Y > 0)
        TranslateImage.Y = -(Rows * FrameStep.Y) + FrameStep.Y;
    else if (!WrapRows && TranslateImage.Y > 0) TranslateImage.Y = 0;
```

To finish out the function, the current mouse position is stored in the OldMouse variable for usage the next time through:

```
    OldMouse = CurrentMouse;
```

Using the control: single-plane

Let's take a look at how to get the control into a project and make use of it.

1. Open the **SLVRBed** project. This project contains an empty 800✕800 main canvas that we are going to add a SLVR control to.

2. In Solution Explorer, right-click the SLVRBed item and select Add ➤ Existing Item from the menu, as shown in Figure 11-8.

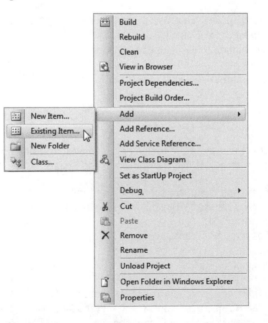

Figure 11-8. The Add ➤ Existing Item option in Visual Studio

3. Navigate to the SLVR Control folder for Chapter 11, and select the SLVR.xaml file. The control is now part of your project, but needs to have the class name updated to match the project.

4. Open the SLVR.xaml file and edit the first line. Remove the SLVRSingleImage text:

   `<UserControl x:Class="SLVRSingleImage.SLVR"`

   and replace it with the name of your project: SLVRBed, like so:

   `<UserControl x:Class="SLVRBed.SLVR"`

5. Open the SLVR.xaml.cs file. Update the namespace near the top of the file the same way. Change the following code:

   `namespace SLVRSingleImage`

   to this:

   `namespace SLVRBed`

6. The control is now ready for use. The next thing we need to do is add the image we will be using. Create a folder in Solution Explorer by right-clicking the SLVRBed item and selecting Add ➤ New Folder. Name the folder images.

7. Right-click the images folder and select Add ➤ Existing Item. Navigate to the bed contact sheet you created earlier. If you don't have it available, I placed a file called BedAll.jpg in the inhabit_bed folder for Chapter 11.

8. This step is very important—if you skip it, the control will throw an error when it tries to load the image. Select the image in the images folder, and look at the Properties panel. Under Build Action, select Content. In Copy to Output Directory, select Copy always. This will compile the image into the package that Silverlight creates when this application is compiled. By compiling the image into the package, your Silverlight application will become larger. The trade-off is that once it's downloaded to the client, the application is ready to go—no extra clicks or waiting.

9. All that's left to do is create an instance of the control and assign some parameters. Open the Page.xaml.cs file for editing, and add an object declaration before the Page() constructor:

   `SLVR Bed;`

10. Inside the Page() constructor, beneath the InitializeComponent(); line, type Bed = new SLVR(. Visual Studio's IntelliSense will open a list of the properties that are needed to instance the SLVR object, as shown in Figure 11-9.

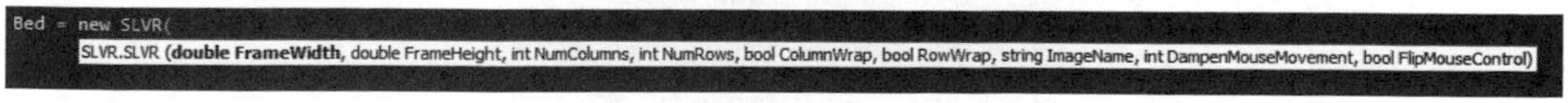

```
Bed = new SLVR(
    SLVR.SLVR (double FrameWidth, double FrameHeight, int NumColumns, int NumRows, bool ColumnWrap, bool RowWrap, string ImageName, int DampenMouseMovement, bool FlipMouseControl)
```

Figure 11-9. Visual Studio's IntelliSense helps with the SLVR object declaration.

11. All you need to do is type each value, separated by commas. For FrameWidth and FrameHeight, we know the bed images were 600×600, so type 600, 600,.

12. For NumColumns and NumRows, we know there were 21 source images in a single row, so type 21, 1,.

13. Since it's a single row, ColumnWrap will be on, but RowWrap will be off, so type true, false,.

14. For the image name, we can see the image in the images folder, so type the full path. You may have a different file name if you created your own earlier, but I'll use "images/BedAll.jpg", (including the quotes).

15. For DampenMouseMovement, 3 should work well on this image, so type 3,.

16. Finally, for FlipMouseControl, type true, and then finish with);. The final code looks like the following:

```
Bed = new SLVR(600,
              600,
              21,
              1,
              true,
              false,
              "images/BedAll.jpg",
              3,
              true);
```

17. All that's left is to position the SLVR object and add it to the main canvas:

```
Canvas.SetLeft(Bed, 100);
Canvas.SetTop(Bed, 100);
LayoutRoot.Children.Add(Bed);
```

Press F5 to compile and run the project. The browser will open, and you'll see the bed, as shown in Figure 11-10. Drag the mouse over the object to spin it. Keep in mind that the frames for the bed are pretty good-sized, and the application is 600×600. If your browser doesn't fit the entire application on the screen, you may see a scrollbar for the browser and another for the div containing the Silverlight application. Plan accordingly when creating your own VR objects to provide the best possible experience for your end users.

©2008 photospherix.com

Figure 11-10. The SLVR object in the browser

Earlier, I mentioned that it's possible to override the starting position for an object. In our case, maybe we've decided that we don't want the application to load with the front of the bed showing, and would prefer the side. The fifth image in our series is a nice side view of the bed, so before the code to position the bed on canvas, we can add a line of code to prime, or preset, the position:

```
Bed.TranslateImage.X = -3000;
```

Remember to use a negative number in order to slide the image to the left.

The code for this example is in the **SLVRBedCompleted** project.

Using the control: multiplane

The bed was a nice example of a single-plane SLVR object. Let's take a look at how to set up a multi-plane object.

1. Open the **SLVRFigure** project. This project contains the SLVR object, but no image. (I figured you might like a little practice adding images to a project.)

2. Right-click the SLVRFigure item in Solution Explorer and select Add ➤ New Folder. Name the folder images.

3. Right-click the images folder you just added and select Add ➤ Existing Item. Navigate to the WoodenFigure folder for Chapter 11 and locate the WoodenFigure.jpg file inside. This is a 12000✕3000-pixel image that contains 20 columns and 5 rows of a wooden figure.

4. With WoodenFigure.jpg selected, change the Build Action to Content and Copy to Output Directory to Copy always on the File Properties panel.

5. Open the Page.xaml.cs file for editing. Before the Page() constructor, declare a new instance of the SLVR object:

```
SLVR Figure;
```

6. Instantiate the SLVR object. Each frame is 600✕600. There are 20 columns and 5 rows. The columns should wrap, but the rows won't. The path to the image is images/WoodenFigure.jpg. Mouse sensitivity is 3, and this time, the mouse control should not be flipped.

```
Figure = new SLVR(600,
                  600,
                  20,
                  5,
                  true,
                  false,
                  "images/WoodenFigure.jpg",
                  3,
                  false);
```

7. Set the position for the object, and add it to the main canvas:

```
Canvas.SetLeft(Figure, 100);
Canvas.SetTop(Figure, 100);
LayoutRoot.Children.Add(Figure);
```

8. Press F5 to compile and run the application. It looks pretty good, and works as expected, but the initial state of the object has the figure with its back kind of turned, as shown in Figure 11-11.

©2008 PhotoSpherix.com

Figure 11-11. The figure loads, but is looking in the wrong direction!

9. If you open the WoodenFigure.jpg file and take a look, the front-facing figure is in the 16th column and 4th row (count from 0 in both cases). To change the default position, add the following two lines of code just before the code added in step 7. 16 × 600 (image width) = 9600. 4 × 600 = 2400. We want to move the image left and up, so the numbers are negative.

```
Figure.TranslateImage.X = -9600;
Figure.TranslateImage.Y = -2400;
```

If you compile and run the program again, you will see the figure sitting cross-legged, facing forward, as shown in Figure 11-12.

©2008 PhotoSpherix.com

Figure 11-12. After priming the starting position, the figure faces forward as expected.

You can do it!

OK, now it's your turn to make a SLVR object from scratch. Open the **SLVRMini** project. This is a skeleton project I created for you.

You will need to add the user control, change the namespace for the XAML and code-behind in the control so it matches this project, add the image, set the image properties, and instance the SLVR object. Use the MiniAll.jpg file in the mini folder for Chapter 11. This image is 20 columns and 6 rows, and each frame is 600×600, resulting in a 12000×3600-pixel image.

For a little extra challenge, set the starting image to the front view of the car.

If you get stuck, I've provided the **SLVRMiniCompleted** project to look at for help with the code if necessary.

About that time travel thing . . .

This is the moment you've been waiting for, right? You worked through the rest of the examples and got to this point to see how Silverlight can help you travel through time.

Here's the answer you're looking for.

Don't lock yourself into thinking of the SLVR user control as a VR "object." You can use it to show the passage of time very easily. Just about everyone has a digital camera. Set yours up on a tripod and use an inexpensive kitchen timer or your watch to snap a photo of something every 30 or 60 seconds. If your camera has an interval timer, it's even easier. Photograph the sun setting, flowers blooming, seeds sprouting, or clouds racing across the sky. Load your images into a SLVR control and enjoy the results. You'll be able to pass hours or days on command. Also consider experimenting with stop-motion animation—children's toys, product packaging, product assembly, and so on.

I've included two example projects that illustrate this concept. The first, shown in Figure 11-13, is called **SLVRCrownPoint**. This is a time-lapse photo series taken at Crown Point, Oregon, at 1 minute intervals. It shows the passage of about 45 minutes around sunset.

Figure 11-13. A still from the SLVRCrownPoint project

The second example, shown in Figure 11-14, is a time-lapse photo series taken near the base of Mt. Adams in Washington State. The photo interval is 30 seconds, as it was quite windy and the clouds were moving past the mountain at a pretty good clip. The project is called **SLVRMtAdams**.

Mt. Adams Timelapse (30 sec. intervals)

Figure 11-14. A still from the SLVRMtAdams project

Summary

In this chapter, you learned about what a VR object is, and how to go about getting images suitable for use in the SLVR user control. To get images, you can photograph your own objects, render them from a 3D animation package, or use a service provider like PhotoSpherix.

Once you have the images of your object, you need to make a contact sheet to assemble the separate frames into a single large image for use in the user control using a program like IrfanView.

When your contact sheet image is ready to go, adding the SLVR object to your application is pretty quick. It involves adding the control to your project, importing your image into the project, and setting up the code that instantiates the SLVR object.

Remember to "think outside the object" when creating VR presentations. While objects are certainly a valid and important use for the technology, find ways to make your applications unique—pass time or try some stop-motion animation.

INDEX

Width property (ReferenceLine element), 323
Windows Presentation Foundation (WPF), 23
writeVectors() function, 187

X

x axis rotation (3D simulation), 295–296
XAML (Extensible Application Markup Language). *See* also Microsoft Expression Blend
  basics, 9–11
  Canvas element, 14–15
  controls elements, 21
  Ellipse element, 19
  Image element, 15–17
  LayoutRoot element, 14
  Line element, 20–21
  Path element, 17–19
  Rectangle element, 17
  TextBlock element, 19–20
  TextBox element, 19
  using Expression Blend to create, 11–14
XAxis3D project, 295–296
xmlns:x namespace, 13
x:Name property, 15

Y

y axis rotation (3D simulation), 280–283
YAxis3D project, 282–283

Z

z axis rotation (3D simulation), 272–274
Z-order, 115
ZAxis3D project, 272–274